T0235164

Lecture Notes in Computer Science   **10258**

Commenced Publication in 1973
Founding and Former Series Editors:
Gerhard Goos, Juris Hartmanis, and Jan van Leeuwen

More information about this series at http://www.springer.com/series/7407

Wil van der Aalst · Eike Best (Eds.)

Application and Theory
of Petri Nets
and Concurrency

38th International Conference, PETRI NETS 2017
Zaragoza, Spain, June 25–30, 2017
Proceedings

 Springer

Editors
Wil van der Aalst
Department of Mathematics and Computer
 Science (MF 7.103)
Eindhoven University of Technology
Eindhoven, Noord-Brabant
The Netherlands

Eike Best
Carl von Ossietzky Universität Oldenburg
Oldenburg
Germany

ISSN 0302-9743   ISSN 1611-3349   (electronic)
Lecture Notes in Computer Science
ISBN 978-3-319-57860-6   ISBN 978-3-319-57861-3   (eBook)
DOI 10.1007/978-3-319-57861-3

Library of Congress Control Number: 2017938160

LNCS Sublibrary: SL1 – Theoretical Computer Science and General Issues

Printed on acid-free paper

This Springer imprint is published by Springer Nature
The registered company is Springer International Publishing AG
The registered company address is: Gewerbestrasse 11, 6330 Cham, Switzerland

Preface

This volume constitutes the proceedings of the 38th International Conference on Application and Theory of Petri Nets and Concurrency (Petri Nets 2017). This series of conferences serves as an annual meeting place to discuss progress in the field of Petri nets and related models of concurrency. These conferences provide a forum for researchers to present and discuss both applications and theoretical developments in this area. Novel tools and substantial enhancements to existing tools can also be presented. This year, the satellite program of the conference comprised five workshops, two Petri net courses, two advanced tutorials, and a model-checking contest.

Petri Nets 2017 was colocated with the Application of Concurrency to System Design Conference (ACSD 2017). Both were organized by the Aragón Institute of Engineering Research of Zaragoza University. The conference took place at the School of Engineering and Architecture of Zaragoza University during June 25–30, 2017. We would like to express our deepest thanks to the Organizing Committee chaired by José Manuel Colom for the time and effort invested in the local organization of this event.

This year, 33 papers were submitted to Petri Nets 2016 by authors from 25 different countries. Each paper was reviewed by three reviewers. The discussion phase and final selection process by the Program Committee (PC) were supported by the EasyChair conference system. The PC selected 16 papers for presentation: nine theory papers, four application papers, and three tool papers. The number of submissions was a bit lower than expected. However, we were pleased that several highly innovative and very strong papers were submitted. After the conference, some of these authors were invited to submit an extended version of their contribution for consideration in a special issue of a journal.

We thank the PC members and other reviewers for their careful and timely evaluation of the submissions and the fruitful constructive discussions that resulted in the final selection of papers. The Springer LNCS team (notably Anna Kramer and Alfred Hofmann) and Uli Schlachter provided excellent and welcome support in the preparation of this volume. We are also grateful to the invited speakers for their contributions:

- Thomas Henzinger, Institute of Science and Technology (IST) Austria, who delivered the Distinguished Carl Adam Petri Lecture
  "Promises and Challenges of Reactive Modeling: A Personal Perspective"
- Josep Carmona, Universitat Politècnica de Catalunya, Barcelona, Spain
  "The Alignment of Formal, Structured and Unstructured Process Descriptions"
- Christos Cassandras, Boston University, USA
  "Complexity Made Simple (at a Small Price)"
- Irina Lomazova, National Research University Higher School of Economics, Moscow, Russia
  "Resource Equivalences in Petri Nets"

Alongside ACSD 2017, the following workshops were colocated: the Workshop on Petri Nets and Software Engineering (PNSE 2017), the Workshop on Modeling and Software Engineering in Business and Industry (MoSEBIn 2017), the Workshop on Algorithms and Theories for the Analysis of Event Data (ATAED 2017), the Workshop on Structure Theory of Petri Nets (STRUCTURE 2017), and the Workshop on Healthcare Management and Patient Safety Through Modelling and Simulation. Other colocated events included: the Model Checking Contest, the Petri Net Course, and an Advanced Tutorial on Process Mining (A Tour In Process Mining: From Practice to Algorithmic Challenges).

We hope you will enjoy reading the contributions in this LNCS volume.

June 2017   Wil van der Aalst
                                                                         Eike Best

Organization

Steering Committee

W. van der Aalst, The Netherlands
G. Ciardo, USA
J. Desel, Germany
S. Donatelli, Italy
S. Haddad, France
K. Hiraishi, Japan
J. Kleijn, The Netherlands
F. Kordon, France
M. Koutny, UK (Chair)
L.M. Kristensen, Norway
C. Lin, China
W. Penczek, Poland
L. Pomello, Italy
W. Reisig, Germany
G. Rozenberg, The Netherlands
M. Silva, Spain
A. Valmari, Finland
A. Yakovlev, UK

Program Committee

Wil van der Aalst (Co-chair)	Eindhoven University of Technology, The Netherlands
Gianfranco Balbo	University of Turin, Italy
Robin Bergenthum	FernUniversität in Hagen, Germany
Eike Best (Co-chair)	Carl von Ossietzky Universität Oldenburg, Germany
Hanifa Boucheneb	Polytechnique Montréal, Québec, Canada
Didier Buchs	CUI, University of Geneva, Switzerland
Lawrence Cabac	University of Hamburg, Germany
José Manuel Colom	University of Zaragoza, Spain
Dirk Fahland	Eindhoven University of Technology, The Netherlands
David de Frutos Escrig	Universidad Complutense de Madrid, Spain
Gilles Geeraerts	Université Libre de Bruxelles, Belgium
Henri Hansen	Tampere University of Technology, Finland
Petr Jancar	Technical University Ostrava, Czech Republic
Ryszard Janicki	McMaster University, Canada
Gabriel Juhas	Slovak University of Technology, Bratislava, Slovakia
Fabrice Kordon	LIP6/UPMC, Paris, France
Lars M. Kristensen	Bergen University College, Norway
Hiroshi Matsuno	Yamaguchi University, Japan
Łukasz Mikulski	Nicolaus Copernicus University, Toruń, Poland

Andrew Miner	Iowa State University, USA
Daniel Moldt	University of Hamburg, Germany
G. Michele Pinna	Università di Cagliari, Italy
Pascal Poizat	Paris Ouest University and LIP6, France
Sylvain Schmitz	LSV, CNRS, and ENS de Cachan, France
Pawel Sobocinski	University of Southampton, UK
Yann Thierry-Mieg	LIP6/UPMC, Paris, France
Irina Virbitskaite	Russian Academy of Sciences, Novosibirsk, Russia
Matthias Weidlich	Humboldt-Universität zu Berlin, Germany
Karsten Wolf	Universität Rostock, Germany

Workshops and Tutorials Chairs

Lars M. Kristensen	Bergen University College
Wojciech Penczek	Polish Academy of Sciences

Organizing Committee

José Manuel Colom (Chair)	University of Zaragoza
José Ángel Bañares	University of Zaragoza
Fernando Tricas	University of Zaragoza
Santiago Velilla	University of Zaragoza
Víctor Medel	University of Zaragoza

Tools Exhibition Chair

Unai Arronategui	University of Zaragoza

Publicity Chair

Rafael Tolosana-Calasanz	University of Zaragoza

Additional Reviewers

Junaid Babar
Kamila Barylska
Marco Beccuti
Béatrice Bérard
Paul Brunet
Maximilien Colange
Giuliana Franceschinis
Anna Gogolinska
Serge Haddad
Michael Haustermann
Thomas Hujsa
Stefan Klikovits

Eiji Konaka
Kahloul Laïd
Alban Linard
Benjamin Meis
David Mosteller
Marcin Piątkowski
Dimitri Racordon
Fernando Rosa-Velardo
Igor Tarasyuk
Valentin Valero
Rui Wang

Distinguished Carl Adam Petri Lecture

Promises and Challenges of Reactive Modeling: A Personal Perspective

Thomas A. Henzinger

IST (Institute of Science and Technology) Austria, Am Campus 1,
3400 Klosterneuburg, Austria

Abstract. Reactive models offer a fundamental paradigm for predicting the behavior of highly concurrent event-based systems, which includes all systems with significant software components. While much historical emphasis has been put on the analysis and comparison of different models for concurrency, several additional capabilities of reactive models have come into focus more recently: the heterogeneous combination of computational and analytical models, of worst-case and best-effort techniques; interface languages for the decomposition of a system into multiple viewpoints, in addition to temporal, spatial, and hierarchical structuring mechanisms; reasoning about strategic choice, in addition to non-deterministic and probabilistic choice; computing quantitative fitness measures vis-à-vis boolean requirements, in addition to measures of time and resource consumption; design for robustness properties, in addition to correctness and performance properties; theories of approximation in addition to theories of abstraction; methods for system synthesis in addition to model analysis. We review some results and outline some challenges on these topics.

This research is supported in part by the Austrian Science Fund (FWF) under grants S11402-N23 (RiSE/SHiNE) and Z211-N23 (Wittgenstein Award).

Contents

Invited Talks

The Alignment of Formal, Structured and Unstructured Process Descriptions

Josep Carmona[(✉)]

Universitat Politècnica de Catalunya, Barcelona, Spain
jcarmona@cs.upc.edu

Abstract. Nowadays organizations are experimenting a drift on the way processes are managed. On the one hand, formal notations like Petri nets or Business Process Model and Notation (BPMN) enable the unambiguous reasoning and automation of designed processes. This way of eliciting processes by manual design, which stemmed decades ago, will still be an important actor in the future. On the other hand, regulations require organizations to store their process executions in structured representations, so that they are known and can be analyzed. Finally, due to the different nature of stakeholders within an organization (ranging from the most technical members, e.g., developers, to less technical), textual descriptions of processes are also maintained to enable that everyone in the organization understands their processes.

In this paper I will describe techniques for facilitating the interconnection between these three process representations. This requires interdisciplinary research to connect several fields: business process management, formal methods, natural language processing and process mining.

1 Introduction

With the aim of having individuals from various levels examine their operations, organizations maintain different representations of their processes: while *textual descriptions* of processes are well-suited for non-technical members, they are less appropriate for describing precise aspects of the underlying process [1]. In contrast, *formal and graphical process notations* are unambiguous representations which can be the basis for automating the corresponding processes within the organization [2], but they are oriented to specialized members. Recent studies have not concluded a clear superiority between neither of the two aforementioned notations [3,4]. Finally, the current trend to store all kinds of digital data has made organizations to become more than ever data-oriented, thus dependent on the available techniques to extract value from the data. Process mining is an emerging field which focuses on analyzing the *event logs* corresponding to process executions, with the purpose of extracting, analyzing and enhancing evidence-based process models [5].

In this context, due to the evolving nature of processes, there is a high risk of having deviations between these three different representations, a problem that may have serious consequences for any organization [6]. To have these different

© Springer International Publishing AG 2017
W. van der Aalst and E. Best (Eds.): PETRI NETS 2017, LNCS 10258, pp. 3–11, 2017.
DOI: 10.1007/978-3-319-57861-3_1

descriptions aligned to ensure that everybody shares the same version of the process is not only a desired feature, but also a real challenge originated by the contrasting nature of each process representation.

Likewise, organizations need to keep track of the deviations between different versions of the same process under the same representation (e.g., the winter sales process vs. the summer sales process, or the incorporation of a new form of payment in a process), to bound the flexibility and variability of a running process, or simply to be aware of the evolution of a process over time.

In this paper I will provide an overview of the milestones and current challenges that arise when trying to align these three different process descriptions. I will mainly focus on the algorithmic support for computing alignments across different process descriptions, and only will briefly discuss the case where the process descriptions are the same.

2   Descriptions of Processes

Here we informally describe three types of descriptions to report processes used in organizations. The reader can find a wider view in (which also includes spreadsheets and business rules) in [6].

Graphical Models. There exist a plethora of formal and graphical notations to model processes, like BPMNs [7], EPCs [8], Petri Nets [9], YAWL [10], and many others. In this paper, we will informally use one of them: BPMN. BPMN models are composed from three types of nodes: events, activities and gateways. *Events* (represented as circles) denote something that happens (e.g., time, messages, . . .), rather than *Activities* which are something that is done (represented as rounded-corner rectangles). Finally, the *gateways*, represented as diamond shapes, are used to route the control flow. These elements can be partitioned into pools or lanes, to group activities performed by the same actor (person, department, institution, etc.). An example of BPMN is shown in Fig. 1. We consider graphical models a formal process description.

Textual Descriptions. Textual descriptions of processes can often be found in organizations [1]. A possibility is to use *written use cases* [11], but those already introduce some structuring that limits the flexibility of the description. Instead, unrestricted textual descriptions like the one shown in Fig. 1 can be created by anyone with knowledge on the process. In general, textual descriptions assume a linear description of the sequence of tasks carried out, while concurrency, iteration and other control-flow patterns are expressed in a less precise manner. We consider text as an unstructured process description.

Event Logs. Event logs represent the footprints left by process executions, stored by an information system [5]. As minimal requirement, event logs are formed from *events*, that assign activities to process executions (cases). Additionally, other information can be associated to an event like its timestamp, resource, cost, etc. Part of an event log is reported in Table 1. While in the two previous descriptions, the process is explicitly described, an event log describe

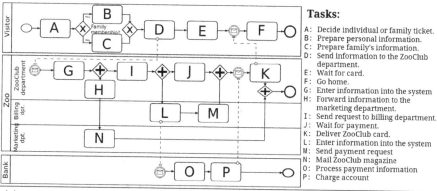

Tasks:

A: Decide individual or family ticket.
B: Prepare personal information.
C: Prepare family's information.
D: Send information to the ZooClub department.
E: Wait for card.
F: Go home.
G: Enter information into the system
H: Forward information to the marketing department.
I: Send request to billing department.
J: Wait for payment.
K: Deliver ZooClub card.
L: Enter information into the system
M: Send payment request
N: Mail ZooClub magazine
O: Process payment information
P: Charge account

(1) *When a visitor wants to become a member of Barcelona's ZooClub, the following steps must be taken.* (2) *First of all, the customer must decide whether he wants an individual or family membership.* (3) *If he wants an individual membership, he must prepare his personal information.* (4) *If he wants a family membership instead, he should prepare the information for its spouse and spawn as well.* (5) *The customer must then give this information to the ZooClub department.* (6) *The ZooClub enters the visitor's personal data into the system and takes the payment request to the Billing department.* (7) *The ZooClub department also forwards the visitor's information to the marketing department.* (8) *On receiving the request, the billing department also enters the visitor's personal data into their local database.* (9) *After that, the billing department sends the payment request to the bank.* (10) *The bank processes the payment information and, if everything is correct, charges the payment into user's account.* (11) *Once the payment is confirmed, the ZooClub department can print the card and deliver it to the visitor.* (12) *In the meantime, the Marketing department makes a request to mail the Zoo Club's magazine to the visitor's home.* (13) *Once the visitor receives the card, he can go home.*

Fig. 1. Graphical and textual description of the Zoo process.

implicitly the process, by providing example of its possible executions. We regard event logs as an structured process description.

3 The Alignment Graph: An Algorithmic Tour

Van der Aa *et al.* recently reported on the fragmentation organizations have with respect to the description of the processes [6]. This will only get worse in the near future, since process-related data in any of the considered forms will become ubiquitous. Hence, automation will be a crucial element to allow stakeholders to catch up with the evolving and flexible nature of processes.

In particular, algorithms for the computation of alignments between (different) process representations will be needed. One possibility, that it is not contemplated here, is to use transformations between the different representations. For instance, there are mature techniques that transform an event log into a

Table 1. Part of an event log for the Zoo process.

Event	Case id	Activity	Timestamp	Person	Dept	Data
1	1	A	10-04-2015 9:08 am	Miquel	–	–
2	2	A	10-04-2015 10:03 am	Sandra	–	–
3	2	B	10-04-2015 10:05 am	Sandra	–	Personal
4	1	C	10-04-2015 9:09 am	Miquel	–	Family
5	1	D	10-04-2015 9:10 am	Miquel	–	–
6	1	G	10-04-2015 9:12 am	Ruth	ZooClub	Family
7	1	H	10-04-2015 9:12 am	Ruth	ZooClub	Family
8	2	D	10-04-2015 10:06 am	Sandra	ZooClub	Personal
9	1	I	10-04-2015 9:18 am	Ruth	ZooClub	–
10	1	N	10-04-2015 10:03 am	Pere	Marketing	–
11	1	L	10-04-2015 11:32 am	Teresa	Billing	34567-e
12	1	J	10-04-2015 2:01 pm	Ruth	–	–
13	1	M	10-04-2015 7:06 pm	Teresa	–	–

process model [5]. Likewise, recent techniques have appeared to transform a textual description into a process model [1] and back [12]. Although they represent a very useful toolbox that may help into integrating different sources of process information, these transformations do not always guarantee the preservation of the main aspects of the original process description.

For the three process representations described in the previous section, we now show the main techniques available for facilitating the matching between process representations. Figure 2 summarizes them into the *alignment graph*.

Formal Models vs. Event logs. The seminal work in [13] proposed the notion of alignment between process models described as Petri nets and event logs, and developed a technique to compute optimal alignments for a particular class of process models. For each trace σ in the log, the approach consists on exploring the synchronous product of model's state space and σ. In the exploration, the shortest path is computed using the A^* algorithm, once costs for model and log moves are defined. Several optimizations have been proposed to the basic approach: for instance, the use of Integer Linear Programming (ILP) techniques on each visited state to prune the search space [13]. Alternatively, an approach based on partial orders which verbalizes the differences computed has been proposed in [14]. Recently, an approach fully based on ILP has been presented, which significantly reduces the complexity of computing alignments [15] at the expense of dropping the optimality guarantee. Some heuristics that cannot guarantee always the derivation of real alignments but work well in practice can be found in the literature [16–18].

Textual Descriptions vs. Formal Models. The seminal work [19,20] was the first one in proposing an algorithm for aligning textual descriptions and process models, with the particular aim of detecting inconsistencies between both representations. The technique uses a linguistic analysis (NLP) previous to a *best-first search* technique to compute an optimal alignment. In contrast to [19,20], the approach in [21] encodes the problem of computing an alignment as the resolution of an ILP model, representing a significant reduction (of several orders of magnitude) in the time requirements for computing an alignment.

Textual Descriptions vs. Event logs. This is a less explored field. However, techniques applied in related problems may be applicable here. For instance, linguistic techniques for extracting the temporal relations between the main events in a text can be used to derive the behavioral patterns [22,23], which can then be compared to the *log-based ordering relations* of a log [5]. Those can be the inputs to ILP matching techniques similar to the ones applied to the previous problems.

The previous family of techniques focused on techniques for aligning across different process descriptions. For completeness, we now report some of the techniques used for aligning process descriptions on the same notation.

Formal Models vs. Formal Models. There has been a plethora of techniques in the last decade to facilitate the matching between process models. For BPMN notation, for instance, the reader can find a good summary in [24]. The techniques have been extensively applied in the context of process model repositories, e.g. [25]. Overall, the techniques range from graph-edit distance, event structures, behavioral profiles and many more.

Event Logs vs. Event Logs. In the last years some contributions have focused into aligning event logs, in order to extract differences that may represent expected or unexpected process variations. The work in [26] uses event structures to verbalize differences, while less fine-grained techniques can also be used by comparing log-based ordering relations. On a different perspective, the use of concept-drift techniques based on statistical tests together with adaptive windowing [27] can also be used to detect inconsistencies between event logs [28].

Textual Descriptions vs. Textual Descriptions. Again, in the scope of textual descriptions of processes this is a less explored family of techniques. Due to the widespread use of textual documentations of processes in organization, techniques for automatically providing inconsistencies between textual descriptions can be a very important tool to improve the understandability of the processes [4]. As for previous techniques that need to deal with textual descriptions, the use of linguistic analysis as an input for later matching techniques (e.g., ILP) may be a promising direction. On a more general setting, computing the semantic similarity between two texts is a classical task in NLP and Information Retrieval (IR) fields. In IR, this is typically tackled by term-frequency based approaches, that compare distributions of words in the documents, so documents are considered similar if they contain similar words in a similar distribution. In NLP field, approaches based on n-gram occurrences in both texts have also been used to evaluate results of Machine Translation (BLEU [29]) or Summarization

(ROUGE [30] systems, by comparing them to gold standard human-produced documents for the same tasks. More recently, more accurate semantic comparison of texts has been approached by tasks such as Textual Entailment [31] (decide whether one text implies the other or not) and Semantic Textual Similarity [32] (decide to which extent two texts are equivalent –they say the same, one is contained in the other, one implies the other, they talk about the same topic but do not say the same, they are unrelated...). For this more advanced comparison, heavier NLP machinery is required (syntactic parsers, semantic analyzers, ontologies, word embeddings, etc.).

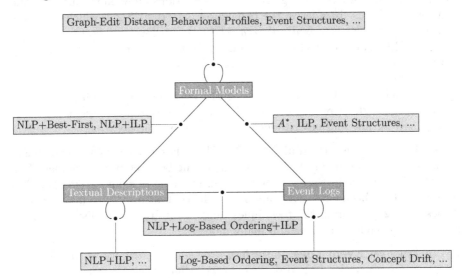

Fig. 2. The alignment graph.

4   Outlook

In this paper I have summarized the current algorithmic support for the alignment of different process descriptions. Overall, these techniques often need to combine several disciplines, like linguistic analysis, graph-based techniques, mathematical optimization, statistics, machine learning, to name a few.

In spite of some successful cases, most of the techniques need to be improved or reconsidered in some particular scenarios: when the quality of the alignments derived needs to be secured, when the techniques are meant to be applicable on the large, or in an online setting.

The progress in the techniques enumerated in this paper will have a direct impact in the way organizations deal with their processes, enabling the continuous awareness of the processes by any agent. For particular fields like healthcare, education, administration and similar, the influence can be even stronger, due to the enormous importance processes have in parallel with the heterogeneity of the existing stakeholders.

Acknowledgements. I would like to thank to the organization of the Petri Nets and ACSD conferences for both the invitation to give a keynote and to write an article in the conference proceedings.

I would like to thank some researchers that collaborate with my group on some of the topics of this paper: Han van der Aa, Andrea Burattin, Thomas Chatain, Boudewijn van Dongen, Henrik Leopold, Hajo A. Reijers and Barbara Weber. Likewise, I would like to thank the local collaborators LLuís Padró, Josep Sànchez-Ferreres, David Sanchez-Charles and Farbod Taymouri.

This work has been partially supported by funds from the Spanish Ministry for Economy and Competitiveness (MINECO), the European Union (FEDER funds) under grant COMMAS (ref. TIN2013-46181-C2-1-R).

References

1. Leopold, H., Mendling, J., Polyvyanyy, A.: Supporting process model validation through natural language generation. IEEE Trans. Softw. Eng. **40**(8), 818–840 (2014)
2. Dumas, M., Rosa, M.L., Mendling, J., Reijers, H.A.: Fundamentals of Business Process Management. Springer, Heidelberg (2013)
3. Ottensooser, A., Fekete, A.D.: Comparing readability of graphical and sentential process design notations: data analysis report. University of Sydney, School of Information Technologies (2010)
4. Ottensooser, A., Fekete, A., Reijers, H.A., Mendling, J., Menictas, C.: Making sense of business process descriptions: an experimental comparison of graphical and textual notations. J. Syst. Softw. **85**(3), 596–606 (2012)
5. van der Aalst, W.M.P.: Process Mining - Discovery, Conformance and Enhancement of Business Processes. Springer, Heidelberg (2011)
6. van der Aa, H., Leopold, H., Mannhardt, F., Reijers, H.A.: On the fragmentation of process information: challenges, solutions, and outlook. In: Proceedings of Enterprise, Business-Process and Information Systems Modeling - 16th International Conference, BPMDS 2015, 20th International Conference, EMMSAD 2015, Held at CAiSE 2015, Stockholm, Sweden, 8–9 June 2015, pp. 3–18 (2015)
7. OMG: Business process model and notation (BPMN) version 2.0 (2011)
8. Scheer, A.W.: ARIS-Business Process Modeling. Springer, Heidelberg (1998)
9. Murata, T.: Petri nets: properties, analysis and applications. Proc. IEEE **77**(4), 541–574 (1989)
10. van der Aalst, W.M.P., ter Hofstede, A.H.M.: YAWL: yet another workflow language. Inf. Syst. **30**(4), 245–275 (2005)
11. Cockburn, A.: Writing Effective Use Cases. Addison-Wesley Longman, Boston (2000)
12. Friedrich, F., Mendling, J., Puhlmann, F.: Process model generation from natural language text. In: Mouratidis, H., Rolland, C. (eds.) CAiSE 2011. LNCS, vol. 6741, pp. 482–496. Springer, Heidelberg (2011). doi:10.1007/978-3-642-21640-4_36
13. Adriansyah, A.: Aligning observed and modeled behavior. Ph.D. thesis, Technische Universiteit Eindhoven (2014)
14. Armas-Cervantes, A., Baldan, P., Dumas, M., García-Bañuelos, L.: Diagnosing behavioral differences between business process models: an approach based on event structures. Inf. Syst. **56**, 304–325 (2016)

15. van Dongen, B., Carmona, J., Chatain, T., Taymouri, F.: Aligning modeled and observed behavior: a compromise between complexity and quality. In: Advanced Information Systems Engineering - 29th International Conference, CAiSE 2017, Essen, Germany, 12–16 June 2017, Proceedings (2017, in press)

16. Rozinat, A., van der Aalst, W.M.P.: Conformance checking of processes based on monitoring real behavior. Inf. Syst. **33**(1), 64–95 (2008)

17. Taymouri, F., Carmona, J.: A recursive paradigm for aligning observed behavior of large structured process models. In: La Rosa, M., Loos, P., Pastor, O. (eds.) BPM 2016. LNCS, vol. 9850, pp. 197–214. Springer, Cham (2016). doi:10.1007/978-3-319-45348-4_12

18. Verbeek, H.M.W., van der Aalst, W.M.P.: Merging alignments for decomposed replay. In: Kordon, F., Moldt, D. (eds.) PETRI NETS 2016. LNCS, vol. 9698, pp. 219–239. Springer, Cham (2016). doi:10.1007/978-3-319-39086-4_14

19. van der Aa, H., Leopold, H., Reijers, H.A.: Detecting inconsistencies between process models and textual descriptions. In: Motahari-Nezhad, H.R., Recker, J., Weidlich, M. (eds.) BPM 2015. LNCS, vol. 9253, pp. 90–105. Springer, Cham (2015). doi:10.1007/978-3-319-23063-4_6

20. van der Aa, H., Leopold, H., Reijers, H.A.: Comparing textual descriptions to process models - the automatic detection of inconsistencies. Inf. Syst. **64**, 447–460 (2016)

21. Sànchez-Ferreres, J., Carmona, J., Padró, L.: Aligning textual and graphical descriptions of processes through ILP techniques. In: Advanced Information Systems Engineering - 29th International Conference, CAiSE 2017, Essen, Germany, 12–16 June 2017, Proceedings (2017, in press)

22. UzZaman, N., Llorens, H., Derczynski, L., Allen, J., Verhagen, M., Pustejovsky, J.: Semeval-2013 task 1: Tempeval-3: evaluating time expressions, events, and temporal relations. In: Second Joint Conference on Lexical and Computational Semantics (*SEM), vol. 2: Proceedings of the Seventh International Workshop on Semantic Evaluation (SemEval 2013), Atlanta, Georgia, USA, Association for Computational Linguistics, pp. 1–9, June 2013

23. Mirza, P.: Extracting temporal and causal relations between events. Ph.D. thesis, International Doctorate School in Information and Communication Technologies, University of Trento (2016)

24. Becker, M., Laue, R.: A comparative survey of business process similarity measures. Comput. Ind. **63**(2), 148–167 (2012)

25. Rosa, M.L., Dumas, M., Ekanayake, C.C., García-Bañuelos, L., Recker, J., ter Hofstede, A.H.M.: Detecting approximate clones in business process model repositories. Inf. Syst. **49**, 102–125 (2015)

26. van Beest, N.R.T.P., Dumas, M., García-Bañuelos, L., Rosa, M.: Log delta analysis: interpretable differencing of business process event logs. In: Motahari-Nezhad, H.R., Recker, J., Weidlich, M. (eds.) BPM 2015. LNCS, vol. 9253, pp. 386–405. Springer, Cham (2015). doi:10.1007/978-3-319-23063-4_26

27. Bifet, A., Gavaldà, R.: Learning from time-changing data with adaptive windowing. In: Proceedings of the Seventh SIAM International Conference on Data Mining, 26–28 April 2007, Minneapolis, Minnesota, USA, pp. 443–448 (2007)

28. Maaradji, A., Dumas, M., Rosa, M., Ostovar, A.: Fast and accurate business process drift detection. In: Motahari-Nezhad, H.R., Recker, J., Weidlich, M. (eds.) BPM 2015. LNCS, vol. 9253, pp. 406–422. Springer, Cham (2015). doi:10.1007/978-3-319-23063-4_27

29. Papineni, K., Roukos, S., Ward, T., Zhu, W.: BLEU: a method for automatic evaluation of machine translation. In: Proceedings of the 40th Annual Meeting of the Association for Computational Linguistics, 6–12 July 2002, Philadelphia, PA, USA, pp. 311–318 (2002)
30. Lin, C.Y.: Rouge: a package for automatic evaluation of summaries. In: Proceedings of the ACL-2004 Workshop. Association for Computational Linguistics, pp. 74–81 (2004)
31. Negri, M., Marchetti, A., Mehdad, Y., Bentivogli, L., Giampiccolo, D.: Semeval-2012 task 8: cross-lingual textual entailment for content synchronization. In: Proceedings of *SEM 2012 (2012)
32. Agirre, E., Banea, C., Cardie, C., Cer, D.M., Diab, M.T., Gonzalez-Agirre, A., Guo, W., Lopez-Gazpio, I., Maritxalar, M., Mihalcea, R., Rigau, G., Uria, L., Wiebe, J.: Semeval-2015 task 2: semantic textual similarity, English, Spanish and pilot on interpretability. In: Proceedings of the 9th International Workshop on Semantic Evaluation, SemEval@NAACL-HLT 2015, Denver, Colorado, USA, 4–5 June 2015, pp. 252–263 (2015)

Complexity Made Simple (at a Small Price)

Christos G. Cassandras$^{(\boxtimes)}$

Division of Systems Engineering, Boston University, Boston 02215, USA
cgc@bu.edu

Abstract. Fundamental complexity limits prevent us from directly solving many design, control, and optimization problems. Yet, there are ways to solve such hard problems by exploiting their specific structure, by asking the "right" questions, and by challenging some conventional approaches. First, slow, inefficient, and intrusive trial-and-error techniques can sometimes be bypassed through simple thought experiments constructed at a "small price." In particular, for Discrete Event Systems this can be systematically accomplished through the theory of Perturbation Analysis. Second, decomposition and abstraction methods can often provide accurate solutions or significantly simplify a hard problem at the "small price" of some loss of accuracy. Finally, conventional time-driven methods for sampling, control, and communication can be replaced by event-driven techniques with the proper events triggering these actions.

1 Complexity Limits

There are a number of problems which are well known for their "complexity." The sources of such complexity may be in the physical nature of the processes involved or in the operational rules imposed to control an engineered system. They may also originate in the stochastic nature of the problem or in its mere dimensionality which limits our computational ability to solve it despite the fastest computational engines at our disposal. In fact, there are at least three fundamental limits that involve complex dynamic systems. First is the well-known $1/\sqrt{T}$ (or $1/\sqrt{N}$) limit best illustrated through the central limit theorem: we cannot learn from data faster than $1/\sqrt{T}$ (or $1/\sqrt{N}$) where T is the time spent to collect data or to simulate a process (equivalently, N is the amount of data collected). Second is the NP-hard limit, i.e., the simple combinatorial fact that the size of a strategy space to be explored is given by N^M where N is the size of the decision space and M is the size of the information space. Third is the so-called "No-Free-Lunch" limit expressed in [9] as a No-Free-Lunch Theorem quantifying the tradeoff between generality and efficiency of an algorithm. This is illustrated, for example, by Linear Programming algorithms which can very efficiently solve a very small (albeit important) class of optimization problems. Still, there are ways to solve many hard

C.G. Cassandras—Supported in part by NSF under grants CNS-1239021, ECCS-1509084, and IIP-1430145, by AFOSR under grant FA9550-15-1-0471, and by The MathWorks.

W. van der Aalst and E. Best (Eds.): PETRI NETS 2017, LNCS 10258, pp. 12–18, 2017.
DOI: 10.1007/978-3-319-57861-3_2

problems by exploiting their specific structure, by asking the "right" questions, and by challenging some conventional approaches.

2   Perturbation Analysis for Discrete Event Systems

Trial-and-error techniques are often used to systematically learn and predict the behavior of a complex system. These are invariably slow, inefficient, and intrusive. However, this learning can sometimes be accomplished at a fraction of the usual brute-force trial-and-error process through simple "thought experiments" constructed at a "small price." This is particularly true for Discrete Event Systems (DES), regardless of the modeling framework (automata, Petri Nets, or other) one chooses to employ. In particular, the theory of *Perturbation Analysis* (PA) [2,5,6] has established that event-driven dynamics give rise to state trajectories (sample paths) from which one can very efficiently and nonintrusively extract sensitivities of state variables (therefore, various performance metrics as well) with respect to at least certain types of design or control parameters. The origin of the key concepts that form the cornerstones of the PA theory are found in a long-standing problem known as the *buffer allocation problem*. In its industrial engineering version, a typical serial transfer line consists of N workstations in tandem, each with different characteristics in terms of its production rate, failure rate and repair time when failing. In order to accommodate this inhomogeneous behavior, a buffer is placed before the ith workstation, $i = 1, \ldots, N$, with B_i discrete slots where production parts can be queued and $\sum_{i=1}^{N} B_i = B$. The problem is to allocate these B buffer slots, i.e., determine a vector $[B_1 \ldots B_N]$, so as to maximize the throughput of the transfer line while also maintaining a low overall average delay of the parts moving from an entry point before the first workstation to an exit point following the Nth workstation. Tackling this problem in a "brute force" manner requires considering all possible buffer allocations, an enormous number (e.g., for a reasonably small problem such as $B = 24$ and $N = 6$, this gives 118,755 possible solutions.) A direct trial-and-error approach where one is allowed to test each allocation for about a week would require about 2300 years. If one were to reduce the initial solution space to only 1000 "good guesses" and use the fastest possible simulation software, the overall task would still require several hours of CPU time.

The approach first taken in [7] was to study the serial transfer line as a dynamic system whose state includes the integer-valued buffer contents along with real-valued "clocks" associated with each workstation as it processes a part. The question then posed was: "what would happen if in a given allocation a specific value B_i were changed to $B_i + 1$?" When part arrival and processing time distributions are unknown, there is no analytical expression relating the system throughput to the parameter vector $[B_1 \ldots B_N]$. Thus, the "brute force" way to answer this question is to first simulate the system under the nominal allocation with the value B_i and estimate the system's performance over a (sufficiently long) time period T which may be denoted by $L_T(B_i)$. Then, repeat the simulation under $B_i + 1$ to obtain $L_T(B_i + 1)$. The difference $\Delta L_T(B_i) = L_T(B_i + 1) - L_T(B_i)$

provides an estimate of the system's performance sensitivity with respect to B_i. However, this is unnecessary: indeed, the initial simulation alone yielding $L_T(B_i)$ and a simple thought experiment can deliver the value of $\Delta L_T(B_i)$. Moreover, the same thought experiment can deliver the entire vector $[\Delta L_T(B_1), \ldots, \Delta L_T(B_N)]$ with minimal extra effort. The key observation is that when B_i is replaced by $B_i + 1$, no change in the state of the system can take place unless one of two "events" is observed at time t: (i) The ith buffer content, say $x_i(t)$, reaches its upper limit, i.e., $x_i(t) = B_i$ and a part is ready to leave the $(i-1)$th workstation. In this case, this upstream workstation is "blocked" since there is no place for the departing part to go. However, in a perturbed system with B_i replaced by $B_i + 1$ that would not happen and one can simply predict a buffer content perturbation $\Delta x_i(t) = 1$. Moreover, one can record when this blocking occurs at time $t \equiv t_{i,B}$ and the next time that a part departs from the ith workstation, $t_{i,D}$. Then, $t_{i,D} - t_{i,B}$ is the amount of time that would be gained (i.e., no blocking would have occurred) in a perturbed system realization. The important observation here is that $t_{i,D}, t_{i,B}$ are directly observed along the nominal system realization. (ii) The $(i+1)$th buffer content reaches its lower limit, i.e., $x_{i+1}(t) = 0$ and a part is ready to leave the ith workstation. In this case, if $\Delta x_i(t) = 1$, i.e., the ith workstation has already gained a part from an earlier blocking event, then this gain can now propagate downstream and we can set $\Delta x_{i+1}(t) = \Delta x_i(t) = 1$. Thus, estimating the effect of replacing B_i by $B_i + 1$ boils down to observing just a few events along the nominal system realization: *blocking events* (when $x_i(t) = B_i$ and a part departure from $i - 1$ takes place) and *idling events* (when $x_i(t) = 0$ at any $i = 1, \ldots, N$.)

This basic idea can be extended to a large class of DES. The general procedure is one where some parameter perturbation $\Delta\theta$ *generates* a state perturbation $\Delta x_i(t)$ when a specific event occurs at time t. Subsequently, the system dynamics dictate how $\Delta x_i(t)$ *propagates* through the system by affecting $\Delta x_i(t)$ or $\Delta x_j(t)$ for $j \neq i$. Depending on a performance metric of interest, this ultimately yields $\Delta L_T(\Delta\theta)$, the estimated change in performance due to $\Delta\theta$. To illustrate this process, we consider the case of a simple First-In-First-Out (FIFO) queuing system with a single server preceded by a queue. Let $\{A_k\}$ be the sequence of (generally random) arrival times, $k = 1, 2, \ldots$, and $\{D_k\}$ be the corresponding sequence of departure times from the system. If Z_k denotes the service time of the kth entity (customer) processed, then the Lindley equation

$$D_k = \max(A_k, D_{k-1}) + Z_k \qquad (1)$$

describes the departure time dynamics with $k = 1, 2, \ldots$ Suppose that all (or just some selected subset) of the service times are perturbed by ΔZ_k, $k = 1, 2, \ldots$ Let $I_k = A_k - D_{k-1}$ and observe that when $I_k > 0$ it captures an idle period (since the server must wait until $A_k > D_{k-1}$ to become busy again) and when $I_k < 0$ it captures the waiting time $D_{k-1} - A_k$ of the kth arriving entity in the system. It is easy to obtain from (1) the following departure time perturbation equation:

$$\Delta D_k = \Delta Z_k + \begin{cases} \Delta D_{k-1} & \text{if } I_k \leq 0, \ \Delta D_{k-1} \geq I_k \\ 0 & \text{if } I_k > 0, \ \Delta D_{k-1} \leq I_k \\ I_k & \text{if } I_k \leq 0, \ \Delta D_{k-1} \leq I_k \\ \Delta D_{k-1} - I_k & \text{if } I_k > 0, \ \Delta D_{k-1} \geq I_k \end{cases} \tag{2}$$

where ΔD_k can be obtained from the generated perturbations ΔZ_k and directly observed data in the form of I_k. Next, observe that if we select $\Delta Z_k > 0$ to be sufficiently small so that $\Delta D_{k-1} > 0$ can never exceed the finite value of $I_k > 0$, then this reduces to

$$\Delta D_k = \Delta Z_k + \begin{cases} \Delta D_{k-1} & \text{if } I_k \leq 0 \\ 0 & \text{otherwise} \end{cases} \tag{3}$$

which is much simpler, requiring only the detection of an idling interval when $I_k > 0$, at which time the departure time perturbation is reset to $\Delta D_k = \Delta Z_k$. Naturally, the question is: "How small do perturbations need to be before the IPA equation can be used?" In a stochastic system, the answer to this question is generally dependent on the specific realization based on which ΔD_k is evaluated. Thus, it is logical to extend the question of estimating $\Delta D_k(\Delta\theta)$, $k = 1, 2, \ldots$, the departure time perturbations, to estimating the derivative $\frac{dD_k(\theta)}{d\theta}$ by allowing $\Delta\theta \to 0$. When $\Delta\theta \to 0$, this leads to *Infinitesimal Perturbation Analysis* (IPA) and one obtains derivatives (sensitivities) of the form $\frac{dL(\theta)}{d\theta}$ for performance metrics which can be expressed as a function of the departure times, i.e., $L(D_1(\theta), D_2(\theta), \ldots)$ These derivatives can be combined with standard gradient-based optimization techniques to solve hard stochastic optimization problems exploiting the fact that $dL(\theta)/d\theta$ can be shown under certain conditions to be an unbiased estimate of $dE[L(\theta)]/d\theta$, the derivative of an objective function $E[L(\theta)]$. When these conditions do not hold, several PA methods have been developed to still obtain unbiased estimates of $dE[L(\theta)]/d\theta$ at the expense of additional observed sample path data [2].

3   Decomposition and Abstraction

These are complementary approaches that can often provide accurate solutions or significantly simplify a hard problem at the "small price" of some loss of accuracy. Decomposition naturally arises in networks consisting of multiple nodes (often referred to as "agents") that cooperate to control their individual state so as to optimize a common objective. To accomplish this, the nodes need to communicate with each other to exchange state information. Since communication costs can be significant and reliance on a single central coordinator is highly complex, we seek conditions under which the optimization process can be decomposed and distributed over the nodes: each node performs its own optimization with communication carried out only when absolutely necessary and limited to its neighbors. The "absolutely necessary" condition is specified by events defined to occur when some state estimation error function at a node exceeds a threshold, thus drastically reducing the overall communication cost. One such scheme is based on node j maintaining an estimate of every neighboring node i's state, denoted by x_j^i. Assuming node i knows this estimate, it notifies node j of its true state x_i only when $\left\| x_i - x_j^i \right\| > \theta_i(t)$ where $\theta_i(t)$ is some threshold (possibly time-varying) and $\left\| \cdot \right\|$ is an appropriately defined norm that measures this state estimation error. This type of asynchronous, event-driven scheme can be shown to still guarantee convergence to an optimum even in the presence of communication delays as long as they are bounded [10].

On the abstraction side, the key idea is to replace a complex model by a simpler one that retains the salient features of the problem that one wishes to address. In the case of DES, this is possible by preserving only "significant" events and replacing the system's activity in between these events by continuous time-driven surrogates. A good example of this approach arises when a queueing system is abstracted by a *Stochastic Flow Model* (SFM) [3,4] where the "significant" events occur when the queue either becomes empty or it ceases to be empty following an idle period. The SFM framework essentially consists of fluid queues which forego the notion of the individual customer and focus instead on the aggregate flow. In such a fluid queue, traffic and service processes are characterized by instantaneous flow rates as opposed to the arrival, departure, and service times of discrete customers. The SFM qualifies as a stochastic hybrid system with bi-layer dynamics: event-driven dynamics at the upper layer and time-driven dynamics at the lower layer. The discrete events are associated with changes in traffic-flow processes, such as the reaching or leaving the boundaries of busy periods at the queues. In contrast, the time-driven dynamics describe the continuous evolution of flow rates between successive discrete events, usually through differential equations. Performance metrics that are natural to SFMs typically reflect quantitative measures of flow rates, like average throughput, buffer workload, and loss.

It is important to point out that the abstraction process serves the purpose of control and optimization rather than performance analysis. In this case, the "right" question to ask is "what is the value of a parameter that delivers the optimal performance?" and not "what is the optimal performance?" The SFM abstraction captures only those features of the underlying "real" system that are needed to lead to the correct answer to this question, even though the corresponding optimal performance may not be accurately estimated. Even if the exact solution cannot be obtained by such lower-resolution models, one can still obtain near-optimal points that exhibit robustness with respect to certain aspects of the model they are based on.

4   Event-Driven vs. Time-Driven Methods

The emergence of DES has brought to the forefront an alternative viewpoint to the traditional *time-driven* paradigm in which time is an independent variable and, as it evolves, so does the state of a dynamic system. The *event-driven* paradigm offers an alternative, complementary look at modeling, control, communication, and optimization [1,8]. The key idea is that a clock should not be assumed to dictate actions simply because a time step is taken; rather, an action should be triggered by an "event" specified as a well-defined condition on the system state or as a consequence of environmental uncertainties that result in random state transitions. Observing that such an event could actually be defined to be the occurrence of a "clock tick," it follows that this framework may in fact incorporate time-driven methods as well. On the other hand, defining the proper events requires more sophisticated techniques compared to simply reacting to time steps. In the development of DES, such events are seen as the natural means to drive the dynamics of a large class of systems (e.g., computer networks, manufacturing systems, supply chains.) More generally, however, it is evident that most interesting dynamic systems are in fact "hybrid" in nature, i.e., at least some of their state transitions are caused by (possibly controllable) events. *Stochastic hybrid systems* form the broadest class of dynamic systems one can envision (the SFM framework mentioned above is a special class of such systems.) As an example, a *hybrid* Petri net is one whose transition firing times are dependent on time-driven processes describing the evolution of continuous state variables associated with places: when a state variable exceeds a given threshold, this contributes to enabling one or more transitions in the output set of that place.

The IPA theory mentioned earlier for DES can be extended to hybrid systems, giving rise to a general-purpose *IPA Calculus* [4] which is the foundation of a gradient estimation methodology: it is based on a set of equations which provide state sensitivities of the form $dx(t; \theta)/d\theta$ for any model parameter θ (more generally, the gradient $\nabla x(t; \theta)$ with respect to a parameter vector θ.) For any performance metric $E[L(\theta)]$, this also provides sensitivities of the form $dE[L(\theta)]/d\theta$ through the sample path derivatives $dL(\theta)/d\theta$ which in turn depend on the stochastic processes $\{dx(t; \theta)/d\theta\}$. As in the case of DES, these can be obtained on line in an efficient non-intrusive manner. Moreover, they can be shown to be unbiased under very mild technical conditions and they possess a number of practically important properties. One of these properties stems from the fact that since the gradient estimation procedure is entirely event-driven, it is *scalable in the size of the event space* as opposed to the generally much larger state space of a system. Another important property is that the resulting estimators are independent of the random processes involved; at worst, they require only minimal effort to estimate simple statistics in the neighborhood of certain observable events.

References

1. Cassandras, C.G.: The event-driven paradigm for control, communication, and optimization. J. Control Decis. **1**(1), 3–17 (2014)
2. Cassandras, C.G., Lafortune, S.: Introduction to Discrete Event Systems, 2nd edn. Springer, US (2008)
3. Cassandras, C.G., Wardi, Y., Melamed, B., Sun, G., Panayiotou, C.G.: Perturbation analysis for on-line control and optimization of stochastic fluid models. IEEE Trans. Autom. Control **47**(8), 1234–1248 (2002)

4. Cassandras, C.G., Wardi, Y., Panayiotou, C.G., Yao, C.: Perturbation analysis and optimization of stochastic hybrid systems. Eur. J. Control **16**(6), 642–664 (2010)
5. Glasserman, P.: Gradient Estimation via Perturbation Analysis. Kluwer Academic Publishers, Dordrecht (1991)
6. Ho, Y.C., Cao, X.R.: Perturbation Analysis of Discrete Event Dynamic Systems. Kluwer Academic Publishers, Dordrecht (1991)
7. Ho, Y.C., Eyler, A., Chien, D.T.: A gradient technique for general buffer storage design in a serial production line. Int. J. Prod. Res. **17**, 557–580 (1979)
8. Miskowicz, M. (ed.): Event-Based Control and Signal Processing. CRC Press/Taylor and Francis, Boca Raton (2015)
9. Wolpert, D.H., Macready, W.G.: No free lunch theorems for optimization. IEEE Trans. Evol. Comput. **1**(1), 67–82 (1997)
10. Zhong, M., Cassandras, C.G.: Asynchronous distributed optimization with event-driven communication. IEEE Trans. Autom. Control **55**(12), 2735–2750 (2010)

Resource Equivalences in Petri Nets

Irina A. Lomazova$^{(\boxtimes)}$

National Research University Higher School of Economics,
20 Myasnitskaya ul., Moscow 101000, Russia
ilomazova@hse.ru

Abstract. Tokens in Petri net models may represent a control flow state, or resources produced/consumed by transition firings. From the resource perspective a part of a Petri net marking can be considered as a store needed for ensuring some future system behavior. The talk is devoted to the study of several types of resource equivalence in Petri nets. A resource is defined as a part (submultiset) of a Petri net marking and two resources are called equivalent iff replacing one of them by another in any reachable marking does not change the observable Petri net behavior. We investigate decidability of resource equivalences, present an algorithm for computing its finite approximation, and discuss applicability of resource equivalences to state space reduction and adaptive system processing.

1 Introduction

In Petri net models, places may be interpreted as resource repositories, and tokens represent resource availability, or resources themselves. A transition firing in its turn may be considered as resource handling, relocation, elimination, and creation. Thus Petri nets have a clear resource perspective, and are widely used for modeling and analysis of different kinds of resource-oriented systems, such as manufacturing systems, resource allocation systems etc.

In open nets special resource places are used for modeling a resource interface of the system [2,7,13,21]. In workflow nets resource places represent resources that can be consumed and produced during the business process execution. Obviously, resource places not only demonstrate a resource flow, but may substantially influence the system control flow [6,27].

As a mathematical formalism Petri nets are closely connected with the Girard's linear logic [12], which also has a nice resource interpretation, and for different classes of Petri nets it is possible to express a Petri net as a linear logic formula [8,9].

Here we consider resources as parts of Petri nets markings (bags of tokens residing in Petri net places) and study the possibility to replace one resource by another in any reachable marking without changing the observable net behavior.

This work is supported by the Basic Research Program at the National Research University Higher School of Economics and Russian Foundation for Basic Research, project No. 16-01-00546.

W. van der Aalst and E. Best (Eds.): PETRI NETS 2017, LNCS 10258, pp. 19–34, 2017.
DOI: 10.1007/978-3-319-57861-3_3

An observable system behavior is captured by the bisimulation equivalence [23]. Two states are bisimilar, if their behavior cannot be distinguished by an external observer. It was proved by P. Jančar [16] that marking (state) bisimulation is undecidable for Petri nets.

In [1] C. Autant and Ph. Schnoebelen studied the place bisimulation and proved that this relation is decidable. Roughly speaking, two places in a Petri net are bisimular, if in any marking a token in one place can be replaced by a token in another one without violating the characteristic property of the bisimulation equivalence — the transfer property. As a consequence we get that replacing tokens in bisimilar places does not change the observable net behavior. Also bisimilar places can be merged, and place bisimulation can be used for the equivalent reduction of the net.

Ph. Schnoebelen and N. Sidorova introduced in [26] the equivalence relation on places, called place fusion. It is defined as an equivalence on Petri net places, which allows to replace a token in one place by a token in the other one in any marking without changing the net observable behavior. It was proved in [26] that place fusion is undecidable.

In [3] we presented the notion of the resource similarity. A resource in a Petri net is a part of a marking. Two resources are similar for a given Petri net if replacing one of them by another in any marking does not change the observable net behavior. The resource similarity can be considered as a generalization of the place fusion equivalence, in the sense that the place fusion is the resource similarity for one-token resources. Hence, the resource similarity is undecidable.

However, the resource similarity, as well as some other interesting resource equivalences, can be generated by a finite basis. We prove that the resource similarity is closed under addition of resources and transitivity, and can be generated as the additive and transitive closure of some finite relation (AT-basis). The similar result in terms of congruences in commutative semigroups was obtained by L. Redei [24] and Y. Hirshfeld [15] (a shorter proof). However, our proof is constructive and explicitly defines a minimal AT-basis.

The study we describe here, in particular constructing the finite AT-basis, is based on well-quasi-orderings (wqo's). The wqo, defined as the component-wise comparison of integers, can be naturally defined on Petri net markings, and many substantial results are based on this ordering and the monotonicity property of transition firings, e.g. the classical coverability tree by Karp and Miller [17].

In the more general setting of infinite-state systems with wqo on states and the monotonicity property the theory of well-structured transition systems [10,11] was developed and continues to be a source of interesting results on decidability for extensions of Petri nets, such as nested Petri nets [19,20,22], and Petri nets with data [18,25]. For comparing resources we use the wqo different from the usual ordering on markings in Petri nets, since we need to enforce not monotonicity of transition firings, but monotonicity of resource addition.

This paper presents a survey on resource equivalences in Petri nets and contains results and parts of texts of papers [3–5], written jointly with Vladimir Bashkin. Though these papers were written more than ten years ago, we consider the topic still interesting and perspective for the theory of Petri nets. There are still open problems and questions that can be a source for further research.

2   Resource Similarity

We consider classical place/transition Petri nets.

By $\mathbb{N}$ we denote the set of natural numbers. A *multiset* m over a set S is a mapping $m : S \to \mathbb{N}$, i.e. a multiset may contain several copies of the same element. For two multisets m, m' over S the inclusion relation and the sum of two multisets are defined as usual: $m \subseteq m'$ iff $\forall s \in S : m(s) \leq m'(s)$, and $\forall s \in S : m + m'(s) = m(s) + m'(s)$. By $\mathcal{M}(S)$ we denote the set of all finite multisets over S.

A *Petri net* $N = (P, T, W)$ is a tuple, where P is a finite set of *places*, T — a finite set of *transitions*, and $W : (P \times T) \cup (T \times P) \to \mathbb{N}$ — an arc-weight function. To observe a net behavior transitions are marked by special labels representing observable actions or events. Let Act be a set of action names. A *labeled Petri net* is a tuple $N = (P, T, W, l)$, where (P, T, W) is a Petri net and $l : T \to Act$ is a labeling function.

A *marking* in a Petri net is a function $M : P \to \mathbb{N}$ mapping each place to some natural number (possibly zero), i.e. $M \in \mathcal{M}(P)$. Pictorially, P-elements are represented by circles, T-elements by boxes, and the flow relation F by directed arcs. Places may carry tokens represented by filled circles. A current marking M is designated by putting $M(p)$ tokens into each place $p \in P$. Tokens residing in a place are often interpreted as resources of some type consumed or produced by a transition firing.

For a transition $t \in T$ an arc (x, t) is called an *input arc* and an arc (t, x) — an *output arc*; the *preset* $^{\bullet}t$ and the *postset* $t^{\bullet}$ are defined as the multisets over P such that $^{\bullet}t(p) = W(p, t)$ and $t^{\bullet}(p) = W(t, p)$ for each $p \in P$. A transition $t \in T$ is *enabled* in a marking M iff $\forall p \in P \; M(p) \geq W(p, t)$. An enabled transition t may *fire* yielding a new marking $M' =_{\text{def}} M - {^{\bullet}t} + t^{\bullet}$, i.e. $M'(p) = M(p) - W(p, t) + W(t, p)$ for each $p \in P$ (denoted $M \xrightarrow{t} M'$).

Two markings (states) in a Petri net are considered equivalent, if they generate the same observable behavior. Finding equivalent states may be very helpful for reducing the state space of a Petri net when analyzing its behavioral properties. The classical observable equivalence for Petri nets is a marking bisimulation [23].

Let $N = (P, T, W, l)$ be a labeled Petri net. We say that a relation $R \subseteq \mathcal{M}(P) \times \mathcal{M}(P)$ satisfies the *transfer property* iff for all $(M_1, M_2) \in R$ and for every firing $M_1 \xrightarrow{t} M_1'$, there exists an imitating firing $M_2 \xrightarrow{u} M_2'$, such that $l(t) = l(u)$, and $(M_1', M_2') \in R$. The transfer property can be represented by the following diagram:

$$
\begin{array}{ccc}
M_1 & R & M_2 \\
\downarrow t & & \downarrow u \qquad l(u) = l(t) \\
M_1' & R & M_2'
\end{array}
$$

A relation R is called a *marking bisimulation*, if both R and R^{-1} satisfy the transfer property.

For every labeled Petri net there exists the largest marking bisimulation (called bisimilarity and denoted by $\sim$) and this bisimulation is an equivalence.

Intuitively, two markings in a Petri net are bisimilar iff replacement one of them by another does not change the observable system behavior. It was proved by P. Jančar [16], that marking bisimulation is undecidable for Petri nets. Then it would be interesting to look for decidable approximations of marking bisimilarity.

Ph. Schnoebelen and N. Sidorova studied in [26] an equivalence on Petri net places, which allows to replace a token in one place by a token in the other one in any marking without changing the net observable behavior. This equivalence is called *place fusion*, since merging two equivalent places gives the net with the same observable behavior. Unfortunately, as it was proved in [26], place fusion is also undecidable.

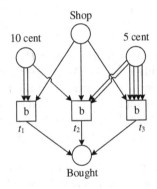

Fig. 1. Buying goods for 20 cents

Here we consider a more general case of replacing not just one token, but a larger part of a marking without changing the system behavior. We define these submarkings as *resources*, and the definition of a resource coincides with the definition of a marking, since submarking is a marking itself. Markings and resources are differentiated further because of their different substantial interpretation. Resources in our considerations are not just tokens, but multisets of tokens residing in their places. They are parts of markings which may or may not provide this or that kind of net behavior, e.g. the Petri net in Fig. 1 two ten-cent coins form a resource — enough to buy an item of goods.

Then formally, for a labeled Petri net $N = (P, T, W, l)$, a *resource* $R \in \mathcal{M}(P)$ is a multiset over the set of places P.

Two resources r and s in N are called *similar* (denoted $r \approx s$) iff for every marking $R \in \mathcal{M}(P)$, $r \subseteq R$ implies $R \sim R - r + s$. Thus if two resources are similar, then in every marking each of these resources can be replaced by another without changing the observable system's behavior. E.g. buying an item of goods according to the process modeled by the Petri net in Fig. 1 can be done with two ten-cent coins, or one ten-cent and two five-cent coins, or fore five-cent coins. In all these cases we have the same observable behavior, and all these three bags of coins form similar resources.

It can be easily checked that resource similarity is an equivalence, and is more strong than the marking bisimulation: $m \approx m' \Rightarrow m \sim m'$. The converse implication is obviously not true (cf. Fig. 2). In other words $(\approx) \subset (\sim)$.

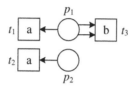

Fig. 2. The resource similarity does not coincide with the marking bisimulation: $p_1 \sim p_2$, but $p_1 \not\approx p_2$

On the other hand, place fusion is a special case of resource similarity for resources of capacity 1. Hence, undecidability of place fusion implies undecidability of resource similarity.

Though the resource similarity is undecidable, it has some nice properties and can be represented by a finite basis.

First of all, being equivalence relation, resource similarity is closed under *transitivity*. More interesting, it is closed under *addition of resources*, i.e. for any resources r, s, u, v in a Petri net N we have

$$r \approx s \ \& \ u \approx v \ \Rightarrow \ r + u \approx s + v$$

Let R^{AT} denote the additive-transitive closure (AT-closure) of the relation $R \subseteq \mathcal{M}(P) \times \mathcal{M}(P)$ (the minimal congruence, containing R). Then resource similarity $\approx$ coincides with its AT-closure $(\approx)^{AT}$.

Let $B \subseteq \mathcal{M}(P) \times \mathcal{M}(P)$ be a binary relation on resources. A relation B' is called an *AT-basis* of B iff $(B')^{AT} = B^{AT}$. An AT-basis B' is called *minimal* iff there is no $B'' \subset B'$ such that $(B'')^{AT} = B^{AT}$.

Thus an AT-basis completely specifies the relation. So, when a relation has a finite AT-basis, it has a nice and helpful finite representation. Further we show that the resource similarity has a finite AT-basis. For constructing this basis we use a special well-quasi ordering on resources.

Recall that a *well-quasi-ordering* (a wqo) is any quasi-ordering $\leq$ such that, for any infinite sequence $x_0, x_1, x_2, \ldots$, in X, there exist indexes $i < j$ with $x_i \leq x_j$. The classical property of wqo's states that the set of minimal w.r.t. a wqo elements is finite.

Now we define a special wqo on pairs of Petri net resources, and minimal elements in this wqo will form a minimal AT-basis for the resource similarity relation.

Note that for a given Petri net its markings (and resources) are integer vectors of a fixed length. So, by Higman's lemma [14] sequence (coordinate-wise) partial ordering on the set of a Petri net markings is a wqo. This ordering is very helpful for analysis of Petri nets as well-structured transition systems [11] and, in particular, for techniques based on constructing a coverability tree/graph. However, for constructing AT-basis for resource similarity relation we need another ordering.

So, we define a partial order $\sqsubseteq$ on the set $B \subseteq \mathcal{M}(P) \times \mathcal{M}(P)$ of pairs of resources as follows:

1. For identity pairs let

$$(r_1, r_1) \sqsubseteq (r_2, r_2) \overset{def}{\Leftrightarrow} r_1 \subseteq r_2;$$

2. For two non-identity pairs, the maximal identity parts and the addend pairs of disjoint resources are compared separately:

$$(r_1 + o_1, r_1 + o'_1) \sqsubseteq (r_2 + o_2, r_2 + o'_2) \overset{def}{\Leftrightarrow}$$

$$\overset{def}{\Leftrightarrow} o_1 \cap o'_1 = \emptyset \ \& \ o_2 \cap o'_2 = \emptyset \ \& \ r_1 \subseteq r_2 \ \& \ o_1 \subseteq o_2 \ \& \ o'_1 \subseteq o'_2.$$

3. An identity pair and a non-identity pair are always incomparable.

Let then B_s denote the set of all elements of B^{AT}, which are minimal with respect to $\sqsubseteq$.

Theorem 1 ([3]). *Let $B \subseteq \mathcal{M}(P) \times \mathcal{M}(P)$ be a symmetric and reflexive relation. Then B_s is an AT-basis of B^{AT} and B_s is finite.*

We call B_s the *ground basis* of B.

As a direct consequence of this theorem we obtain that for any symmetric and reflexive relation all its minimal AT-bases are finite.

A similar to Theorem 1 result (in terms of congruences in commutative semigroups) was obtained by L. Redei [24] in 1965 and Y. Hirshfeld [15] (a shorter proof) in 1994. However, the proof in [3] differs from their proofs, and, what is more important, is based on the explicitly defined wqo, i.e. it is constructive. The wqo described here is used further for constructing the ground bases for some other resource equivalences.

The main implication of Theorem 1 for our considerations is that for every Petri net its resource similarity relation can be represented by a finite number of pairs. Hence, though resource similarity is undecidable, if we by any means find some similarity pairs, we can obtain new similarities by applying transitivity and addition, and may hope to sufficiently approximate resource similarity relation.

3   Resource Bisimulation

The resource similarity relation is a narrowing of the marking bisimilarity, which is closed under addition of resources and transitivity, i.e. if a relation B is a resource similarity, then $B = B^{AT}$. We know also that, being finitely based, resource similarity is undecidable, and hence its finite basis cannot be computed effectively. Then looking for a computable approximation of the marking bisimilarity we define one more relation on Petri net markings (resources).

An equivalence $B \subseteq \mathcal{M}(P) \times \mathcal{M}(P)$ is called a *resource bisimulation* iff B^{AT} is a marking bisimulation.

First of all we state several important properties of resource bisimulations. Let N be a labeled Petri net. Then

1. if B_1, B_2 are resource bisimulations for N then $B_1 \cup B_2$ is a resource bisimulation for N;
2. there exists the largest resource bisimulation, denoted by $\simeq$, such that for every resource bisimulation B we have $B \subseteq (\simeq)$.
3. for a given Petri net the resource bisimilarity is a narrowing of the resource similarity relation, i.e. for each two resources r and s:

$$r \simeq s \Rightarrow r \approx s.$$

By the definition the relation $\simeq$ is a symmetric and reflexive relation, closed under transitivity and addition of resources. Then by Theorem 1 above the maximal resource bisimulation has a finite ground AT-basis, consisting of minimal w.r.t. the wqo relation $\sqsubseteq$. The main implication of this for our considerations is that for every Petri net its largest resource bisimulation can be represented by a finite number of pairs.

The AT-closure of a resource bisimulation is a marking bisimulation, and marking bisimulations are characterized by the transfer property. We show now that resource bisimulations can be characterized by a weak variant of the transfer property, when only 'relevant' markings are considered for a transition t. The weak variant of the transfer property for place bisimulation was defined in [1]. The following definition generalizes it for arbitrary resources.

Thus we say that a relation $B \subseteq \mathcal{M}(P) \times \mathcal{M}(P)$ satisfies *the weak transfer property* iff for all $(r, s) \in B$, for all $t \in T$, s.t. ${}^\bullet t \cap r \neq \emptyset$, there exists an imitating step $u \in T$, s.t. $l(t) = l(u)$ and, writing M_1 for ${}^\bullet t \cup r$ and M_2 for ${}^\bullet t - r + s$, we have $M_1 \xrightarrow{t} M_1'$ and $M_2 \xrightarrow{u} M_2'$ with $(M_1', M_2') \in B^{AT}$.

The weak transfer property can be represented by the following diagram:

$$r \quad \approx_B \quad s$$

$${}^\bullet t \cup r \qquad\qquad {}^\bullet t - r + s$$

$$\downarrow t \qquad\qquad\qquad \downarrow (\exists)u,\ l(u) = l(t)$$

$$M_1' \quad \sim_{B^{AT}} \quad M_2'$$

The following theorem gives an important characterization of resource bisimulation relations.

Theorem 2 ([3]). *A relation $B \subseteq \mathcal{M}(P) \times \mathcal{M}(P)$ is a resource bisimulation iff B is an equivalence and it satisfies the weak transfer property.*

This characterization can be used for checking whether a given finite relation B is a resource bisimulation, since for a finite relation the weak transfer property can be directly verified.

Moreover, the largest resource bisimulation for resources with a bounded number of tokens can be computed by the following algorithm.

Let $N = (P, T, F, l)$ be a labeled Petri net and $\mathcal{M}_q(P)$ denote the set of all its resources, containing not more then q tokens (residing in all places).

Algorithm

Input: a labeled Petri net $N = (P, T, F, l)$, a positive integer q.
Output: the relation $B(N, q)$
Step 1: Let $C = \{(\emptyset, \emptyset)\}$ be an empty set of pairs (considered as a relation over $\mathcal{M}_q(P)$).
Step 2: Let $B = (\mathcal{M}_q(P) \times \mathcal{M}_q(P)) \setminus C$.
Step 3: Compute a ground basis B_s. Denote by B_s^{nr} the set of all non-identity elements of B_s.
Step 4: Check if B_s conforms to the weak transfer property (it is sufficient to check only B_s^{nr}). If the weak transfer property is valid, then stop. The current B is $B(N, q)$. Otherwise, there exists a pair $(r, s) \in B_s^{nr}$ and a transition $t \in T$ with $\bullet t \cap r \neq \emptyset$ such that $\bullet t \cup r \xrightarrow{t} M_1'$ cannot be imitated from $\bullet t - r + s$. Then add pairs $(r, s), (s, r)$ to C and return back to the step 2.

For each Petri net N the resource bisimilarity $\simeq$ is an infinite relation, and for a natural number q the bisimulation relation $B(N, q)$ is a finite approximation for $\simeq$. We obviously have

$$B(N, 1) \subseteq B(N, 2) \subseteq B(N, 2) \subseteq \cdots \subseteq \simeq,$$

and hence

$$B(N, 1)^{AT} \subseteq B(N, 2)^{AT} \subseteq B(N, 3)^{AT} \subseteq \cdots \subseteq \simeq .$$

But since the resource bisimilarity has a finite AT-basis, there exists a natural number q_0 such that

$$B(N, 1)^{AT} \subseteq B(N, 2)^{AT} \subseteq \cdots \subseteq B(N, q_0)^{AT} = B(N, q_0 + 1) = \cdots = \simeq .$$

Then the problem is to compute, or evaluate q_0. It is easy to see that computing an upper bound for q_0 is equivalent to computing an AT-basis for the resource bisimilarity. However, the **question**, *whether the largest resource bisimulation can be effectively computed*, is still **open**.

Note that if for some q we have $B(N, q) = B(N, q+1)$, it does not imply that the sequence has stabilized. Consider e.g. the Petri net in Fig. 3. For this net we have $B(N, 1) = B(N, 2) = \{(0,0), (1,1)\}$, $B(N, 3) = \{(0,0), (1,1), (2,3), (3,2)\}$, and $B(N, 1)^{AT} = B(N, 2)^{AT} \subset B(N, 3)^{AT} = \simeq$.

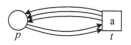

Fig. 3. A Petri net, for which the largest resource bisimulation has an AT-basis of size three

One more **open problem** is *whether the largest resource bisimulation of a Petri net coincides with its resource similarity*:

$$(\simeq) \overset{?}{=} (\approx)$$

Since resource similarity is undecidable, the answer 'yes' to this problem implies that resource bisimilarity is undecidable as well.

We *conjecture* the positive answer to the last question. Our attempts to find an example of a resource similarity which is not a resource bisimilarity have failed, though we cannot prove that resource similarity and resource bisimilarity coincide. If this conjecture is true, than an upper bound for q_0 also cannot be effectively computed.

However, for practical applications an upper bound for q_0 can be evaluated either by experts in the application domain, or by analysis of the concrete net. Then the algorithm for computing $B(N, q)$ can be applied and $B(N, q)$ can be used as an AT-basis for approximating resource bisimilarity.

4   Conditional Resource Similarity

A natural modification of the resource similarity relation evolves when we would like to replace a part of some resource. We call it the *conditional similarity*. In words, two resources are conditionally similar if replacing one of them by another in any marking in the presence of some additional resources does not change the observable net behavior. For many applications the notion of the conditional resource similarity is even more natural than unconditional one. For instance, one can replace an excessive memory subsystem by a smaller one with the required maximal capacity provided.

More formally, for resources $r, s, b \in \mathcal{M}(P)$ two resources r and s are called *similar under a condition b* (denoted $r \approx_{|b} s$) iff for every resource $m \in \mathcal{M}(P)$ s.t. $b \subseteq m$ we have $m + r \sim m + s$.

Resources r and s are called *conditionally similar* (denoted $r \approx_| s$) iff there exists $b \in \mathcal{M}(P)$ s.t. $r \approx_{|b} s$.

Examples of conditionally similar resources are given in Fig. 4. Here for the Petri net in (a) the resources p_1 and p_2 are similar only when the additional resource q is available. For the Petri net in (b) the conditional similarity means that adding more resources to p does not change the net behavior.

The plain and conditional similarities are connected in the straightforward way. For each two similar resources $m \approx m'$ and two arbitrary resources $r, s \in \mathcal{M}(P)$ we have $m + r \approx m' + s$ iff $r \approx_{|m} s$.

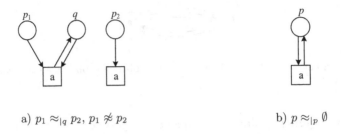

a) $p_1 \approx_{|q} p_2$, $p_1 \not\approx p_2$ b) $p \approx_{|p} \emptyset$

Fig. 4. Examples of conditionally similar resources

The conditional similarity is closed under addition of resources. Let $r, r', m, m', b_1, b_2 \in \mathcal{M}(P)$. If $m \approx_{|b_1} m'$ and $r \approx_{|b_2} r'$, then $m + r \approx_{|b_1 \cup b_2} m' + r'$.

The conditional similarity is an equivalence and has some nice properties. Let $r, s, b, b', m, m' \in \mathcal{M}(P)$. Then the following implications are valid:

1. $r \approx_{|b} s$, $b \subseteq b' \Rightarrow r \approx_{|b'} s$.
2. $m + r \approx_{|b} m + s \Leftrightarrow r \approx_{|b+m} s$.
3. $m + r \approx_| m + s \Leftrightarrow r \approx_| s$.
4. $m \approx m'$, $m + r \approx m' + s \Rightarrow r \approx_| s$.
5. $m \approx_| m'$, $m + r \approx_| m' + s \Rightarrow r \approx_| s$.

Here the first implication says that the conditional resource similarity is invariant modulo the condition enlargement. Claims 2 and 3 state that the common parts can be removed from both similar resources. Claims 4 and 5 state that the difference of similar, as well as conditionally similar, resources is also conditionally similar.

Thus, the conditional similarity, as well as plain similarity, is closed under addition of resources, and unlike the plain similarity, it is closed under the subtraction of similar resources. These properties allow constructing an additive base for the conditional similarity relation.

A pair $r \approx_| s$ of conditionally similar resources is called *minimal* if it cannot be decomposed into a sum of two other non-empty conditionally similar pairs, i.e. for every non-empty pair $r' \approx_| s'$ of conditionally similar resources $r = r' + r''$ and $s = s' + s''$ implies $r = r'$ and $s = s'$.

The Claim 5 from the above list of conditional similarity properties immediately implies that every pair of conditionally similar resources can be decomposed into a sum of minimal pairs of conditionally similar resources.

Recall that for the 'plain' similarity a special wqo $\sqsubseteq$ was needed for constructing the AT-basis of the relation. The plain similarity is not closed under subtraction of similar resources, and that is why it cannot be represented by additive closure of some basis. The case of the conditional similarity turns to be more simple. Minimal pairs in the conditional similarity relations are minimal double-length vectors w.r.t. the standard coordinate-wise ordering $\leq$.

By Higman's lemma the coordinate-wise ordering $\leq$ on vectors of natural numbers is a wqo. Hence, for every Petri net the set of minimal pairs of conditionally similar resources is finite. And hence, we get that the set of all pairs of conditionally similar resources is an *additive closure* of the finite set of all minimal pairs of conditionally similar resources.

By Claim 1 from the above list of the conditional similarity properties the set of conditions for a pair of conditionally similar resources is upward closed. These conditions are represented by integer vectors of the same length, and then obviously for every pair $r \approx_| s$ of conditionally similar resources the set of all its minimal conditions (w.r.t. the coordinate-wise comparison) is finite.

Let $R \subseteq \mathcal{M}(P) \times \mathcal{M}(P)$ be some set of pairs of conditionally similar resources ($r \approx_| s$ for every $(r, s) \in R$). Let

$$B = \{ (u, v) \in \mathcal{M}(P) \times \mathcal{M}(P) \mid u \approx v \ \wedge \ \forall (r, s) \in R \ \ u + r \approx v + s \}$$

be a set of all common conditions for R. By $Cond(R)$ we denote the set of all minimal elements of B (w.r.t. $\leq$, considering B as a set of vectors of length $2|P|$).

Now let us consider more closely the relationship between plain and conditional similarities. Now we call a pair $r \approx s$ of similar resources *minimal* iff it cannot be decomposed into a sum of a pair of similar resources and a pair of conditionally similar resources, i.e. for every non-empty pair $r' \approx s'$ of similar resources $r = r' + r''$ and $s = s' + s''$ implies $r = r'$ and $s = s'$.

Immediately from the definition we obtain that every pair of similar resources can be decomposed into the sum of one minimal pair of similar resources and several minimal pairs of conditionally similar resources.

Let $R \subseteq \mathcal{M}(P) \times \mathcal{M}(P)$. By $lc(R)$ we denote the set of all *linear combinations* over R, i.e. $lc(R) = \{(r, s) \mid (r, s) = (r_1, s_1) + \ldots + (r_k, s_k), (r_i, s_i) \in R, i = 1, \ldots, k\}$.

Let also $S \subseteq \mathcal{M}(P) \times \mathcal{M}(P)$. By $R + S$ we denote the set of all sums of pairs from R and S, i.e. $R + S = \{(u, v) \mid (u, v) = (r + r', s + s'), (r, s) \in R, (r', s') \in S\}$.

The following theorem shows the connection between the plain resource similarity and the conditional resource similarity.

Theorem 3 ([4]). *Let N be a Petri net, $(\approx)$ — the set of all pairs of similar resources for N, $(\approx_|)$ — the set of all pairs of conditionally similar resources for N. The set $(\approx)$ is semilinear. Specifically, there exists a finite set $R \subseteq (\approx_|)$ s.t.*

$$(\approx) = \bigcup_{\mathcal{R} \in 2^R} [Cond(\mathcal{R}) + lc(\mathcal{R})],$$

where 2^R is the set of all subsets of R.

Note that a sum of conditionally similar pairs may have a smaller minimal condition than its components. So, the minimal conditionally similar pairs may be not enough for the additive decompositions of unconditionally similar resources. It could be that some other pairs, depending on decomposed resources, are also needed in this decomposition.

Undecidability of the resource similarity implies that the conditional resource similarity is also undecidable for Petri nets. This means that it is impossible to construct an algorithm, answering whether a given pair of resources is similar under a given condition. To find conditionally similar resources one can compute finite resource bisimulations, as described above, to approximate resource similarity and then subtract similar (or identity) parts in pairs of similar resources in accordance to the Claim 4 of the property list above: $m \approx m'$, $m + r \approx m' + s \Rightarrow r \approx_| s$. Since the conditional resource similarity has a finite additive basis, we may hope to chose the right size of the finite bisimilarity relation to compute the additive basis of the conditional resource bisimilarity.

5   Generalized Resource Similarity

Finding interchangeable resources may be useful not only for reducing the state space of the system, but also for adaptive controlling of the process execution. Then the question is whether it is possible to replace some resources together with changing the next activity step. In this case we consider two kinds of resources: a bag of tokens is a (passive) *material resource*, while a bag of activities forms a (dynamic) *activity resource*. Of course, an activity resource should be secured by the necessary material resources.

Thus we define a *generalized resource*. It includes not only statical but also dynamical components. Generalized resource is a pair of multisets: a multiset of places and a multiset of transitions. A multiset of places defines a *material resource*, a multiset of transition defines an *activity resource*.

Meaningfully, two generalized resources are called *similar*, iff in any state of the system we can replace tokens and firings of one generalized resource by tokens and firings of another not changing the observable system behavior. Here all transitions in the activity part of a generalized resource are supposed to fire independently (in one parallel step).

For defining generalized resources we consider parallel transition firings. The transitions may *fire in parallel* (simultaneously), if there are enough tokens for all of them. In particular, the transition may fire in parallel with itself. The simultaneous firing of the multiset of transitions is called *a parallel step*. The precondition and the postcondition for a multiset $\alpha \in \mathcal{M}(T)$ of transitions are defined as follows:

$$^\bullet\alpha =_{def} \sum_{t \in \alpha} {}^\bullet t, \qquad \alpha^\bullet =_{def} \sum_{t \in \alpha} t^\bullet.$$

Note that if a transition t occurs n times in α then its precondition $^\bullet t$ occurs n times in $^\bullet\alpha$. Obviously,

$$^\bullet(\alpha + \beta) = {}^\bullet\alpha + {}^\bullet\beta, \qquad (\alpha + \beta)^\bullet = \alpha^\bullet + \beta^\bullet.$$

A labeling function $l : T \to Act$ can be generalized to multisets:

$$\text{for } \alpha \in \mathcal{M}(T) \qquad l(\alpha) =_{def} \sum_{t \in \alpha} l(t).$$

Again, we use not a union but a sum of multisets.

Formally, let $N = (P, T, F, l)$ be a labeled Petri net. A pair (r, α) s. t. $r \in \mathcal{M}(P), \alpha \in \mathcal{M}(T)$ and $^\bullet\alpha \subseteq r$ is called a *generalized resource* of a Petri net N. The set of all generalized resources of N is denoted by $\Phi(N)$.

The requirement $^\bullet\alpha \subseteq r$ for a generalized resource (r, α) is very natural and guarantees that materials necessary for enabling activity part of the resource are always included into its material part. Note that by definition $^\bullet\alpha$ contains enough tokens for *parallel* firing of *all* transitions in α. Hence α can be always considered as a parallel step.

Generalized resources (r, α) and (s, β) are called *similar* iff

1. $l(\alpha) = l(\beta)$;
2. for every marking $M \in \mathcal{M}(P)$, if $M + r \xrightarrow{\alpha} M'$ and $M + s \xrightarrow{\beta} M''$, then $M' \sim M''$.

By abuse of notation we use the same relation symbol $\approx$ for the similarity of generalized resources as for the plain resource similarity, and write $(r, \alpha) \approx (s, \beta)$, when the generalized resources (r, α) and (s, β) are similar.

Figure 5 gives an example of similar generalized resources.

$$(p_1, t_1) \approx (p_1 + p_2, t_2)$$

Fig. 5. An example of two similar generalized resources

The generalized resource similarity has a natural interpretation. Consider a situation when a process represented by a Petri net is controlled by a supervisor. This supervisor may choose one of the enabled steps to fire. Then if a step α is enabled in a current marking M, generalized resources (r, α) and (s, β) are similar, and $r \subseteq M$, the supervisor may change the resource r for s and fire β instead of α without changing the observable net behavior. Note that this replacement does not replace transitions in the net's graph. Figure 5 shows an example of similar generalized resources.

Special cases of generalized resource similarity allows to express some interesting system properties. Here are some examples:

$(r, \alpha) \approx (r, \beta)$ Activities α and β are **equivalent** in any state of the system, when a resource r is available.

$(r, \alpha) \approx (s, \alpha)$ Resources r and s are **equivalent**, if α is certainly executed.

$(r, \alpha) \approx (r + s, \beta)$ Activity α is more **efficient** than β.

$(r, \emptyset) \approx (r + s, \emptyset)$ Resource s is **redundant**.

The generalized resource similarity has some nice properties. First of all, it is an equivalence. Then for each two steps $\alpha, \beta \in \mathcal{M}(T)$. we have

$$l(\alpha) = l(\beta) \quad \Rightarrow \quad (^\bullet\alpha + \beta^\bullet, \alpha) \approx (^\bullet\beta + \alpha^\bullet, \beta).$$

There are two special kinds of generalized resources. A generalized resource of the form $(r, \emptyset)$ is called a *material resource*. A generalized resource of the form $(^\bullet\alpha, \alpha)$ is an *activity resource*.

The material resource similarity coincides with the plain resource similarity, studied above, i.e. for $r, s \in \mathcal{M}(P)$ we have

$$r \approx s \quad \Leftrightarrow \quad (r, \emptyset) \approx (s, \emptyset).$$

Similarity of activity resources also can be expressed via the plain resource similarity, precisely, for $\alpha, \beta \in \mathcal{M}(T)$ we have

$$(^\bullet\alpha, \alpha) \approx (^\bullet\beta, \beta) \quad \Leftrightarrow \quad (\alpha^\bullet, \emptyset) \approx (\beta^\bullet, \emptyset).$$

This means that activity steps can be interchanged, iff they produce equivalent material resources.

The plain consequence of this is that the generalized resource similarity is undecidable for labeled Petri nets, since the plain resource similarity is undecidable.

However, the generalized resource similarity inherits not only bad, but good properties of the plain similarity relation. Namely, the generalized resource similarity is closed under the addition of pairs of resources, i.e. for $(r, \alpha), (s, \beta), (u, \gamma), (v, \delta) \in \Phi(N)$ we have

$$(r, \alpha) \approx (s, \beta) \,\&\, (u, \gamma) \approx (v, \delta) \Rightarrow (r + u, \alpha + \gamma) \approx (s + v, \beta + \delta).$$

Note that the generalized resource similarity is not closed under the subtraction of pairs of resources. Moreover, the difference of two generalized resources may be itself not a generalized resource, since the material part of the resource may not enable its activity part after subtraction.

Thus, the generalized resource similarity is closed under addition of resources and transitivity, and hence coincides with its own AT-closure. Being equivalence it is also a symmetric and reflexive relation. So, we can apply Theorem 1 and conclude that the generalized similarity has a finite AT-basis.

To construct the ground AT-basis for the generalized resource similarity we follow the scheme, used for plain similarity, and define a partial order on pairs of generalized resources (by abuse of notation we denote it $\sqsubseteq$) as follows:

$$\Big((r, \alpha), (s, \beta)\Big) \sqsubseteq \Big((u, \gamma), (v, \delta)\Big) \;\stackrel{def}{\Leftrightarrow}\; (r, s) \sqsubseteq (u, v) \,\&\, (\alpha, \beta) \sqsubseteq (\gamma, \delta).$$

Let $R(N) \subseteq \Phi(N) \times \Phi(N)$ denote the generalized resource similarity relation for a Petri net N. To prove that minimal w.r.t. $\sqsubseteq$ elements of the set $R(N)$ form an AT-basis for $R(N)$, we are to check additionally that each generalized resource (r, α) in these minimal elements meets the requirement ${}^\bullet\alpha \subseteq r$. Luckily, it turns to be true, and the method of proof used for the plain similarity can be adapted for the generalized resource similarity.

So, we denote the set of all minimal (w.r.t. $\sqsubseteq$) elements of $R(N)$ by $R_s(N)$ and call it the *ground basis* of $R(N)$. Then similar to Theorem 1 we get

Theorem 4. *Let N be a labeled Petri net. Then $R(N) = R(N)^{AT}$, the ground basis $R_s(N)$ is an AT-basis of $R(N)$, and $R_s(N)$ is finite.*

It was stated earlier that special kinds of generalized resource similarity, consisting of only material, or only activity resources, can be reduced to plain resource similarity. For these special cases the described above technique for computing approximations of resource bisimulation can be used to find some pairs of similar generalized resources. The **question** whether the notion of resource bisimulation and related theory can be extended to generalized resources remains **open**.

Acknowledgment. I would like to thank Vladimir Bashkin for the many years of collaborative research, of which this paper presents just a part.

References

1. Autant, C., Schnoebelen, P.: Place bisimulations in Petri nets. In: Jensen, K. (ed.) ICATPN 1992. LNCS, vol. 616, pp. 45–61. Springer, Heidelberg (1992). doi:10.1007/3-540-55676-1_3
2. Baldan, P., Bonchi, F., Gadducci, F.: Encoding asynchronous interactions using open Petri nets. In: Bravetti, M., Zavattaro, G. (eds.) CONCUR 2009. LNCS, vol. 5710, pp. 99–114. Springer, Heidelberg (2009). doi:10.1007/978-3-642-04081-8_8
3. Bashkin, V.A., Lomazova, I.A.: Petri nets and resource bisimulation. Fundam. Inf. **55**, 101–114 (2003). http://content.iospress.com/articles/fundamenta-informaticae/fi55-2-02
4. Bashkin, V.A., Lomazova, I.A.: Resource similarities in Petri net models of distributed systems. In: Malyshkin, V.E. (ed.) PaCT 2003. LNCS, vol. 2763, pp. 35–48. Springer, Heidelberg (2003). doi:10.1007/978-3-540-45145-7_4
5. Bashkin, V.A., Lomazova, I.A.: Similarity of generalized resources in Petri nets. In: Malyshkin, V. (ed.) PaCT 2005. LNCS, vol. 3606, pp. 27–41. Springer, Heidelberg (2005). doi:10.1007/11535294_3
6. Bashkin, V.A., Lomazova, I.A.: Decidability of k-soundness for workflow nets with an unbounded resource. In: Koutny, M., Haddad, S., Yakovlev, A. (eds.) Transactions on Petri Nets and Other Models of Concurrency IX. LNCS, vol. 8910, pp. 1–18. Springer, Heidelberg (2014). doi:10.1007/978-3-662-45730-6_1
7. Dong, X., Fu, Y., Varacca, D.: Place bisimulation and liveness for open Petri nets. In: Fränzle, M., Kapur, D., Zhan, N. (eds.) SETTA 2016. LNCS, vol. 9984, pp. 1–17. Springer, Cham (2016). doi:10.1007/978-3-319-47677-3_1
8. Farwer, B.: A linear logic view of object Petri nets. Fundam. Inf. **37**(3), 225–246 (1999). http://dl.acm.org/citation.cfm?id=2377296.2377299
9. Farwer, B., Lomazova, I.: A systematic approach towards object-based Petri net formalisms. In: Bjørner, D., Broy, M., Zamulin, A.V. (eds.) PSI 2001. LNCS, vol. 2244, pp. 255–267. Springer, Heidelberg (2001). doi:10.1007/3-540-45575-2_26

10. Finkel, A.: The ideal theory for WSTS. In: Larsen, K.G., Potapov, I., Srba, J. (eds.) RP 2016. LNCS, vol. 9899, pp. 1–22. Springer, Cham (2016). doi:10.1007/978-3-319-45994-3_1

11. Finkel, A., Schnoebelen, P.: Well-structured transition systems everywhere!. Theoret. Comput. Sci. **256**(1), 63–92 (2001). http://www.sciencedirect.com/science/article/pii/S030439750000102X

12. Girard, J.Y.: Linear logic. Theoret. Comput. Sci. **50**(1), 1–101 (1987). http://www.sciencedirect.com/science/article/pii/0304397587900454

13. Heckel, R.: Open Petri nets as semantic model for workflow integration. In: Ehrig, H., Reisig, W., Rozenberg, G., Weber, H. (eds.) Petri Net Technology for Communication-Based Systems. LNCS, vol. 2472, pp. 281–294. Springer, Heidelberg (2003). doi:10.1007/978-3-540-40022-6_14

14. Higman, G.: Ordering by divisibility in abstract algebras. Proc. Lond. Math. Soc. **s3-2**(1), 326–336 (1952). http://dx.doi.org/10.1112/plms/s3-2.1.326

15. Hirshfeld, Y.: Congruences in commutative semigroups. Technical report ECS-LFCS-94-291, Department of Computer Science, University of Edinburgh (1994)

16. Jančar, P.: Decidability questions for bisimilarity of Petri nets and some related problems. In: Enjalbert, P., Mayr, E.W., Wagner, K.W. (eds.) STACS 1994. LNCS, vol. 775, pp. 581–592. Springer, Heidelberg (1994). doi:10.1007/3-540-57785-8_173

17. Karp, R.M., Miller, R.E.: Parallel program schemata. J. Comput. Syst. Sci. **3**(2), 147–195 (1969). http://www.sciencedirect.com/science/article/pii/S0022000069800115

18. Lasota, S.: Decidability border for Petri nets with data: WQO dichotomy conjecture. In: Kordon, F., Moldt, D. (eds.) PETRI NETS 2016. LNCS, vol. 9698, pp. 20–36. Springer, Cham (2016). doi:10.1007/978-3-319-39086-4_3

19. Lomazova, I.A.: Nested Petri nets - a formalism for specification and verification of multi-agent distributed systems. Fundam. Inf. **43**(1), 195–214 (2000). http://www.scopus.com/inward/record.url?eid=2-s2.0-0034250902&partnerID=40&md5=8a9efd42010e494aaaa3a09b99e97f25

20. Lomazova, I.A.: Nested Petri nets: multi-level and recursive systems. Fundam. Inf. **47**(3–4), 283–293 (2001). http://dl.acm.org/citation.cfm?id=1220035.1220044

21. Lomazova, I.A., Romanov, I.V.: Analyzing compatibility of services via resource conformance. Fundam. Inf. **128**(1–2), 129–141 (2013). http://dx.doi.org/10.3233/FI-2013-937

22. Lomazova, I.A., Schnoebelen, P.: Some decidability results for nested Petri Nets. In: Bjøner, D., Broy, M., Zamulin, A.V. (eds.) PSI 1999. LNCS, vol. 1755, pp. 208–220. Springer, Heidelberg (2000). doi:10.1007/3-540-46562-6_18

23. Milner, R.: Communication and Concurrency. Prentice-Hall Inc., Upper Saddle River (1989)

24. Rédei, L.: The Theory of Finitely Generated Commutative Semigroups. Oxford University Press, New York (1965)

25. Rosa-Velardo, F., de Frutos-Escrig, D.: Decidability and complexity of Petri nets with unordered data. Theoret. Comput. Sci. **412**(34), 4439–4451 (2011). http://www.sciencedirect.com/science/article/pii/S0304397511003896

26. Schnoebelen, P., Sidorova, N.: Bisimulation and the reduction of Petri Nets. In: Nielsen, M., Simpson, D. (eds.) ICATPN 2000. LNCS, vol. 1825, pp. 409–423. Springer, Heidelberg (2000). doi:10.1007/3-540-44988-4_23

27. Sidorova, N., Stahl, C.: Soundness for resource-constrained workflow nets is decidable. IEEE Trans. Syst. Man Cybern.: Syst. **43**(3), 724–729 (2013)

Simulation of Colored Petri Nets

Faster Simulation of (Coloured) Petri Nets Using Parallel Computing

Franck Pommereau[✉] and Jordan de la Houssaye

IBISC, University of Évry, 23 Boulevard de France, 91037 Évry Cedex, France
{franck.pommereau,jordan.delahoussaye}@ibisc.univ-evry.fr

Abstract. Fast simulation, *i.e.*, automatic computation of sequential runs, is widely used to analyse Petri nets. In particular, it enables for quantitative statistical analysis by observing large sets of runs. Moreover, fast simulation may be used to actually run a Petri net model as a (prototype) implementation of a system, in which case such a net would embed fragments of the code of the system. In both these contexts, being able to perform faster simulation is highly desirable.

In this paper, we propose a way to accelerate fast simulation by exploiting parallel computing, targeting both the multi-core CPUs available nowadays in every laptop or workstation, and larger parallel computers including those with distributed memory (clusters). We design an algorithm to do so and assess in particular its correctness and completeness through its formal modelling as a Petri net whose state space is analysed. We also present a benchmark of a prototype implementation that clearly shows how our algorithm effectively accelerates fast simulation, in particular in the case of large concurrent coloured Petri nets, which is precisely the kind of nets that are usually slow to simulate.

Keywords: Petri nets · Fast simulation · Parallel computing

1 Introduction

Fast simulation is a widely used technique that consists in computing a run of a Petri net. Such a run is built automatically, as fast as possible, contrasting with interactive simulation for which the user is requested to chose the next of every step in the run. Fast simulation allows the modeller to make direct observations of the behaviour of a Petri net, just like developers run their programs to observe them. How fast is fast simulation becomes crucial when one wants to build large sets of runs on which various properties may be measured in order to perform quantitative statistical analysis, as done in [4] for example. This is a widely used technique that nicely complements qualitative analysis through state-space analysis (in particular, model-checking). Moreover, considering coloured Petri nets more specifically, one may embed in a Petri net model parts of the functional fragments of system under design, *i.e.*, the Petri net may be equipped with code that performs actual computation and is intended to be integrated into the final

© Springer International Publishing AG 2017
W. van der Aalst and E. Best (Eds.): PETRI NETS 2017, LNCS 10258, pp. 37–56, 2017.
DOI: 10.1007/978-3-319-57861-3_4

system. In such a case, the Petri net is used both for analysis and for simulating the non-functional parts of the system that may be complicated to implement (which is true in particular for distributed system). Such a model may thus be used as an implementation of the system, or just considered as a prototype that may be simulated to observe runs or perform tests in the environment where the system is expected to operate. In such a case also, being able to accelerate simulation is very interesting.

In this paper we propose a parallel algorithm to accelerate simulation, designed in such a way that it can be implemented using a wide variety of programming languages, and targeting shared memory as well as distributed memory computer. This makes it suitable for being used on laptops or workstations equipped with multi-core CPUs (that is, all of them nowadays) as well as on dedicated computers like clusters. The main idea behind this algorithm is to compute a run of a Petri net from a sequential pseudo-concurrent process (*i.e.*, using *cooperative multitasking* within a single thread of execution) that delegates some computation to external processes through remote procedure calls. We present our algorithm, called *Medusa*, and we assess its properties resorting to formal modelling and analysis, then we present a prototype implementation and a benchmark of its performances. Doing so we show that Medusa is *correct* (it only builds legal runs), *complete* (it can build any run of the simulated Petri net), and *fair* (it has no bias that would favour some runs over others). The benchmark shows that our choice of a cooperative multitasking algorithm requesting worker processes (or threads) can be easily and effectively implemented. Moreover, we observe that Medusa's acceleration grows linearly with the number of processes, up to some point where it amortises, which depends on the intrinsic concurrency in the Petri net and on the work load necessary to compute the successors of a marking through one transition. Consequently, we can conclude that Medusa is well suited for large and concurrent coloured Petri nets, which is exactly the case where faster simulation is the most needed.

The next section provides the definition of the Petri nets we use in the rest of the paper. Then, Sect. 3 presents Medusa algorithm and its formal analysis. Section 4 describes the prototype implementation and its benchmark, and a detailed analysis of the results obtained from the latter. The paper ends on a conclusion with a discussion about related and future works.

2   Petri Nets

To start with, we need to define multisets and various operations between them.

Definition 1. *A* multiset *A over of set X is a function $X \to \mathbb{N}$ where for every $x \in X$, $A(x)$ is the number of occurrences of x in A. For A and B two multisets over X, we define:*

- *$A \leq B$ iff $A(x) \leq B(x)$ for all $x \in X$;*
- *$A + B$ is the multiset over X such that $(A + B)(x) \stackrel{\text{df}}{=} A(x) + B(x)$ for all $x \in X$;*

– $A - B$, defined iff $B \leq A$, is the multiset over X such that $(A - B)(x) \stackrel{\mathrm{df}}{=} A(x) - B(x)$ for all $x \in X$.

A (coloured) Petri net involves values, variables and expressions. These objects are defined by a *colour domain* that provides data values, variables, operators, a syntax for expressions, possibly typing rules, etc. For instance, one may use integer arithmetic or Boolean logic as colour domains. Usually, more elaborated colour domains are useful to ease modelling, in particular, one may consider a functional programming language or the functional fragment (expressions) of an imperative programming language. We consider here an abstract colour domain with the following pairwise disjoint sets:

– $\mathbb{D}$ is the set of *data* values;
– $\mathbb{V}$ is the set of *variables*;
– $\mathbb{E}$ is the set of *expressions*, involving values, variables and appropriate operators. Let $e \in \mathbb{E}$, we note by $\mathsf{vars}(e)$ the set of variables from $\mathbb{V}$ involved in e. Moreover, variables or values may be considered as (simple) expressions, *i.e.*, we assume that $\mathbb{D} \cup \mathbb{V} \subset \mathbb{E}$.

We make no assumption about the typing or syntactical correctness of expressions; instead, we assume that any expression can be evaluated, possibly to $\bot \notin \mathbb{D}$ (undefined). More precisely, a *binding* is a partial function $\beta : \mathbb{V} \to \mathbb{D}$. Let $e \in \mathbb{E}$ and β be a binding, we note by $\beta(e)$ the evaluation of e under β. The application of a binding to evaluate an expression is naturally extended to sets and multisets of expressions.

Take for instance $\beta \stackrel{\mathrm{df}}{=} \{x \mapsto 0\}$, we may have distinct evaluations of various expressions depending on the chosen colour domain:

– in Python, C and JavaScript: $\beta(x + 1) = 1$;
– in Python, $\beta(x + \texttt{"hello"}) = \bot$ because of a type exception, in C it is the address of string $\texttt{"hello"}$, while in JavaScript it is the string $\texttt{"0hello"}$ because an automatic coercion is performed;
– in Python and JavaScript $\beta(x + y) = \bot$ because of an exception complaining that y is not defined, and in C also but because of a compilation error.

We can now define a variant of coloured Petri nets that is independent of the annotation language.

Definition 2. *A Petri net is a tuple (S, T, ℓ) where:*

– *S is the finite set of places;*
– *T, disjoint from S, is the finite set of transitions;*
– *ℓ is a labelling function such that:*
  - *for all $s \in S$, $\ell(s) \subseteq \mathbb{D}$ is the type of s, i.e., the values that s is allowed to carry as tokens,*
  - *for all $t \in T$, $\ell(t) \in \mathbb{E}$ is the guard of t, i.e., a condition for its execution,*
  - *for all $(x, y) \in (S \times T) \cup (T \times S)$, $\ell(x, y)$ is a multiset over $\mathbb{E}$ and defines the arc from x towards y.*

For all $x \in T \cup P$ we define $\bullet x \overset{\mathrm{df}}{=} \{y \in P \cup T \mid \ell(y,x) \neq \emptyset\}$ and $x^\bullet \overset{\mathrm{df}}{=} \{y \in P \cup T \mid \ell(x,y) \neq \emptyset\}$. These notations are naturally extended to sets of nodes.

Then we define the dynamic aspect of Petri nets, i.e., the markings and the firing of transitions. Note that we also introduce a notion of *token flow* that will be needed to define our algorithm.

Definition 3. Let $N \overset{\mathrm{df}}{=} (S, T, \ell)$ be a Petri net. A marking M of N is a function on S that maps each place s to a finite multiset over $\ell(s)$ representing the tokens held by s. For two markings A and B, we define:

- $A \leq B$ iff $A(s) \leq B(s)$ for all $s \in S$;
- $A + B$ is the marking such that $(A+B)(s) \overset{\mathrm{df}}{=} A(s) + B(s)$ for all $s \in S$;
- $A - B$, defined iff $B \leq A$, is the marking such that $(A-B)(s) \overset{\mathrm{df}}{=} A(s) - B(s)$ for all $s \in S$.

Let $t \in T$ be a transition, M a marking and β a binding. The token flow generated by t and β at M is a pair of markings $sub_{M,t,\beta} \overset{\mathrm{df}}{=} \{s \mapsto \beta(\ell(s,t)) \mid s \in S\}$ and $add_{M,t,\beta} \overset{\mathrm{df}}{=} \{s \mapsto \beta(\ell(t,s)) \mid s \in S\}$. Then, t is enabled for β at M, which is noted by $M[t, \beta\rangle$, iff the following conditions hold:

- M has enough tokens, i.e., $sub_{M,t,\beta} \leq M$;
- the guard is satisfied, i.e., $\beta(\ell(t))$ is true;
- place types are respected, i.e., $add_{M,t,\beta}$ is a valid marking of N.

If $t \in T$ is enabled for binding β at marking M, then t may fire and yield a marking M' defined by $M' \overset{\mathrm{df}}{=} M - sub_{M,t,\beta} + add_{M,t,\beta}$, which is noted by $M[t, \beta\rangle M'$. Finally, we note by $\lceil M\rangle$ the set of all the markings reachable from a marking M through arbitrary sequences of transitions and bindings.

3 Medusa: A Concurrent Simulation Algorithm

In order to distinguish the transitions in a Petri net from the corresponding data structures used in Medusa algorithm, we call the latter *players*; by extension, we shall call player as well the activity that handles this data structure (i.e., we may adopt an object-oriented point of view, which fits with our implementation). Moreover, each player belongs to a *team* that consists of the other players with which it is in competition to fire its transitions. More precisely, for every transition we define a corresponding *player* to record information about this transition as follows:

```
1   struct player :
2       trans : transition    # the player's transition
3       team  : set[player]    # its team (a set of players)
4       out   : set[player]    # its output (a set of players)
5       busy  : bool           # is the player currently working?
6       retry : bool           # should the player retry its current work?
```

Then, for each transition (and the corresponding player), we define its *team* as the set of transitions (and players) with which it is in conflict (including the transition itself), and its *output* as the set of transition for which it may produce a token. Formally:

Definition 4. *Let* $N \stackrel{\mathrm{df}}{=} (S, T, \ell)$ *be a Petri net, then for all* $t \in T$ *we define* team$(t) \stackrel{\mathrm{df}}{=} (^\bullet t)^\bullet$ *and* out$(t) \stackrel{\mathrm{df}}{=} (t^\bullet)^\bullet$. *Let* p *be a player, then* $p.team$ *is the set of players such that* team$(p.transition) = \{q.transition \mid q \in p.team\}$, *and* $p.out$ *is the set of players such that* out$(p.transition) = \{q.transition \mid q \in p.out\}$.

Finally, a Petri net *run* is a list r of markings (this may be enriched easily) whose latest item is noted as r.last, and we use an operation "**append** m **to** r" to add a marking m at the end of r. Moreover, [] represents the empty run.

3.1   Concurrency Model

We consider an interleaving concurrency model in which the simulation engine is executed on a single computation unit (*e.g.*, one core of one CPU) on which multiple sequential threads of execution are interleaved. Other computation units exist and are exploited to execute code through *remote procedure calls* (RPC). Moreover, a thread has to explicitly release the control so that another can be scheduled, that is, we assume so called cooperative multitasking. Consequently, there is no need for lock primitives to guarantee consistent accesses to data structures. To express this we use two primitives:

- "**call** fun$(\cdots)$" invokes a function fun asynchronously, *i.e.*, its execution starts in a new thread but it is not scheduled immediately, instead, the caller is able to continue its own execution. This requires that "fun" returns no value because the caller has no way to get it;
- "**rpc** fun$(\cdots)$" is similar to **call** but the caller is blocked until the result is returned. Moreover, the execution of fun is performed on another computation unit so that, while the caller is waiting, another thread can be scheduled and executed in the simulation.

The goal is to achieve speedup by allowing this sequential engine to be executed in parallel with the remote procedures it calls. In the implementation, a limited pool of worker processes will be used to execute the RPC calls, which means that not all those calls can be executed in parallel but some are sequentialised. But this has no consequence on the definition of the algorithm.

3.2   Medusa Algorithm

Figure 1 shows Medusa algorithm. The entry point is function **startup** that creates a new run and launches in parallel one instance of procedure work for each player. Players are marked as busy and they all share the same run just created.

The main procedure is thus work. Line 9, it computes the token flows available from the current marking by calling remote procedure getflows. Note that this

```
 1   def startup (players) :
 2       run ← []
 3       for player in players :
 4           player.busy ← True
 5           call work(player, run)
 6
 7   def work (player, run) :
 8       player.retry ← False
 9       flows ← {f in rpc getflows(player.trans, run.last) | f.sub ≤ run.last}
10       if player.retry and flows = ∅ :
11           call work(player, run)
12       elif flows = ∅ :
13           player.busy ← False
14       else :
15           choose flow in flows
16           append run.last − flow.sub + flow.add to run
17           player.busy ← False
18           for other in player.team ∪ player.out :
19               if not other.busy :
20                   other.busy ← True
21                   call work(other, run)
22               elif other.busy and other in player.out :
23                   other.retry ← True
```

Fig. 1. Medusa algorithm, where remote procedure getflows(t,m) returns the set of token flows for a transition t at a marking m.

call is initiated using the latest marking in the run, and it may take some time during which other instances of work will be scheduled. When flows are returned and this instance of work is scheduled again, they are filtered by keeping only those that are applicable to the current latest marking. This may not be the same marking as when getflows has been called if another work instance from the same team has fired its transition (thus removing tokens). Line 10, if the player has been told to retry and found no usable flow, work is called again. Otherwise, line 12, if there is no usable flow then the player becomes idle. Finally, line 14, the player has a usable flow and fires its transition by computing a new marking that is added to the run. Then it is marked idle (line 17) and it has to inform all the player in its team or in its output that their input markings has been changed: in the team we have removed tokens, in the output, we have added tokens. If such a player is not busy, it is put to work (lines 20–21), otherwise, if this is a player in the output, it is told to retry because it is waiting for getflows and will retrieve an outdated result since we just added tokens to its input places. Retry is actually attempted (line 13) only is no valid flow is available, this is necessary to avoid a deadlock, but not mandatory since there are already usable flows. Remember that we assume cooperative multitasking, so when an instance of work finds another player to be busy, then the work instance for this latter player *must* by paused because of the call to getflows.

3.3   Formal Analysis

To assess Medusa's expected properties, we have conducted two actions. On the one hand, during our benchmark presented below, every run computed has been checked to be a correct run of the executed Petri net. On the other hand, we have built a formal model of Medusa using the ABCD specification language [15] and analysed its state space, which is reported now. We have not enough room to present the model (available here [16]) but we describe it here in terms of its Petri net semantics, that we call the *model-net* to distinguish it from the *simulated-net* for which it computes a run:

- a place holds the players structures, initially at the state they have at the end of startup, plus a field state to record which step of work this player is currently handling. So, simulating **call** work(player, run) just requires to put player.state at the appropriate value;
- instead of the whole computed run, only run.last is stored, into a dedicated place, because it is the only marking we need and because this allows one to keep a finite state space (provided that the simulated-net itself has a finitely many markings);
- one transition models the beginning of work, picking a player, updating it and putting in another place the flows obtained from getflows (this piece of code is named *rpc*). These flows will be retrieved by one of the following transitions;
- a second transitions models the end of line 9 that filters the flows and the execution of line 11 (code piece *retry*);
- a third transition models also the end of line 9, but now together with line 13 (code piece *idle*);
- finally, a fourth transition models the end of line 9 together with lines 15–23 (code piece *fire*).

Instances of these transitions for the different players are interleaved when the model-net is executed, which models cooperative multitasking.

We have computed the state space of this model-net when its fires the transitions of simulated-nets like those depicted in Fig. 2. In Fig. 3, we show the resulting marking graph for simulated-net (3). Slightly larger nets have been analysed as well, with the same results as presented below, but the state space of the model becomes quickly intractable for nets with more that 4–5 transitions. However, the nets depicted in Fig. 2 have been carefully chosen to focus on the analysed aspects: correctness, completeness, deadlocks, progression, and fairness.

To check these properties, we consider the marking graph G_m of the model-net in which: every node is replaced by the marking of the simulated-net that is stored in run.last in this state of the model-net; every edge that corresponds to the *fire* piece of code is labelled by the transition that is fired (*i.e.*, on black edges in Fig. 3, the gray parts of the labels are removed); other edges (the gray ones) are labelled by τ. Then, let G_m/τ be G_m in which all the τ transitions have been collapsed (*i.e.*, whenever $x \xrightarrow{\tau} y$ we merge nodes x and y and remove the resulting τ-labelled side-loop). We have checked that for each simulated-net,

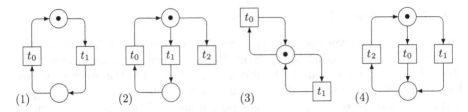

Fig. 2. Examples of simulated-nets used to analyse the model of Medusa. From the left to the right, these simulated-nets yield model-nets with state spaces with respectively 18, 135, 8, and 126 states. The state space for net (3) is depicted in Fig. 3.

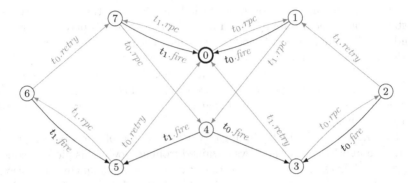

Fig. 3. The state space of the model-net for simulated-net (3) from Fig. 2 where the initial state is 0. Edges are labelled with the player's transition for which procedure work is active followed by the name of the code piece that is executed. Gray arcs are those whose label is replaced by τ to check weak bisimilarity.

its marking graph G_s and G_m/τ are isomorphic, from which we have that the model-net and the simulated-net are *weak bisimilar* [5]. Consequently, we obtain:

- *correctness*: every run constructed by the model-net is a valid run of the simulated-net;
- *completeness*: for every run of the simulated-net, there is an execution of the model-net that constructs this run;
- *deadlocks equivalence*: the simulated-net and the model-nets have exactly the same deadlocks, if any, *i.e.*, every deadlock in one net corresponds to a deadlock in the other net with the same marking of the simulated-net;
- *progression*: we have checked that there is no loop with only τ edges in G_m, which means that the model-net cannot progress unboundedly without executing an instance of the *fire* piece of code;
- *fairness equivalence*: a fair (resp. unfair) run of the simulated-net can be constructed only by a fair (resp. unfair) run of the model-net because both nets have bisimilar executions and the model-net has to progress. So considering for example G_m for simulated-net (3) that is shown in Fig. 3, a fair execution of Medusa cannot always favour loops like $0 \leftrightarrow 1$ where transition t_1 is completely excluded, or $1 \to 4 \to 3 \to 2 \to 1$ where transition t_1 is considered but never allowed to fire. We will discuss fairness from a quantitative point of view in the next section.

4   Towards an Efficient Implementation

We have made a prototype implementation of Medusa using SNAKES [14] for the Petri net aspects and gevent [2] for the cooperative multitasking aspects. The simulator consists of one main process that executes Medusa and a bunch of worker processes to which computation tasks are delegated through RPC. The implementation of Medusa itself is in Python and is very close to the pseudo-code presented above, the implementation of **call** and **rpc** on the top of gevent requires less than 100 additional lines of code. All this code is available in [16].

We have exercised this prototype on a choice of parametrised models depicted in Fig. 4. Each model is designed as a reversible net so that we can run arbitrary long simulations without encountering a deadlock. Models StarFlower and HyperLoops have both conflicts and concurrency, while Cycle has no conflict and its concurrency is limited to the number of tokens, finally, Parallel has no conflicts but maximal concurrency. Each model has also a parameter $chroma \geq 0$ that allows to simulate the effect of having coloured Petri nets for which firing transitions takes more time: each transition is equipped with a guard that is always true but spends $chroma/10$ s using the CPU intensively. To do so it computes the BZip2 compression of the SHA512 hash of a random value, and repeatedly on the result. This loop involves two CPU-intensive algorithms and using a random seed plus a strong cryptographic hash ensure that we avoid potential effects of the computer's caches.

We have built more than 700 instances of these models with various parameters and ran about 22 k simulations of these instances that we have split into five classes according to their number of transitions, as shown in Fig. 5. Note that we have also ran simulations for much larger nets with up to 115 k transitions but there are too few to present smooth results, however, they are so far consistent with what we present here. These simulations allowed to observe various aspects:

- how adding more worker processes speeds-up the simulation;
- how the simulation speed is influenced by the amount of computation required to fire transitions as captured by parameter $chroma$;
- how Medusa behaves when the number of transitions grows;
- how theoretical "fairness equivalence" can be observed on an implementation.

This benchmark have been run on a computer equipped with two 64 bits Intel® Xeon® hexacore CPUs at 2.67 GHz, sharing 44 Gb of RAM, which allows to run up to 12 processes independently so we have limited our benchmark to 10 worker processes in order to leave enough CPU for Medusa main process and the operating system. On the software side, we have used Debian 8.6 with Linux kernel 4.4.19, Python 2.7.9, gevent 1.1.2 (for cooperative multitasking) [2], gipc 0.6.0 (simplified IPC for gevent) [8], psutil 4.3.1 (measure the CPU and memory usage of processes) [17], and SNAKES 0.9.21 [14].

4.1   Performance Analysis

Let us first remark that the time necessary to build a set of players from a Petri net is always negligible and thus not analysed here. Moreover, by design, Medusa

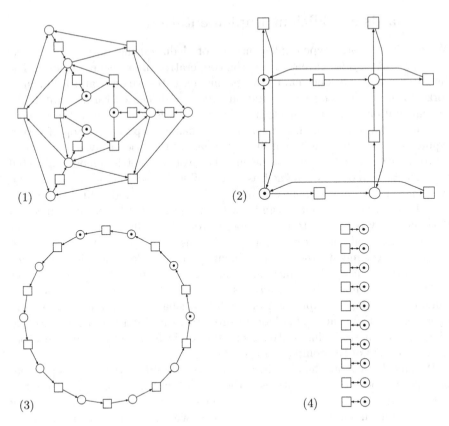

Fig. 4. Instances of the models used for the benchmark. (1) *StarFlower*(*depth* = 2, *num* = 3) is organised as a series of concentric connected rings of places and transitions, where *depth* is the number of rings and *num* is the number of pairs of places and transitions on a ring. (2) *HyperLoop*(*dim* = 2, *width* = 2) is organised as an hyper-cube of dimension *dim* where *width* is the number of transitions on one edge. (3) *Cycle*(*length* = 10, *tokens* = 4) is organised as a loop, where *length* is the number of transitions and *tokens* the number of tokens. (4) *Parallel*(*length* = 10) is organised as a series of independent side-loops, where *length* is the number of transitions.

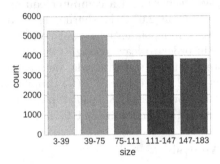

Fig. 5. Distribution of the simulated instances by size (number of transitions).

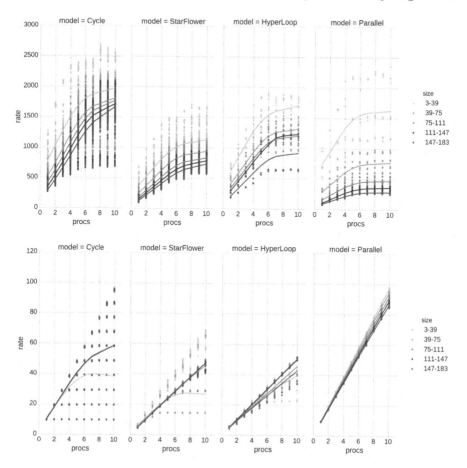

Fig. 6. Firing rates with respect to the number of worker processes, for *chroma* = 0 (top) and *chroma* = 1 (bottom). Higher is better.

cannot accelerate the simulation of Petri nets that have no concurrency at all because it can only parallelise the firing of concurrent transitions.

That said, Fig. 6 shows how many transitions per second Medusa can fire, with respect to the number of worker processes and to the size of the nets, for *chroma* ∈ {0, 1}, decomposed by model. We observe in general a linear speedup until 5 or 6 processes, where it starts to amortise. For uncoloured models, firing rate is better for smaller nets and it decreases with the size of the nets. For coloured models, rates are of course much lower because every transition firing takes 0.1 s, but larger nets globally have better rates. Moreover, for models with more concurrency between transitions (*i.e.*, larger models or those with less conflicts) Medusa scales better with the number of processes. See in particular the curves for the coloured instances of Parallel.

We explain these observations by the overhead introduced by Medusa that is more important in the uncoloured case than in the coloured case where most of the time is spent computing token flows. This is not surprising that an algorithm that is designed to parallelise computation tasks is more efficient when these tasks take more time. Furthermore, having more concurrent nets yields more such tasks so it allows to better use worker processes that are always fed with token flows to compute, in such a way that we maximise parallel efficiency.

To confirm this, we have programmed a very simple sequential simulator directly based on SNAKES that repeatedly chooses and fires a transition (see its pseudo-code in Fig. 7). We have exercised this simulator on the same instances and compared it with Medusa (using 6 to 10 worker processes).

The results are provided in Fig. 8. We can observe that SNAKES simulation is better than Medusa for uncoloured nets (except on model Cycle), but that Medusa is much faster than SNAKES for coloured nets. In the former case, this is explained again by the additional cost of IPC and the relatively bigger complexity of Medusa algorithm, which cannot be compensated by parallel computation because token flows require very little computation time. In the latter case, parallel computation becomes effective and Medusa is actually able to compute in parallel the token flows for several transitions, which is the most clearly observed in the case of Parallel.

Another confirmation that worker processes are efficiently exploited can be obtained by decomposing the time spent in IPC into three classes: (1) waiting: when Medusa is waiting for a worker process to be available, during which another task in Medusa may be active (for instance to fire a transition); (2) communication: the time spent in sending a request from Medusa to a worker process, or in receiving the answer; (3) computation: the time spent by the worker process to compute the token flows, during which Medusa may be busy handling other players. This is shown in Fig. 9 where we observe that waiting time is largely dominant when there is not enough worker processes, but quickly decreases with the number of processes. Moreover, communication time is always negligible and not visible in this graph. Note also that we obtain identical plots if we separate cases by *chroma* or net sizes. This waiting time that never disappears shows that Medusa is always fast compared to the worker processes. So, the fact that firing rates do not grow linearly after some point does not come from the overhead of the parallel processing, but it must come from the insufficient intrinsic concurrency in the simulated nets, which does not occur with Parallel.

This is also illustrated on Fig. 10 where we focus on coloured instances of model Cycle: in this model, the number of tokens is exactly the maximum number of transitions that may fire concurrently (but if several tokens are located in the same place, concurrency is lower because Medusa does not consider auto-concurrency). In Fig. 10 we clearly observe that Medusa has exactly the same performance than the SNAKES-based simulator when only one token is available (*i.e.*, 10 transitions per second as each transition takes 0.1 s), but it accelerates with the number of tokens.

```
 1  def simul (net) :
 2      deadlock ← False
 3      while not deadlock :   # simulate until a deadlock is found
 4          deadlock ← True  # assume the current marking is a deadlock
 5          for trans in shuffle (net. transitions ) : # try to fire each transition
 6              flows ← getflows(trans, net.marking)
 7              if flows ≠ ∅ : # choose one flow and fire
 8                  choose flow in flows
 9                  net.marking ← net.marking − flow.sub + flow.add
10                  deadlock ← False # actually we did not reach a deadlock
11                  break              # quit for loop ⇒ restart while loop
```

Fig. 7. The simple SNAKES-based simulator used for comparison with Medusa.

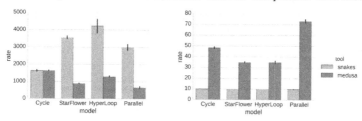

Fig. 8. Compared mean firing rates of SNAKES and Medusa (for 6–10 processes), by models, and for *chroma* = 0 (left) and *chroma* = 1 (right). Higher is better.

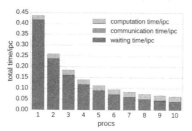

Fig. 9. Decomposition of the time spent in IPCs with respect to the number of worker processes.

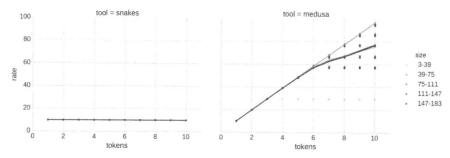

Fig. 10. Mean firing rates of SNAKES and Medusa (for 6–10 processes) on the Cycle model for *chroma* = 1 with respect to the number of tokens.

Finally, in Fig. 11 we show how Medusa behaves when the size of the simulated Petri net grows. The rate of the SNAKES simulator is plotted also for comparison. As previously observed, adding transitions allows to add concurrency, which yields better rates, especially when we use more processes. We can indeed see how the initial slope is steeper when there are more worker processes. Then, after this initial growth, the rates stabilises and only depends on the number of workers. We can also observe that, for a fixed number of workers, the rates stay constant when the nets get larger. However, model Parallel is different since the rate decreases with the size of the nets. Actually, the smallest instances we have used have 10 concurrent transitions, which is already enough to keep 10 workers fully busy, and indeed, we reach 100 firings per second for 10 workers and 10 transitions whose firing costs 0.1 s each. But the workers are already fully busy and cannot absorb more, so increasing the number of transitions only results in increasing the overhead to manage them. Similarly, for a fixed number of transitions, adding more workers only results in increasing the overhead to manage them as well.

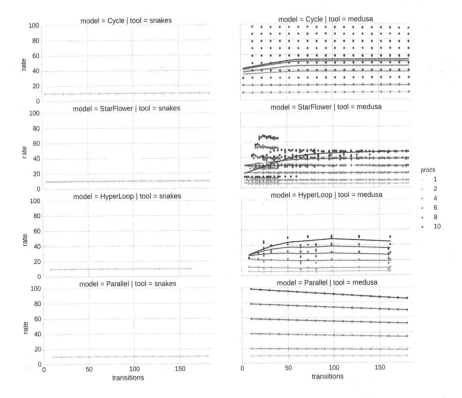

Fig. 11. Mean firing rates of SNAKES and Medusa for *chroma* = 1 with respect to the number transitions, decomposed by tool, model, and number of worker processes.

From all these experiments, we observe that for a better overall performance, we need to have: (1) more worker processes to reduce the waiting time; (2) more concurrent Petri nets to always be able to feed these worker processes and use them as much as possible; (3) more CPU-intensive activity when computing token flows to reduce the overhead introduced by Medusa, which is the case with coloured nets that may perform high-level computation in their arcs and in their guards. So we conclude that Medusa is well suited to accelerate the simulation of large coloured Petri nets involving CPU-intensive computation, which is the typical case that requires acceleration (the other cases being naturally fast to simulate).

4.2   Analysing the Design of Medusa

Medusa is designed to be "as concurrent as possible", *i.e.*, every player is given a chance to fire its transition, even if its work may be invalidated by another player firing a transition (which yields a retry, *i.e.*, the execution of lines 10–11 in Fig. 1).

To observe how this design impacts the execution, we have counted the number of retries performed by Medusa with respect to the number of firings, which is plotted in Fig. 12. This shows that the number of retries highly depends on the model (from lines 18 and 22 in Fig. 1: a retry is possible only if a player is working on a transition that is given tokens from another, but may have had tokens stolen by another player in the team). But in any case it remains proportional to (and lower than or equal to) the number of firings.

Fewer retries would be desirable because they correspond to wasted work. But it currently looks like they are hard to avoid without resorting to a higher-level scheduler that would choose which player is given a chance to fire its transition. But doing so is not necessarily more efficient because such an arbiter cannot know in advance which player will actually succeed in firing its transition.

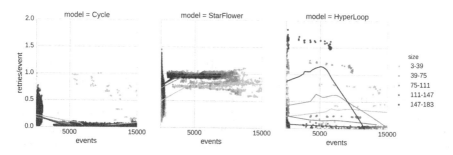

Fig. 12. Number of retries with respect to the number of firings. Lower is better. Model Parallel is not depicted because it requires no retry at all.

4.3 Fairness Analysis

To analyse the fairness of Medusa from a quantitative perspective, we have compared it to the SNAKES simulator (presented above, see Fig. 7) using both small and large instances of each model. Each instance has been simulated using both simulators for growing lengths of simulations (measured as the number of firings). For each pair of simulation, we have counted the frequency of firing for each transition and computed the distance between these two vectors. Both simulators use the same random number generator. The result is rendered in Fig. 13 from which we observe that, for every model, the two simulators converge to the same distribution of the transitions they choose as the number of firing grows. However, we have used nets whose transitions need all the same time to fire, it is likely that if some transitions need less time than others, they are more likely to be chosen by Medusa that is designed to fire transitions "as soon as possible", which is not the case for a sequential simulator that first chooses a transitions to fire regardless of the time it will take.

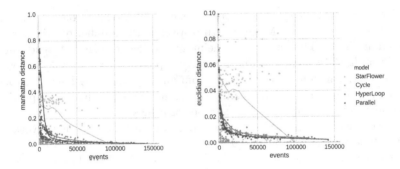

Fig. 13. Distances between SNAKES and Medusa simulations with respect to the number of firings (events). Lower is better.

5   Conclusion

In this paper we have presented a parallel algorithm to compute a sequential run of a Petri net. This algorithm is based on cooperative multitasking and thus is actually sequential, but it delegates computation to other processes which allows to keep it simple while achieving acceleration by launching computation in parallel processes. This architecture is well suited for multi-core CPUs or multi-CPUs computers, as well as for distributed computers where inter-process communication is made over the network. Moreover, our Python prototype shows that Medusa can be implemented successfully even with a language that is notoriously bad with concurrency and whose default implementation (that we have used) cannot exploit more than one core or CPU.

We have presented a formal analysis of Medusa, as well as a prototype implementation with a benchmark. This allowed to show that Medusa is well suited to accelerate the simulation of large coloured Petri nets with concurrency, that is, exactly the kind of nets that are usually slow to simulate and for which faster simulation is highly desirable. Moreover, Medusa scales well and is able to execute very large nets with thousands of transitions. We have only limited experiment for these cases but the systematic bench we have presented is still in progress processing larger nets. Preliminary results are fully consistent with what we have presented above. Moreover, we have shown in our benchmark that the firing rate does not depend on the size of the nets (except in pathological cases like model Parallel). Finally, Medusa has been proved correct and complete on a limited but varied set of simulated nets.

We have also identified some limitations of Medusa, and of our analysis. First, it is designed to compute random runs by fire transitions "as soon as possible", consequently, it may be a big change to design a variant with, for instance, priorities between transitions. Such variants have been tested and involve a higher-level scheduling, which works correctly but slows down simulation because we try to fire transitions in one order that is not necessarily available Moreover, on the one hand, we have shown that Medusa does not generate unfair runs of the simulated Petri net from fair runs of the simulation. But on the other hand, unfair runs of the simulation are likely to occur with nets whose transitions do not all require the same computation time considering that Medusa will tend to fire the first one for which this computation completes. Finally, we have seen that Medusa introduces an important overhead on small uncoloured Petri nets and that it cannot accelerate a Petri net that has no concurrency because it is just as concurrent as the simulated Petri net. To do so we would need a radically different algorithm focusing on parallelising the firing of a single transition. This is however not really a limitation but rather a design choice, and actually, having simultaneously two levels of concurrency can be envisaged.

Despite these limitations, we believe that we have demonstrated strong arguments to convince that Medusa has a clear potential to lead to efficient implementations of faster simulators.

5.1   Related Works

The question of executing a Petri net has been long standing. In [11], the author propose a sophisticated solution based on places invariants to extract processes from a Petri net in order to distribute its execution on Ada threads. This is necessary because a naive implementation that would put one thread for each transition would quickly collapse as the number of transitions would grow (threads or processes do not scale well). This highlights a crucial aspect of our proposal: we rely on cooperative multitasking instead of threads, which we have tested to scale happily to hundreds of thousands of pseudo-concurrent activities. Building such a net or loading it in memory takes a lot of time, but we have tested that once this is done, simulation is as fast as with smaller nets, even faster if more transitions means more concurrency.

In [12], the question of parallel simulation of *timed* Petri nets is solved using also a sophisticated partitioning of the Petri net to distribute its nodes on the computation units (CPU + memory), and a complex communication protocol to synchronise the distributed timed execution in order to ensure that it remains globally correct. The problem solved is substantially distinct from ours: [12] distributes a *timed uncoloured* Petri net and ensures the synchronisation the timed executions of its resulting parts, while we distribute the computation that arises from the execution of a centralised *untimed coloured* Petri net. We end up with a much simpler approach that has probably a much lower overhead and can be executed even on a modest multi-core CPU while [12] is designed for distributed-memory parallel computers.

Reference [19] is a 3-pages paper in which, among other things, the authors describe a parallel simulation engine that relies on partitioning a Petri nets into a set of sub-nets, being then processed in parallel. However, this topic is treated only briefly in a paper that is already very short, so it gives no further details about the parallel algorithm itself. Moreover, we have found no further reference to this paper, including no available software.

Finally, as stated on Renew's web page [18], "[its] simulation engine is capable of true concurrency and supports symmetric multi-processor architectures". Considering that Renew is able to execute Java code attached to the transitions of the Petri nets it simulates [3], this makes it very comparable to SNAKES equipped with Medusa. (Note that, like Renew, SNAKES is able to execute nets-within-nets as shown in [13].) However, we've found no description of this concurrent simulation algorithm but a comparison with Medusa should be very interesting.

5.2   Future Works

In the future, we intend to combine Medusa with the compilation of Petri nets as performed by Neco [6]. In the current prototype, we indeed rely on SNAKES to compute the token flows and so, the simulated net is interpreted (*i.e.*, it is represented as a data structure that is requested and on which generic algorithms are executed). What Neco does is to compile a Petri net into a set of specialised data structures and algorithms so that the Petri net structure disappears and the algorithms can be optimised on a per-transition basis. Experiments have showed that this yields a dramatic improvement in the performances for the computation of state spaces. Neco is currently operating on steps that are coarser than we need, being able to compute the successors of a marking, but not the tokens flows. To make them available to Medusa, we will need to refine Neco.

That done, we should be able to experiment with other finer-grains algorithms. In particular, we envisage to randomise the iterations on the tokens of input places in order to compute a single random token flow, instead computing all the possible flows before to chose one randomly. This should greatly alleviate the work load of worker processes, making them available for more computation (thus reducing the waiting times we have observed in Fig. 9). But at the same time, this should also increase the number of retries as a single flow is more likely to be invalidated by a concurrent firing than a whole set of flows. In this new algorithm, a retry would however only consist in requesting the next random flow and so should be less time consuming than in the current setting.

We also want to experiment with other implementation languages, we think in particular about the Go language [1,9] that features native cooperative multi-tasking (through so called *goroutines*) with compiler that generates native code that is able to efficiently exploit multi-core CPUs. Go programs are expected to run at the speed of C, even with hundreds of thousands of goroutines started simultaneously. So we expect a Go implementation of Medusa to have a low overhead whose performance on sequential Petri nets could be comparable to a simpler sequential simulator like that outlined in Fig. 7.

Coming back to our current prototype, we would like to perform a finer analysis of the effect of colours. Choosing parameter *chroma* in $\{0, 1\}$ as considered in this paper turned out to be much too coarse, and we should have designed our benchmark with much smaller delays (*e.g.*, *chroma*/100 s instead of *chroma*/10) but when we have had enough data to analyse the benchmark and discovered this, it was to late to restart it from scratch. Furthermore, we should experiment with real cases of coloured Petri nets instead of the artificial ones we have used here. We shall also consider more varied models, in particular those from the model-checking contest [10] should be good candidates as they already come with scaling parameters.

Analysis of fairness should also be refined, first by defining properly what would fairness mean in the context of the "as soon as possible" execution policy on which Medusa has been built. This definition should be general enough to allow for a comparison with other policies, and we would like to adapt Medusa to allow it to be parametrised by such policies.

A more theoretical work will be to provide a formal mechanised proof of Medusa algorithm. We expect to be able to adapt the techniques used in [7] where the authors prove BSP-parallel programs. Such programs are structured as sequences of *super-steps*, each of which being the parallel run of independent sequential blocks of code. The proof technique relies on the fact that the blocks being independent, they may be run sequentially in any order that respect the order of the super-steps; so the proof is reduced to that of a sequential program. Like a BSP program, Medusa algorithm is also organised a set of sequential blocks that are already scheduled sequentially, so we see no major obstacle to reuse the techniques from [7].

Supplementary Material

The ABCD model of Medusa, the scripts to analyse it, and the prototype implementation of Medusa are available as free software under the GNU GPL licence at http://github.com/fpom/PETRINETS-2017-supplementary [16].

Acknowledgements. We warmly thank Camille Coti (LIPN) for her help in understanding our hardware and how to exploit it correctly for our benchmark.

References

1. The Go programming language. http://golang.org
2. Bilenko, D.: gevent contributors: gevent. http://www.gevent.org
3. Cabac, L., Haustermann, M., Mosteller, D.: Renew 2.5 – towards a comprehensive integrated development environment for petri net-based applications. In: Kordon, F., Moldt, D. (eds.) PETRI NETS 2016. LNCS, vol. 9698, pp. 101–112. Springer, Cham (2016). doi:10.1007/978-3-319-39086-4_7
4. Chaou, S., Utard, G., Pommereau, F.: Evaluating a peer-to-peer storage system in presence of malicious peers. In: Proceedings of HPCS 2011. IEEE Computer Society (2011)
5. Fernandez, J.-C., Mounier, L.: "On the fly" verification of behavioural equivalences and preorders. In: Larsen, K.G., Skou, A. (eds.) CAV 1991. LNCS, vol. 575, pp. 181–191. Springer, Heidelberg (1992). doi:10.1007/3-540-55179-4_18
6. Fronc, Ł., Pommereau, F.: Building petri nets tools around Neco compiler. In: Proceedings of PNSE 2013 (2013)
7. Gava, F., Fortin, J., Guedj, M.: Deductive verification of state-space algorithms. In: Johnsen, E.B., Petre, L. (eds.) IFM 2013. LNCS, vol. 7940, pp. 124–138. Springer, Heidelberg (2013). doi:10.1007/978-3-642-38613-8_9
8. Gehrcke, J.P.: gipc: child processes and IPC for gevent. http://gehrcke.de/gipc
9. Kincaid, J.: Google's Go: a new programming language that's Python meets C++. (2009). http://techcrunch.com/2009/11/10/google-go-language
10. Kordon, F., Garavel, H., Hillah, L.M., Hulin-Hubard, F., Chiardo, G., Hamez, A., Jezequel, L., Miner, A., Meijer, J., Paviot-Adet, E., Racordon, D., Rodriguez, C., Rohr, C., Srba, J., Thierry-Mieg, Y., Trinh, G., Wolf, K.: Complete Results for the 2016th Edition of the Model Checking Contest (2016). http://mcc.lip.6.fr/2016/results.php
11. Kordon, F.: Prototypage de systèmes parallèles à partir de réseaux de Petri colorés. Ph.D. thesis, UPMC (1992)
12. Nicol, D.M., Mao, W.: Automated parallelization of timed petri-net simulations. J. Parallel Distrib. Comput. **29**(1), 60–74 (1995)
13. Pommereau, F.: Nets in nets with SNAKES. In: Proceedings of MOCA 2009. Universität Hamburg, Department of Informatik, Hamburg (2009)
14. Pommereau, F.: SNAKES: a flexible high-level petri nets library (Tool paper). In: Devillers, R., Valmari, A. (eds.) PETRI NETS 2015. LNCS, vol. 9115, pp. 254–265. Springer, Cham (2015). doi:10.1007/978-3-319-19488-2_13
15. Pommereau, F.: ABCD: a user-friendly language for formal modelling and analysis. In: Kordon, F., Moldt, D. (eds.) PETRI NETS 2016. LNCS, vol. 9698, pp. 176–195. Springer, Cham (2016). doi:10.1007/978-3-319-39086-4_12
16. Pommereau, F., de la Houssaye, J.: Supplementary material. http://github.com/fpom/PETRINETS-2017-supplementary
17. Rodola, G.: A cross-platform process and system utilities module for Python. http://github.com/giampaolo/psutil
18. The Theoretical Foundations Group of the Department for Informatics of the University of Hamburg: Renew, the reference net workshop - highlights. http://www.informatik.uni-hamburg.de/TGI/renew/highlights.html
19. Wang, B., Zhao, C.: A petri net simulation kernel with extendibility, convenient modeling and fast simulation engine. In: Proceedings of ICCT 2003, vol. 2. IEEE (2003)

Evaluating and Improving SIP Non-INVITE Transaction to Alleviate the Losing Race Problem

Junxian Liu[1(✉)], Lin Liu[2], and Tao Chen[1]

[1] Science and Technology on Information Systems Engineering Laboratory,
National University of Defense Technology,
Changsha 410073, Hunan, People's Republic of China
18674864900@163.com, kd_chentao@163.com
[2] School of Information Technology and Mathematical Sciences,
University of South Australia, Adelaide, SA 5095, Australia
Lin.Liu@unisa.edu.au

Abstract. SIP (Session Initiation Protocol) is developed by IETF for creating and managing sessions such as Internet calls. The exchange of SIP messages is controlled by two types of transactions: INVITE transaction for session setup; non-INVITE transaction (NIT) for other purposes, e.g. canceling a session. NIT was identified to have a race condition under which it will fail if a final response by server is not received by the client in time. An update to NIT thus has been proposed by IETF to reduce the risk of NIT losing the race. Although the update has been implemented in some SIP products, no report on the effectiveness of the update has been seen. In this paper, firstly the performance of the update is evaluated by simulation using Coloured Petri Nets (CPNs). The results show that the update does not improve the situation in most cases. Therefore we examine the causes of the losing race problem and propose an improvement to enhance the performance of NIT under the race condition. The analysis suggests that the improvement can effectively alleviate the losing race problem. We hope that this research can contribute to the SIP community and demonstrate the usefulness of CPNs in protocol development.

Keywords: Session Initiation Protocol · Protocol design · Protocol verification · Performance analysis · Coloured Petri Nets · Signed Digraph

1 Introduction

When Voice over IP (VoIP) is now becoming a reality of our daily life at work, at home, and on the move, a cornerstone of VoIP technology, the Session Initiation Protocol (SIP), is on the way to celebrate its 14th anniversary as a proposed Internet standard (RFC 2543 [1]). SIP was developed by IETF (Internet Engineering Task Force), originally as part of its Internet multimedia conferencing architecture [2], for initializing multimedia conferences including voice calls,

© Springer International Publishing AG 2017
W. van der Aalst and E. Best (Eds.): PETRI NETS 2017, LNCS 10258, pp. 57–77, 2017.
DOI: 10.1007/978-3-319-57861-3_5

over the Internet. It was also developed with the goal of being a general-purpose signaling protocol for creating, maintaining and terminating Internet sessions regardless of the types of the sessions [1].

It turns out that, instead of conferencing, VoIP is now the most popular application of SIP. With the merging of the Internet and mobile networks, VoIP with SIP has gone beyond the Internet, and SIP has become an essential component of the IMS (IP Multimedia Subsystem) of the 3GPP (the 3rd Generation Partnership Project) [3,4]. SIP has also been used for non-voice/video applications such as instant messaging [5].

With its increasing deployment and applications, SIP has been undergoing continuous development. The second version of SIP (RFC 3261 [6]) was released in 2002, not long after the publication of the first version (RFC 2543 [1]). Over the years, a number of updates to RFC 3261 have been proposed. Among these updates, RFC 4320 [7] presents a solution to the issues identified for the non-INVITE transaction (NIT) of SIP.

SIP transactions are the most important components of the protocol for the control of SIP message exchange. A SIP transaction comprises a client transaction and a server transaction at the client and server sides respectively. There are two types of SIP transactions: INVITE and non-INVITE. The former is used for creating a session, and the latter is used for all other purposes, including canceling an ongoing session, terminating a completed session, and registering a SIP entity with a SIP registrar with its location to allow other entities to find where this entity is via the registrar.

In RFC 4321 [8], it was identified that the NIT, as defined in RFC 3261, may fail due to a race condition, i.e. the final response generated by the server transaction may not be able to reach the client side before the timer of the client transaction expires. In this case, the client transaction will have been destroyed when the response arrives, hence no matching client transaction can be found for the response and the NIT fails. In RFC 4320 [7], an update to SIP is proposed to alleviate the racing problem.

For an important protocol like SIP, particularly given its rising popularity, it is necessary to assure that it functions correctly and performs effectively. With SIP NIT, the increasingly challenging network conditions (e.g. congestion) have made it more likely to lose the race, therefore an in-depth analysis and assessment of the update proposed in RFC 4320 is highly desirable.

Considering SIP in general, the major research efforts can be divided into three broad categories: (1) Extension or enhancement of SIP (RFC 3261) for its use in various settings, such as peer-to-peer networks and wireless networks [9–13]; (2) Evaluation or improvement of SIP performance [14–19]; and (3) Security analysis and countermeasures [20,21].

With NIT specifically, there has been little research focusing on it, except for [22], which evaluates the performance of NIT (considering the update in RFC 4320), in terms of a measure known as Quality of Signaling (QoSg). However, the QoSg measure is for evaluating the overall performance of NIT, instead of the effect of the update in RFC 4320 on solving the losing race problem. Interestingly, with the update in RFC 4320, although it has been implemented in some SIP products [23], so far no report has been seen on their effectiveness from these implementations either.

Therefore this paper will fill in this gap. The aim of this paper is to answer the following questions about the update in RFC 4320: (1) Does the update work at all? (2) How effective the update is in alleviating the losing race problem? (3) If the update does not perform well, what is a better solution?

The work of this paper is also motivated by the goal of pushing the boundaries of the applications of formal methods in solving real world protocol design problems. The formal method of our interest is Coloured Petri Nets (CPNs) [24]. CPNs have been proved to be useful for analyzing the functional or logical correctness of network protocols [24–26]. With SIP, a collection of papers have been published on analyzing the protocol with CPNs [9, 27–31]. However, the simulation based performance analysis technique of CPNs [24] has had very limited applications to protocol analysis, including SIP. In [32], we proposed an extension to a commonly used [25], CPN based methodology for protocol functional analysis, with a performance analysis component, and analyzed the functional properties and performance of NIT following the extended methodology. On the basis of the work in [32], in this paper we evaluate the effectiveness of the update in RFC 4320 and our proposed improvement for NIT.

For the evaluation, performance analysis is started from identifying and specifying the performance measures for assessing the update in RFC 4320, and the factors possibly affecting the measures. Next, based on the CPN model of the original NIT (i.e. the NIT specified in RFC 3261 without the update in RFC 4320), the settings of CPN simulations are determined for collecting information about the performance measures. Then the simulations are conducted to evaluate the performance measures and their relationships with the affecting factors. In the next stage, the CPN model of the original NIT is revised to reflect the update in RFC 4320, and similar performance analysis of the updated model is conducted. Then we are able to compare the performance of the original NIT with the updated NIT based on the values of the measures. A hypothesis test is used to find out whether the update has significantly improved the performance of NIT regarding the race condition. Furthermore, we examine in depth the losing race problem and its causes by means of Signed Digraphs [33], and devise an improvement to NIT. The same evaluation process is then carried out for the NIT with our proposed update to see whether it can effectively alleviate the losing race problem.

The contribution of this paper is threefold. Firstly, we show that the update in RFC 4320 is not able to effectively alleviate the losing race problem of NIT. Thus we propose an improvement, and use CPN simulations to demonstrate its working. We hope the result will contribute to the development and consolidation of SIP specification. Secondly, we have applied CPN simulation based performance analysis to assist protocol design, and the outcome of the paper shows that CPN is an effective tool in performance analysis, which may complement the commonly used approaches based on network simulators, such as

NS-2. Thirdly, a method of system engineering, the Signed Digraph method, is used to analyze the key factors affecting the protocol performance, which shows that the combination of CPN Tools and the Signed Digraph method can be used to crack down on some specific problem in protocol analysis in a structured way.

The rest of the paper is organized as follows. Section 2 describes the losing race problem, as well as the update in RFC 4320. The CPN models of NIT are presented in Sect. 3. In Sect. 4 we describe the measures for the evaluation, and conduct CPN simulations to analyze the effect of the update in RFC 4320. In Sect. 5, we analyze and identify the possible causes of the losing race problem, to further discuss the feasibility and possible limitations of the update in RFC 4320. Then we propose a solution to the problem, and CPN simulations performed to show its effectiveness. Finally Sect. 6 discusses the results and concludes the paper.

2   Losing Race Problem and the Update of SIP NIT

The introduction of SIP NIT could be find in RFC 3261 [6]. The state machines of SIP NIT for the non-INVITE client transaction (NICT) and the non-INVITE server transaction (NIST) are shown in Figs. 1 and 2.

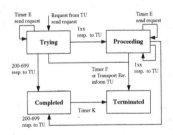

Fig. 1. State machine for NICT

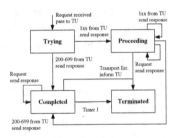

Fig. 2. State machine for NIST

A number of issues of the NIT were identified and presented in RFC 4321 in 2006 [8], and the losing race problem is a major one. Figure 3 shows the race condition, under which the client and the server have conflicting views about the NIT: the server believes that the transaction has succeeded as it responded to the request, but the client believes the transaction has failed since the final response reached the client after NICT had been terminated. The race in Fig. 3 is important as SIP will cache the timeout failures [8]. If the server loses the race, i.e. it fails to respond as quickly as enough, it will be blacklisted for some period of time.

From the design of the protocol, one cause of the race condition is the use of provisional responses. When the client receives a provisional response in the *Trying* state, it transits to the *Proceeding* state immediately. A consequence of

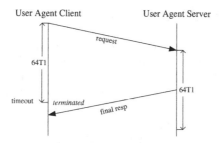

Fig. 3. Race condition of NIT presented in RFC 4321 [8]

this state transition is that Timer E will be set to $T2$ (i.e. $8T1$) after it fires for the first time in the *Proceeding* state, which would have been set to $2T1$ if a provisional response had not been received and the NICT was still in its *Trying* state (see Fig. 4 [8]). If a final response sent after this provisional response is lost, the interval of retransmitting the final response is $T2$, as the retransmission has to be triggered by a request that is retransmitted when Timer E fires. Hence the arrival of the final response will be delayed at the client side, and the possibility of losing the race will increase.

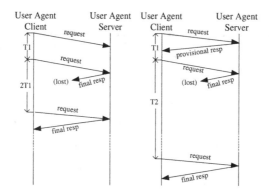

Fig. 4. Provisional response's influence on the race condition [8]

To alleviate the problem, an update by better utilizing the provisional responses is presented in RFC 4320 [7]. The update states that: (1) The use of all provisional responses except the 100 response is prohibited; (2) With unreliable transport, a 100 response must not be sent before the amount of time taken for Timer E to be reset to $T2$; (3) With reliable transport, a 100 response may be sent when a request is received; (4) Regardless of transport, the server must respond to a request with a 100 response if the request has not been otherwise responded to after the amount of time taken for Timer E to be reset to $T2$.

3   Modelling NIT Using CPNs

As described in the Introduction, to evaluate the updates to NIT, the CPN models need to be created for the different versions of the NIT: the NIT originally defined in RFC 3261, the NIT with the update in RFC 4320, and the NIT with our proposed update. As the CPN models of the updated NITs are obtained by revising the model of the original NIT created in [32], to save space and also because the focus of the paper is on performance analysis, this section only presents a brief description of the CPN model for the original NIT to provide necessary background to readers.

Figure 5 shows the top level CPN model, which contains five substitution transitions, and each is a collapsed CPN modeling a module as its name suggests. This part of the model is created by following the parameterized channel modeling method in [34], so it can be switched to represent a reliable transport or an unreliable transport, based on the need of the analysis. The CPN model of NICT is shown in Fig. 6, which is the substitution transition *Client_Transaction* in Fig. 5 after unfolding. Figure 7 is the submodule of the *Server_Transaction* transition in Fig. 5. More details of the model could be find in [32].

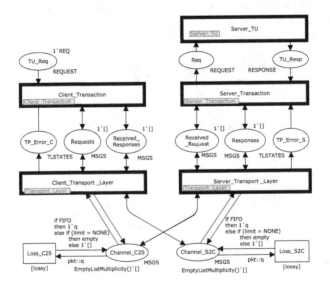

Fig. 5. Top level CPN model for SIP NIT, each rectangle with thick border is a collapsed CPN modeling a module as its name suggests [32]

4   Evaluating the Update in RFC 4320

4.1   Performance Measures for Evaluation

When a NIT is completed, both NICT and NIST are in their *Terminated* state. As described in Sect. 2, due to the race condition, the NIT fails when it loses

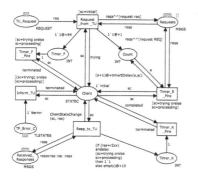

Fig. 6. CPN model for NICT

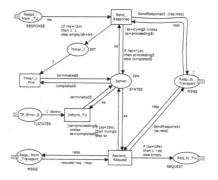

Fig. 7. CPN Model for NIST

the race, i.e. it is completed and both NICT and NIST are terminated, but the NICT never receives a final response. Therefore there are two cases for the completion of a NIT: (1) Success: the NICT has received a final response before being terminated, i.e. the NIT wins the race; (2) Failure: no final response is received by the NICT, i.e. the NIT loses the race.

Hence the performance of the NIT under the race condition can be evaluated by the probability (ratio) of NIT terminating when losing the race. The lower the probability is, the higher the performance. To measure the probability, we present a performance measure named the Losing Race Ratio (LRR), which is defined as:

$$LRR = \frac{TR - SR}{TR},\qquad(1)$$

where TR (Terminating Rate) is the proportion of NITs that have completed, i.e. both NICT and NIST have reached their *Terminated* state, out of all the NITs that are started in a CPN simulation experiment; SR (Success Rate) is the proportion of NITs that have completed successfully, out of all the started NITs in the CPN simulation experiment.

It should be noted that not all NITs started are able to complete, for example, if the request can never reach the server, then the NICT will reach its *Terminated* state, but the NIST is never been created (in our CPN model the NIST will be still in the assumed *Idle* state).

The success of a NIT depends on whether a final response is able to arrive at the client side in time, so that if we assume the Transaction User (TU) of NIST is well-behaved, i.e. it always generates a final response, then LRR is influenced by the loss rate of the transport medium, and the delay of generating and transmitting the final response. Therefore the factors affecting the value of LRR can be abstracted to the following four parameters:

1. *Final Response Processing Delay (fPD)* [22]: the time required by the TU of NIST to process the request and generate a final response.
2. *Provisional Response Processing Delay (pPD)* [22]: the time required by the TU of NIST to process the request and generate a provisional response.

3. *Transmission Delay (TD)*: the end-to-end delay of transmitting a message over the medium.
4. *Loss Rate of Channel (LRC)*: the loss rate of the transport medium, i.e. the probability of losing a message by the medium.

4.2   Assumptions and CPN Model Configuration

The following assumptions or simplifications are made for the CPN simulations:

1. As NIT needs to complete rapidly [8], assume that if the TU of NIST generates a provisional response, it SHOULD generate the response without any delay, i.e. $pPD = 0$ s;
2. In the general case TD is about half of the round trip delay, i.e. approximately $T1/2$ seconds, so the effect of TD on LRR is small comparing to the other parameters. So for the convenience of simulations and analysis, we assume that $TD = 0$ s;
3. There is no transport error, so SIP transport layer does not report any transport error to NIT;
4. The losses of messages by the channels of the two directions (client to server and server to client) are independent of each other, but the loss rates (LRCs) of the channels are the same;
5. As CPN Tools we used (v3.4.0) [35] does not support time in float numbers, we use a CPN time unit to represent $T1$ (500 ms);
6. As NICT enters its *Terminated* state within $64T1$ seconds (i.e. 64 CPN time units), the range of the value of fPD is restricted to be $[0, 64]$.

The CPN model is revised and configured based on the above assumptions. To calculate the values of LRR using Eq. (1) for different settings of the parameters fPD and LRC, CPN data collection monitors [24] are added to collect the simulation data of TR and SR.

4.3   Simulation Results and Analysis

To compare the performance of the original NIT and the NIT with the update in RFC 4320, two sets of simulations were conducted for 500 times each using CPN Tools [35], one with the original NIT model and one with the modified model for the NIT with the update. For each sets of simulations, the values of TR, SR and LRR are averaged over the 500 simulations, and the relationships between each of the average values and the two parameters fPD and LRC are displayed in Figs. 8, 9 and 10. With each of the figures, the diagrams on the left are for the original NIT and the diagrams on the right are for the updated NIT.

From Fig. 8 we see that in both cases (original NIT and updated NIT), TRs, the rates of terminating, have the same characteristics. This is expected as the update in RFC 4320 (see Sect. 2) only changes the timing of sending provisional responses, and the sequence of operations of NIT is not changed, that is, in both cases, as long as a request can arrives at the server side and the NIST user is

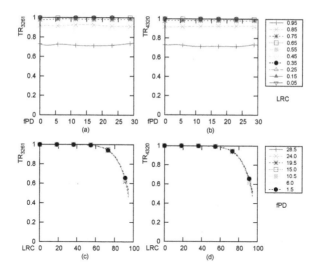

Fig. 8. Relationships among TR and fPD, LRC. (a) and (b) are (TR vs. fPD) when LRC has different values, (c) and (d) are (TR vs. LRC) when fPD has different values.

well-behaved, the NICT and NIST will reach their *Terminated* states. This also explains why in Fig. 8, diagrams (a) and (b) show that TR is independent of fPD, but from diagrams (c) and (d) TR decreases with the increase of LRC. When LRC is less than 60%, TR is nearly equal to 1, however when LRC is greater than 60%, TR decreases rapidly.

With Fig. 9, comparing diagrams (a) and (c) with (b) and (d), we see that overall the SRs are similar in both cases (original and updated NITs), although there are slight differences between them. From Fig. 10 we can draw similar conclusion for LRR, i.e. the difference between the $LRRs$ in the two cases are slight.

Given the limited information that we can obtain from the direct observation of the $LRRs$ in both cases, in order to find out whether the update of RFC 4320 works for the losing race problem, we conduct a two-proportion z-test to determine the statistic significance of the difference of the $LRRs$ in the two cases, for each configuration (value assignment) of the pair (LRC, fPD). In the following, we denote the value of LRR as LRR_{3261} and LRR_{4320} in the two cases.

As the update in RFC 4320 is expected to resolve the losing race problem, it is reasonable to believe that $LRR_{3261} > LRR_{4320}$. Therefore we state the null hypothesis (H_0) and an alternative hypothesis (H_a) as:

$$H_0 : LRR_{3261} \leq LRR_{4320}; \; H_a : LRR_{3261} > LRR_{4320}.$$

We need to find out all possible configurations of (LRC, fPD) that reject H_0 at some significance level. For a configuration of (LRC, fPD), for the original NIT, let the number of simulations (NITs) that lose the race be m_1 and the number of simulations that terminate be n_1; and for the updated NIT, let the

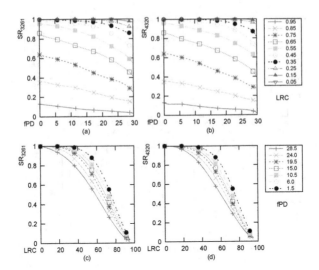

Fig. 9. Relationships among *SR* and *fPD*, *LRC*. (a) and (b) are (*SR* vs. *fPD*) when *LRC* has different values, (c) and (d) are (*SR* vs. *LRC*) when *fPD* has different values.

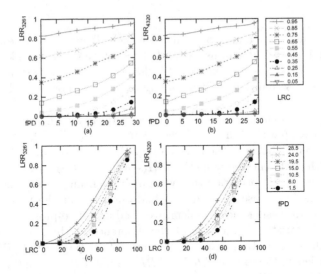

Fig. 10. Relationships among *LRR* and *fPD*, *LRC*. (a) and (b) are (*LRR* vs. *fPD*) when *LRC* has different values, (c) and (d) are (*LRR* vs. *LRC*) when *fPD* has different values.

number of simulations that lose the race be m_2 and the number of simulations that terminate be n_2. Then the z-score can be calculated as follows [36]:

$$z = \frac{p_1 - p_2}{\sqrt{p(1-p)(\frac{1}{n_1} + \frac{1}{n_2})}}, \tag{2}$$

where

$$p_1 = \frac{m_1}{n_1}, \quad p_2 = \frac{m_2}{n_2}, \quad p = \frac{m_1 + m_2}{n_1 + n_2}.$$

In this paper we select $\alpha = 0.05$ as the significance level. Since the above test is an one-tailed test, the related critical value is $z_{0.05} = 1.645$. When the z-score is less than $z_{0.05}$, we accept H_0 at significance level 0.05, which means the effect of the update in RFC 4320 is not significant. When the z-score is greater than $z_{0.05}$, we reject H_0 at the significance level 0.05, which means the effects of the update may be significant.

Figure 11 tabulates the results of the z-tests for all possible configurations of (LRC, fPD). The row headers are the values of fPD (in seconds or half CPN time units) and the column headers are the values of LRC (in %). A table cell shows the result of the z-test for the corresponding configuration, where 1 represents H_0 is rejected, and 0 represents H_0 is accepted.

fPD\LRC	0	5	10	15	20	25	30	35	40	45	50	55	60	65	70	75	80	85	90	95
0	0	0	0	0	0	0	0	0	0	0	0	0	0	0	0	0	0	0	0	0
1.5	0	0	0	0	0	0	0	0	0	0	0	0	1	0	0	0	0	0	0	0
3	0	0	0	0	0	0	0	0	0	0	0	0	0	0	0	0	0	0	0	0
4.5	0	0	0			0	0	0	0	0	0	0	0	0	0	0	0	1	0	
6	0	0	0	0	0	0	0	0	0	0	0	0	0	0	1	0	0	0	0	0
7.5	0	0	0	0	0	0	0	0	0	0	0	0	0	0	0	0	0	0	0	0
9	0	0	0		0	0	0	0	0	0	0	0	0	0	0	0	0	0	0	0
10.5	0	0	0	0	0	0	0	1	0	0	0	0	0	0	0	0	0	0	0	0
12	0	0	0	0	0	0	0	0	0	0	0	0	0	0	0	0	0	0	0	0
13.5	0	0	0	0	0	0	0	0	0	0	0	1	0	0	0	0	0	0	0	0
15	0	0	0	0	0	0	0	0	0	0	0	0	0	0	0	0	0	0	0	0
16.5	0	0	0	0	0	0	0	0	0	0	0	0	0	0	0	0	0	1	0	0
18	0	0	0	0	0	0	0	0	0	0	0	0	0	1	0	0	0	0	0	0
19.5	0	0	0	0	0	0	1	0	0	0	0	1	0	0	0	0	0	0	0	0
21	0	0	0	0	0	0	0	0	1	0	0	0	0	0	0	0	1	0	0	0
22.5	0	0	0	0	0	0	0	0	1	0	0	0	0	1	0	0	0	0	0	0
24	0	0	0	0	0	0	1	0	0	1	0	0	0	0	0	0	0	0	0	0
25.5	0	0	0	0	0	0	0	0	0	0	0	0	0	0	0	0	0	1	0	0
27	0	0	0	1	1	0	0	0	0	0	0	0	1	0	1	0	0	0	0	0
28.5	0	0	0	1	1	0	0	0	0	1	1	1	0	0	0	0	0	0	0	0
30	0	0	0	0	0	0	0	0	0	0	0	1	0	0	0	0	0	0	0	0

Fig. 11. Results of z-test at $\alpha = 0.05$, 1 represents the update of RFC 4320 works for the losing race problem.

From Fig. 11 we see that when LRC is less than 35% and fPD is less than 18 s (Area A in the table), the effect of the update is not significant (H_0 : $LRR_{3261} \le LRR_{4320}$ is accepted). When fPD is greater than 18 s, the update may take effect when LRC is in the range of [15%, 55%] (Area B). For most of other configurations, we cannot see that the update significantly alleviates the race problem.

To summarize, in the normal operation settings of NIT, low to medium loss rate and final response process delay (i.e. area A in Fig. 11), the update in RFC 4320 does not make significant difference regarding the losing race problem, and in most other settings, the update does not take significant effect either. To reduce the risk of NIT losing the race, we need a more effective approach to alleviate the problem.

5   Proposing New Updates to NIT

In this section, the cause of the losing race problem is analyzed in depth firstly. Based on the analysis, a new update to RFC 3261 is developed, together with the analytical results and performance evaluation using CPNs of the update.

5.1   An In-depth Analysis of the Losing Race Problem

Figure 12 shows the interactions of NICT, NIST and the TU of NIST, where solid lines indicate successful message transmissions and dashed lines for failed transmissions (messages are lost). UUD (User to User Delay) is the time interval from sending the first request until the (re)transmission of the request being received by NIST for the first time. $pRpD$ (Provisional Response Delay [22]) indicates the time interval from sending the first request until the transmission or a retransmission of the provisional response being received by NICT for the first time, and $fRpD$ (Final Response Delay [22]) is the time interval from sending the first request until the transmission or a retransmission of the final response being received by NICT for the first time. $fWindow$ indicates the time interval from NIST sending a final response until NICT times out and terminates without receiving a final response.

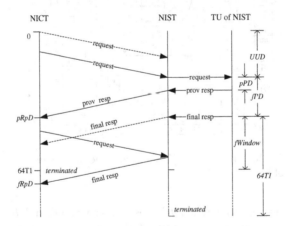

Fig. 12. Interactions among NICT, NIST and the TU of NIST

From Fig. 12, it can be seen that a NIT will lose the race when $fRpD$ is greater than $64T1$. The length of $fRpD$ is related to many factors, such as fPD, UUD and $fRpT$ (*Final Responses Transmitted*). $fRpT$ is the number of final responses sent by server, the more final responses sent, the shorter the $fRpD$, as the NICT will have more chance to receive a final response given a lossy channel. LRC affects $fRpD$ too, as lower LRC can result in a shorter $fRpD$. In turn, these factors are influenced by other parameters.

In order to find out the factors that have significant impact on *fRpD*, thus determine *LRR*, we examined the parameters step by step and summarized their relationships to a Signed Digraph [33] in Fig. 13. In this diagram, an arc from a node A to a node B with the sign "+" or "−" means that node B's value increases or decreases with the increasing of node A's value. *RT* (*Requests Transmitted*) is the number of requests sent by NICT, and *pRpT* (*Provisional Responses Transmitted*) is the number of provisional responses sent by NIST [22].

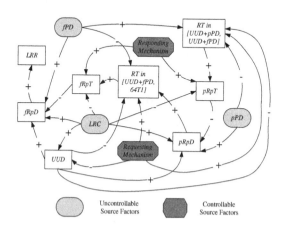

Fig. 13. Signed Digraph for analyzing the causes of the losing race problem

It is noticed that the sink node of the diagram is *LRR*, and there are five source nodes: *fPD, pPD, LRC, Requesting Mechanism (ReqM)* and *Responding Mechanism (RespM)*. Between the source nodes and the sink node are *pRpT, pRpD, fRpT, fRpD, RT* and *UUD*. Source nodes are the original factors that influence *LRR*, in which *fPD, pPD* and *LRC* are objective and uncontrollable by NIT. Therefore the possible way to improve NIT is to change the rules of *ReqM* and *RespM*. *ReqM* specifies when and how many times the request needs to be retransmitted, and *RespM* specifies the timing and frequency of transmitting and retransmitting the responses at the server side.

In order to see all possible approaches to solve the losing race problem, we remove all the uncontrollable source factors from Fig. 13, and obtain the reduced Signed Digraph in Fig. 14. It is noticed that smaller *fRpD* leads to lower *LRR*, and reducing *UUD* or raising *fRpT* are the ways to reduce *fRpD*. Therefore the possible ways are to improve *ReqM* or *RespM*.

The first approach is to change *ReqM* to increase the numbers of retransmissions of the request. It is useful in reducing *UUD*. However changing *UUD* and *ReqM* will influence *RT* directly and indirectly. From Fig. 12 we know that the client should avoid increasing the number of retransmissions during $[UUD + pPD, UUD + fPD]$, otherwise the number of retransmissions of provisional responses will increase and thus delay the recovery from lost final

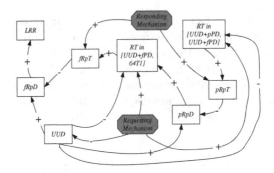

Fig. 14. Reduced Signed Digraph without the uncontrollable source factors

responses. Since the client does not know the exact time the server begins to transmit the final response, this approach is hard to implement.

The second way is to improve *RespM* to raise *fRpT* but reduce *pRpT* (the number of provisional responses sent), as increasing *pRpT* will decrease *pRpD* and then decrease *fRpT* indirectly. We see that this approach is easy to implement and the effect is direct.

5.2   Further Analysis for the Updates in RFC 4320

To find out the reason why the update in RFC 4320 does not have a significant effect on the losing race problem, in Fig. 14 we trace the path from node *RespM* to *LRR* via *pRpT*, and obtain the reduced Signed Digraph in Fig. 15.

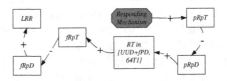

Fig. 15. Reduced Signed Digraph for the update in RFC 4320

This graph shows that the update in RFC 4320 focuses on increasing *LRR* by reducing *pRpT* only, and it essentially functions by means of increasing *fRpT*. However, since the path from *RespM* to *fRpT* contains quite a number of factors, the strength of the influence of *RespM* can wear off along the path, so the values of *fRpT* may not increase much when the responding mechanism is adjusted. To see this, we calculated the values of *fRpT* with respect to different *fPD* and *LRC* by using simulation data. The results are shown in Fig. 16. From this figure, we see that after the update (Fig. 16(b) and (d)), the values of *fRpT* have not increased significantly compared to its values in the case of the original NIT.

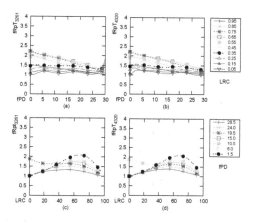

Fig. 16. Values of *fRpT* with and without the update in RFC 4320, (a) and (c) are for the case without update, (b) and (d) are for the case with update

5.3   New Updates to NIT for the Losing Race Problem

Based on the above analysis, we will focus on the second approach, i.e. raising *fRpT* meanwhile reducing *pRpT*, when proposing our improvement.

The current *RespM* with respect to the final response is: NIST transmits the final response received from its TU and retransmits the response only when it receives a retransmission of the request. The main idea of our proposal is to retransmit the final response proactively during the *fWindow*, instead of waiting for an external trigger (a request). The purpose is to increase the chance for the client to receive a final response before NICT is terminated. There are two questions about the idea though: (1) How to determine the number of retransmissions? (2) How to spread the retransmissions over the period of *fWindow*?

We use a "Dynamic Balancing Strategy" in answering the first question. Let n_{rt} be the number of requests that have been (re)transmitted when the NIST receives a request for the first time. "Balancing" means that the number of extra retransmissions on top of those triggered by the retransmitted requests should be made the same as n_{rt}, as the influence of the loss of the channel is the same on the (re)transmissions of requests and responses. "Dynamic" means that n_{rt} is calculated dynamically based on the timestamp of the received request for each NIT.

Using this strategy, the total number of retransmissions of the final response is $n_0 + n_{te} + n_{plus} + n_{rt}$, where n_0 is always 1 (the initial transmission of the final response); n_{te} is the number of retransmissions triggered by the received (retransmitted) requests, which is the number of the retransmissions specified for the original NIT; n_{plus} is a fixed number for adjusting the total number, which will be analyzed in Sect. 5.4.

The value of n_{rt} can be approximated using the following formula:

$$n_{rt} = max\{i \mid \delta_i T1 \leq UUD - 0.5T1, 1 \leq i \leq 11\}. \tag{3}$$

Details of calculating δ_i and UUD in the above formula is be discussed later in this section.

With the second question, two possible schemes can be used to spread the $n_{plus} + n_{rt}$ extra retransmissions. One is to use equal intervals. As the interval between adjacent retransmissions should not be over $T1$ (estimated round trip time), we can set the interval to $T1$. The second scheme is to use the exponential backoffs on the retransmission, similar to the setting of firing Timer E. Using the first scheme the NIT may have higher probability of success than using the second scheme because the latter uses longer internals, which may not work well when the $fWindow$ is small. Therefore we will select the first scheme.

Based on the above discussions, we propose the following updates to the original NIT, which also incorporate the update in RFC 4320:

1. Follow the update in RFC 4320 for the transmission of provisional responses (see Sect. 2);
2. When an unreliable transport is in use, once NIST transmits a final response for the first time, it retransmits the response up to $n_{plus} + n_{rt}$ times at the interval of $T1$, over the period of $fWindow$.

Note that the update to response retransmission is on top of the retransmission process of the original NIT, so for the updated NIT, when NIST receives a retransmission of the request in this period, it still retransmits the final response as specified in RFC 3261.

According to the above proposal, the state machine of NIST is revised by adding a timer (called Timer L). When the NIST enters its *Completed* state, it MUST set Timer L to fire in $T1$ seconds if an unreliable transport is in use; When Timer L fires, it will be reset to $T1$ if it has not fired for more than $n_{plus} + n_{rt}$ times.

5.4 Simulations and Comparative Analysis

According to the proposed improvement, we modify the CPN model of the original NIST to analyze the effect of the proposal. The other settings for each of the simulation in the series is the same to those described in Sects. 4.2 and 4.3. A series of simulations were conducted for $n_{plus} = 0, 1, 2, 3$ respectively. Figure 17 shows the average values of LRR in the form of contour maps. The two maps in the top row are for the original NIT and the NIT with the update in RFC 4320 respectively, and the maps in the next two rows are for the NIT with our proposed update, when $n_{plus} = 0, 1, 2, 3$ respectively.

For the convenience of describing the maps, we introduce the symbol $A_{k,\gamma}$ to represent the range of (fPD, LRC) that satisfies $LRR(fPD, LRC) \leq \gamma$, where k stands for the different versions of NIT, and the possible values of k are: 3261 (original NIT), 4320 (NIT with the update in RFC4320), and $0, 1, 2, 3$ are for NIT with the new updates when $n_{plus} = 0, 1, 2, 3$ respectively. From Fig. 17, when $\gamma = 0.1, 0.2, 0.3, 0.4$ (refer to the four contours at the bottom of each map), comparing $A_{3261,\gamma}$ with $A_{n_{plus},\gamma}$ ($n_{plus} = 0, 1, 2, 3$), we see that our

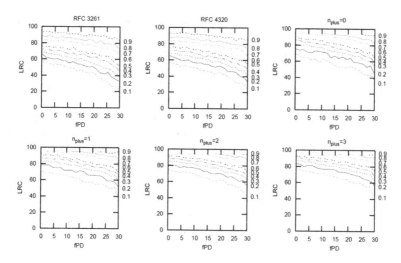

Fig. 17. Comparison of *LRRs* for different retransmission schemas of the final response, n_{plus} indicates the extra-retransmission times relative to that in RFC 3261 and 4320

proposed improvement significantly decreases the risk of losing the race, as the contours for $A_{n_{plus},\gamma}$ all stand closer to the top of their maps. This suggests that the NIT with our proposed improvement will unlikely to lose the race given the same values of (*fPD*, *LRC*) for which the original NIT or the NIT with the update in RFC 4320 will have very high probabilities (*LRRs*) to lose the race.

To select an appropriate value of n_{plus} for the improved NIT, we analyze the effects of improvement with different values of n_{plus}. We calculate the difference of *LRRs* for the original NIT and the improved NIT for $n_{plus} = 0, 1, 2, 3$ respectively and the results are shown in Fig. 18.

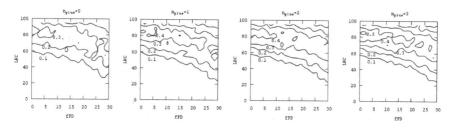

Fig. 18. Comparison of $LRR_{3261} - LRR_{n_{plus}}$ for different retransmission schemas of the final response

We use $B_{n_{plus},\beta}$ to represent the range of (*fPD*, *LRC*) satisfying $LRR_{3261} - LRR_{n_{plus}} \le \beta$. From Fig. 18 we see that the impact of n_{plus} on *LRR* depends on the value of (*fPD*, *LRC*).

When $\beta \leq 0.2$, the values of $B_{n_{plus},\beta}$ for $n_{plus} = 0, 1, 2, 3$ (the bottom two contours in each map) are similar. This means that the decrement of LRR could reach 20% when (fPD, LRC) locates in $B_{0,0.2}$. Noted that $A_{3261,0.3}$ is similar to $B_{n_{plus},0.2}$ ($n_{plus} = 0, 1, 2, 3$), which implies that the impacts of different values of n_{plus} are similar, i.e. there is no difference for different n_{plus} values when (fPD, LRC) locates in $A_{3261,0.3}$.

When $\beta > 0.2$, $B_{n_{plus},\alpha}(n_{plus} = 0, 1, 2, 3)$ are clearly different. Figure 18 shows that the differences are most significant when (fPD, LRC) changes from $(0, 80)$ to $(30, 60)$, and the larger n_{plus} is, the more significant the improvement.

Therefore, we can select appropriate values for n_{plus} based on the network condition (i.e. LRC) and the estimated delay of the TU of NIST for generating a response (fPD). At the same time we need to balance the level of performance improvement and the value of n_{plus} to avoid overload the network with too many retransmissions.

6   Conclusion

By using CPN modeling and simulation based performance analysis, the effect of the update in RFC 4320 to the SIP NIT regarding the losing race problem has been studied. The analysis shows that the update in RFC 4320 has only a small effect on alleviating the problem. By hypothesis tests we found out that under the common setting of the protocol, i.e. LRC (channel loss rate) is less than 35% and fPD (time taken for a server to generate a response) is less than 18 s, the effect is not significant; when fPD is larger than 18 s, the update may take effect if LRC is fairly large.

To propose a more effective solution to the losing race problem, we created a Signed Digraph that describes the relationships of the factors related to the race condition. By excluding the uncontrollable source factors (including the loss rate of the channel and the response processing delay), we identified the factors that may be improved to reduce the chance losing the race, which are the responding mechanism of the server and the requesting mechanism of the client. The responding mechanism can be selected as the target for improvement because changing the requesting mechanism is hardly practical.

RFC 4320 focuses on reducing the times of retransmissions of provisional responses to alleviate the losing race problem. Simulation results and theoretical analysis by Signed Digraph have shown that this approach does not work well. The reason is that it does not increase the times of retransmissions of final responses effectively. Therefore our proposed update focuses on increasing proactive retransmissions of the final response by adding a timer to the NIST state machine. The number of times of firing the timer is determined by the server in real time according to a "Dynamic Balancing Strategy".

The analytical study and simulation analysis undertaken in this paper also have shown that our proposed update significantly alleviates the losing race problem. It can reduce the probability of losing the race up to 30%. If the loss rate of the channel is especially high (such as 80%), one or two additional retransmissions of the final response will reduce the probability of losing the race effectively, up to 45%.

In addition, with our work, we have found that CPN performance analysis is useful in protocol design and improvement. The techniques can be used effectively to produce quick and formal results for protocol analysis, which may complement the commonly used approaches based on network simulations.

References

1. Handley, M., Schulzrinne, H., Schooler, E., Rosenberg, J.: SIP: Session Initiation Protocol. RFC 2543 (Proposed Standard, obsoleted by RFC 3261), March 1999
2. Handley, M., Crowcroft, J., Bormann, C., Ott, J.: The Internet Multimedia Conferencing Architecture. Internet Draft (expired), July 2000
3. 3GPP: 3GPP Website - Technologies. http://www.3gpp.org/Technologies. Last accessed 20 Jan 2013
4. Camarillo, G., García-Martín, M.: The 3G IP Multimedia Subsystem (IMS): Merging the Internet and the Cellular Worlds. Wiley, Chichester (2011)
5. Rosenberg, J., Schulzrinne, H., Huitema, C., Gurle, C.: Session Initiation Protocol (SIP) Extension for Instant Messaging. RFC 3428, December 2002
6. Rosenberg, J., Schulzrinne, H., Camarillo, G., Johnston, A., Peterson, J., Sparks, R., Handley, M., Schooler, E.: SIP: Session Initiation Protocol. RFC 3261 (2002)
7. Sparks, R.: Actions Addressing Identified Issues with the Session Initiation Protocol's (SIP) Non-INVITE Transaction. RFC 4320, January 2006
8. Sparks, R.: Problems Identified Associated with the Session Initiation Protocol's (SIP) Non-INVITE Transaction. RFC 4321, January 2006
9. Ahson, S.A., Ilyas, M.: SIP Handbook: Services, Technologies, and Security of Session Initiation Protocol, 1st edn. CRC Press Inc., Boca Raton (2008)
10. Shi, J., Wang, Y., Gu, L., Li, L., Lin, W., Li, Y., Ji, Y., Zhang, P.: A hierarchical peer-to-peer SIP system for heterogeneous overlays interworking. In: 2007 Global Telecommunications Conference, GLOBECOM 2007, pp. 93–97. IEEE, November 2007
11. Zheng, X., Oleshchuk, V.: A survey on peer-to-peer SIP based communication systems. Peer-to-Peer Netw. Appl. **3**, 257–264 (2010)
12. Fathi, H., Chakraborty, S., Prasad, R.: Optimization of SIP session setup delay for VoIP in 3G wireless networks. IEEE Trans. Mob. Comput. **5**(9), 1121–1132 (2006)
13. Vidal, I., Garcia-Reinoso, J., Soto, I., Valera, F.: Evaluating extensions to IMS session setup for multicast-based many-to-many services. Comput. Netw. **55**(3), 600–621 (2011)
14. Camarillo, G., Kantola, R., Schulzrinne, H.: Evaluation of transport protocols for the session initiation protocol. Netw. Magzine Glob. Internetworking **17**(5), 40–46 (2003)
15. Gurbani, V.K., Jagadeesan, L.J., Menditratta, V.B.: Characterizing session initiation protocol (SIP) network performance and reliability. In: Malek, M., Nett, E., Suri, N. (eds.) ISAS 2005. LNCS, vol. 3694, pp. 196–211. Springer, Heidelberg (2005). doi:10.1007/11560333_16
16. Liao, J., Wang, J., Li, T., Wang, J., Wang, J., Zhu, X.: A distributed end-to-end overload control mechanism for networks of SIP servers. Comput. Netw. **56**(12), 2847–2868 (2012)

17. Pack, S., Park, G., Lee, K., Lee, W.: Analysis of SIP transfer delay in multi-rate wireless networks. IEEE Commun. Lett. **14**(10), 918–920 (2010)
18. Shen, C., Schulzrinne, H.: On TCP-based SIP server overload control. In: Principles, Systems and Applications of IP Telecommunications, IPTComm 2010, pp. 71–83. ACM, New York (2010)
19. Sisalem, D., Liisberg, M., Rebahi, Y.: A theoretical model of the effects of losses and delays on the performance of SIP. In: 2008 Global Telecommunications Conference, IEEE GLOBECOM 2008, pp. 1–6. IEEE (2008)
20. Keromytis, A.: A Comprehensive survey of voice over IP security research. IEEE Commun. Surv. Tutorials **14**(2), 514–537 (2012). Quarter
21. Sisalem, D., Floroiu, J., Kuthan, J., Abend, U., Schulzrinne, P.H.: SIP Security. Wiley, Chichester (2009)
22. Happenhofer, M., Egger, C., Reichl, P.: Quality of signalling: a new concept for evaluating the performance of Non-INVITE SIP transactions. In: 2010 22nd International Teletraffic Congress (ITC), pp. 1–8, September 2010
23. Wiki, S.: SIPit Summaries. https://www.sipit.net/SIPitSummaries. Last accessed 20 Jan 2013
24. Jensen, K., Kristensen, L.M.: Coloured Petri Nets - Modelling and Validation of Concurrent Systems. Springer, Heidelberg (2009)
25. Billington, J., Gallasch, G.E., Han, B.: A coloured Petri Net approach to protocol verification. In: Desel, J., Reisig, W., Rozenberg, G. (eds.) ACPN 2003. LNCS, vol. 3098, pp. 210–290. Springer, Heidelberg (2004). doi:10.1007/978-3-540-27755-2_6
26. Kristensen, L.M., Simonsen, K.I.F.: Applications of coloured Petri Nets for functional validation of protocol designs. In: Jensen, K., Aalst, W.M.P., Balbo, G., Koutny, M., Wolf, K. (eds.) Transactions on Petri Nets and Other Models of Concurrency VII. LNCS, vol. 7480, pp. 56–115. Springer, Heidelberg (2013). doi:10.1007/978-3-642-38143-0_3
27. Ding, L.G., Liu, L.: Modelling and analysis of the INVITE transaction of the session initiation protocol using coloured Petri Nets. In: Hee, K.M., Valk, R. (eds.) PETRI NETS 2008. LNCS, vol. 5062, pp. 132–151. Springer, Heidelberg (2008). doi:10.1007/978-3-540-68746-7_12
28. Ding, Y., Su, G.: Intrusion detection system for signal based SIP attacks through timed HCPN. In: IEEE Computer Society ARES, pp. 190–197 (2007)
29. Kizmaz, S., Kirci, M.: Verification of session initiation protocol using timed colored Petri Net. International Journal of Computer Network and Security **4**(3), 170–179 (2011)
30. Liu, L.: Verification of the SIP transaction using coloured Petri Nets. In: The 32nd Australasian Computer Science Conference. CRPIT, vol. 91, pp. 63–72. Australian Computer Society (2009)
31. Liu, L.: Uncovering SIP vulnerabilities to DoS attacks using coloured Petri Nets. In: International Joint Conference of IEEE TrustCom/IEEE ICESS/FCST, Los Alamitos, CA, USA, pp. 29–36. IEEE Computer Society (2011)
32. Liu, J., Liu, L.: A coloured Petri Net approach to the functional and performance analysis of SIP Non-INVITE transaction. In: Koutny, M., Haddad, S., Yakovlev, A. (eds.) Transactions on Petri Nets and Other Models of Concurrency IX. LNCS, vol. 8910, pp. 147–177. Springer, Heidelberg (2014). doi:10.1007/978-3-662-45730-6_8

33. Forrester, J.: Principles of Systems. System Dynamics Series. Productivity Press, Portland (1990)
34. Billington, J., Vanit-Anunchai, S., Gallasch, G.E.: Parameterised coloured Petri Net channel models. In: Jensen, K., Billington, J., Koutny, M. (eds.) Transactions on Petri Nets and Other Models of Concurrency III. LNCS, vol. 5800, pp. 71–97. Springer, Heidelberg (2009). doi:10.1007/978-3-642-04856-2_4
35. CPN Group: CPN Tools homepage. http://cpntools.org/start. Last accessed 20 Jan 2013
36. Kanji, G.K.: 100 Statistical Tests. One Hundred Statistical Tests. SAGE Publications, London (2006)

Performance and Replica Consistency Simulation for Quorum-Based NoSQL System Cassandra

Xiangdong Huang[1,2]([✉]), Jianmin Wang[1,2], Jialin Qiao[1,2], Liangfan Zheng[1], Jinrui Zhang[1], and Raymond K. Wong[3]

[1] School of Software, Tsinghua University, Beijing 100084, China
`huangxd12@mails.tsinghua.edu.cn`, `jimwang@tsinghua.edu.cn`
[2] National Engineering Laboratory for Big Data System Software, Beijing 100084, China
[3] School of Computer Science and Engineering, University of New South Wales, Sydney, Australia
`wong@cse.unsw.edu.au`

Abstract. Distributed NoSQL systems such as Cassandra are popular nowadays. However, it is complicated and tedious to configure these systems to achieve their maximum performance for a given environment. This paper focuses on the application of a Coloured Petri Net-based simulation method on a quorum-based system, Cassandra. By analyzing the read and write process of Cassandra, we propose a CPN model, which can be used for performance analysis, optimization, and replica consistency detection. To help users understanding the NoSQL well, a CPN-based simulator called QuoVis is developed. Using QuoVis, users can visualize the read and write process of Cassandra, try different hardware parameters for performance simulation, optimizing system parameters such as timeout and data partitioning strategy, and detecting replica consistency. Experiments show our model fits the real Cassandra cluster well.

1 Introduction

By facilitating high availability for large volumes of data, distributed NoSQL systems have been becoming popular nowadays. For example, Apple company stores over 10 PB of data with over 75,000 Cassandra nodes, and Uber company stores all the GPS data of cars with about 300 Cassandra nodes. Many such systems, e.g., Cassandra [19], Riak [8] and Voldemort [11], are designed as quorum-based systems [28] to support high availability and guarantee replica consistency.

To support different workloads in different environments, NoSQL systems usually have many parameters for users to set. Setting these parameters correctly may have a huge impact on the system performance. For instance, Cassandra (v2.0) has more than 70 parameters, and users may need to tune many of them, e.g., concurrent writes, timeout value and memtable size, to achieve the best performance for their environment; while tuning the I/O parameters in HBase can improve the throughput several times [4].

© Springer International Publishing AG 2017
W. van der Aalst and E. Best (Eds.): PETRI NETS 2017, LNCS 10258, pp. 78–98, 2017.
DOI: 10.1007/978-3-319-57861-3_6

However, tuning the system parameters can be complicated and tedious because it requires users to modify the configuration, then restart and benchmark the system. This process needs to repeat until the targeted performance is achieved. For example, to determine the best table size in memory in Cassandra (i.e., `max_memtable_threshold`), users need to try a particular memory size and apply this new size to all the nodes, then restart the cluster and run some benchmark tests. It needs to repeat until the overall performance is satisfied. The above steps cost a lot of time: just starting up an n-nodes Cassandra cluster, we need at least $2n$ minutes (called as "two minutes rule"[1]). Besides, users have to care about the "cold start" problem in their tests. Worst still, if users are not experts of the target system, they may be confused about what the bottleneck is under the current system configuration or why some exceptions happen (e.g., violating "two minutes rule").

Furthermore, when evaluating or analyzing complex features what NoSQL systems claimed, such as strong consistency guarantee, users or developers need to cover as many as possible situations. However, it is difficult to cover all possible scenarios in a given environment for evaluation purposes. For example, the convergence speed of replicas (from inconsistency to consistency) can be impacted by the network conditions. However, it is almost impossible to adjust the network settings to simulate all possible network performances. Finally, there is no easy way to observe the consistency and monitor the running status of the cluster or specific data values in real-time. Users have to collect distributed logs to track the running trace of the cluster and this method has some fundamental limitations [21].

To address the above issues, we propose building a Coloured Petri Net (i.e., CPN) model for simulating quorum-based NoSQL databases, and then using the model to evaluate and analyze the system. In the paper, we consider Cassandra as an example. Firstly, we analyze the read and write process of Cassandra, and then build a CPN model for the system. The model abstracts the data partitioning strategy, data transitions, network transfer and quorum-based replica control protocol. Secondly, we propose how to use the model for performance evaluation, consistency analysis and evaluation.

To help users (who have little knowledge about CPN) understanding the work process of quorum-based NoSQL systems and tuning them, we developed a visual simulator for Cassandra, called QuoVis. QuoVis can simulate the local data transition in a node, data propagation between nodes. It provides a set of plugins specifically for tuning and analyzing Cassandra. For example, some default plugins allow users to simulate the hardware performance (such as the time cost of each step in a read or write process), and modify the system parameters (such as data partitioning strategy, timeout, etc.). These plugins help us to simulate cluster behavior, especially during message communications, in different scenarios. Based on the plugins, users can simulate and determine appropriate system parameters for a particular production environment. There are also other more specific plugins for more advanced usages. For example, one of them is to detect whether the replicas are consistent at a particular time, or whether a

---

[1] https://issues.apache.org/jira/browse/CASSANDRA-2434.

protocol can make the replica consistent eventually in a given system configuration. Additional plugins can be built by users and added to the simulator to support more analysis ability.

To the best of our knowledge, the model for Cassandra is the first CPN model for NoSQL systems which provides many analysis applications. QuoVis is the first simulator tool for NoSQL clusters. Though the CPN model is built based on Cassandra, we believe that it is also useful for guiding readers to build models for other quorum-based systems, e.g., Riak and Voldemort, and other NoSQL systems.

2   Related Works

Petri Net has been used in many applications. For example, Quentin Gaudel et al. proposed using Hybrid Particle Petri Nets to diagnose the health status of a hybrid system [12]. Petri Net has also been used in the molecular programming area, such as verifying DNA walker circuits using Stochastic Petri Nets [5]. These applications show the power of Petri Net.

As for big data system performance optimization and correction verification areas, there are two kinds of methods: modifying parameters and workloads on real clusters for performance tuning, or using simulation results to analyze the real system. For example, to optimize the performance of jobs on MapReduce, MRTuner [26] was proposed. MRTuner gave a new cost model which considering the holistic optimization, and designed a fast search method to find the optimal execution plan. Similarly, Apache Spark was also optimized by similar methods [25]. Other works, such as Starfish [15] was also proposed. Some simulation works using PeerSim [23,30], Gloudsim [10] and others. However, all of these works do not consider recent popular NoSQL systems as targets.

Though many works were done using (Coloured) Petri Net for system evaluation [20,22,29], using Petri Net to model recent big data systems is still emerging [1,24]. HDFS was modeled in [1] while Cassandra was targeted in [24]. [1] proposed using a CP-net to build the behaviour of HDFS. Using this model, a special scenario, which data nodes leave from the cluster and join into the cluster back frequently, was discussed. In [24], Osman et al. used a QP-net to model the replica of Cassandra. They used the model to evaluate the quorum mechanism. However, the model lacks of ability for analyzing some different consistency metrics of NoSQL, such as data-centric and client-centric consistency metrics [6]. Comparing with QP-net, CPN is more suitable for analyzing the replica consistency. It is because that in the CPN model, users can observe the values of tokens, so that it is easy to determine whether the replicas of a data item are consistent or not. Besides, the model does not fit Cassandra well in some processes. For example, Cassandra splits its reading process as "read digests" and "read original values", while the model does not consider that.

The Quorum-based system has a long history. Quorum can be traced back to 1979 [13], and now many NoSQL systems use it. In brief, suppose one data item has k replicas. Quorum-based systems allow only w replicas to update successfully, and r replicas return responses for a reading request. If $w + r > k$, then clients can read the latest version of the data item.

3   The CPN Model

In this section, we first investigate the write process of Cassandra, and then build a CPN model according to that.

3.1   Writing Operation

We use Cassandra as an example to describe the writing operation. The reason that we choose Cassandra is that it combines the design of Dynamo-like and BigTable-like NoSQL systems [19] and it is popular in the world. We have used Cassandra solving the data management problems for meteorological data and time series data.

In a Cassandra cluster, each data item has k replicas. k is configurable. Therefore, given a writing request, there are at least k servers will be involved. We define 3 kinds of nodes (i.e., servers) for each request: *coordinator*, *participator* and *other*s. The coordinator is the node which the client sends the request to. It is also the node which gives the response to the client. The participator is the node which receives a forwarded request. Except for the coordinator, all the nodes which have replicas of the requested data item are participators. Other nodes in the cluster which do not handle the query or writing operation are others. For a request, we only care about the coordinator and participators.

Figure 1 shows a Cassandra cluster with 5 nodes ($s_1 \sim s_5$) and each data item has two replicas: s_1 and s_2 store item A. A client sends a writing request for A to s_1. In this case, s_1 is the coordinator and s_2 is a participator. Both $s_3 \sim s_5$ are other nodes.

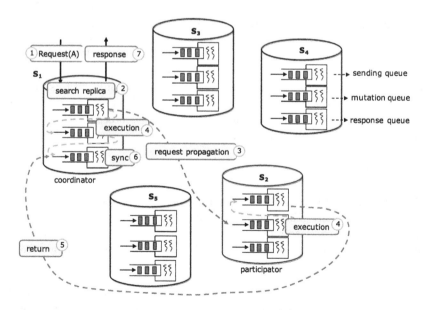

Fig. 1. Writing operation between two nodes in a 5-nodes Cassandra cluster

Figure 1 splits a writing operation of Cassandra into 7 steps (① ~ ⑦). There are two branches: a *remote branch*, which is ① → ② → ③ → ④ → ⑤ → ⑥ → ⑦; and a *local branch*, which is ① → ② → ④ → ⑥ → ⑦. If the replica number $k > 1$, then at least one remote branch will be fired. If the coordinator has one replica of the requested data item, the local branch will be fired. Otherwise the local branch will be not fired. A detailed description about these steps can be found in our previous work [16] and Osman et al.'s work [24] has a similar discussion.

⑥ is for synchronizing writing acknowledgements. In Cassandra, for each writing request, it will be propagated to k servers (which the coordinator may be one of), but the coordinator only accepts w ($w \leq k$ and w is also user-defined) writing acknowledgements. That is why Cassandra claims it is a consistency-tunable system.

Because requests may come in faster than they can be digested, a temporary space to cache the requests is necessary. For each node-to-node connection, the coordinator has a *propagation queue* to cache the requests for sending them out. Except for the propagation queue, each node has a *mutation queue* to cache the requests from clients or coordinators for executing local writing operations. Similarly, each node has a *reading queue* for reading operations. After finishing the reading or writing operation locally, the node sends a response message to the coordinator. The step is also handled by the propagation queue. To handle received response messages, a *response queue* is needed.

3.2 Query Operation

The query operation is similar to the writing operation. To describe a query operation step by step, we just need to rename the "execution" in Fig. 1 as "query", and modify the time costs of transitions. In detail, a query process has two stages: read data digest, and read data values. Some works such as [24] do not consider that. We have implemented the two stages with CPN language[2].

The outputs of "search replica" and "sync" also need to be modified. "search replica" in the writing operation generates k tasks, while only r tasks are generated in the query operation ($r \leq k$ and r is a user-defined value). Similarly, "sync" in the writing operation only accepts w response messages while it needs r response messages for query operations.

3.3 CPN Model

Model with 2 Nodes. Firstly, we use a CP-net to describe the two branches in Sect. 3.1. When converting the two branches to a CP-net model, we can use a multi-choice pattern [9] to represent ②. Similarly, ⑥ is a synchronizing merge pattern [9] in CP-net form. Other steps can be modeled by a sequence pattern [9].

---

[2] How to model the two stage is not shown in this paper, but the source code of the model and all the source codes of CPN models in this paper can be found from the Github website: https://github.com/jixuan1989/color-petri-net-cassandra.

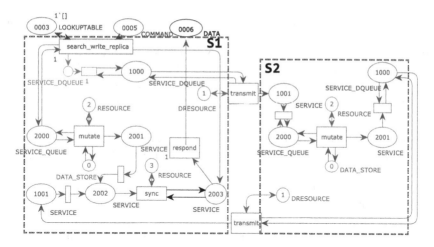

Fig. 2. Using CP-net to describe a writing operation between two nodes

Figure 2 shows a CP-net model for a writing operation instance between two nodes. In the figure, "search write replica" transition represents step ②, "transmit" transition represents step ③ or ⑤, "mutate" is step ④, "sync" is step ⑥, and "respond" is step ⑦. ① is a token in the "0005" place. The definitions of col_set, expressions and functions are omitted here, and users can get them in a ".cpn" file from Github.

Cassandra uses consistent hashing ring [18] as its data partitioning strategy [19]. The tokens in the "0003" place represent the information of the consistent hashing ring. In our model, the ring is modeled using a numeric space K, e.g., $[0,100]$. Each node is responsible for some ranges of the space, e.g., node s_1 may be responsible for ranges $[40,50)$ and $[50,60)$.

The data item is modeled as a triple $item = (key, value, version)$, where $hash(key) \in K$. A request is a quintuple $req = (type, key, value, version, clevel)$ where $type$ is READ or WRITE, and $clevel$ is the required consistency level (i.e., the value of the quorum parameter w or r). So, if a client sends a request (WRITE, 45, 3, 2, 1), i.e., the key is 45, value is 3, version is 2 and the required consistency level is $w = 1$, then the request will be propagated to node s_1 and other replicas.

Tokens in the "2003" are callbacks which count how many acknowledgements that have been received. Tokens in the "0006" place represent the results that clients receive. Tokens in the "0" place represent the persistent data items on disk in Cassandra nodes.

As described in Sect. 3.1, there are 3 queues in our system. In the figure, place "1000", "2000" and "2003" are the *sending queue*, the *mutation queue* and the *response queue*. We implement the queues by the List in the CPN Tools. By using hd list, tl list and $\wedge\wedge$ operations, we can implement the FIFO strategy of a queue[3]. That is why the arcs between the place "2000" (or "1000", "2003") and

---

[3] http://cpntools.org/documentation/tasks/editing/constructs/queuesstacks.

its adjacent transitions are round arrows. Tokens in the place "2" are concurrent write threads. If there are t tokens totally in the place "2", then the place "2", "2000" and the "mutate" transition form a queueing system which has t service counters. Place "1" and "3" are similar with "2". In this model, all the anonymous transitions can be simplified by merging its input place and output place. We draw them for generating the folded model in the rest of this paper.

Modeling a Cluster. Next, we extend Fig. 2 to describe a cluster. We use a 5-nodes cluster as an example. By copying the model structure of s_1 (s_2 is a sub-model of s_1's structure), we get CP-net structures for $s_2 \sim s_5$. As shown in Figure 3, we organize the structures of $s_1 \sim s_5$ together by connecting the "input" (i.e., "1001") and "output" (i.e., "1000") places with anonymous transitions.

Figure 3 shows the architecture of a cluster clearly. A client can choose any node as the coordinator. Data will be stored in k "0" places eventually (k is the replica number).

It is hard to use the model in Fig. 3 for modeling arbitrary sized clusters. For example, to simulate a cluster with n nodes, we need to construct a model which is similar with Fig. 3 by copying, pasting and some minor modifications. To solve the problem, a folded Petri Net model is built based on Fig. 3. Figure 4 shows

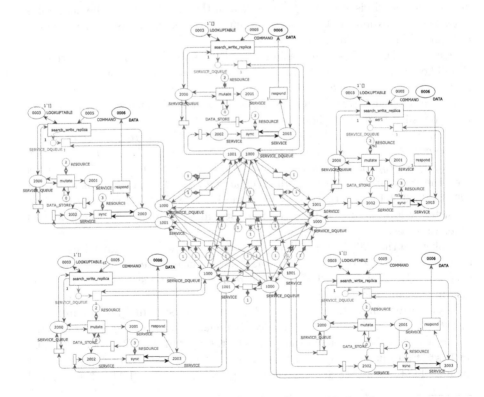

Fig. 3. Replicating two nodes to a cluster with 5 nodes

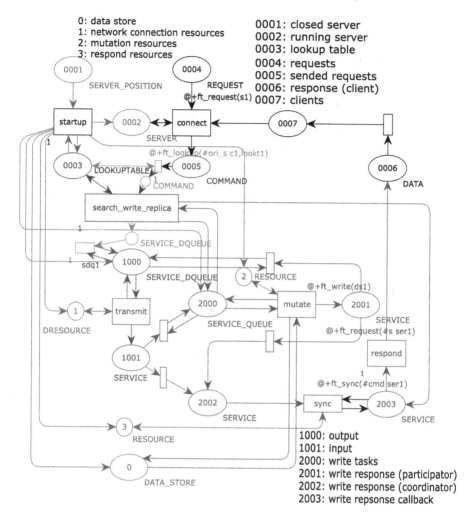

Fig. 4. A folded model for represent a cluster with any number of nodes (Color figure online)

the model. The model is drew by CPN Tools and users can download the source code of the model from Github. The elements (i.e., places and transitions) tinged with green color refer to the initiation process of servers, so that many resources are initialized. The dark color elements refer to determining which nodes having replicas. The purple color elements refer to the network propagation. The blue elements refer to the local write process and the synchronization process.

The model defines 15 col_sets and 16 complex functions (except for simple expressions on arcs). To make the model readable, we omit the expressions or functions on arcs, the guard functions on transitions, and the definition of col_sets. However, the time costs of important transitions are reserved. Place 0001, 0003, 0004, and 0007 have initial tokens. Users can read detailed model on Github.

4 Model Analysis

4.1 Performance Simulation

In CPN Tools, transitions in a model can have a property, time cost. It is introduced by Timed Petri Net. Suppose a transition has that property, and the time cost is t, then it means that when the transition is fired, it generates the output tokens after t time units. Using that property, we can simulate the time cost of a write process in the real cluster. Before simulation, users need to define the time costs of each transition in our model.

To simulate a cluster with n nodes using the model in Fig. 4, we just need to put n tokens with different values into the place "0001". In default, the consistent hashing ring will be generated automatically and stored in the place "0003" when the transition "startup" is fired. To simulate m requests, we need to put m tokens into the place "0004". After the simulation, Data items (i.e., tokens) will be stored in the place "0".

Suppose $\sigma_r(t)$ is the number of tokens in the place "0004" at time t (the clock is controlled by the CP-net model rather than a real clock in the real world), and $\sigma_i(t)$ is the number of tokens which belong to the node s_i in the place "0" at time t. Then the throughput T_{s_i} of the node s_i between time t_1 to t_2 is:

$$T_{s_i} = \frac{\sigma_i(t_2) - \sigma_i(t_1)}{t_2 - t_1}$$

The throughput T of the cluster is:

$$T = \frac{\sigma_r(t_2) - \sigma_r(t_1)}{t_2 - t_1} \tag{1}$$

Given a request, we mark that its related token d is put into the place "0004" at time $t_{req}(d)$, and generated into the place "0" at time $t_{res}(d)$. Then given a request set R, the average latency of requests is:

$$L(R) = \frac{\sum_{r \in R} (t_{res}(r) - t_{req}(r))}{|R|} \tag{2}$$

4.2 Parameter Tuning

A model which can be used for tuning parameters needs to have two characteristics: (1) the model can reflect the current configurations of a real system; (2) the model can tune parameters which users focus on. In our model, the first characteristic is implemented by the settings of time costs of each transition: we collect system log from real systems and then analyze the time costs of each events; then we use the time costs as transitions' time costs. After that, the model can reflect the performance of the real system well. In this way, though we do not know the specific values of all the parameters, the model has the ability to reflect the impact of current parameters' values.

As for the second characteristic, the model in this paper can only be used for tuning (1) the numbers of the concurrent write threads, the network connections, and concurrent synchronization threads; (2) the timeout parameter; (3) different workloads and quorum settings; and (4) data partitioning configuration. The first one can be achieved by modifying the number of tokens in the place "2", "1" and "3". The second one is not shown in Fig. 4. Users can find the related transitions in a more complex model on Github. The third one can be achieved by adding different tokens in the place "0004". By setting the tokens with different time values, we can control the number of concurrent requests. By setting the tokens with different "key" values, we can control the data distribution of requests. By setting the tokens with different *clevel* values, we can control the quorum settings. The 4th one can be achieved by modifying tokens in the place "0003".

4.3   Consistency Detection

By checking all the tokens in the place "0" on each servers, we can detect whether there is replica inconsistency easily. If a data item has two replicas, then it needs to be stored on the places "0" of two servers. Given a data item (key, value, version)= (k, v, vr), we suppose the replicas of it are on server s_i and s_j, and the related tokens in the places 0 of s_i and s_j are $token_i = (k, v_i, vr_i)$ and $token_j = (k, v_j, vr_j)$. then there are 3 situations:

(1) Neither $token_i$ or $token_j$ exists, which means both the two servers s_i and s_j have not finished the writing operation.
(2) $token_i$ (or $token_j$) does not exist, which means s_i (or s_j) has not finished the writing operation while s_j (or s_i) has finished it. If $token_i$ does not exist, we consider that s_j has the latest version of the data item. Otherwise s_i has the latest version.
(3) $v_i \neq v_j$ or $vr_i \neq vr_j$, which means the two replicas are not consistent. If $vr_i > vr_j$, then s_i has the latest version, otherwise s_i has a stale version.

Figure 5 shows an example of the third situation. In the figure, we omit the irrelevant part of the model. The data item whose key is b has two

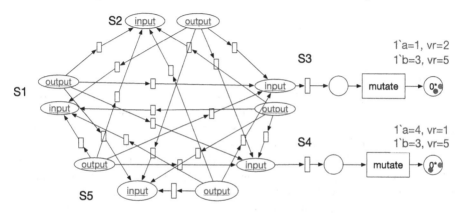

Fig. 5. An example of inconsistent data items

consistent replicas. The data item whose key is a has two inconsistent replicas. Because data item a on server s_4 has a smaller version than s_3, we consider that the data item on s_4 is more stale. The reason of the inconsistency may be that server s_4 lost one or more writing operations for the data item.

Detecting the consistency of replicas is meaningful because it helps us accelerating the reading process. Normally, Cassandra provides eventual consistency for high availability and low latency [2]: as described in Sect. 2, if $w + r > k$, where k is the number of replicas, users can get a strong consistent result. However, for each reading requests, it requires the cluster reads r replicas, where the $r - 1$ reading results are meaningless if all of the replicas are consistent. Therefore, if we know the replicas are consistent, we can set $r = 1$ to accelerate reading processes while maintaining the strong consistency property. Therefore, monitoring whether the replicas are consistent and when they become consistent are important.

By monitoring the changes of tokens of place 0 on all the servers, we can observe the inconsistency of all the data items. It is easy to be implemented by CPN language and CPN Tools, while some other Petri Net languages which do not have the concept of "colour" are hard to support it. That is one of the main reason that we choose CPN.

4.4 Consistency Measurement

Because of the importance of replica consistency, many consistency metrics are proposed. From the client-centric view, there are k-staleness, t-visibility [3], session consistency [27] and so on. These metrics are a little easier than data-centric metrics, it is because they consider the target systems as black boxes. From the data-centric view, there are atomicity, regularity, and safeness [14]. Besides, inconsistency time window is also proposed in [7,16] respectively, while the definitions of them are slightly different. In this paper, we use the CPN model to show what the inconsistency time window in [16] is and how to measure it.

Inconsistent time window: It refers to the duration time of the inconsistent between two replicas. Given a writing operation $W[x]1$ (i.e., set item $x = 1$), and the item x has two replica s_i and s_j, if s_i finished $W[x]1$ at time t_i while s_j finished it at t_j, we say the inconsistent time window of s_i and s_j on data item x is

$$itw_x(s_i, s_j) = |t_i - t_j|. \tag{3}$$

Figure 6 shows an example. Similar with Fig. 5, the irrelevant part of the model is omitted. The figure is a snapshot that the blue and red tokens $token_b$ and $token_r$ have been written successfully in server s_4 at time t_0. At that time, $token_b$ and $token_r$ were not written in server s_3. Therefore, it belongs to the second inconsistency situation. There are two cases: the token ($token_r$) has enqueued the mutation queue, but it is waiting for enjoying service; the token ($token_b$) has not been propagated to the server (s_3). By monitoring the changes of place 0, we will know the exact time that the tokens are written successfully. Then we can calculate the inconsistency time window by Eq. 3.

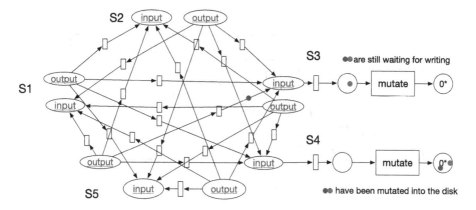

Fig. 6. An example of inconsistent time window (Color figure online)

5   Application: QuoVis

To help users understanding the read and write process of Cassandra well, we build a visualization simulator[4]. The tool is driven by our CPN model and CPN Tools's execution engine (by using Access/CPN library [31][5]). Besides, the tool provides some analysis plugins for helping users simulating and tuning the performance, and analyzing the consistency.

We firstly introduce the architecture of QuoVis. Then we describe the basic simulation and visualization of QuoVis. Then we demonstrate 3 analysis plugins. The first plugin shows how to simulate the hardware performance and tune the system parameters with QuoVis (Sects. 5.3 and 5.4). The second plugin helps users to choose a better data partitioning strategy by quantitatively comparing the performance difference (Sect. 5.5). With the third plugin, we illustrate how to use the model for consistency detection (Sect. 5.6). Besides, we discuss about that whether the quorum protocol can always guarantee eventual consistency in Cassandra.

5.1   System Design

QuoVis is designed based on a modular architecture with an extensible plugin interface, as shown in Fig. 7. The underlying model is the kernel of the simulator. The simulator engine has the ability to execute the model step-by-step and can provide the runtime information to other modules. When executing the model, the simulator maintains a virtual global clock (i.e., the time in CPN Tools execution engine) to simulate the time elapsed for each step in a read or

---

[4] A demo video is available from https://www.youtube.com/watch?v=nvIBDUubFvM.

[5] We found the performance is terrible for simulating a large scale clusters, and thereby we have built a faster execution engine. The engine is not the focus of this paper so that we omit it.

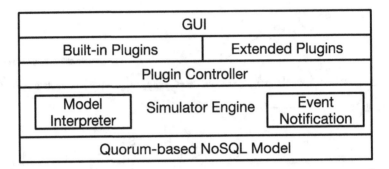

Fig. 7. QuoVis system architecture

write process. The elapsed time is irrelevant to the real-world time. Hence, the simulation result is independent on the performance on the underlying hardware which QuoVis runs on.

The abilities of tuning Cassandra parameters and other analysis are provided as plugins. Some built-in plugins have been developed. Users can create new plugins to extend the built-in abilities. Plugin controller is responsible for plugin registration and management. Plugins can be loaded dynamically. To avoid plugins asking information from the simulator frequently, an event notification module is in place to allow plugins to subscribe only the transitions and their binding data values (i.e., tokens) of their interests. The GUI module is designed to visualize the running status of the model. Plugins can also customize the GUI.

5.2 Process Visualization

This section demonstrates how QuoVis simulates a Cassandra cluster with an arbitrary number of nodes and settings, and can be used to visualize each step of a read or write process. A screenshot of the main screen of the simulator is shown in Fig. 8. Users can configure the number of servers, clients and other details on the left pane. Users can customize the reading and writing requests via an advanced menu there. By setting the starting time of the first read request, QuoVis can simulate a cluster which has loaded data before the read workload comes. Users can also control the simulation progress step by step through the simulation, and watch the simulation trace details on the right pane.

The animation of the simulation is shown on the middle pane for visualization purposes. Users can, for example, animate and monitor how the cluster with the consistent hashing ring is constructed and how a read or write process is running. For each node, there are nine circles that represent some important places in the model. Normally, these places represent queues in Cassandra model. Users can observe how many items in a queue and even obtain the details of the items there when the mouse pointer is placed on top of its corresponding circle. When a message moves from one queue to a queue of another node, an animation of a small blue bubble moving from its corresponding circle to another circle will be played to reflect this message propagation. The blue bubble represents a token

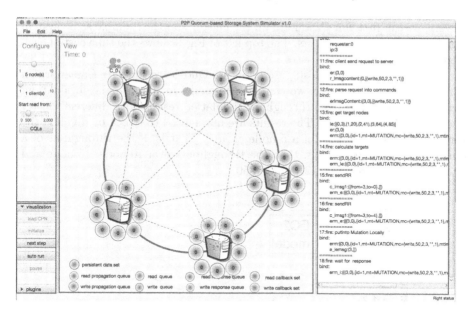

Fig. 8. The main screen of the simulator (Color figure online)

in our model. Overall this simulation and visualization demonstrate the most common application of our simulator.

5.3   Performance Simulation

When a user uses the simulator to simulate a NoSQL cluster in a production environment, the user needs to input the hardware parameters to describe the production environment at first. In QuoVis, we use the time costs of each step to describe hardware performance. For example, if we want to use QuoVis to simulate and analyze a Cassandra cluster on Amazon EC2 with 5 *t2.small*

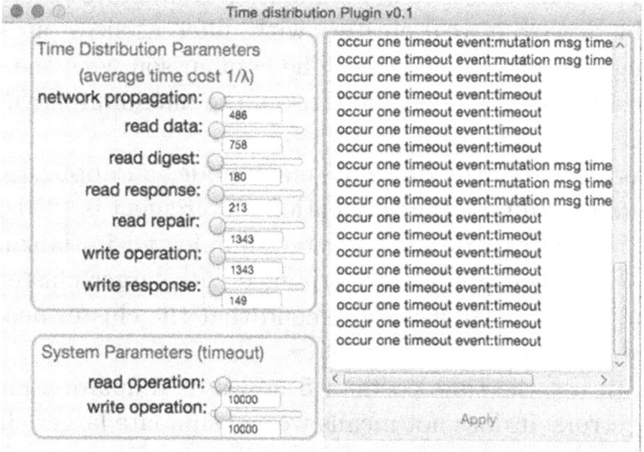

Fig. 9. The plugin for tuning time cost and timeout.

servers, we can first run Cassandra on the cluster and then sample some system logs to calculate the time costs. The top left of Fig. 9 shows the time cost of each step on the cluster.

After getting the time costs, users can use QuoVis to simulate Cassandra on Amazon EC2. For example, we can use the model for performance evaluation. Figure 10 demonstrates the throughput simulation results with different cluster sizes by the CP-net model. The results are normalized to $[1, \infty)$ by dividing the throughput result by that of a 5-node cluster. That is, if the throughput of a 5-node cluster is 1000 ops/s, then the throughputs of a 10-node, 15-node and 20-node clusters are 1190, 1210 and 1350.

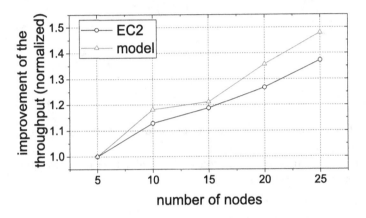

Fig. 10. Throughput prediction of clusters with different sizes and a comparison with real systems

In this experiment, the time distributions are collected and calculated by system log in a 5-nodes cluster. When we change the size of the cluster in our model, we do not change the time distributions of each transition. The above approach may make some errors to our simulation results. However, we think the error is minor: by deploying real clusters with different sizes on Amazon EC2, we get the throughput on real clusters. The comparison with the model is also shown in Fig. 10. According to the comparison, the maximum error of the model is about 9% (i.e., the cluster with 25 nodes).

Using our model, we can predict how many nodes an application needs. For example, in Figure 10, suppose the application requirement is 1250 ops/s. Firstly, we can deploy a 5-nodes cluster and collect system log for initializing our model. Then we use the model to predict performance with larger clusters. According to the prediction in Figure 10, we recommend that the cluster needs more than 20 nodes (1350 > 1250).

Though we can use the time costs of 5 nodes to simulate a cluster with 25 nodes within 9% errors, it does not means we can simulate larger cluster without modifying the time costs while keeping a small error. For example, if we want to predict the performance of a cluster with 60 nodes, we would better to get the real time costs of each transition on a 30-nodes cluster first. Fortunately, it is acceptable in practice: scaling out a cluster is iterative, and it is unlikely that scaling out a cluster from 5 nodes to 500 nodes one round.

5.4   Parameter Optimization: Timeout

To get the best performance, users need to determine various system parameters such as timeout value, maximum number of threads, etc. We consider the timeout value as a specific example. A high timeout value delays the detection of system exception or node failure, and a low timeout value can misjudge a normal process as an exception that affect the system correctness. Since the cluster is newly setup, users are unlikely to identify suitable values for the system parameters quickly. Instead of trial and error, restart and benchmark the system, it would be desirable to be able to just enter different parameter values and simulate the benchmarks.

With QuoVis, users can easily try different parameter values to simulate different scenarios of a NoSQL cluster. Firstly, users need to initialize the QuoVis model by entering the hardware performance (i.e., the time costs) as above. After the initialization, we can use QuoVis to find the suitable system parameters. For example, in Fig. 9, we set the timeout value to 10000, which leads to too many timeout events. As a result, more than 1/10 of the writing requests fail. Therefore, many write operations have not been successfully replicated in all the replicas, i.e., the replicas are inconsistent. Users can then increase the timeout value until an acceptable number of timeout events is resulted.

5.5   Parameter Optimization: Consistent Hashing Ring

How data items are placed in a cluster can significantly affect the overall performance [17], and users can control the data partitioning strategy by modifying the consistent hashing ring. Using QuoVis, we can easily compare different data partitioning strategies and visualize the results. In this section, we use QuoVis to simulate different data partitioning strategies and predict the throughput. The plugin GUI is omitted here because of the limitation of pages.

To calculate the accuracy of the simulation result, we benchmark Cassandra throughput using 5 data partitioning strategies on Amazon EC2. Figure 11 shows the comparison results. The results are normalized to 0~1 by dividing the throughput with the first partition strategy $P1$. Prediction from QuoVis is consistent with the throughput of the actual cluster. For example, QuoVis predicts that the throughput of the cluster with $P2$ strategy is about 86% of the throughput from the uniform strategy ($P1$). The result in the real cluster shows that the percentage is about 83%. By observation, the maximum error is about 8% ($P5$).

In addition, we can also use QuoVis to find out the reason that causes the decline of throughput. Via the visual process shown of $P5$ in QuoVis, we found that the mutation queues of node s_1 and s_5 are long and the sizes of the persistent

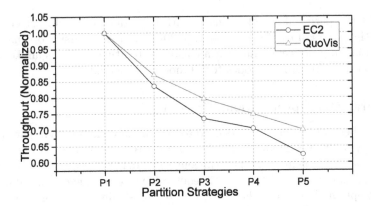

Fig. 11. data partitioning strategies - a real cluster vs QuoVis with 2 replicas. The results are normalized. The data partitions of servers $s_1:s_2:s_3:s_4:s_5$ are: uniform (P1), 15:15:15:15:40 (P2), 12:12:13:13:50 (P3), 10:10:10:10:60 (P4) and 7:7:8:8:70 (P5).

data sets of s_1 and s_5 are the largest. Therefore, we conjecture that s_1 and s_5 are the performance bottlenecks. This comparison has two implications: a uniform data partitioning is better in these settings; or node s_1 and s_5 should be upgraded; or the *concurrent write number* parameters on s_1 and s_5 should be optimized to achieve better performance if we must use this data partitioning strategy.

5.6 Consistency Detection

Eventual consistency history plugin supports detecting the replica consistency. Figure 12 shows the screenshot of the plugin. For each data item, if any replica contains a different value, we label the data item as inconsistent. When the *persistent data set* of a node changes, the plugin records the number of inconsistent data items and displays the records in a line chart (i.e., the red line with 'x' symbol in the chart).

Figure 12 shows an example that the system is not yet consistent after all writing requests are finished. In Fig. 12, sometimes the up and down of the red line means that some data inconsistencies are temporary. If the number of inconsistencies is greater than 0 at the end, it means that some data items are inconsistent permanently. For example, for a writing request, the message will queue up in a propagation queue, a write queue, the propagation queue again and then a response queue in turn. Since each node has its own progress in digesting its messages (e.g., some may have more messages), so temporary inconsistencies will occur.

However, the timeout parameter limits the waiting time for a writing operation, the message has to depart from the queue if the time is up. If a message is timeout, the replica will be inconsistent permanently. Therefore, to keep replicas consistent eventually, we need to set the timeout value big enough or run on high performance hardware and network.

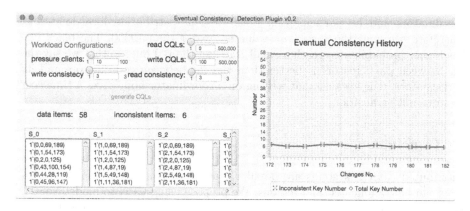

Fig. 12. A case of that not all the replicas eventually reach to consistent status (Color figure online)

The timeout strategy indicates that eventual consistency is not satisfied with only writing operations. Most systems address this issue by triggering a repair when they receive read requests. For example, Cassandra uses *read repair* mechanism to repair these inconsistent data items automatically. However, this repair always incurs performance penalty. We can use QuoVis to tune the timeout parameters to avoid this data consistency issue.

By using Eq. 3, we can calculate the inconsistency time window. In this simulation, each data item has 3 replicas. The write consistency level is 2. There are 20000 different data items. When one node finishes writing a replica of a data item, we calculate the inconsistency time window by Eq. 3. After all the data items are written, we draw the inconsistency time window distribution for visualization.

Figure 13 shows the result. The black line is the distribution of the *itw*s between two participators. The red line is the distribution of the *itw*s between

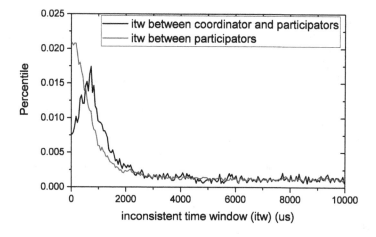

Fig. 13. The distribution of the inconsistent time window (Color figure online)

coordinators and its participators. Both the *itw* distribution have long-tails. Therefore, we omit the *itw* whose value is greater than 10000. The black line has higher probability to reach a small *itw* than the red line, so that we say the *itw* between participators is better than the *itw* between coordinators and its participators. It is because that writing on a coordinator node saves a time cost of "transmit" transition.

6   Conclusion

Distributed NoSQL systems are popular, but tuning and analyzing these systems can be complicated and tedious. We propose using CPN to model NoSQL systems and for performance and consistency analysis. We have presented our recently built simulator called QuoVis for analyzing and tuning a quorum-based NoSQL system, Cassandra. The simulator is supported by the engine of CPN Tools and Access/CPN. Several usage scenarios have been presented to show the effectiveness of our simulator for deploying, maintaining (including visualizing and monitoring) a distributed NoSQL system. Since our simulator is built based on an extensible (plugin-based), modular architecture, its functionalities can be easily extended. Finally, although the underlying model of our simulator is based on Cassandra, we believe that it can be easily customized for other NoSQL systems.

Acknowledgement. The paper is supported by The National Key R&D Program of China (2016YFB1000701) and NSFC (61325008).

References

1. Aguilera-Mendoza, L., Llorente-Quesada, M.T.: Modeling and simulation of hadoop distributed file system in a cluster of workstations. In: Cuzzocrea, A., Maabout, S. (eds.) MEDI 2013. LNCS, vol. 8216, pp. 1–12. Springer, Heidelberg (2013). doi:10.1007/978-3-642-41366-7_1
2. Bailis, P., Ghodsi, A.: Eventual consistency today: limitations, extensions, and beyond. Commun. ACM **56**(5), 55–63 (2013)
3. Bailis, P., Venkataraman, S., Franklin, M.J., Hellerstein, J.M., Stoica, I.: Probabilistically bounded staleness for practical partial quorums. VLDB **5**(8), 776–787 (2012)
4. Bao, X., Liu, L., Xiao, N., Zhou, Y., Zhang, Q.: Policy-driven configuration management for NoSQL. In: 2015 IEEE 8th International Conference on Cloud Computing (CLOUD), pp. 245–252, June 2015
5. Barbot, B., Kwiatkowska, M.: On quantitative modelling and verification of DNA walker circuits using stochastic Petri Nets. In: Devillers, R., Valmari, A. (eds.) PETRI NETS 2015. LNCS, vol. 9115, pp. 1–32. Springer, Cham (2015). doi:10.1007/978-3-319-19488-2_1
6. Bermbach, D.: Benchmarking Eventually Consistent Distributed Storage Systems. KIT Scientific Publishing, Karlsruhe (2014)

7. Bermbach, D., Tai, S.: Eventual consistency: how soon is eventual? An evaluation of amazon s3's consistency behavior. In: Proceedings of the 6th Workshop on Middleware for Service Oriented Computing, p. 1. ACM (2011)

8. Bushik, S.: A Vendor-Independent Comparison of NoSQL Databases: Cassandra, HBase, MongoDB, Riak. Network World, 22 October 2012

9. van Der Aalst, W.M., Ter Hofstede, A.H., Kiepuszewski, B., Barros, A.P.: Workflow patterns. Distrib. Parallel Databases 14(1), 5–51 (2003)

10. Di, S., Cappello, F.: GloudSim: Google trace based cloud simulator with virtual machines. Softw. Pract. Experience 45(11), 1571–1590 (2015)

11. Feinberg, A.: Project voldemort: reliable distributed storage. In: Proceedings of the 10th IEEE International Conference on Data Engineering (2011)

12. Gaudel, Q., Ribot, P., Chanthery, E., Daigle, M.J.: Health monitoring of a planetary rover using hybrid particle Petri Nets. In: Kordon, F., Moldt, D. (eds.) PETRI NETS 2016. LNCS, vol. 9698, pp. 196–215. Springer, Cham (2016). doi:10.1007/978-3-319-39086-4_13

13. Gifford, D.K.: Weighted voting for replicated data. In: Proceedings of the Seventh ACM Symposium on Operating Systems Principles, pp. 150–162. ACM (1979)

14. Golab, W., Li, X., Shah, M.A.: Analyzing consistency properties for fun and profit. In: Proceedings of the 30th Annual ACM SIGACT-SIGOPS Symposium on Principles of Distributed Computing, pp. 197–206. ACM (2011)

15. Herodotou, H., Lim, H., Luo, G., Borisov, N., Dong, L., Cetin, F.B., Babu, S.: Starfish: a self-tuning system for big data analytics. CIDR 11, 261–272 (2011)

16. Huang, X., Wang, J., Bai, J., Ding, G., Long, M.: Inherent replica inconsistency in Cassandra. In: 2014 IEEE International Congress on Big Data, pp. 740–747. IEEE (2014)

17. Huang, X., Wang, J., Zhong, Y., Song, S., Yu, P.S.: Optimizing data partition for scaling out NoSQL cluster. Concurrency Comput. Pract. Experience 17, 5793–5809 (2015)

18. Karger, D., Lehman, E., Leighton, T., Panigrahy, R., Levine, M., Lewin, D.: Consistent hashing and random trees: distributed caching protocols for relieving hot spots on the world wide web. In: Proceedings of the 29th ACM Symposium on Theory of Computing, pp. 654–663. ACM (1997)

19. Lakshman, A., Malik, P.: Cassandra: a decentralized structured storage system. ACM SIGOPS Operating Syst. Rev. 44(2), 35–40 (2010)

20. Liao, W., Hou, K., Zheng, Y., He, X.: Modeling and simulation of troubleshooting process for automobile based on Petri Net and flexsim. In: Qi, E., Shen, J., Dou, R. (eds.) The 19th International Conference on Industrial Engineering and Engineering Management, pp. 1141–1153. Springer, Heidelberg (2013). doi:10.1007/978-3-642-38391-5_121

21. Mace, J., Roelke, R., Fonseca, R.: Pivot tracing: dynamic causal monitoring for distributed systems. In: Proceedings of the 25th SOSP, pp. 378–393. ACM (2015)

22. Majidi, F., Harounabadi, A.: Presentation of an executable model for evaluation of software architecture using blackboard technique and formal models. JACST 4(1), 23–31 (2015)

23. Montresor, A., Jelasity, M.: Peersim: A scalable P2P simulator. In: 2009 IEEE Ninth International Conference on Peer-to-Peer Computing, pp. 99–100. IEEE (2009)

24. Osman, R., Piazzolla, P.: Modelling replication in NoSQL datastores. In: Norman, G., Sanders, W. (eds.) QEST 2014. LNCS, vol. 8657, pp. 194–209. Springer, Cham (2014). doi:10.1007/978-3-319-10696-0_16

25. Shi, J., Qiu, Y., Minhas, U.F., Jiao, L., Wang, C., Reinwald, B., Özcan, F.: Clash of the titans: MapReduce vs. Spark for large scale data analytics. VLDB **8**(13), 2110–2121 (2015)

26. Shi, J., Zou, J., Lu, J., Cao, Z., Li, S., Wang, C.: MRTuner: a toolkit to enable holistic optimization for MapReduce jobs. VLDB **7**(13), 1319–1330 (2014)

27. Terry, D.B., Demers, A.J., Petersen, K., Spreitzer, M.J., Theimer, M.M., Welch, B.B.: Session guarantees for weakly consistent replicated data. In: 1994 Proceedings of the Third International Conference on Parallel and Distributed Information Systems, pp. 140–149. IEEE (1994)

28. Thomas, R.H.: A majority consensus approach to concurrency control for multiple copy databases. ACM Trans. Database Syst. (TODS) **4**(2), 180–209 (1979)

29. Wagenhals, L.W., Liles, S.W., Levis, A.H.: Toward executable architectures to support evaluation. In: 2009 International Symposium on Collaborative Technologies and Systems, pp. 502–511, May 2009

30. Wang, K., Kulkarni, A., Lang, M., Arnold, D., Raicu, I.: Using simulation to explore distributed key-value stores for extreme-scale system services. In: Proceedings of the International Conference on High Performance Computing, Networking, Storage and Analysis, p. 9. ACM (2013)

31. Westergaard, M.: Access/CPN 2.0: a high-level interface to coloured Petri Net models. In: Kristensen, L.M., Petrucci, L. (eds.) PETRI NETS 2011. LNCS, vol. 6709, pp. 328–337. Springer, Heidelberg (2011). doi:10.1007/978-3-642-21834-7_19

Petri Net Tools

travis - An Online Tool for the Synthesis and Analysis of Petri Nets with Final States

Benjamin Meis$^{(\boxtimes)}$, Robin Bergenthum, and Jörg Desel

Department of Software Engineering and Theory of Programming,
FernUniversität in Hagen, Hagen, Germany
{benjamin.meis,robin.bergenthum,joerg.desel}@fernuni-hagen.de

Abstract. This paper introduces the online tool *travis*. The main application of *travis* is the synthesis and the analysis of Petri net models with final states. Using *travis* we can load or specify a labeled transition system and toggle an arbitrary set of states to be final. *travis* can also load and handle event logs to start the synthesis procedure. Fix a transition system or an event log, *travis* is able to synthesize a k-bounded Petri net model with a set of final markings related to the set of specified final states. Furthermore, *travis* can synthesize a so-called neat place for any k-bounded Petri net model at hand if such a place exists. A neat place is marked if and only if the Petri net is in a final state. The computation of neat places is a strong tool to analyze final states of process models.

1 Introduction

travis is an online tool for the synthesis and the analysis of Petri nets with final states. The tool runs in a browser without being downloaded or installed. *travis* can easily be accessed at http://www.fernuni-hagen.de/sttp/travis. *travis* is developed in Java, using the Google Web Toolkit (GWT). GWT is an open source development kit for browser-based applications. The GWT compiler can generate HTML, CSS and JavaScript from Java code. Thus, *travis* is pure HTML, CSS and JavaScript. The *travis* homepage at http://www.fernuni-hagen. de/sttp/forschung/travis.shtml provides a description of *travis*, all example files used in this tool paper, and a short documentation of the usage and the functionalities of *travis*. The core of *travis* are algorithms presented in [16,17]. These papers introduce synthesis and analysis algorithms for k-bounded Petri nets with final states. *travis* can be applied in an educational context to teach different concepts of distributed final states, as well as in the context of business process modeling to identify and indicate final states of process models. Several tools for Petri net synthesis and analysis have been implemented, e.g. LoLA, GENET, Petrify, VipTool, and APT. LoLA is a very strong tool for the analysis of place/transition nets [19], GENET is a tool for the synthesis and mining of Petri nets from automata [8], Petrify is a tool for the synthesis of Petri nets and asynchronous circuits [11], VipTool is a tool for modeling, simulation, validation and verification of systems using place/transition Petri nets [4], and APT is a tool for synthesis and the analysis of Petri nets and transition systems [5].

© Springer International Publishing AG 2017
W. van der Aalst and E. Best (Eds.): PETRI NETS 2017, LNCS 10258, pp. 101–111, 2017.
DOI: 10.1007/978-3-319-57861-3_7

travis has two different kinds of editors: a transition system editor including an event log loader and a Petri net editor. Figure 1 depicts an overview of the main features of *travis* where each editor is depicted by a framed box.

The event log loader loads log-files of the standard XES file format [18]. A user can simply drag-and-drop a stored file into the event log loader. Thus, *travis* has a simple interface to import files created by other tools handling and creating event logs. The most popular one of such tools is called ProM [1]. ProM is a framework that supports a wide variety of process mining techniques. The transition system editor loads, creates, and edits labeled transition systems with final states. Of course, *travis* supports all standard editing features for states, labels, and transitions, as well as, alignment and graph drawing algorithms. We can toggle any arbitrary set of states to be final. *travis* adapts the file format of the APT framework [5] to handle labeled transition systems with final states.

The Petri net editor loads, creates, simulates, and edits Petri nets with final states. Again, *travis* supports all standard editing features and graph drawing algorithms. A final state of a Petri net is a marking. *travis* has a small built-in options dialog. With this dialog, final markings can be created, deleted, edited, and highlighted in the Petri net at hand. *travis* uses the PNML file format [15] to handle Petri nets and their sets of final markings. Using this format, *travis* is able to share Petri net files with analysis tools like VipTool, Charlie [14] and WoPeD [13].

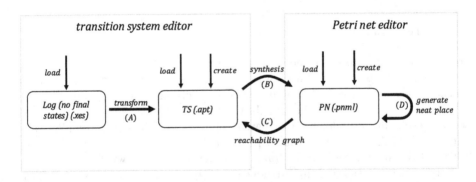

Fig. 1. Overview of the functionalities of *travis*

Figure 1 depicts the core algorithms of *travis* as bold arcs: (A) folding of an event log into a labeled transition system with final states, (B) synthesis of a Petri net with final states from a labeled transition system with final states, (C) unfolding of a Petri net with final states to a labeled transition system with final states, and (D) adding a so-called neat place to a Petri net with final states. Applying (A), we can fold a loaded event log into a labeled transition system with final states. Every case of the log is a trace in the related transition system where similar prefixes of traces will be merged. If the event log does not include explicitly specified final states, *travis* will add a final state at the end of every case. Remark, using this method a prefix of a case can as well lead to a final state if this prefix is equal to another case of the loaded event log. Thus, we can express arbitrary sets of final states using logs.

Executing (B), we can synthesize a k-bounded Petri net with final states from a labeled transition system with final states. In a first step, *travis* constructs the Petri net applying the region-based synthesis algorithm introduced in [9]. In a second step, *travis* will synthesize the related set of final markings applying the algorithm presented in [17].

Performing (C), we can unfold a bounded Petri net with final states to a labeled transition system with final states. This is a rather easy task because we consider the Petri net to be bounded, i.e. the Petri net has a finite set of states.

Processing (D), we can add a so-called neat place to a Petri net with final states. This algorithm is introduced in [17]. Like algorithm (B) this algorithm is based on the theory of regions. For an introduction to region theory we refer the reader to [3,6,7,9,10,12]. Roughly speaking, whenever performing (D), *travis* calculates a suitable set of set-operations forming the final states of the transition system related to the Petri net at hand using only regions. If this is possible *travis* adds a neat place to the specified Petri net. A neat place is only marked if the Petri net is in a final state. In other words, we see locally – at the neat place – whether the net is in a global final marking or not.

Altogether, *travis* supports the analysis and synthesis of final states for Petri net models. The analysis is based on the notion of neat places. In an educational context, *travis* can support teaching. Calculating a neat place highlights the notion of (final) markings and exploits the difference between distributed and local states. In a business process context, *travis* can analyze models whenever final states are crucial for the validity of the process model.

In the remainder, we present two examples demonstrating the features of *travis*. In the first example (Sect. 2), we synthesize a 3-bounded Petri net with a general neat place from a labeled transition system with final states. In the second example (Sect. 3), we synthesize a 1-bounded Petri net with a 1-bounded neat place from an event log obtained from a BPMN model. Section 3 concludes the paper and presents future work.

2 Synthesis of K-bounded Petri Nets with Final States from Transition Systems

In this section, we synthesize a k-bounded Petri net with final states from a transition system with *travis*. The rather technical example of this section was introduced in [16,17]. A related .apt file can be downloaded from the *travis* website.

Figure 2 depicts a browser running the transition system editor of *travis*. This editor consists of a canvas together with a toolbar and a sidebar. Using *travis* is simple. With the toolbar we can create a new, load, save, center, and align a transition system. Furthermore, we can switch to the Petri net editor of *travis* and can start the different algorithms like a simple spring embedder or the synthesis algorithm. The sidebar is for editing the transition system. We can add, delete, and move states and transitions. Moreover, we can toggle states to be intermediate, initial, or final. A user can edit the labels of states and events by double-clicking on the related text elements in the canvas.

The depicted transition system has 17 states connected by transitions labeled by A, B, C, D or E. In this example, s_0 is the initial state and s_6 and s_{16} are two final states of the model. Of course, there can only be one initial state, but any number of final states. The initial state is drawn white and every final state is encircled black.

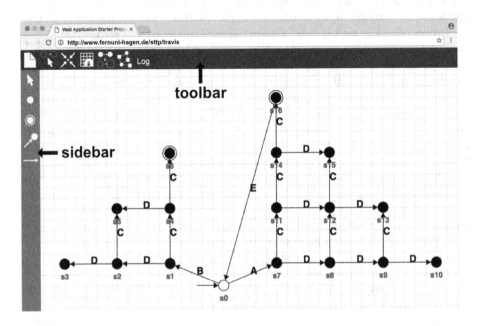

Fig. 2. Transition system editor of *travis*.

In the transition system editor, the button for the synthesis algorithm opens a small options dialog. This dialog is depicted on the right hand side of Fig. 3. We set a bound of three for the synthesis algorithm and start the synthesis procedure. *travis* implements the synthesis algorithm introduced by Carmona, Cortadella and Kishinevsky (see [9]) to generate a related 3-bounded Petri net model.

As soon as we start the synthesis algorithm, *travis* will open its Petri net editor. Figure 3 depicts the Petri net editor showing the result of the synthesis algorithm. The Petri net editor is structured just like the transition system editor. Of course, all algorithms and editing features of the toolbar and the sidebar are updated to the Petri net features of *travis*.

The result of the synthesis procedure using the transition system of Fig. 2 as an input is depicted in the canvas of the Petri net editor in Fig. 3. It is a 3-bounded Petri net with the transitions A, B, C, D, and E and the places p_1,

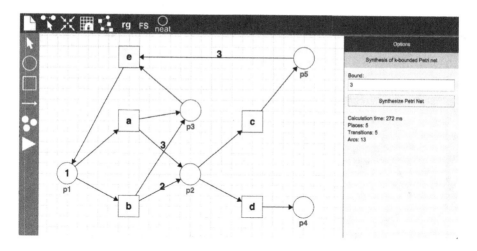

Fig. 3. Petri net editor with synthesized 3-bounded Petri net.

p_2, p_3, p_4, and p_5. The initial marking of this net is one token in the place p_1. In the initial marking, the transitions A and B are enabled. After firing transition A, we can three times choose to fire transition C or transition D. After firing transition B, we can two times choose to fire transition C or transition D. Only firing the sequence A, C, C, C will enable transition E. Firing transition E will again lead to the initial marking.

In addition to the synthesis method of [9], *travis* is also able to synthesize the set of final states (see [17] for details). Each final state of the transition system relates to a multiset of places in the related Petri net model. Sets of multisets are a bit tricky to visualize. Therefore, *travis* offers another options dialog to choose from the set of final sets. To visualize a fixed final state, *travis* highlights the places with a positive multiplicity and indicates the respective multiplicity on top of the place.

The right hand side of Fig. 4 depicts this options dialog. In this example, the result of the synthesis has two final states. The first is p_3 and three times p_5. This state relates to s_{16} of the transition system depicted in Fig. 2. It is reachable by firing transition A and three times transition C. The second final state is p_3 and two times p_5. This state relates to s_6 of the transition system depicted in Fig. 2. It is reachable by firing transition B and two times transition C. Figure 4 depicts the first final state, i.e. *travis* highlights both places p_3 and p_5 and tags them with the numbers one and three.

One of the main features of *travis* is to check whether there exists a neat place for a Petri net with final states or not. If such a place exists and is not already in the Petri net at hand, *travis* constructs and adds a neat place. The related button to start the construction of a neat place is located in the toolbar of the Petri net editor. Roughly speaking, a neat place is one single place which carries some fixed numbers of tokens if and only if the Petri net is in a final state. Like mentioned above, it is quite troublesome to highlight final markings

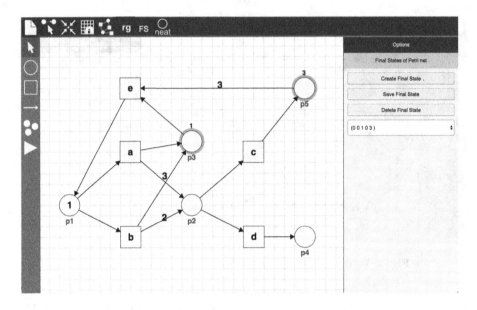

Fig. 4. Visualization of a final state in a Petri net.

of a Petri net. If there is a neat place, only this single neat place needs to be highlighted and checked to see if the net is in a final state. For all the details of neat places we refer the reader to [16,17], but sketch the ideas behind neat places with the help of our example.

Figure 5 depicts the Petri net of Fig. 4 after *travis* was used to construct an additional neat place. In the Petri net editor this place is labeled *neat* and highlighted. On a mouse-over the neat place shows a pop-up window showing a set of numbers. Every time this place carries one of these numbers of tokens, the net is in a final state. In Fig. 5 place *neat* is denoted by three. The synthesized net is in a final state if and only is the number of tokens in *neat* is three. Such a neat place helps a user to immediately see whenever a net is in a final state or not. Especially having large and complex nets or distributed multisets of final markings, a neat place aids the problem of indicating final markings.

Altogether, in this rather technical example, we modeled a transition system with final states and we synthesized a 3-bounded Petri net with a set of related final states. After the synthesis, we asked *travis* to add a so-called neat place. This place clearly highlights the set of final states of this generated Petri net model.

3   Synthesis of 1-bounded Petri Nets with Final States from Event Logs

In this section, we synthesize a 1-bounded Petri net with final states from an event log with *travis*. The example of this section is inspired by a BPMN model of

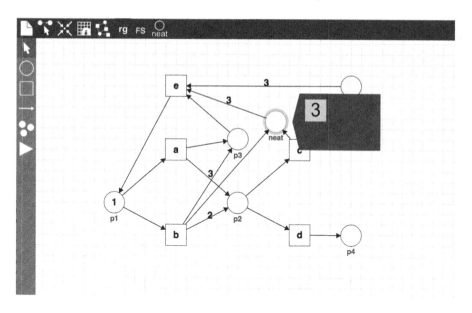

Fig. 5. Synthesized Petri net with a neat place

an article of Thomas Allweyer [2]. The model is depicted in Fig. 6. We executed this model multiple times to generate a related log file. The respective .xes file can be downloaded from the *travis* website.

In Fig. 6, a customer sends a request to an agency. As the request is received, the agency creates an offer. After the offer is sent to the customer, the agency has to wait for a response. If the agency receives some change requests, it has to revise the offer, recreate it, and resend it to the customer. If the agency

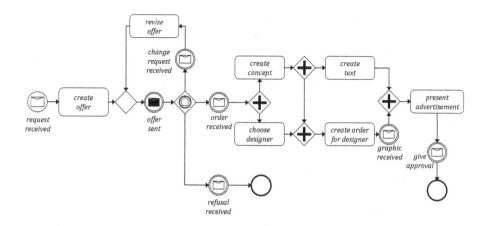

Fig. 6. BPMN diagram of an advertising agency process

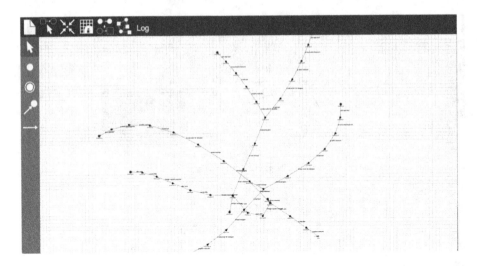

Fig. 7. Transition system loaded from a log file

receives a refusal, the process ends. If the customer accepts the offer, he sends an order to the agency. After the order is received, the agency creates a concept and chooses a graphic designer. In a next step, the agency creates the text for the advertisement, prepares the order for the graphic designer, and receives the graphic from the designer. Finally, the agency presents the finished advertisement to the customer and the process ends after the customer gives the approval. The BMPN model of Fig. 6 has two distinguished final events. One event at the bottom of the model right behind the event *refusal received* and another event at the bottom right side of the model right behind the event *give approval*. Every final event is depicted by a bold circle.

We built an event log from observations of this BPMN model, added a third final event by defining *offer sent* to be final and loaded the related XES-file with *travis*. This is done by dragging the file into the event log loader – a pop-up window of the transition system editor. *travis* loads the event log and automatically builds a related transition system. Whenever a case of the event log ends, the respective state of the constructed transition system is toggled to be a final state. The resulting transition system is depicted in Fig. 7.

We start the synthesis method of *travis* to automatically generate a Petri net with the same behavior as described by the loaded log file. This time we set the bound of the generated Petri net to one. After the construction of this net we also add a neat place.

Figure 8 depicts the synthesized 1-bounded Petri net with the generated 1-bounded neat place. The place is labeled *neat* and in this example, the neat place is marked by one token whenever the net is in a final state.

Only the two transitions *offer sent* and *give approval* add a token to the neat place. Both transitions *change requests received* and *order received* consume one token. If the transition *refusal received* fires, there is no need to add a token to

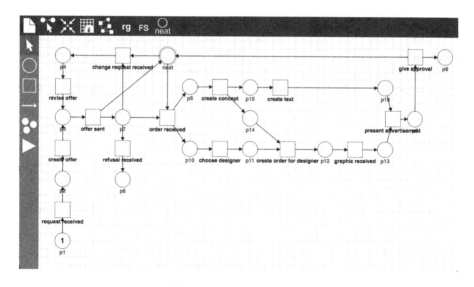

Fig. 8. Synthesized Petri net with neat place

the neat place, because *refusal received* is only enabled if the Petri net is already in a final state and the marking of the neat place does not change.

Altogether, in this second example, we loaded an event log to create a transition system with final states. We synthesized a 1-bounded Petri net with a neat place. This neat place indicates all possible ending points of the business process at hand. Like for workflow nets or modern business process modeling languages, neat places are a very handy notion for the analysis of final states of general Petri nets and of one-safe (workflow net-like) Petri nets.

4   Conclusion and Future Work

This paper presents the new online tool *travis*. *travis* can be executed simply in a browser and is free from any registration. It includes two editors: an editor for labeled transition systems with final states including an event log loader and an editor for Petri nets with final states. *travis* is able to handle the XES format for log-files, the APT format for labeled transition systems and the PNML format for Petri nets. *travis* core features implement the main algorithms presented in [16,17]. The main goal of *travis* is to support the analysis of final states of Petri net models by calculating neat places. Furthermore, *travis* can synthesize a Petri net with final states from an event log or from a labeled transition system with final states. In an educational context, *travis* can support teaching. In a context of business process modeling, *travis* analyzes models whenever consideration of final states is crucial for the validity of the process model.

For future work we will consider to extend *travis* by a set of more general analysis features for Petri nets. Until now, *travis* focuses on the synthesis and on the analysis of final states. But since there are many other well developed tools dealing with more general properties of Petri nets, it may not be necessary to extend *travis* in such a direction. Another important task is to enable *travis* to support specifications including partial ordered behavior. Many region based synthesis methods have been developed but we still miss how the notion of final states can effectively be generalized to partial languages.

References

1. van der Aalst, W.M.P., van Dongen, B.F., Günther, C.W., Rozinat, A., Wei-jters, T.: ProM: the process mining toolkit. In: de Medeiros, A.K.A., Weber, B. (eds.) Proceedings of the Business Process Management Demonstration Track (BPMDemos 2009), Ulm, Germany, 8 September 2009, vol. 489. CEUR. http://www.promtools.org/doku.php
2. Allweyer, T.: Kollaborationen, Choreographien und Konversationen in BPMN 2.0 - Erweiterte Konzepte zur Modellierung übergreifender Geschäftsprozesse. Working Paper. Kaiserslautern University of Applied Sciences Kaiserslautern (2009)
3. Badouel, E., Bernardinello, L., Darondeau, P.: Petri Net Synthesis. Texts in Theoretical Computer Science. Springer, Heidelberg (2015)
4. Bergenthum, R., Desel, J., Lorenz, R., Mauser, S.: Synthesis of Petri nets from scenarios with VipTool. In: Hee, K.M., Valk, R. (eds.) PETRI NETS 2008. LNCS, vol. 5062, pp. 388–398. Springer, Heidelberg (2008). doi:10.1007/978-3-540-68746-7_25
5. Best, E., Schlachter, U.: Analysis of Petri nets and transition systems. In: Knight, S., Lanese, I., Lluch-Lafuente, A., Vieira, H.T. (eds.) Proceedings 8th Interaction and Concurrency Experience, ICE 2015, Grenoble, France, 4–5, vol. 189, pp. 53–67. EPTCS (2015). https://github.com/CvO-Theory/apt
6. Carmona, J., Cortadella, J., Kishinevsky, M., Kondratyev, A., Lavagno, L., Yakovlev, A.: A symbolic algorithm for the synthesis of bounded Petri nets. In: Hee, K.M., Valk, R. (eds.) PETRI NETS 2008. LNCS, vol. 5062, pp. 92–111. Springer, Heidelberg (2008). doi:10.1007/978-3-540-68746-7_10
7. Carmona, J., Cortadella, J., Kishinevsky, M.: A region-based algorithm for discovering Petri nets from event logs. In: Dumas, M., Reichert, M., Shan, M.-C. (eds.) BPM 2008. LNCS, vol. 5240, pp. 358–373. Springer, Heidelberg (2008). doi:10.1007/978-3-540-85758-7_26
8. Carmona, J., Cortadella, J., Kishinevsky, M.: Genet: a tool for the synthesis and mining of Petri nets. In: Ninth International Conference on Application of Concurrency to System Design, ACSD 2009, Augsburg, Germany, 1–3 July 2009
9. Carmona, J., Cortadella, J., Kishinevsky, M.: New region-based algorithms for deriving bounded Petri nets. IEEE Trans. Comput. 59(3), 371–384 (2010)
10. Cortadella, J., Kishinevsky, M., Lavagno, L., Yakovlev, A.: Deriving Petri nets from finite transition systems. IEEE Trans. Comput. 47(8), 859–882 (1998)
11. Cortadella, J., Kishinevsky, M., Kondratyev, A., Lavagno, L., Yakovlev, A.: Petrify: a tool for manipulating concurrent specifications and synthesis of asynchronous controllers. IEICE Trans. Inf. Syst. E80–D(3), 315–325 (1997). http://www.cs.upc.edu/ jordicf/petrify/
12. Desel, J., Reisig, W.: The synthesis problem of Petri nets. Acta Informatikca 33, 279–315 (1996)
13. Eckleder, A., Freytag, T.: WoPeD - a tool for teaching, analyzing and visualizing workflow nets. Petri Net Newslett. 75 (2008). http://woped.dhbw-karlsruhe.de/woped/

14. Heiner, M., Schwarick, M., Wegener, J.-T.: Charlie – an extensible Petri net analysis tool. In: Devillers, R., Valmari, A. (eds.) PETRI NETS 2015. LNCS, vol. 9115, pp. 200–211. Springer, Cham (2015). doi:10.1007/978-3-319-19488-2_10. http://www-dssz.informatik.tu-cottbus.de/DSSZ/Software/Charlie
15. Kindler, E.: PNML: concept, status and future directions. Entwurf Komplexer Automatisierungssysteme (EKA) **9**, 35–55 (2006)
16. Meis, B., Bergenthum, R., Desel, J.: Synthesis of elementary net systems with final configurations. In: van der Aalst, W.M.P., Bergenthum, R., Carmona, J. (eds.) Workshop on Algorithms & Theories for the Analysis of Event Data (ATAED 2016), Torun, Poland, pp. 47–57 (2016)
17. Meis, B., Bergenthum, R., Desel, J.: Synthesis of Petri nets with final states. Submitted
18. Verbeek, H.M.W., Buijs, J.C.A.M., Dongen, B.F., Aalst, W.M.P.: XES, XESame, and ProM 6. In: Soffer, P., Proper, E. (eds.) CAiSE Forum 2010. LNBIP, vol. 72, pp. 60–75. Springer, Heidelberg (2011). doi:10.1007/978-3-642-17722-4_5
19. Wolf, K., Lohmann, N.: LoLA - a low level petri net analyzer (2014). http://home.gna.org/service-tech/lola/

An Integrated Environment for Petri Net Slicing

Marisa Llorens, Javier Oliver, Josep Silva, and Salvador Tamarit[✉]

Universitat Politècnica de València, Camí de Vera S/N, 46022 València, Spain
{mllorens,fjoliver,jsilva,stamarit}@dsic.upv.es

Abstract. Petri net slicing is a technique to automatically isolate the part of a marked Petri net that influences or is influenced by a given set of places. There exist different algorithms for Petri net slicing with different objectives. Nevertheless, they have never been evaluated or compared from a practical point of view. In fact, because there does not exist a public implementation of some of them, their performance and scalability have remained unknown. In this paper we present three tools for the analysis and transformation of Petri nets. The three tools are complementary, and they allow us to extract from a Petri net a set of slices that preserve a given set of properties (e.g., boundedness, reversibility, etc.). For this, they include the first public, free, and open-source implementation of the most important algorithms for Petri net slicing, including a new algorithm that reduces the size of the slices. Our implementation of the algorithms allowed us to compare all of them and to measure and report for the first time about their individual performance.

1 Introduction and Objectives

Petri net slicing [2] is a technique to extract the part of a Petri net that is relevant with respect to a so-called *slicing criterion*. In general, the slicing criterion is a set of places of a marked Petri net, and the slice produced is a new Petri net that contains the subset of the original Petri net that can contribute tokens to the slicing criterion. The main motivation for Petri net slicing is lessening the state space explosion problem for model checking [2–4,6,7]. As a reduction technique, it is supposed to preserve some properties, so the sliced net (which ideally has a smaller state space) can be model checked instead of the original net. Additionally, Petri net slicing is useful to enhance reachability analyses [3,4,6], for Petri net comprehension [5], and for debugging [5,7], among others.

Example 1. Consider the Petri net of Fig. 1(a), where the slicing criterion is the set of places in grey color (places $\{p_6, p_9\}$). The Petri nets shown in Figs. 1(a)–(e) are slices computed with different algorithms. This example is a contribution

---

This work has been partially supported by MINECO/AEI/FEDER (EU) under grants TIN2013-44742-C4-1-R and TIN2016-76843-C4-1-R, and by the *Generalitat Valenciana* under grant PROMETEO-II/2015/013 (SmartLogic). Salvador Tamarit was partially supported by the *Conselleria de Educación, Investigación, Cultura y Deporte de la Generalitat Valenciana* under the grant APOSTD/2016/036.

W. van der Aalst and E. Best (Eds.): PETRI NETS 2017, LNCS 10258, pp. 112–124, 2017.
DOI: 10.1007/978-3-319-57861-3_8

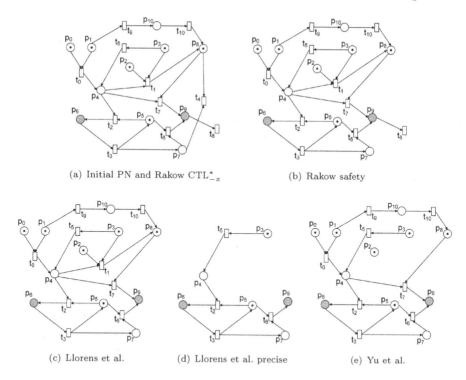

(a) Initial PN and Rakow CTL*_−x   (b) Rakow safety

(c) Llorens et al.   (d) Llorens et al. precise   (e) Yu et al.

Fig. 1. Five different slices (a)–(e) of the same Petri net (a).

by itself because it presents a Petri net whose slices computed with the five algorithms described are pairwise different. In order to find this Petri net and its slicing criterion we used our implementation.

Petri net slicing was first defined in [1]. Since then, several other techniques have appeared with different interpretations about what a Petri net slice is, and how it should be computed [5–7]. A recent survey on Petri net slicing [2] compares the algorithms proposed so far from a theoretical perspective and it reveals that they are complementary. Unfortunately, some of these algorithms have been only proposed theoretically, and no public implementation of any of them exists. Therefore, they have not been empirically evaluated or compared, and thus, their performance and precision is unknown in practice.

In this paper we present three complementary tools for the analysis and transformation of Petri nets. The first tool, **pn_slicer**, includes the first public, free, and open-source implementation of the most important algorithms for Petri net slicing, including a new algorithm that reduces the size of the slices. This tool is not only a standard slicer, but it is also able to extract from a Petri net a set of slices that preserve a given set of properties (e.g., liveness, boundedness, etc.), using LoLA[1] and APT[2]. The second tool, **pn_prop**, allows us to compare

---
[1] LoLA - Low Level Petri Net Analyzer: http://home.gna.org/service-tech/lola/.
[2] APT - Analysis of Petri nets and labelled transition systems: https://github.com/CvO-theory/apt.

a Petri net and its slice by analyzing what properties have been preserved or not after the slicing transformation. The third tool, pn_tools, implements many useful features such as Petri net animation, Petri net format conversion, and an algorithm for Petri net slicing based on a firing sequence.

Besides the three tools presented, we provide the first empirical evaluation and comparison of the main Petri net slicing algorithms. We also study what properties are kept by each algorithm. We use as benchmarks the whole *Model Checking Contest @ Petri Nets 2017*[3].

2   Petri Net Slicing Algorithms

There exist two important dimensions that must be considered when selecting a Petri net slicing algorithm:

- **static/dynamic**: A static slicing algorithm does not consider any initial marking for the Petri net being sliced. Contrarily, a dynamic slicing algorithm does consider a concrete initial marking. Hence, in general, dynamic slicing algorithms can produce smaller slices than their static counterparts.
- **backward/forward**: A backward slicing algorithm computes the part of the Petri net that can contribute tokens to the slicing criterion. A forward slicing algorithm computes the part of the Petri net to which the slicing criterion can contribute tokens.

In the rest of this section, we review and summarize the most important Petri net slicing techniques that can be found in the literature [5–7].

Rakow - CTL$^*_{-x}$ Slicing [6]: static backward slicing approach preserving any property expressed in CTL$^*_{-x}$, i.e., CTL* without next-time operator. The slicing criterion is a set of places (which may, for instance, be the places that a CTL$^*_{-x}$ property φ refers to). This algorithm starts in the criterion places and, iteratively, builds the sliced net by taking all the incoming and outgoing non-reading transitions (those that change the marking of a place) together with their input places. Rakow's CTL$^*_{-x}$ algorithm computes all the paths P of the Petri net that could change (increase or decrease) the token count of any place of the slicing criterion, and also those paths that can enable or disable the transitions in P.

Rakow - Safety Slicing [6]: static backward slicing approach that preserves stutter-invariant linear-time safety properties. The slicing criterion is also a set of places Q. This algorithm takes all non-reading transitions connected to Q and all their input places and, iteratively, takes only transitions that increase the token count on places in the sliced net and their input places. Rakow's safety algorithm computes all the paths of the Petri net that contribute tokens to the slicing criterion, in such a way that the places in the slice contain at least as many tokens as the original net, and the same token count on the slicing criterion.

---

[3] Model Checking Contest @ Petri Nets 2017: http://mcc.lip6.fr/models.php.

Llorens et al. [5]: It was the first dynamic slicing approach, and combines both backward and forward slicing. The slicing criterion is a pair $\langle M_0, Q \rangle$, being M_0 an initial marking and Q a set of places. The algorithm iteratively computes a backward slice by taking all the incoming transitions together with their input places. Then, the algorithm computes a forward slice by collecting first all places that are marked in M_0 and all transitions initially enabled in M_0 and, iteratively, it moves forwards adding their outgoing places and the transitions whose input places are in the set of collected places. The final slice is obtained as the intersection of the backward and forward slices. Llorens et al.'s algorithm computes all the paths of the Petri net that could increase the token count of any place of the slicing criterion from the initial marking.

Llorens et al. - precise: The precision of the algorithm by Llorens et al. can be improved if we compute the smallest path that could increase the token count of the slicing criterion (instead of all paths). Also, if the forward slice is only computed for the resultant Petri net obtained from the backward slice. We have implemented an improved version of this algorithm. It is integrated into the Petri net slicer.

Yu et al. [7]: dynamic backward slicing approach based on the Structural Dependency Graph (SDG). It uses two algorithms: Algorithm 1 takes a set of places Q as the slicing criterion, and it constructs the $SDG(N)$ with a backward traversal process from Q. Algorithm 2 takes $SDG(N)$, and the slicing criterion $\langle M_0, Q \rangle$, and it extracts the dynamic slice, a subnet that can dynamically affect the slicing criterion from the initial marking M_0. If the initial marking M_0 cannot affect the slicing criterion, the dynamic slice is set to null and this means that there does not exist a dynamic slice that can transport tokens to the places of interest. Yu et al.'s algorithm computes one single path of the Petri net that could increase the token count of at least one place of the slicing criterion from the initial marking.

Example 2. Consider the Petri net of Fig. 1(a), where the user wants to produce a slice w.r.t. the slicing criterion $\{p_6, p_9\}$. With Rakow's CTL^*_{-x} algorithm, the slice obtained is the original net (Fig. 1(a)). Figure 1(b) shows the safety slice obtained in Rakow's safety algorithm. The slice obtained by Llorens et al. is shown in Fig. 1(c). Figure 1(d) shows the slice obtained with the improved version of Llorens et al.'s algorithm. Finally, Fig. 1(e) shows the slice obtained with the algorithm by Yu et al.

3   A Universal Tool for Petri Net Slicing

In this section, we present PN-Suite, a system prepared to implement, combine, compare, and evaluate Petri net slicing algorithms. Roughly, this system can be seen as a workbench that implements the currently most important algorithms for Petri net slicing, and it is prepared to easily integrate more algorithms into it. This system provides a new functionality that is particularly useful for the analysis and optimization of Petri nets: it combines all the slicing algorithms with the analysis of properties in such a way that one can reduce the size of a Petri net producing a slice that preserves some desired properties.

PN-Suite implements interfaces to communicate with other systems such as LoLA and APT. This means that it takes advantage of LoLA and APT analyses to report about the properties kept or lost by the slices produced. Hence, they are only invoked, through their public interfaces, when a property must be validated.

In the rest of this section we describe the main features and functionality of PN-Suite, and its architecture.

3.1 Installation and Usage

PN-Suite is free and open-source, and it is publicly available[4]. There are two prerequisites to use this tool, and both are free: Graphviz[5] and the Erlang/OTP framework[6]. The (free) system LoLA is optional: it enables the use of LoLA expressions as properties to preserve when performing slicing. Listing 1.1 shows the few steps needed to have PN-Suite installed in a Unix system.

Listing 1.1. Installation of the tool

```
$ git clone https://github.com/tamarit/pn_suite.git
$ cd pn_suite/
$ make
$ sudo make install
```

The first step clones the GitHub's repository to the local system. Then, make is used to compile source files and, finally, three executables (pn_slicer, pn_prop, and pn_tools) are generated and installed by make install.

The independence of these three tools is an important design decision. Separating their functionality increases their cohesion because each tool is specific for a concrete task. This allows other tools to use a single command that produces exactly what they need, or to combine them, if they need a more complex result. In particular, the tools pn_slicer and pn_prop are independent because the former is in charge of producing slices, and the later studies the preservation of properties of the slices produced.

pn_slicer. This tool allows us to extract slices using one of the algorithms, or to extract all the slices (using all algorithms) that preserve a given set of properties.

Listing 1.2. pn_slicer command format

```
$ pn_slicer PNML_FILE SLICING_CRITERION [PROPERTY_LIST | ALGORITHM] [-json]
```

where SLICING_CRITERION is a quoted list of places separated with commas. PROPERTY_LIST is optional. It accepts both APT properties and LoLA expressions. Valid APT properties can be found at the GitHub's repository of our tool.

---

[4] https://github.com/tamarit/pn_suite.

[5] Graphviz - Graph Visualization Software: http://www.graphviz.org/.

[6] http://www.erlang.org/.

LoLA expressions are preceded by `lola:`, e.g., `lola:EF DEADLOCK`. `ALGORITHM` is also optional. If not specified, all algorithms will be used. To choose a slicing algorithm we have to write `alg:ALGORITHM` (no quotes required). The names of the algorithms are: `rakow_ctl`, `rakow_safety`, `llorens`, `llorens_prec`, and `yu`.

For instance, all the slices in Fig. 1 can be computed with the following command (observe that they all preserve the property `conflict_free` and the same deadlock freedom, i.e., `lola:EF DEADLOCK`).

Listing 1.3. `pn_slicer` command usage

```
$ pn_slicer pn_example.xml "P6,P9" "conflict_free,lola:EF DEADLOCK"
Petri net named pn_example successfully read.
Slicing criterion: [P6, P9]
1.- Llorens et al's slicer precise -> Reduction: 54.55 %
2.- Llorens et al's slicer -> Reduction: 9.09 %
3.- Rakow's slicer CTL -> Reduction: 0.00 %
4.- Yu et al's slicer -> Reduction: 13.64 %
5.- Rakow's slicer safety -> Reduction: 4.55 %
```

Each slice is stored in a file named `output/<PNML_NAME>_<OUTPUT_NUMBER>.pnml`, where `<OUTPUT_NUMBER>` indicates the algorithm used (1.-Llorens, 3.-Rakow, 4.-Yu, etc.). For example, Yu's slice generated in Listing 1.3 can be found at `output/example_4.pnml`. A PDF file is also generated. If flag `-json` is used, a JSON output is generated with exact details about locations and other data.

pn_prop. This tool allows us to study the preservation of properties of a slice.

Listing 1.4. `pn_prop` command format

```
$ pn_prop PNML_FILE PNML_FILE [PROPERTY_LIST]
```

Given two Petri nets (often a Petri net and its slice), it shows a list of properties that hold in both Petri nets, and a list of properties that only hold in the original Petri net. It is also possible to specify some specific properties, and only them will be analyzed. For the analysis of properties, **pn_prop** conveniently communicates with either LoLA, or APT, or both. With the information provided by these tools, it decides whether the required properties are preserved. For instance, Listing 1.5 shows that both properties, `simply_live` and `EF DEADLOCK`, are preserved between the two Petri nets given as arguments.

Listing 1.5. `pn_prop` command usage examples

```
$ pn_prop pn_example.xml output/example_1.pnml
Preserved properties:
weakly_connected, output_nonbranching, strongly_connected, free_choice, pure,
plain, strongly_live, k-marking, s_net, nonpure_only_simple_side_conditions,
simply_live, t_net, weakly_live, restricted_free_choice, homogeneous,
isolated_elements, bounded, reversible, conflict_free
Changed properties:
backwards_persistent, num_places, bicf, persistent, bcf, num_tokens,
asymmetric_choice, num_arcs, num_transitions, num_labels, safe, k-bounded

$ pn_prop pn_example.xml output/example_1.pnml "simply_live,lola:EF DEADLOCK"
true
```

Pn_tools. This tool is interactive and it can be used to animate a Petri net, slice it, or convert it to several formats.

Listing 1.6. pn_tools command usage

```
$ pn_tools pn_example.xml
Petri net example successfully read.

These are the available options:
1 .- Run the Petri Net
2 .- Export the Petri Net
3 .- Slicing Llorens et al.
4 .- Slicing Llorens et al. (precise)
5 .- Slicing Llorens et al. (for a given transition seq.)
6 .- Slicing Yu et al.
7 .- Slicing Rakow CTL
8 .- Slicing Rakow Safety
What do you want to do?
[1/2/3/4/5/6/7/8]:
```

Animation: The Petri net can be animated either manually or randomly. If manual animation is chosen, the system iteratively shows to the user the enabled transitions, and they can select the transitions that must be fired. As a visual support, the Petri net that is being animated can be found at output/<PN_NAME>_run.pdf. In this PDF, the enabled transitions are highlighted in red, so the user can see them clearly. In the random animation we can specify the number n of random steps to be performed, and the Petri net fires n random transitions, or until no more transitions can be fired (Listing 1.7).

Slicing: The user can select from a menu a slicing algorithm. Then, according to the chosen algorithm, the user can specify a slicing criterion. The Petri net is then automatically sliced and a new Petri net (the slice) is produced. It is important to highlight that this tool implements another slicing algorithm (option 5 in Listing 1.6) besides those of **pn_slicer**. This algorithm allows us to extract a slice from a Petri net considering a specific firing sequence (instead of all possible firing sequences as all the other algorithms do).

Output: The output of PN-Suite can be produced in many different formats, including standard PNML[7] (compatible with PIPE5[8]), LoLA, APT, DOT and more than 50 other formats provided by Graphviz (Listing 1.8).

---

[7] The Petri Net Markup Language reference site: http://www.pnml.org/.
[8] The Platform Independent Petri Net Editor version 5: http://sarahtattersall.github. io/PIPE/.

Listing 1.7. The Petri net can be animated either randomly or manually

```
[1/2/3/4/5/6/7/8]:   1
Available modes:
0.- Manually
n.- n random steps (at most)
How do you want to run the PN? $ 10
Selected transition: T5
Selected transition: T9
Selected transition: T10
Selected transition: T7
Selected transition: T8
There is not any fireable transition.
Execution:
T5,T9,T10,T7,T8
```

Listing 1.8. Output formats

```
[1/2/3/4/5/6/7/8]:   2
1 .- pdf
2 .- dot
3 .- PNML (compatible with PIPE)
4 .- LoLA
5 .- APT
6 .- Other formats
What format do you need?
[1/2/3/4/5/6]:   1
```

Even though we strongly encourage all users to install PN-Suite, we have implemented an online web interface[9]. This interface allows for testing many features of PN-Suite without the need to install it. It includes the five Petri net slicing algorithms that can be studied and compared with any PNML Petri net or with a collection of Petri nets available in the interface. For security reasons, the runtime has been limited to 2 s. Figure 2 shows a screenshot of the web interface showing the slice of the Petri net in Example 1(a).

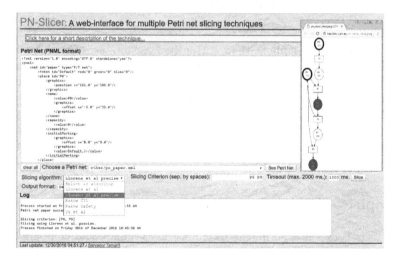

Fig. 2. Screenshot of PN-Suite web-interface with the slice of Fig. 1(d).

3.2 Architecture

The internal architecture of our system is depicted in Fig. 3. In the figure, the white rectangles are files or text (e.g., the original Petri net, its slice, the slicing criterion, or reports about properties preserved after the transformation), whereas dark rectangles represent modules of the system.

---

[9] http://kaz.dsic.upv.es/pn_slicer.

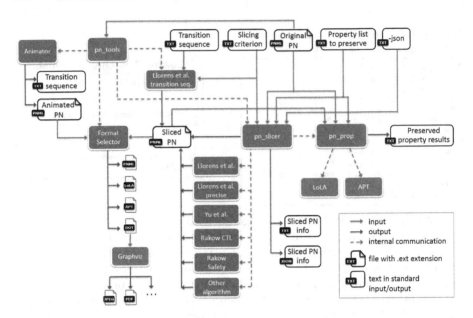

Fig. 3. Architecture of PN-Suite.

It is important to highlight that, currently, PN-Suite uses five different slicing algorithms, but it is prepared to easily integrate more algorithms. For this, it contains interfaces that allow the system to invoke the slicing algorithm with given inputs, and receive the answer with a specified format. The *Other algorithm* dark rectangle in Fig. 3 represents this scenario. Hence, the system can be extended by other researchers that want to include their slicing algorithms, and it can be used to compare future slicing algorithms against the current empirical evaluation (see Sect. 4).

4   Empirical Evaluation

We conducted several experiments to empirically evaluate and compare all the Petri net slicing algorithms. For the evaluation we used the suite *Model Checking Contest @ Petri Nets 2017*. For each one of the 43 Petri nets used, we produced 20 random slicing criteria with a size between 1 and 5 places. Hence, in total we produced 860 slicing criteria. Each slicing criteria with its associated Petri net was then used to produce a slice with each of the five slicing algorithms implemented. The Petri nets of the benchmarks can be found, classified by year, in folder **examples/mcc_models** at: https://github.com/tamarit/pn_suite. For the replicability and validation of the experiments, all data, including the slicing criteria is available, classified by year, in folder **data**.

In order to evaluate the performance of our tool, all benchmarks were executed in the same hardware configuration: Intel® Core™ i7-3520M (2 cores,

4 MB Cache, 2.90 GHz) with 8 GB RAM. During the execution of the benchmarks, all processes of the system except PN-Suite were stopped to avoid interference of external programs.

We produced the set of measures shown in Table 1. This table compares the five slicing algorithms, one in each column: Llorens et al. (L), Llorens et al. precise (LP), Rakow CTL^*_{-x} slicing (RC), Rakow Safety slicing (RS), and Yu et al. (Y). The rows have been divided into two sections.

1. *Property preservation.* The upper part of the table studies the preservation of properties—a document in our repository[10] contains a short description of these properties—after the slicing process carried out with each algorithm. Of course, given a Petri net where a specific property (e.g., *strong liveness*) is preserved, there can coexist slices of this Petri net where the property is preserved and where the property is not preserved. Therefore, we are interested in statistical information. Specifically, we want to know, for each property and algorithm, the ratio of slices produced by the algorithm that do preserve the property. This information is useful to select one slicing algorithm if one is interested in preserving some specific properties in the slice. Note that this information is complementary to theoretical results that prove whether an algorithm preserves or not certain property, i.e., a boolean value. With our study, we are not providing a boolean value, instead a trusting ratio. For instance, although according to the theory the property *backwards persistent* would not be preserved by any algorithm, here we show that by using Rakow CTL^*_{-x} slicing we can get a slice where this property is preserved in 99% of the cases. Moreover, the results obtained can lead new theoretical proofs, since new property preservations can be discovered and then proved. To design this experiment, we sliced all the benchmarks with each algorithm, and evaluated the percentage of times that each property holds in the slice. In each row, the best value is in bold.

2. *Performance and efficiency.* In the bottom part of the table we first measure the percentage of times that the slice is equal to the original Petri net, considering the number of places, tokens, transitions, and labels. Row `Size` shows the proportion of the size of the slice with respect to the original net. For this, it considers places and transitions. Finally, row `Time` shows the average time needed by each of the algorithms to compute a slice.

In the table we can see that the algorithm whose slices do preserve more properties is Rakow's CTL^*_{-x} algorithm. It presents the best values in all cases except in two. This algorithm preserves all properties with a probability higher than 0.9 except for one case: *traps*. This is an expected result, because slices usually destroy traps when they remove transitions. However, 58% of the traps were preserved with this algorithm.

Another interesting information is that those cells where the value is not 1.00 do ensure that the corresponding algorithm does not always preserve the property (we found a counterexample). The opposite is not true: those cells with a value of 1.00 do not necessarily ensure that the property will be preserved in all cases by the algorithm.

---

[10] https://github.com/tamarit/pn_suite/blob/master/doc/glossary.pdf.

Table 1. Benchmark results showing statistical information about the preservation of properties by the different slices.

Property preservation		L	LP	RC	RS	Y
Behavioural	*strongly-live*	**1.00**	0.80	**1.00**	**1.00**	0.95
	weakly-live	**1.00**	0.91	**1.00**	**1.00**	0.92
	simply-live	**0.91**	**0.91**	**0.91**	**0.91**	0.78
	deadlock free	**1.00**	0.82	**1.00**	**1.00**	**1.00**
	persistent	0.89	0.61	**1.00**	0.97	0.57
	backwards persistent	0.98	0.47	**0.99**	0.98	0.77
	bounded	**1.00**	**1.00**	**1.00**	**1.00**	**1.00**
	k-bounded	**1.00**	0.85	**1.00**	**1.00**	0.88
	safe	**1.00**	0.88	**1.00**	**1.00**	**1.00**
	k-marking	**1.00**	**1.00**	**1.00**	**1.00**	**1.00**
	reversible	**1.00**	0.80	**1.00**	**1.00**	0.95
	binary conflict free	0.89	0.61	**1.00**	0.97	0.57
	behaviourally conflict free	0.89	0.61	**1.00**	0.97	0.57
Structural	*strongly-connected*	**1.00**	0.81	**1.00**	**1.00**	0.80
	weakly-connected	0.99	0.88	**1.00**	**1.00**	0.71
	isolated elements	0.99	0.98	**1.00**	**1.00**	0.77
	free-choice	0.90	0.67	**0.94**	0.92	0.83
	restricted-free-choice	0.97	0.97	**0.98**	**0.98**	0.87
	asymmetric-choice	0.89	0.75	**1.00**	0.92	0.86
	siphons	0.91	0.51	**0.94**	0.90	0.63
	traps	0.52	0.12	**0.58**	**0.58**	0.24
	pure	**1.00**	0.95	0.94	0.94	**1.00**
	nonpure-only-simple-side-conditions	**1.00**	0.95	0.94	0.94	**1.00**
	conflict free	0.89	0.61	**1.00**	0.97	0.57
	output-nonbranching	0.89	0.61	**1.00**	0.97	0.57
	s-net	0.94	0.94	**0.95**	**0.95**	0.94
	t-net	0.90	0.61	**1.00**	0.97	0.69
Performance and efficiency		L	LP	RC	RS	Y
num_places		0.52	**0.12**	0.50	0.50	0.24
num_tokens		0.91	**0.62**	0.94	0.90	0.91
num_arcs		0.52	**0.12**	0.50	0.50	0.23
num_transitions		0.52	**0.12**	0.53	0.50	0.23
num_labels		0.52	**0.12**	0.53	0.50	0.23
Size (% reduction of the slice)		0.78	0.53	0.84	0.80	**0.50**
Time (runtime in milliseconds)		10.77	774.95	7.11	**7.03**	14.39

In the second part of the table we see that computing slices is an efficient task (less than 1 s in all cases). Almost all algorithms have similar time values (between 7 and 14 ms.) except for the improved version of Llorens et al.'s algorithm, with a runtime of two orders of magnitude more. This algorithm is much more exhaustive than the others (i.e., it computes all possible paths and takes the smaller one). For this reason, its computational cost is significantly higher, but the size of its slices is usually smaller.

Finally, the size of the slices is a very interesting result. It ranges over 50% and 84% of the size of the original Petri net. We provide five rows num_X to give an idea of the slice's size considering places, transitions, etc.

5   Conclusions

We have presented PN-Suite, a suite that includes three independent and complementary tools to analyse Petri nets. Specifically, our implementation includes animation and analysis tools, and the most powerful Petri net slicer in the current state of the art, which integrates the implementation of the main slicing algorithms. The implementation of all the algorithms is necessary and useful, because they have different purposes, and they retain different properties in their slices.

The implementation of the main slicing algorithms have produced another important result: their first empirical evaluation and comparison. Until our implementation, some of the algorithms were only theoretical results, and no public implementation existed. Thus, their individual performance and scalability remained unknown. Their relative efficiency was also unknown. The evaluation of the algorithms have produced the first measures of their average runtime, the relative size of the slices, and the properties that they preserve.

There are two other side results of our work: in the theoretical side, we have proposed (and implemented) a new algorithm that improves the dynamic slicing algorithm by Llorens et al. [5]. In the practical side, we have implemented a web interface to test the suite and compare the algorithms without the need to install the system. All our research and implementation is public, free and open-source. This includes our experiments and empirical evaluation.

References

1. Chang, C., Wang, H.: A slicing algorithm of concurrency modeling based on petri nets. In: Proceedings of the International Conference on Parallel Processing, ICPP 1986, pp. 789–792. IEEE Computer Society Press (1986)
2. Khan, Y., Guelfi, N.: Survey of Petri Nets Slicing. Technical report, University of Luxembourg, Faculty of Science, Technology and Communication (FSTC), Computer Science and Communications Research Unit (CSC), Luxembourg (2013). http://hdl.handle.net/10993/13606
3. Khan, Y., Risoldi, M.: Optimizing algebraic petri net model checking by slicing. In: International Workshop on Modeling and Business Environments, ModBE 2013, pp. 275–294 (2013). (associated with Petri Nets 2013)

4. Lee, W., Cha, S., Kwon, Y., Kim, H.: A slicing-based approach to enhance petri net reachability analysis. J. Res. Pract. Inform. Technol. **32**(2), 131–143 (2000)
5. Llorens, M., Oliver, J., Silva, J., Tamarit, S., Vidal, G.: Dynamic slicing techniques for petri nets. Electron. Notes Theor. Comput. Sci. **223**, 153–165 (2008)
6. Rakow, A.: Safety slicing petri nets. In: Haddad, S., Pomello, L. (eds.) PETRI NETS 2012. LNCS, vol. 7347, pp. 268–287. Springer, Heidelberg (2012). doi:10.1007/978-3-642-31131-4_15
7. Yu, W., Ding, Z., Fang, X.: Dynamic slicing of petri nets based on structural dependency graph and its application in system analysis. Asian J. Control **17**(4), 1403–1414 (2015). http://dx.doi.org/10.1002/asjc.1031

Petri Nets Repository: A Tool to Benchmark and Debug Petri Net Tools

Lom Messan Hillah[1] and Fabrice Kordon[2(✉)]

[1] Univ. Paris Nanterre, LIP6 CNRS UMR 7606, 75005 Paris, France
`lom-messan.hillah@lip6.fr`
[2] Sorbonne Universités, UPMC Univ. Paris 06,
LIP6 CNRS UMR 7606, 75005 Paris, France
`Fabrice.Kordon@lip6.fr`

Abstract. For a given scientific community, being able to use a common and rich accepted benchmark for the evaluation of algorithms and prototypes is an added value. The goal of this paper is to present Petri Nets Repository, an open Petri nets models database. It offers two main ways to navigate through the benchmark using criteria related to Petri net properties: a Web interface, and a Web service API (REST). So far, this database embeds the models from the Model Checking Contest, as well as those of the discontinued Petriweb.

A placeholder is available to store, when possible, the outputs of the Model Checking Contest; then for the corresponding models there will be formulas and their accepted results available too. We believe this would help the community to easily create oracles to debug new algorithms and tools.

1 Introduction

Motivation. Today, it is much easier, and more requested, to provide reproducible and comparable data when evaluating one's contribution. Thus, there is a strong need for common benchmarks that are shared by a given community. Moreover, when prototype tools are not only proofs-of-concepts, but also a key entry to process industrial problems, there is a need to ensure quality of developed software, which can be partially achieved by using benchmarks whose results are already known.

Petri Nets Repository (PNR) Objectives. To achieve the goal stemming from the first motivation, communities have elaborated competitions where programs of a given area are tested against the same benchmarks and rated. There are established major events concerning different areas: the SAT competition[1] (9 editions since 2002), the Satisfiability Modulo Theories Competition[2]

---

[1] http://www.satcompetition.org.
[2] http://smtcomp.sourceforge.net/.

© Springer International Publishing AG 2017
W. van der Aalst and E. Best (Eds.): PETRI NETS 2017, LNCS 10258, pp. 125–135, 2017.
DOI: 10.1007/978-3-319-57861-3_9

(11 editions since 2005), the Hardware Model Checking Contest[3] (8 editions since 2007), the Rigorous Examination of Reactive Systems Challenge[4] (6 editions since 2010), the Timing Analysis Contest[5] (4 editions since 2011), and the Competition on Software Verification[6] (5 editions since 2012). The existence of these long-lasting events is a clear indication of interest and usefulness. In most cases, benchmarks are freely available to the involved communities.

In the Petri net Community, the Model Checking Contest [9,10] was created in 2011 and reaches its 7th edition in 2017. As for other competitions, it provides an evolving benchmark composed, in 2016, of 664 models dispatched among 67 Petri nets.

However, achieving the goal stemming from the second motivation requires more: we need a way to query models according to identified characteristics that could allow us to check performances of an algorithm for known conditions. This requires a sophisticated environment allowing to extract sub-benchmarks with dedicated specificities.

This is the main objective of Petri Nets Repository (PNR). It is built on top of a Petri net model database that anybody can query. PNR can be accessed either manually via a Web browser interface or programmatically via a REST interface [5]. It contains models from the Model Checking Contest, but we also imported Petri nets from a previously existing database: Petriweb [7]. PNR is not only a database than can be queried via a web interface as Petriweb was. It also offers an API to automate queries, thus enabling its use in the context of tool testing and benchmarking (as detailed in Sect. 4).

Contents. Section 2 details the architecture of PNR, and Sect. 3 presents some technical characteristics of the tool. Section 4 illustrates the typical use of PNR, and Sect. 5 sketches our perspectives in extending PNR before a conclusion in Sect. 6.

2   Architecture

Petri Nets Repository (PNR) is a Web application that currently offers a large collection of Petri net models provided by the community.

Figure 1 depicts the architecture of PNR. It is composed of a front end that exposes two interfaces to end users (through a browser and a REST API), a middle end and a back end. Figure 1 also shows typical clients of PNR, indicating that they can interact with it in two ways, over HTTP. The client with a Web browser interacts with PNR through the graphical interface and those with other specific tools (*e.g.* a terminal or a Petri net tool) can communicate with PNR using the exposed REST API. In any case, all clients including browsers use the REST API.

---

[3] http://fmv.jku.at/hwmcc15/index.html.
[4] http://rers-challenge.org.
[5] https://sites.google.com/site/taucontest2015/.
[6] https://sv-comp.sosy-lab.org.

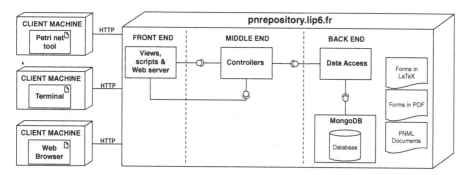

Fig. 1. Overview of the architecture of Petri Nets Repository

The front end Web interface. The Web front end is composed of a set of views encoded in templatized Scala/HTML files and a Web server that serves these compiled views to any browser. We additionally developed some client-side processing scripts to complement the dynamic rendering of the views in the browser. These scripts are written in CoffeeScript [2] and then compiled into Javascript.

The browser shows the content of the Petri net metadata in a table, fetched from PNR. Metadata typically is composed of a model name, type (*i.e.* P/T or Colored net), size, whether it has parameters, and the values of the statically defined properties (*e.g.* deadlock: false) in the LaTeX file used as a model submission template in the model submission kit[7] of the Model Checking Contest. All metadata from PNR are structured in JavaScript Object Notation (JSON) [4].

End users can filter the content of the table over the defined properties, or even provide an ad hoc query formulated as a logical expression. The search function this type of query triggers is performed locally, on the client side. Finally, end users can also open the PDF forms of the models from the table and download the archive containing their PDF forms or PNML [8] documents, upon selection.

The front end REST API. The concept of route encodes the URLs of the REST API in a text file. A route is composed of three parts: the HTTP method (*e.g.* GET, POST), the path of the queried resource, and the fully-qualified name of the program handling the request. For example, `GET/mcc/models/all/metadata.jsoncontrollers.MCCBrowser.browse()` specifies the Java method that handles the querying metadata about all the Petri net models in the MCC collection. All paths are relative to the base URL of PNR (*i.e.* http://pnrepository.lip6.fr).

Some routes return the views along with data used in the client-side scripts to render them in the browser. For example, `/mcc/models/all/browser.html` returns the HTML used to render the collection of all the models in the MCC, along with the list of statically defined properties found in their LaTeX

---

[7] http://mcc.lip6.fr/archives/ModelSubmissionKit.tar.gz.

description files. Some routes only return data in JSON, for example, the public URL to the PNML file of a given model identifier in a GET request: /mcc/models/:id/pnml.json. Other routes return raw data, for example, an archive containing the PNML files of a set of models: /mcc/pnml/*file. The client-side scripts use these routes.

The API, whose reference documentation is published on /api/apiref.html[8], is useful for any user or client tool to query the collections: fetch metadata, download PDF or PNML files of models according to some search criterion. For instance, using a command line tool like cURL [1], one can fetch the metadata of all the models in the MCC collection in a JSON array with:

Listing 1.1. Command line to fetch the metadata of all the models in the MCC collection

```
curl -o pnr-mcc-metadata.json
    http://pnrepository.lip6.fr/mcc/models/all/metadata.json
```

The resulting JSON array contains records encoded as JSON objects. Each record describes a Petri net in the queried collection, like the DES model shown in Listing 1.2.

The middle end. The middle end is composed of the business logic programs (in Java) that handle the requests to the exposed REST API, configuration, logging, and access to the database, the PDF, and the PNML files of the models. A key feature of our REST API is the search function over a particular collection of models (*e.g.* /pweb/search.json for the Petriweb collection), or over all of them (*i.e.* /all/search.json). This search API can potentially inflict a heavy workload upon the back end and the database depending on the frequency and complexity of the requests. Consequently, we have conditioned its successful invocation to providing valid Java Web Tokens (JWT) [12] that we emit upon request, to the interested end users for their own usage.

Listing 1.2. The metadata of the DES model in JSON

```
{"modelName":"DES (Data Encryption Standard)","modelType":"PT",
"authorName":"Wendelin Serwe and Hubert
    Garavel","authorContact":"wendelin.serwe@inria.fr",
"modelOrigin":"Company{NIST (USA)}","modelShortDescription":"These nets are
    derived from the LNT specification of the DES (Data Encryption Standard)
    symmetric-key encryption algorithm.",
"scalingParamName":"(N, V)","parameterised": "TRUE","modelFixedSize":"null",
"ordinary":"True","simpleFreeChoice":"False","extendedFreeChoice":"False",
"stateMachine":"False","markedGraph":"False","connected":"True",
"stronglyConnected":"False","sourcePlace":"True","sinkPlace":"Unknown",
"sourceTransition":"False","sinkTransition":"Unknown","loopFree":"Unknown",
"subConservative":"False","conservative":"False","nestedUnits":"True",
"safe":"True","deadlock":"Unknown","reversible":"Unknown","quasiLive":"Unknown",
"live":"Unknown","year":"2016","lastUpdated":"2016-06-07T20:53:38",
"modelID":"DES","modelBase":"MCC","links": [
{"rel":"self","href":"http://pnrepository.lp6.fr/mcc/models/DES/metadata.json"},
{"rel":"pnml","href":"http://pnrepository.lp6.fr/mcc/models/DES/pnml.json"},
{"rel":"pdf","href":"http://pnrepository.lp6.fr/mcc/models/DES/pdf.json"}]}
```

---

[8] The JSON version of the API reference documentation is at /api/apiref.json.

The back end. The back end consists of both the database containing the metadata about the Petri nets in the collections mentioned above, and the component handling the corresponding data and interfacing the middle end with the database. This back end component also builds the metadata from parsing the LaTeX files describing the Petri nets. These LaTeX files provided by model submitters are thus the primary source of the data model of the Petri nets. Their design has been refined over the years by the MCC model Committee in agreement with the community. We also used it to integrate the imported Petri nets from Petriweb. PNR is powered by MongoDB [13].

We have organized PNR in separate collections: MCC [9,10], Petriweb, and soon, the "Very Large Petri Nets" Benchmark Suite [6]. Firstly, we then show their different backgrounds and purposes, thus maintaining their history. Secondly, we distinguish the specific services offered on top of each collection according to its background. For instance, the MCC collection outputs yearly results that will soon be linked to the models. However, queries can be dispatched over all the collections, and all the models share the same statically defined properties. The authors of these collections have provided their formal agreement to publishing their models in PNR.

3   Technical Characteristics of the Tool

We rely on Play [11], an open source Web application framework, to design the architecture of Petri Nets Repository. Play provides the standard model-view-controller architectural pattern upon which we built our three-tier Web-based enterprise application. Being stateless, RESTful, asynchronous, modular, and full of other carefully designed features, Play enables rapid Web application prototyping and simplifies its deployment.

In the following sections, we provide information about the content of the database and some scalability metrics.

Content of the database. The database was elaborated from the outputs of the community. First, the discontinued Petriweb was gathered by several colleagues and published via a Web site. Second, the collection coming from the Model Checking Contest has been progressively elaborated, year after year since 2011. The result is a heterogeneous collection of Petri nets coming from various areas: distributed algorithms, protocols, hardware systems, biological systems, etc. Moreover, they are issued from both academic and industrial case studies. This variety ensures a sound fairness for evaluation purposes, due to the variants in the application and modeling choices.

Figure 2 (left) shows that we have a significant number of colored Petri nets associated with their equivalent P/T nets, which is useful when comparing the efficiency of algorithms on colored nets, versus others on P/T nets. Figure 2 (right) also shows that, if some optimizations are considered for models having some identified structural characteristics (*e.g.* safe, or reversible), it is easy to select the corresponding subsets of models. This is also useful when evaluating the impact of an algorithm in such situations. Moreover, numerous models

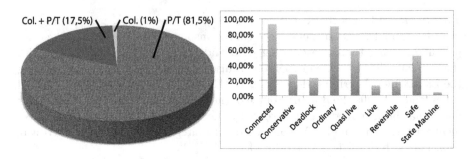

Fig. 2. Distribution of P/T versus colored (left) and according to some typical properties (right).

from the Model Checking Contest have scaling parameters, allowing to generate instances with an increasing complexity. This provides a way to experimentally evaluate the complexity of an algorithm.

We also aim at integrating the models from the "Very Large Petri Nets" Benchmark Suite (this is detailed in Sect. 5).

Scalability of the server. To observe how PNR[9] would perform when a large number of clients connect, we first tested the MCC collection Web page (`/mcc/models/all/browser.html`) with 5000 clients over 1 min. The average response time was 87 ms, with min/max at 80/1141 ms, and 0 error rate. We then tested the API endpoint `/mcc/models/all/metadata.json` with 1000 clients over 1 min. The average response time was 205 ms, with min/max at 160/890 ms, and 0 error rate.

We then wanted to observe the behavior under a number N of requests every second and under a constant load of clients over a time duration T. We tested the endpoint `/mcc/models/all/metadata.json` with 100 clients per second over 1 min. The average response time was 95 ms, with min/max at 81/964 ms, and 0 error rate. We then tested the same endpoint with a load from 250 to 1000 clients over 1 min. The average response time was 319 ms, with min/max at 81/3114 ms, and 0 error rate.

These test cases showed that, under normal circumstances, PNR is fairly scalable. Its native HTTP server is robust enough to support reasonable workloads (*e.g.* the one we can expect from the community).

4   Typical Use of Petri Nets Repository

Using a browser. The Web page displaying the collection of all the models in the MCC has tabbed content. The first tab, "MCC Collection Content", displays the list of Petri nets in a table, along with their properties. When hovering the mouse over a model name, its short description is shown in a small pop-up

---

[9] The PNR HTTP server is based on Netty (http://netty.io/).

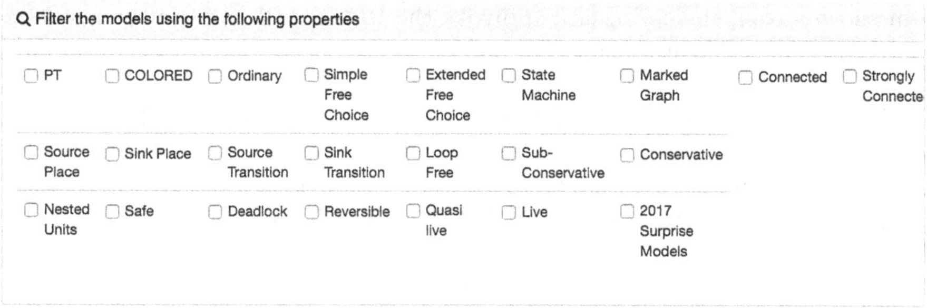

Fig. 3. The quick selection panel of the MCC Collection

window. Clicking on the model name brings up a modal window that displays the "model form" (in PDF).

The user can filter the content of the table using the properties displayed in the quick selection panel "Filter the models using the following properties" (shown in Fig. 3). While this search method only allows the conjunction of properties, the "Advanced Search" feature (search field in the top-right corner above the table) allows any logical expression combining the properties using the connectors && (AND), || (OR), ! (NOT), and ? (UNKNOWN). For example, one can search for sub-conservative or reversible models with subconservative || reversible. Any other arbitrary string that is not a logical expression can also be used to search the table, *e.g.* the name of an author to look for models s/he has submitted. The content of the table is updated as you type. The Reset feature resets the search, displaying the table back in its original state. The CSV and PDF feature exports the content into CSV and PDF files, respectively. The content of the table is paginated so that each page initially displays ten rows to keep a reasonable overall length of the visible page in the browser. However, the user can bypass this setting by choosing how many rows to display. Therefore, it is possible to display all rows in a single page. It is also possible to arrange the columns visibility by selecting which ones to hide or show. Finally, once one or more models have been selected, the user can request to download their forms (in PDF) or PNML documents in an archive. The button to ask the download is located in the bottom-left corner below the table.

The "MCC Collection Cover Flow" tab displays the thumbnails of the models PDF forms, allowing another kind of navigation that is more visualization oriented. The "MCC Contributors" tab displays the list of model submitters, and relates them to the models they have submitted. Finally, the "Metrics" tab shows charts on the contents of the MCC Collection.

The page displaying the collection of Petri nets from Petriweb has the same layout as the one for the MCC, except it has not a list of individual contributors since this information was not provided in the data we had recovered.

Using a proprietary tool. We refer to a "proprietary" tool in this context as, for instance, a command line tool like cURL, or a specific Petri net tool.

Using such a tool, the end user can invoke the REST API and use the result to build whatever application suits his purpose by using the data from Petri Nets Repository.

The same set of actions that the user can perform through a browser can also be achieved directly using the REST API of PNR. In Sect. 2, we showed an example in which we fetch the metadata of all models in the MCC collection, using the command line tool cURL. Next, we detail two more examples using cURL again, combined with other command line tools, in particular jq [3] which allows the processing of the resulting JSON data.

For example, to download the PNML documents of Diffusion2D, the command line is the one in Listing 1.3 (using a GET):

Listing 1.3. Command line to download the PNML documents of Diffusion2D in an archive

```
curl http://pnrepository.lip6.fr/mcc/models/Diffusion2D/pnml.json |
  jq'.href' | xargs -I % curl -o Diffusion2D-pnml.tar.gz
  http://pnrepository.lip6.fr%
```

In the first part of the command, the server responded to the initial request with JSON data specifying the URL to the archive containing the PNML documents. Using jq, we extracted the value of the path field in the second part of the command and fed it to cURL in the last part of the command to download the archive.

We can also perform a search on all the collections in PNR using a query formulated in a JSON payload structured like in Listing 1.4. The `expression` field contains a logical expression that is formulated in the same way as the "Advanced Search" feature allows in the browser. Alternatively, the `fields` contains a mapping to the exact values that the specified properties must have on the matched models (*i.e.* ordinary = True AND live = False AND safe = Unknown). The query in the `expression` field has precedence over the one in `fields`. To have the search function consider the mappings in `fields` instead, it suffices to set the `expression` field to null.

The command line to send a search query on all the collections with the payload of Listing 1.4 is the one in Listing 1.5 (using a POST):

Listing 1.4. A search query payload

```
{"expression" : "(!live && ordinary) || (safe && quasilive)",
  "fields": [{"ordinary": "True"}, {"live": "False"}, {"safe": "Unknown"}]
  }
```

Listing 1.5. Command line to request a search on all collections of PNR

```
curl -H "Content-Type: application/json" -H "uuid: ..." -H "Authorization:
  Bearer ..." -X POST --data @Search-Payload.json
  http://pnrepository.lip6.fr/all/search.json -o resultset.json
```

The search query payload is stored in a file named `Search-Payload.json`. The required Authorization header carries the JSON Web Token that will be first checked before the search query is granted. The uuid header carries the unique identifier issued to the user who has requested the authorization token from us. That identifier must be associated with the token in the request to the API. The result set, saved in `resultset.json`, is structured like in Listing 1.6

Listing 1.6. The result set yielded by the search query in Listing 1.5

```
{ "code": 200, "status": "success", "size": 49, "resultset": [{...},
    {...}, ...] }
```

It shows that the result set contains 49 models that matched the logical expression in Listing 1.4. The `resultset` field is an array of JSON objects, each one describing a matching model with the same structure as in Listing 1.2. The interested user can then loop through this result set and, for example, download the corresponding PDF or PNML documents with subsequent invocations of the API.

Listing 1.7. An oracle for MyTool written in bash

```
#Query PNR to get the list of models with deadlocks
curl -s -H "Content-Type: application/json" -H "uuid: ..." -H
    "Authorization: Bearer ..." -X POST --data '{"expression": "deadlock"}'
    http://pnrepository.lip6.fr/all/search.json -o /tmp/fetch.json
#Get model ids and put them as arguments for later use in the loop
set $(cat /tmp/fetch.json | jq '.resultset [].modelID' | sed -e 's/"//g')
#List of json files each referring to the URL of the PNML archive for a
    model
cat /tmp/fetch.json | jq'.resultset [].links[] | select(.rel |
    contains("pnml")) | .href' | sed -e's/"//g' > /tmp/pnml_lists
#Loop on selected models (get all their instances and process them)
rm -rf /tmp/checks ; mkdir -p /tmp/checks
cat /tmp/pnml_lists | while read jsonUrl ; do
    echo "--- retrieving PNML files for model $1"
    # Extract the URL for the PNML archive
    url=$(curl -s $jsonUrl | jq '.href' | sed -e 's/"//g')
    curl -s -o /tmp/checks/archive.tar.gz $url
    (cd /tmp/checks # process all instances in a temp directory
    tar xzf archive.tar.gz
    for instance in $1/PT/*.pnml ; do # processing all P/T PNML files
        test=$($MyToolPath -deadlock $instance | grep"deadlock=True")
        if [ -z"$test"] ; then
            echo"    $instance ==> NOT PASSED"
        else
            echo"    $instance ==> PASSED"
        fi
    done)
    shift
done
```

Benchmarking a tool. Dynamic access to a large repository of models is useful for benchmarking. Let us consider the case of MyTool that has a deadlock detection function to be tested. The simple bash script presented in Listing 1.7 sets up an oracle that can automatically test the outputs of MyTool against all the models having deadlocks in PNR (a similar script can be elaborated to test the tool when there are no deadlocks). This script will automatically consider new models inserted in PNR.

This benchmarking example shows that debugging can be easily performed on known computed properties. It will be easy to perform similar tests on the behavioral properties computed in the MCC collection (*e.g.* the size of the state space, or some formulas, etc.) as soon as they are inserted in PNR.

5 Perspectives

There are mainly two features we are planning to enrich PNR with, from a short term to a longer term. The first one deals with the integration of the useful "Very large Petri Nets" (VLPN) Benchmark Suite [6]. The second one is about integrating the yearly results of the Model Checking Contest (MCC).

The VLPN benchmark. This is a collection of several hundreds of Petri nets generated from high-level specifications of meaningful systems. They can contain up to 131 216 places and 16 967 720 transitions. So far, the connection to this collection is performed thanks to a simple link to the original Web site. As soon as the database of VLPN is imported, the services of PNR will be available on it too.

The MCC outputs. Since 2015, the Model Checking Contest has introduced a way to evaluate the quality of results based on the outputs of the participating tools. For a given formula, these outputs are summarized and, when a large majority of tools do agree, it is possible to state that the corresponding result is safe. This is the case of all the examinations proposed in the MCC: size of the state spaces, bounds of the nets, and numerous reachability, LTL and CTL formulae.

We would like to associate all these safe results to the corresponding models in order to provide an even more useful benchmark. If models are associated with a set of checked properties, then they can not only be used for benchmarking tools, but also serve as a basis to elaborate oracles for tools. In fact, such a function was manually set up by some 2016 MCC's tool developers (based on the outputs of the 2015 edition) to increase the reliability of their algorithm. Our objective is to make it possible to retrieve these results automatically from PNR, so that tool developers can use them even if they have not yet participated in the Model Checking Contest.

Towards Performance Benchmarking. Section 4 shows how some benchmarking of tools can be automated to check correctness of properties computation, that could even be enhanced with the exploitation of the outputs from the Model Checking Contest. This could lead to the elaboration of performance checking: tool developers might evaluate the impact of a given change in terms of performances.

Online model submission. Currently, the model submission procedure relies on a yearly call for models in the context of the MCC. Model submitters send their model forms in LaTeX to the model board before a given deadline. With PNR, we will eventually propose an online submission form. It would aim at becoming an easier alternative to submitting model information in a LaTeX file, while we will keep building the final PDF version from LaTeX in the back end since this format provides us with numerous advantages in the management of the models.

6   Conclusion

This paper presents Petri Nets Repository (PNR), a large repository of 109 models, from which 706 instances (*i.e.* individual PNML files with different parameter values, when applicable) are derived. The collections of Petri nets are available to the community through a Web interface and a REST API.

Our objective is twofold. First, we are progressively building a reference benchmark that can be helpful to provide fair comparison between tools. Second, PNR is associated with programmatic ways to query it so that it is possible to elaborate oracles from the provided data. Petri Nets Repository is available at http://pnrepository.lip6.fr.

Acknowledgements. The authors thank Hubert Garavel for his helpful advice during the design of Petri Net Repository.

References

1. cURL. https://curl.haxx.se
2. Ashkenas, J.: CoffeeScript. http://coffeescript.org
3. Dolan, S.: jq. https://stedolan.github.io/jq/
4. ECMA: ECMA-404. The JSON Data Interchange Standard. http://www.json.org
5. Fielding, R.T., Taylor, R.N.: Principled design of the modern web architecture. ACM Trans. Internet Techn. **2**(2), 115–150 (2002)
6. Garavel, H.: The VLPN Benchmarck Suite. http://cadp.inria.fr/resources/vlpn/
7. Goud, R., van Hee, K.M., Post, R.D.J., van der Werf, J.M.E.M.: Petriweb: a repository for petri nets. In: Donatelli, S., Thiagarajan, P.S. (eds.) ICATPN 2006. LNCS, vol. 4024, pp. 411–420. Springer, Heidelberg (2006). doi:10.1007/11767589_24
8. Hillah, L.M., Kindler, E., Kordon, F., Petrucci, L., Trèves, N.: A primer on the Petri net markup language and ISO/IEC 15909-2. Petri Net Newsl. **76**, 9–28 (2009)
9. Kordon, F., Garavel, H., Hillah, L.M., Hulin-Hubard, F., Chiardo, G., Hamez, A., Jezequel, L., Miner, A., Meijer, J., Paviot-Adet, E., Racordon, D., Rodriguez, C., Rohr, C., Srba, J., Thierry-Mieg, Y., Trịnh, G., Wolf, K.: Complete Results for the 2016 Edition of the Model Checking Contest, June 2016. http://mcc.lip6.fr/2016/results.php
10. Kordon, F., Garavel, H., Hillah, L.M., Paviot-Adet, E., Jezequel, L., Rodríguez, C., Hulin-Hubard, F.: MCC'2015 – the fifth model checking contest. In: Koutny, M., Desel, J., Kleijn, J. (eds.) Transactions on Petri Nets and Other Models of Concurrency XI. LNCS, vol. 9930, pp. 262–273. Springer, Heidelberg (2016). doi:10.1007/978-3-662-53401-4_12
11. Lightbend, Z.: Play Framework. https://www.playframework.com
12. Jones, M., Bradley, J., Sakimura, N.: JSON Web Token (JWT), Request for Comments 7519, Internet Engineering TaskForce (2015). https://tools.ietf.org/html/rfc7519
13. MongoDB, Inc: MongoDB. https://www.mongodb.com

Model Checking

Extended Dependency Graphs and Efficient Distributed Fixed-Point Computation

Andreas E. Dalsgaard[1], Søren Enevoldsen[1], Peter Fogh[1], Lasse S. Jensen[1],
Tobias S. Jepsen[1], Isabella Kaufmann[1], Kim G. Larsen[1], Søren M. Nielsen[1],
Mads Chr. Olesen[1], Samuel Pastva[1,2], and Jiří Srba[1(✉)]

[1] Department of Computer Science, Aalborg University, Aalborg East, Denmark
srba@cs.aau.dk
[2] Faculty of Informatics, Masaryk University, Brno, Czech Republic

Abstract. Equivalence and model checking problems can be encoded into computing fixed points on dependency graphs. Dependency graphs represent causal dependencies among the nodes of the graph by means of hyper-edges. We suggest to extend the model of dependency graphs with so-called negation edges in order to increase their applicability. The graphs (as well as the verification problems) suffer from the state space explosion problem. To combat this issue, we design an on-the-fly algorithm for efficiently computing fixed points on extended dependency graphs. Our algorithm supplements previous approaches with the possibility to back-propagate, in certain scenarios, the domain value 0, in addition to the standard back-propagation of the value 1. Finally, we design a distributed version of the algorithm, implement it in an open-source tool, and demonstrate the efficiency of our general approach on the benchmark of Petri net models and CTL queries from the Model Checking Contest 2016.

1 Introduction

Model checking [9], a widely used verification technique for exhaustive state space search, may be both time and memory consuming as a result of the state space explosion problem. As a consequence, interesting real-life models can often be too large to be verified. Numerous approaches have been proposed to address this problem, including symbolic model checking and various abstraction techniques [7]. An alternative approach is to distribute the computation across multiple cores/machines, thus expanding the amount of available resources. Tools such as LTSmin [23] and DIVINE [1] have recently been exploring this possibility, without the need of being committed to a fixed model description language.

It has also been observed that model checking is closely related to the problem of evaluating fixed points [6,20,25,29], as these are suitable for expressing system properties described in the logics like Computation Tree Logic (CTL) [8] or the modal μ-calculus [28]. This has been formally captured by the notion of dependency graphs of Liu and Smolka [29]. A dependency graph, consisting of a finite set of nodes and hyper-edges with multiple target nodes, is an abstract

© Springer International Publishing AG 2017
W. van der Aalst and E. Best (Eds.): PETRI NETS 2017, LNCS 10258, pp. 139–158, 2017.
DOI: 10.1007/978-3-319-57861-3_10

framework for efficient minimum fixed-point computation over the node assignments that assign to each node the value 0 or 1. It has a variety of usages, including model checking [6, 20, 25] and equivalence checking [10]. Apart from formal verification, dependency graphs are also used to solve games based e.g. on timed game automata [5] or to encode Boolean equation systems [24].

Liu and Smolka proved in [29] that dependency graphs can be used to compute fixed points of Boolean graphs and to solve in linear time the P-complete problem HORNSAT [15]. They offered both a global and local algorithm for computing the minimum fixed-point value. The global algorithm computes the minimum fixed-point value for all nodes in the graph, though, we are often only interested in the values for some specific nodes. The advantage of the local algorithm is that it needs to compute the values only for a subset of the nodes in order to conclude about the assignment value for a given node of the graph. In practise, the local algorithm is superior to the global one [20] and to further boost its performance, we recently suggested a distributed implementation of the local algorithm with preliminary experimental results [10] conducted for weak bisimulation and simulation checking of CCS processes.

Our Contributions. Neither the original paper by Liu and Smolka [29] nor the recent distributed implementation [10] handle the problem of negation in dependency graphs as this can break the monotonicity in the iterative evaluation of the fixed points. In our work, we extend dependency graphs with so-called *negation edges*, define a sufficient condition for the existence of unique fixed points and design an efficient algorithm for their computation, hence allowing us to encode richer properties rather than just plain equivalence checking or negation-free model checking. As we aim for a competitive implementation and applicability in various verification tools, it is necessary to offer the user the binary answer (whether a property holds or not or whether two systems are equivalent or not) together with the evidence why this is the case. This can be conveniently done by the use of *two-player games* between Attacker and Defender. In our implementation, it is possible for the user to play the role of Defender while the Attacker (played by the tool) can convince the user why a property does not hold. We formally define games played on the extended dependency graphs and prove a correspondence between the winner of the game and the fixed-point value of a node in a dependency graph.

In order to maximize the computation performance, we introduce a novel concept of *certain zero* value that can be back-propagated along hyper-edges and negation edges in order to ensure early termination of the fixed-point algorithm. This technique can often result in considerable improvements in the verification time and has not been, to the best of our knowledge, exploited in earlier work. To further enhance the performance, we present a *distributed algorithm* for a fixed-point computation and prove its correctness. Last but not least, we implement the distributed algorithm in an extensible open source framework and we demonstrate the applicability of the framework on CTL model checking of Petri nets. In order to do so, we integrate the framework into the tool TAPAAL [11, 21] and run a series of experiments on the Petri net models and queries from the Model Checking Contest (MCC) 2016 [26]. An early single-core prototype of the tool implementing the negation edges and certain zero back-propagation also participated in the 2016 competition and was awarded a silver medal in the category of CTL cardinality verification with 23010 points, while the tool LoLA [31] (using a single core in the CTL category) took the gold medal with 27617 points. As documented by the experiments in this paper, our 4-core distributed algorithm now outperforms the optimized sequential algorithm and hence it will challenge the first place in the next year competition (also given that Lola employs stubborn set reduction techniques and query rewriting that were not yet used in our current implementation).

Related Work. Related algorithms for explicit distributed CTL model checking include the assumption based method [4] and a map-reduce based method [2]. Opposed to our algorithm, which computes a local result, these algorithms often focus on computing the global result. The local and global algorithms by Liu and Smolka [29] were also extended to weighted Kripke structures for weighted CTL model checking via symbolic dependency graphs [20], however, without any parallel or distributed implementation.

LTSmin [23] is a language independent model checker which provides a large amount of parallel and symbolic algorithms. To the best of our knowledge, LTSmin uses a symbolic algorithm based on binary decision diagrams for CTL model checking and even our sequential algorithm outperformed LTSmin at MCC'16 [26] (in e.g. CTL cardinality category LTSmin scored 12452 points compared to 23010 points achieved by our tool). Marcie [18] is another Petri net model checking tool that performs symbolic analysis using interval decision diagrams whereas our approach is based on explicit analysis using extended dependency graphs. Marcie was a previous winner of the CTL category at MCC'15 [27], however, in 2016 it finished on a third place with 18358 points after our tool and LoLA, the winner of the competition that we discussed earlier.

Other related work includes [3,17,22] designing parallel and/or distributed algorithms for model-checking of the alternation-free modal μ-calculus. As in our approach, they often employ the on-the-fly technique but our framework is more general as it relies on dependency graphs to which the various verification problems can be reduced. The notion of support sets as an evidence for the validity of CTL formulae has been introduced in [30] and it is close to a (relevant part of) assignment on a dependency graph, however, the game characterization of support sets was not further developed, as stated in [30]. In our work, we provide a natural game-theoretic characterization of an assignment on general dependency graphs and such a characterization can be used to provide an evidence about the fixed-point value of a node in a dependency graph.

Finally, there are several mature tools like FDR3 [14], CADP [13], SPIN [19] and mCRL2 [16], some of them implementing distributed and on-the-fly algorithms. The specification language of these is however often fixed and extensions of such a language requires nontrivial implementation effort. Our approach relies on reducing a variety of verification problems into extended dependency graphs and then on employing our optimized and efficient distributed implementation,

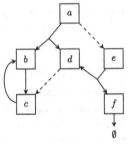

(a) An EDG with $dist(G) = 2$ and $V_0 = \{b, c, f\}$, $V_1 = \{d, e\} \cup V_0$, $V_2 = \{a\} \cup V_1$

	b c f
A_0	0 0 0
$F_0(A_0)$	0 0 1
$F_0(F_0(A_0))$	0 0 1

(b) $A_{min}^{C_0}$ Computation

	b c d e f
A_0	0 0 0 0 0
$F_1(A_0)$	0 0 1 0 1
$F_1(F_1(A_0))$	0 0 1 1 1
$F_1(F_1(F_1(A_0)))$	0 0 1 1 1

(c) $A_{min}^{C_1}$ Computation

	a b c d e f
A_0	0 0 0 0 0 0
$F_2(A_0)$	0 0 0 1 1 1
$F_2(F_2(A_0))$	0 0 0 1 1 1

(d) $A_{min}^{C_2}$ Computation

Fig. 1. An EDG and iterative calculation of its minimum fixed-point assignment

as e.g. demonstrated on CTL model checking of Petri nets presented in this paper or on bisimulation checking of CCS processes [10].

2   Extended Dependency Graphs and Games

We shall now define the notion of extended dependency graphs, adding a new feature of negation edges to the original definition by Liu and Smolka [29].

Definition 1. *An Extended Dependency Graph (EDG) is a tuple $G = (V, E, N)$ where V is a finite set of* configurations, $E \subseteq V \times \mathcal{P}(V)$ *is a finite set of* hyper-edges, *and $N \subseteq V \times V$ is a finite set of* negation edges.

For a hyper-edge $e = (v, T) \in E$ we call v the *source configuration* and $T \subseteq V$ is the set of *target configurations*. We write $v \to u$ if there is a $(v, T) \in E$ such that $u \in T$ and $v \dashrightarrow u$ if $(v, u) \in N$. Furthermore, we write $v \rightsquigarrow u$ if $v \to u$ or $v \dashrightarrow u$. The *successor function* $succ : V \to (E \cup N)$ returns the set of outgoing edges from v, i.e. $succ(v) = \{(v, T) \in E\} \cup \{(v, u) \in N\}$. An example of an EDG is given in Fig. 1(a) with the configurations named a to f, hyper-edges denoted by solid arrows with multiple targets, and dashed negation edges.

In what follows, we consider only EDGs without cycles containing negation edges.

Definition 2. *An EDG $G = (V, E, N)$ is* negation safe *if there are no $v, v' \in V$ s.t. $v \dashrightarrow v'$ and $v' \rightsquigarrow^* v$.*

After the restriction to negation safe EDG, we can now define the negation *distance function* $dist : V \to \mathbb{N}_0$ that returns the maximum number of negation edges throughout all paths starting in a configuration v and is inductively defined as $dist(v) = \max(\{dist(v'') + 1 \mid v', v'' \in V \text{ and } v \to^* v' \dashrightarrow v''\})$ where by convention $\max(\emptyset) = 0$. Note that $dist(v)$ is always finite because every path can visit each negation edge at most once. We then define $dist(G)$ of an EDG G as $dist(G) = \max_{v \in V}(dist(v))$ and for an edge $e \in E \cup N$ where v is its source configuration, we write $dist(e) = dist(v)$.

A *component* C_i of G, where $i \in \mathbb{N}_0$, is a subgraph induced on G by the set of configurations $V_i = \{v \in V \mid dist(v) \leq i\}$. We write V_i, E_i and N_i to denote the set of configurations, hyperedges and negation edges of each respective component. Note that by definition, C_0 does not contain any negation edges. Also observe that $G = C_{dist(G)}$ and that for all $k, \ell \in \mathbb{N}_0$, if $k < \ell$ then C_k is a subgraph of C_ℓ. The EDG G in our example from Fig. 1(a) contains three nonempty components and has $dist(G) = 2$.

An *assignment* A of an EDG $G = (V, E, N)$ is a function $A : V \to \{0, 1\}$ that assigns the value 0 (interpreted as false) or the value 1 (interpreted as true) to each configuration of G. A *zero assignment* A_0 is such that $A_0(v) = 0$ for all $v \in V$. We also assume a component wise ordering $\sqsubseteq$ of assignments such that $A_1 \sqsubseteq A_2$ whenever $A_1(v) \leq A_2(v)$ for all $v \in V$. The set of all assignments of G is denoted by $\mathcal{A}^G$ and clearly $(\mathcal{A}^G, \sqsubseteq)$ is a complete lattice.

We are now ready to define the minimum fixed-points assignment of an EDG G (assuming that a conjunction over the empty set is true, while a disjunction over the empty set is false).

Definition 3. *The* minimum fixed-point assignment *of an EDG G, denoted by $A_{min}^G = A_{min}^{C_{dist(G)}}$ is defined inductively on the components $C_0, C_1, \ldots, C_{dist(G)}$ of G. For all i, $0 \leq i \leq dist(G)$, we define $A_{min}^{C_i}$ to be the minimum fixed-point assignment of the function $F_i : \mathcal{A}^{C_i} \to \mathcal{A}^{C_i}$ where*

$$F_i(A)(v) = A(v) \vee \left[\bigvee_{(v,T) \in E_i} \bigwedge_{u \in T} A(u) \right] \vee \left[\bigvee_{(v,u) \in N_i} \neg A_{min}^{C_{i-1}}(u) \right]. \qquad (1)$$

Note that when computing the minimum fixed-point assignment $A_{min}^{C_0}$ for the base component C_0, we know that $N_0 = \emptyset$ and hence the third disjunct in the function F_0 always evaluates to false. In the inductive steps, the assignment $A_{min}^{C_{i-1}}$ is then well defined for the use in the function F_i. It is also easy to observe that each function F_i is monotonic (by a simple induction on i) and hence by Knaster-Tarski, the unique minimum fixed-point always exists for each i.

In Fig. 1 we show the iterative computation of $A_{min}^{C_0}$, $A_{min}^{C_1}$ and $A_{min}^{C_2}$, starting from the zero assignment A_0. We iteratively upgrade the assignment of a configuration v from the value 0 to 1 whenever there is a hyper-edge (v, T) such that all target configurations $u \in T$ already have the value 1 or whenever there is a negation edge $v \dashrightarrow u$ such that the minimum fixed-point assignment of u (computed earlier) is 0. Once the application of the function F_i stabilizes, we have reached the minimum fixed-point assignment for the component C_i.

Remark 1. The algorithm for computing $A^{C_i}_{min}$ described above, also called the *global algorithm*, relies on the fact that the complete minimum fixed-point assignment of smaller components C_j where $j < i$ must be available before we can proceed with the computation on the component C_i. As we show later on, it is not always necessary to know the whole $A^{C_{i-1}}_{min}$ in order to compute $A^{C_i}_{min}(v)$ for a specific configuration v and such a computation can be done in an on-the-fly manner, using the so-called *local algorithm*.

2.1   Game Characterization

In order to offer a more intuitive understanding of the minimum fixed-point computation on an extended dependency graph G, and to provide a convincing argumentation why the minimum fixed-point value in a given configuration v is 0 or 1 (for the use in our tool), we define a two player game between the players *Defender* and *Attacker*. The *positions* of the game are of the form (v, r) where $v \in V$ is a configuration and $r \in \{0, 1\}$ is a claim about the minimum fixed-point value in v, postulating that $A^G_{min}(v) = r$. The game is played in *rounds* and Defender defends the current claim while Attacker does the opposite.

Rules of the Game: In each round starting from the current position (v, r), the players determine the new position for the next round as follows:

- If $r = 1$ then Defender chooses an edge $e \in succ(v)$. If no such edge exists then Defender loses, otherwise
  - if $e = (v, u) \in N$ then $(u, 0)$ becomes the new current position, and
  - if $e = (v, T) \in E$ then Attacker chooses the next position $(u, 1)$ where $u \in T$, unless $T = \emptyset$ which means that Attacker loses.
- If $r = 0$ then Attacker chooses an edge $e \in succ(v)$. If no such edge exists then Attacker loses, otherwise
  - if $e = (v, u) \in N$ then $(u, 1)$ becomes the new current position, and
  - if $e = (v, T) \in E$ then Defender chooses the next position $(u, 0)$ where $u \in T$, unless $T = \emptyset$ which means that Defender loses.

A *play* is a sequence of positions formed according the rules of the game. Any finite play is lost either by Defender or Attacker as defined above. If a play is infinite, we observe that the claim r can be switched only finitely many times (since the graph is negation safe). Therefore there is only one claim r that is repeated infinitely often in such a play. If $r = 1$ is the infinitely repeated claim then Defender loses, otherwise ($r = 0$) Attacker loses.

The game starting from the position (v, r) is *winning for Defender* if she has a universal winning strategy from (v, r). Similarly, the position is *winning for Attacker* if he has a universal winning strategy from (v, r). Clearly, the game is determined such that only one of the players has a universal winning strategy and from the symmetry of the game rules, we can also notice that Defender is the winner from (v, r) if and only if Attacker is the winner from $(v, 1 - r)$.

Theorem 1. *Let G be a negation safe EDG, $v \in V$ be a configuration and $r \in \{0,1\}$ be a claim. Then $A^G_{min}(v) = r$ if and only if Defender is the winner of the game starting from the position (v, r).*

Proof. By induction on the level of the node v (a node is of level i if it belongs to the component C_i but not to any component C_j where $j < i$), followed by a case analysis. □

Let us now argue that Defender wins from the position $(a, 0)$ in the EDG G from Fig. 1(a). First, Attacker picks either (i) the hyper-edge $(a, \{b, d\})$ or (ii) the negation edge (a, e). In case (i), Defender answers by selecting the configuration b and the game continues from $(b, 0)$. Now Attacker can only pick the hyper-edge $(b, \{c\})$ and Defender is forced to select the configuration c, ending in the position $(c, 0)$ and from here the only continuation of the game brings us again to the position $(b, 0)$. As the play now repeats forever with the claim 0 appearing infinitely often, Defender wins this play. In case (ii) where Attacker selects the negation edge, we continue from the position $(e, 1)$. Defender is forced to select the only available hyper-edge $(e, \{d, f\})$, on which Attacker can answer by selecting the new position $(d, 1)$ or $(f, 1)$. The first choice is not good for Attacker, as Defender will answer by taking the negation edge (d, c) and ending in the position $(c, 0)$ from which we already know that Defender wins. The position $(f, 1)$ is not good for Attacker either as Defender can now select the hyper-edge $(f, \emptyset)$ and Attacker loses as he gets stuck. Hence Defender has a universal winning strategy from $(a, 0)$ and by Theorem 1 we get that $A^G_{min}(a) = 0$.

2.2   Encoding of CTL Model Checking of Petri Nets into EDG

We shall now give an example of how CTL model checking of Petri nets can be encoded into computing fixed-points on EDGs. Let us first recall the Petri net model. Let $\mathbb{N}_0$ denote the set of natural numbers including zero and $\mathbb{N}_\infty$ the set of natural numbers including infinity.

A *Petri net* is a 4-tuple $N = (P, T, F, I)$ where P is a finite set of places, T is a finite set of transitions such that $P \cap T = \emptyset$ and $P \cup T \neq \emptyset$, $F : (P \times T \cup T \times P) \to \mathbb{N}_0$ is the flow function and $I : P \times T \to \mathbb{N}_\infty$ is the inhibitor function. A *marking* on N is a function $M : P \to \mathbb{N}_0$ assigning a number of tokens to each place. The set of all markings on N is denoted $M(N)$. A transition t is enabled in a marking M if $M(p) \geq F((p, t))$ and $M(p) < I(p, t)$ for all $p \in P$. If t is enabled in M, it can fire and produce a marking M', written $M \xrightarrow{t} M'$, such that $M'(p) = M(p) - F((p, t)) + F((t, p))$ for all $p \in P$. We write $M \to M'$ if there is $t \in T$ such that $M \xrightarrow{t} M'$.

In CTL, properties are expressed using a combination of logical and temporal operators over a set of basic propositions. In our case the propositions express properties of a concrete marking M and include the proposition **is_fireable**(Y) for a set of transitions Y that is true iff at least one of the transitions from Y is enabled in the marking M, and arithmetical expressions and predicates over the basic construct **token_count**(X) where X is a subset of places such that

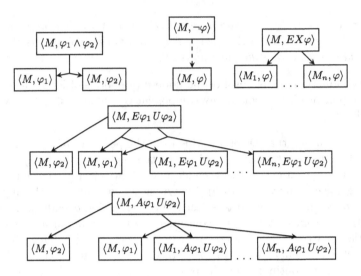

Fig. 2. Construction of EDG where we let $\{M_1, ..., M_n\} = \{M' \mid M \to M'\}$

token_count(X) returns the total number of tokens in the places from the set X in the marking M. The CTL logic is motivated by the requirements of the MCC'16 competition [26] and the syntax of CTL formula φ is

$$\varphi ::= true \mid false \mid \textbf{is\_fireable}(Y) \mid \psi_1 \bowtie \psi_2 \mid \neg\varphi \mid \varphi_1 \wedge \varphi_2 \mid \varphi_1 \vee \varphi_2 \mid$$
$$EG\ \varphi \mid AG\ \varphi \mid EF\ \varphi \mid AF\ \varphi \mid EX\ \varphi \mid AX\ \varphi \mid E\varphi_1 U\varphi_2 \mid A\varphi_1 U\varphi_2$$
$$\psi ::= \psi_1 \oplus \psi_2 \mid c \mid \textbf{token\_count}(X)$$

where $\bowtie\ \in \{<, \leq, =, \geq, >\}$, $X \subseteq P$, $Y \subseteq T$, $c \in \mathbb{N}_0$ and $\oplus \in \{+, -, \cdot\}$. We assume the standard semantics of satisfability of a CTL formula φ in a marking M, written $M \models \varphi$.

For a given marking M and a CTL formula φ, we now construct an EDG with the configurations of the form $\langle M, \varphi \rangle$. If φ is a basic proposition then there is a hyper-edge from $\langle M, \varphi \rangle$ with the empty target set iff $M \models \varphi$. The rules for building EDG for a subset of the temporal operators (the other temporal operators are the derived ones) is given in Fig. 2. Observe that this reduction produces a negation safe EDG. We can then conclude with the following correctness result.

Theorem 2 (Encoding Correctness). *Let N be a Petri net, M a marking on N and let φ be a CTL formula. Let G be the EDG with the root $\langle M, \varphi \rangle$ constructed as described above. Then $M \models \varphi$ iff $A^G_{min}(\langle M, \varphi \rangle) = 1$.*

Remark 2. The reader probably noticed that if the Petri net is unbounded (has infinitely many reachable markings), we are actually producing an infinite EDG. Indeed, CTL model checking for unbounded Petri nets is undecidable [12], so we cannot hope for a general algorithmic solution. However, due to the employment

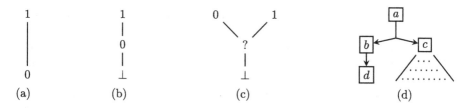

Fig. 3. Comparison of different algorithms for fixed-point computation

of our local algorithm with certain zero propagation, we are sometimes able to obtain a conclusive answer by exploring only a finite part of the (on-the-fly) constructed dependency graph.

3   Algorithms for Fixed-Point Computation on EDG

We shall now discuss the differences of our new distributed algorithm for fixed-point computation of EDG compared to the previous approaches, followed by the description of our algorithm.

Figure 3 shows the partial ordering of the assignment values used by the algorithms. The orderings in the figure show how the configuration values are upgraded during the execution of the algorithms. The global algorithm, described in Sect. 2, only uses the assignment values 0 and 1 as shown in Fig. 3(a). Initially, the whole graph is constructed and all configurations are assigned the value 0. Then it iterates, starting from the component C_0, over all hyper-edges and upgrades the source configuration values to 1 whenever all target configurations are already assigned the value 1. This repeats until no further upgrades are possible and then it uses the negation edges to propagate the values to the higher components until the minimum fixed-point assignment of a given configuration is set to 1 (in which case an early termination is possible) or until the whole process terminates and we can claim that the minimum fixed-point assignment of the given configuration is 0.

The key insight for the local algorithm, as suggested by Liu and Smolka [29] for dependency graphs without negation edges, is that if we are only interested in $A^G_{min}(v)$ for a given configuration v, we do not have to necessarily enumerate the whole graph and compute the value for all configurations in G in order establish that $A^G_{min}(v) = 1$. The local algorithm introduces the value $\perp$ for not yet explored configurations as shown in Fig. 3(b) and performs a forward search in the dependency graph with backward propagation of the value 1. This significantly improves the performance of the global algorithm in case the configuration v gets the value 1. In the case where $A^G_{min}(v) = 0$, the local algorithm must search the whole graph before terminating and announcing the final answer.

Our improvement to the local algorithm is twofold: the handling of negation edges in an on-the-fly manner and the introduction of a new value ?, taking over the previous role of 0, as shown in Fig. 3(c). Here $\perp$ means that a configuration has not been discovered yet, ? that the final minimum fixed-point assignment has not been determined yet, and 0 and 1 mean the final values in the minimum fixed-point assignment. Hence as soon as the given configuration gets the value 0 or 1, we can early terminate and announce the answer. The previous approaches did not allow early termination for the value 0, but as Fig. 3(d) shows, it can save lots of work. Since d has no outgoing hyper-edges, it can get assigned the value 0 (called *certain zero*) and because the single target configuration of the hyper-edge $(b, \{d\})$ is 0, the value 0 can back-propagate to b (we do this by removing hyper-edges that contain at least one target configuration with the value 0 and once a configuration has no outgoing hyper-edges, it will get assigned the certain zero value 0). Now the hyper-edge $(a, \{b, c\})$ can also be removed and as a no longer has any hyper-edges, we can conclude that $A_{min}^G(a) = 0$ without having to explore the potentially large subgraph rooted at c as it would be necessary in the previous algorithms. We moreover have to deal with negation edges where we allow early back-propagation of the certain 0 and certain 1 values, essentially performing an on-the-fly search for the existence of Defender's winning strategy. In what follows, we shall present the formal details of our algorithm, including its distributed implementation.

3.1 Distributed Algorithm for Minimum Fixed-Point Computation

We assume n workers running Algorithm 1 in parallel. Each worker has a unique identifier $i \in \{1, ..., n\}$ and can communicate with any other worker using order preserving, reliable channels. If not stated otherwise, i refers to the identifier of the local worker and j refers to an identifier of some remote worker.

Global Data Structures. Initially, each worker has access to the means of generating a given EDG $G = (V, E, N)$ via the function $succ$, an initial configuration $v_0 \in V$, and a partition function $\delta : V \to \{1, \ldots, n\}$ that splits the configurations among the workers. We say that worker i owns a configuration v if $\delta(v) = i$.

Local Data Structures. Each worker has the following local data structures:

- $W_E^i \subseteq E$ is the waiting list of hyper-edges,
- $W_N^i \subseteq N$ is the waiting list of negation edges,
- $D^i : V \to \mathcal{P}(E \cup N)$ is the dependency set for each configuration,
- $succ^i : V \to \mathcal{P}(E \cup N)$ is the local successor relation such that initially $succ^i(v) = succ(v)$ if $\delta(v) = i$ and otherwise $succ^i(v) = \emptyset$,
- $A^i : V \to \{\bot, ?, 0, 1\}$ is the assignment function (implemented via hashing), initially returning $\bot$ for all configurations,
- $C^i : V \to \mathcal{P}(\{1, \ldots, n\})$ is the set of interested workers who requested the value of a given configuration,
- $M_R^i \subseteq V \times \{1, \ldots, n\}$ is the (unordered) message queue for requests (v, j), where j is the identifier of the worker requesting the assigned value (i.e. 0 or 1) of a configuration v belonging to the partition of worker i, and

---

Algorithm 1. Distributed Certain Zero Algorithm for a Worker i

---

Require: Worker id i, an EDG $G = (V, E, N)$ and an initial configuration $v_0 \in V$.
Ensure: The minimum fixed-point assignment $A_{min}^G(v_0)$
1: **function** DISTRIBUTEDCERTAINZERO(G, v_0)
2:     **if** $\delta(v_0) = i$ **then** EXPLORE(v_0)   ▷ Algorithm 2
3:     **repeat**
4:         **if** $W_E^i \cup W_N^i \cup M_R^i \cup M_A^i \neq \emptyset$ **then**
5:             $task \leftarrow$ PICKTASK($W_E^i, W_N^i, M_R^i, M_A^i$)
6:             **if** $task \in W_E^i$ **then** PROCESSHYPEREDGE($task$)   ▷ Algorithm 2
7:             **else if** $task \in W_N^i$ **then** PROCESSNEGATIONEDGE($task$) ▷ Algorithm 2
8:             **else if** $task \in M_R^i$ **then** PROCESSREQUEST($task$)   ▷ Algorithm 2
9:             **else if** $task \in M_A^i$ **then** PROCESSANSWER($task$)   ▷ Algorithm 2
10:     **until** TERMINATIONDETECTION
11:     **if** $A^i(v_0) = ? \vee A^i(v_0) = 0$ **then return** 0
12:     **else return** 1

– $M_A^i \subseteq V \times \{0, 1\}$ is the (unordered) message queue for answers (v, a), where a is the assigned value of configuration v which has been previously requested by worker i.

For syntactical convenience, we assume that we can add messages to M_R^i and M_A^i directly from other workers.

Global Waiting Lists. When we need to reference the global state in the computation of the parallel algorithm, we can use the following abbreviations.

– The global waiting list of hyper-edges $W_E = \bigcup_{i=1}^n W_E^i$.
– The global waiting list of negation edges $W_N = \bigcup_{i=1}^n W_N^i$.
– The global request message queue $M_R = \bigcup_{i=1}^n M_R^i$.
– The global answer message queue $M_A = \bigcup_{i=1}^n M_A^i$.

Idle Worker. We say that a worker i is idle if it is executing the loop at line 3 through 10 in Algorithm 1, but is not currently executing any of the processing functions on lines 6, 7, 8 or 9.

Pick Task. Algorithm 1 uses at line 5 the function PICKTASK($W_E^i, W_N^i, M_R^i, M_A^i$) that nondeterministically returns:

– a hyper-edge from W_E^i, or
– a message from M_R^i or M_A^i, or
– a negation edge (v, u) from W_N^i provided that $A^i(u) \in \{0, 1, \bot\}$, or
– a negation edge (v, u) from W_N^i if all other workers are idle and v has a minimal distance in all waiting lists and message queues (i.e. for all $(v', x) \in (W_E \cup W_N \cup M_A \cup M_R)$ it holds that $dist(v) \leq dist(v')$).
– If none of the above is satisfied, the worker waits until either a message is received or a negation edge becomes safe to pick. Notice that in this case, W_E^i will remain empty until a message or negation edge is processed.

Algorithm 2. Functions for Worker i Called from Algorithm 1

1: **function** PROCESSHYPEREDGE($e = (v, T)$)   ▷ $e \in E$
2:     $W_E^i \leftarrow W_E^i \setminus \{e\}$
3:     **if** $\forall u \in T : A^i(u) = 1$ **then** FINALASSIGN($v, 1$)   ▷ Edge propagates 1
4:     **else if** $\exists u \in T$ *where* $A^i(u) = 0$ **then** DELETEEDGE(e)
5:     **else if** $X \subseteq T$ *s.t.* $X \neq \emptyset$ *and* $\forall u \in X : A^i(u) = ? \vee A^i(u) = \bot$ **then**
6:         **for** $u \in X$ **do**
7:             $D^i(u) \leftarrow D^i(u) \cup \{e\}$
8:             **if** $A^i(u) = \bot$ **then** EXPLORE(u)

1: **function** PROCESSNEGATIONEDGE($e = (v, u)$)   ▷ $e \in N$
2:     $W_N^i \leftarrow W_N^i \setminus \{e\}$
3:     **if** $A^i(u) = ? \vee A^i(u) = 0$ **then** FINALASSIGN($v, 1$)   ▷ Assign negated value
4:     **else if** $A^i(u) = 1$ **then** DELETEEDGE(e)
5:     **else if** $A^i(u) = \bot$ **then**
6:         $D^i(u) \leftarrow D^i(u) \cup \{e\}; W_N^i \leftarrow W_N^i \cup \{e\};$ EXPLORE(u)

1: **function** PROCESSREQUEST($m = (v, j)$)   ▷ request from worker j
2:     **if** $A^i(v) = 1 \vee A^i(v) = 0$ **then**   ▷ Value of v is already known
3:         $M_A^j \leftarrow M_A^j \cup \{(v, A^i(v))\} ; M_R^i \leftarrow M_R^i \setminus \{m\}$
4:     **else**   ▷ Value of v is not computed yet
5:         $C^i(v) \leftarrow C^i(v) \cup \{j\}$ ▷ Remember that worker j is interested in v
6:         $M_R^i \leftarrow M_R^i \setminus \{m\}$
7:         **if** $A^i(v) = \bot$ **then** EXPLORE(v)

1: **function** PROCESSANSWER($m = (v, a)$)   ▷ $a \in \{0, 1\}$ and $m \in M_A^i$
2:     $M_A^i \leftarrow M_A^i \setminus \{m\}$.
3:     FINALASSIGN(v, a)   ▷ Assign the received answer to v

1: **function** EXPLORE(v)   ▷ $v \in V$
2:     $A^i(v) \leftarrow ?$
3:     **if** $\delta(v) = i$ **then**   ▷ Does worker i own v?
4:         **if** $succ^i(v) = \emptyset$ **then** FINALASSIGN($v, 0$)   ▷ It is safe to propagate 0
5:         $W_E^i \leftarrow W_E^i \cup (succ^i(v) \cap E); W_N^i \leftarrow W_N^i \cup (succ^i(v) \cap N)$
6:     **else**
7:         $M_R^{\delta(v)} \leftarrow M_R^{\delta(v)} \cup \{(v, i)\}$ ▷ If not, request the value from the owner of v

1: **function** DELETEEDGE($e = (v, T)$ *or* $e = (v, u)$)   ▷ $e \in (E \cup N)$
2:     $succ^i(v) \leftarrow succ^i(v) \setminus \{e\}$
3:     **if** $succ^i(v) = \emptyset$ **then** FINALASSIGN($v, 0$)   ▷ It is safe to propagate 0
4:     **if** $e \in E$ **then**
5:         $W_E^i \leftarrow W_E^i \setminus \{e\}$
6:         **for all** $u \in T$ **do** $D^i(u) \leftarrow D^i(u) \setminus \{e\}$
7:     **if** $e \in N$ **then**
8:         $W_N^i \leftarrow W_N^i \setminus \{e\}; D^i(u) \leftarrow D^i(u) \setminus \{e\}$

1: **function** FINALASSIGN(v, a)   ▷ $a \in \{0, 1\}$ and $v \in V$
2:     **if** $v = v_0$ **then return** a and terminate all workers;   ▷ Early termination
3:     $A^i(v) \leftarrow a$
4:     **for all** $j \in C^i(v)$ **do** $M_A^j \leftarrow M_A^j \cup \{(v, a)\}$ ▷ Notify all interested workers
5:     $W_E^i \leftarrow W_E^i \cup \{D^i(v) \cap E\}; W_N^i \leftarrow W_N^i \cup \{D^i(v) \cap N\}$

Even though PICKTASK depends on the global state of the computation to decide whether a negation edge is safe to pick, the rest of the conditions can be decided based on the data that is available locally to each worker. Therefore it is not necessary to synchronise across all workers every time a task should be picked, it is only required if the worker wants to pick a negation edge (v, u) where $A^i(u) = ?$.

Termination of the Algorithm. We utilize a standard TERMINATIONDETECTION function computed distributively that returns *true* if and only if all message queues are empty, all waiting lists are empty (i.e. $W_E \cup W_N \cup M_R \cup M_A = \emptyset$) and all workers are idle. Notice that once the initial configuration v_0 is assigned the final value 0 or 1, the algorithm can terminate early.

We shall now focus on the correctness of the algorithm. By a simple code analysis, we can observe the following lemma.

Lemma 1. *During the execution of Algorithm 1, the value of $A^i(v)$ for any worker i and any configuration v will never decrease (with respect to the ordering from Fig. 3(c)).*

Based on this lemma we can now argue about the termination of the algorithm.

Lemma 2. *Algorithm 1 terminates.*

Proof. To show that the algorithm terminates, we have to argue that eventually all waiting lists become empty and all workers go to idle (unless early termination kicks in before this). By guaranteeing this, the TERMINATIONDETECTION condition will be satisfied and the algorithm terminates.

First, let us observe that if the waiting lists of a worker are empty, the worker will eventually become idle. That is because none of the functions called from the repeat-until loop contain any loops or recursive calls. Also note that in such case, the worker will stay idle until a message is received. In each iteration, an edge is inserted into a waiting list only if the assignment value of some configuration increases. By Lemma 1, the assignment value can never decrease, and since the assignment value can only increase finitely many times, eventually no edges will be inserted into the waiting lists. The same argument applies to request messages as a request can only be sent if an assignment value of a configuration increases from $\perp$ to $?$. The only exception to the considerations above are the answer messages. An answer message can be sent either as a result of an assignment value increase (line 4 of the FINALASSIGN), which only happens finitely many times. However, it can be also sent as a direct response to a request message (line 3 of the PROCESSREQUEST). As we have already shown, each computation can produce only finitely many requests and since each such request can produce at most one answer, the number of answer messages will also be finite.

Finally, we note that as soon as all the messages and hyper-edges are processed by all workers, at least one negation edge becomes safe to pick. Hence if no new messages are sent or edges being inserted into the waiting lists, eventually a negation edge is picked (at most once). Therefore all waiting lists become eventually empty and as a result all workers go idle, satisfying the TERMINATIONDETECTION condition.   □

The main correctness argument is contained in the following loop invariants.

Lemma 3 (Loop Invariants). *For any worker i, the repeat-until loop in Algorithm 1 satisfies the following invariants.*

1. *For all $v \in V$, if $A^i(v) = 1$ then $A^G_{min}(v) = 1$.*
2. *For all $v \in V$, if $A^i(v) = 0$ then $A^G_{min}(v) = 0$.*
3. *For all $v \in V$, if $A^i(v) = ?$ and $i = \delta(v)$ then for all $e \in succ^i(v)$ it holds that $e \in W^i_E \cup W^i_N$ or $e \in D^i(u)$ for some $u \in V$ where $A^i(u) = ?$.*
4. *For all $v \in V$, if $A^i(v) = ?$ and $i \neq \delta(v)$ then one of the following must hold:*
   - $(v,i) \in M^{\delta(v)}_R$,
   - $i \in C^{\delta(v)}(v)$ *and* $A^{\delta(v)}(v) = ?$, *or*
   - $(v,a) \in M^i_A$ *and* $A^{\delta(v)}(v) = a$ *for some* $a \in \{0,1\}$.
5. *If there is a negation edge $e = (v,u) \in W^i_N$ s.t. $A^i(u) = ?$ and all workers are idle and v is minimal in all waiting lists and message queues (i.e. for all $(v',x) \in (W_E \cup W_N \cup M_A \cup M_R)$ it holds that $dist(v) \leq dist(v')$), then $A^G_{min}(u) = 0$.*

Now we can state two technical lemmas.

Lemma 4. *Upon termination of Algorithm 1 at line 11 or line 12, for every negation edge $e = (v,u) \in N$ it holds that either $A^{\delta(v)}(v) \in \{1, \bot\}$ or the negation edge is deleted from $succ^{\delta(v)}$.*

Lemma 5. *Upon termination of Algorithm 1 at line 11 or line 12, for every $i \in \{1, ..., n\}$ and for every $v \in V$ it holds that either $A^i(v) = \bot$ or $A^i(v) = A^{\delta(v)}(v)$.*

We finish this section with the correctness theorem.

Theorem 3. *Algorithm 1 terminates and upon termination it holds, for all i, $1 \leq i \leq n$, that*

- *if $A^i(v_0) = 1$ then $A^G_{min}(v_0) = 1$ and*
- *if $A^i(v_0) \in \{?,0\}$ then $A^G_{min}(v_0) = 0$.*

Proof. By Lemma 2 we know that Algorithm 1 terminates. For a fixed worker i, by Lemma 3, it certainly holds that if $A^i(v) = 1$ or $A^i(v) = 0$ then $A^G_{min}(v) = A^i(v)$. To show that if $A^i(v) = ?$ then $A^G_{min}(v) = 0$, we first construct a global assignment B such that

$$B(v) = \begin{cases} 0 & \text{if there is } i \in \{1, ..., n\} \text{ such that } A^i(v) = ? \text{ or } A^i(v) = 0 \\ 1 & \text{otherwise.} \end{cases} \quad (2)$$

Next we show that B is a fixed-point assignment of G. For a contradiction, let us assume B is not a fixed-point assignment. This can happen in two cases:

- There is a hyper-edge $e = (v, T)$ such that $B(v) = 0$ and $B(u) = 1$ for all $u \in T$. If $A^i(v) = 0$ for some i, it is a direct contradiction with Lemma 3 Condition 2. Otherwise for some i it must hold that $A^i(v) = ?$. By Lemma 5, we get that $A^i(v) = A^{\delta(v)}(v) = ?$. Therefore according to Lemma 3 Condition 3, there exists a configuration u such that $A^{\delta(v)}(u) = ?$ and e is in the dependency set of u. However, $A^{\delta(v)}(u) = ?$ implies that there exists $u \in T$ such that $B(u) = 0$.
- There is a negation edge $e = (v, u)$ such that $B(v) = 0$, and $A^G_{min}(u) = 0$ and e is not deleted. If $A^i(v) = 0$ for some i, it is again a contradiction with Lemma 3 Condition 2. Otherwise for some i it must hold that $A^i(v) = ?$. Then by Lemma 5 we get that $A^i(v) = A^{\delta(v)}(v) = ?$, which is a contradiction with Lemma 4.

Because B is a fixed-point assignment and A^G_{min} is the minimum fixed-point assignment, we get $A^G_{min} \sqsubseteq B$. Therefore if $A^i(v) = ?$ then by the definition of B we have that $B(v) = 0$ and by $A^G_{min}(v) \leq B(v)$ this implies that $A^G_{min}(v) = 0$. □

As a direct consequence of Theorem 3 we get the following corollary.

Corollary 1. *Algorithm 1 terminates and returns $A^G_{min}(v_0)$.*

4   Implementation and Experiments

The single-core local algorithm (local) and its extension with certain zero propagation (czero), together with the distributed versions of czero with non-shared memory and using MPI running on 4 cores (dist-4) and 32 cores (dist-32) have been implemented in an open-source framework written in C++. The implementation is available at http://code.launchpad.net/~tapaal-dist-ctl/verifypn/paper-dist and contains also all experimental data. The general tool architecture was instantiated to CTL model checking of Petri nets by providing C++ code for the initial configuration of the EDG and the successor generator (that for a given configuration outputs all outgoing hyper-edges and negation edges). Optionally, one can also implement a custom-made search strategy or choose it from the predefined ones. In our experiments, we use DFS strategy for both the forward and backward propagation (note that even if each worker in the distributed version runs DFS strategy, depending on the actual order of the request arrivals, this may result in pseudo DFS strategies). The framework also includes a console implementation of the game—the integration into the GUI of the tool TAPAAL is currently under development.

To compare the algorithms, we ran experiments on CTL queries for the Petri nets from MCC'16 [26] on machines with four AMD Opteron 6376 processors, each processor having 16 cores. A 15 GB memory limit per core was enforced for all verification runs. We considered all 322 known Petri net models from the competition, each of them coming with 16 different CTL cardinality queries. As many of these models are either trivial to solve or none of the algorithms are able to provide any answer, we first selected an interesting subset of the models

Table 1. Answered queries within 1 h (out of 784 executions)

Algorithm	Answered queries	Unique answers
Liu and Smolka local, 1 core (local)	475	0
Certain zero local, 1 core (czero)	565	3
Distributed certain zero local, 4 cores (dist-4)	619	4
Distributed certain zero local, 32 cores (dist-32)	670	52

where the slowest algorithm used at least 30 s on one of the first three queries and at the same time the fastest algorithm solved all three queries within 30 min. This left us with 49 models on which we run all 16 CTL queries (in total 784 executions) with the time limit of 1 h.

Table 1 shows how many queries were answered by the algorithms and documents that our certain zero algorithm solved 90 more queries than the one by Liu and Smolka. Running the distributed algorithm on 4 cores further solved 54 more queries and the utilisation of 32 cores allowed us to solve additional 51 queries. The number of unique answers—queries that were solved by a given algorithm but not by any of the remaining three algorithms—clearly shows that adding more workers considerably improves the performance of the distributed algorithm. This is despite the fact that we are solving a P-hard problem [15] and such problems are in general believed not to have efficient parallel algorithms.

In Table 2 we zoom in on a few selected models and show the running time (rounded up to the nearest higher second) for all 16 queries of each model. A dash means running out of resources (time or memory). We can observe a significant positive effect of the certain zero propagation on several queries like A.6, B.7, C.8, D.8 and E.16 and in general a satisfactory performance of this technique. The clear trend with multi-core algorithms is that there is usually a considerable speedup when moving from 1 to 4 cores and a generally nice scaling when we employ 32 cores. Here we can often notice reasonable speedups compared to 1 core certain zero algorithm (A.9, B.1, B.2, B.3, B.12, C.9), sometimes even superlinear speedups like in D.5. On the other hand, occasionally using more cores can actually slowdown the computation like in B.9, E.5 or even E.12 where the distributed algorithms did not find the answer at all. These sporadic anomalies can be explained by the pseudo DFS strategy of the distributed algorithm which means that the answer is either discovered immediately like in D.5 or the workers explore significantly more configurations in a portion of the dependency graph where the answer cannot be concluded from. Nevertheless, these unexpected results are rather rare and the general performance of the distributed algorithms, summarized in Table 1, is compelling.

Finally, we also compare the performance of our verification engine with LoLA, the winner in the CTL category at MCC'16 [26]. We run LoLA on all 784 executions (as summarized for our engines in Table 1) with the same 1 h timeout and 15 GB memory limit. LoLA provided a conclusive answer in 673 cases and given that it is a sequential tool, it won in the comparison with our sequential

Table 2. Verification time in seconds for selected models A: BridgeAndVehicles-PT-V20P20N10, B: Peterson-PT-3, C: ParamProductionCell-PT-4, D: BridgeAndVehicles-PT-V20P10N10, and E: SharedMemory-PT-000010.

	Alg.	1	2	3	4	5	6	7	8	9	10	11	12	13	14	15	16
									Query Number								
A	local	160	447	–	158	234	250	199	1	228	343	229	241	233	1	223	1
	czero	157	453	226	154	229	1	1	1	221	100	227	238	232	1	226	1
	dist-4	82	224	129	86	158	1	1	1	85	1	116	154	133	1	137	1
	dist-32	21	67	1	20	45	1	1	1	11	1	33	36	46	1	33	1
B	local	465	444	453	16	1	1	401	1	1030	1	877	490	3	458	459	1
	czero	452	468	464	16	1	1	1	1	522	1	1	477	3	1	2	1
	dist-4	119	118	125	6	1	1	1	1	180	1	1	144	3	1	1	1
	dist-32	23	22	23	1	1	1	1	1	1270	1	1	28	1	1	1	1
C	local	343	1	183	85	1	1	4	180	–	1	25	1	165	1	173	172
	czero	175	1	172	70	1	1	3	1	333	1	23	1	178	1	1	1
	dist-4	60	1	63	42	3	1	2	1	87	1	12	1	58	1	1	1
	dist-32	20	2	15	18	2	3	1	1	21	1	11	1	13	1	1	1
D	local	263	446	243	236	219	23	204	356	235	164	1	231	279	1	1	13
	czero	1	187	6	228	215	21	188	1	220	1	1	229	257	1	1	11
	dist-4	1	130	6	130	1	12	103	1	122	1	1	124	189	1	1	7
	dist-32	1	45	2	35	1	3	27	1	38	1	1	41	61	1	1	2
E	local	95	137	140	136	139	135	130	139	139	144	148	1	1	138	132	134
	czero	96	143	134	134	137	143	129	134	139	146	141	1	1	137	138	1
	dist-4	33	53	58	53	147	52	50	57	59	65	79	–	1	52	61	1
	dist-32	30	14	15	14	1225	15	20	16	17	18	19	–	1	16	16	9

czero implementation that solved 565 queries. The reason is that about one third of all the 784 queries are actually equivalent to either true or false and hence they can be answered without any state-space exploration by a simple query rewriting technique implemented in LoLA [31]. The problem is that this query simplification implemented in LoLA cannot be turned off for a fair comparison. A detailed analysis revealed that LoLA had 172 exclusive answers compared to 64 exclusive answers of our sequential czero algorithm, however, 58 (34%) of the 172 queries answered exclusively by LoLA were equivalent to either true or false and did not require any state space exploration and further 55 queries (32%) were simplified into a trivial form where LoLA needed to explore less than 1000 markings. After removing these 113 trivial queries, LoLA provided 59 exclusive answers compared to 64 exclusive answers of our sequential czero algorithm. Hence the performance of LoLA is essentially comparable with our sequential algorithm. The main advantage of our approach is that we also provide a distributed implementation that already with 4 cores[1] outperforms the single-core implementation.

5   Conclusion

We extended the formalism of dependency graphs by Liu and Smolka [29] with the notion of negation edges in order to capture nested minimum fixed-point

---

[1] The organizers of MCC'17 allow the tools to utilize 4 cores in the competition.

assignments within the same graph. On the extended dependency graphs, we designed an efficient local algorithm that allows us to back-propagate also certain zero values—both along the normal hyper-edges as well as the negation edges and hence considerably speed up the computation. To further increase the performance and applicability of our approach, we suggested to distribute the local algorithm, proved the correctness of the pseudo-code and provided an efficient, open-source implementation. Now the user can take a verification problem, reduce it to an extended dependency graph and get an efficient distributed verification engine for free. This is a significant advantage compared to a number of other tools that design a specific distributed algorithm for a fixed modeling language and a fixed property language.

We demonstrated the general applicability of our tool on an example of CTL model checking of Petri nets and evaluated the performance on the benchmark of models from the Model Checking Contest 2016. The results confirm significant improvements over the local algorithm by Liu and Smolka achieved by the certain zero propagation and the distribution of the work among several workers. Already the performance of our sequential algorithm with certain zero propagation is comparable with the world leading tool LoLA for CTL model checking of Petri nets (modulo the query transformation rules implemented additionally in LoLA and not related to the actual state-space search). While LoLA implements only a sequential algorithm, we also provide a generic and efficient distribution of the work among a scalable number of workers.

It was observed that for certain models, the search with a large number of workers can be occasionally directed into a portion of the graph where no conclusive answer can be drawn, implying that sometimes just a few workers find the answer faster. In the future work, we shall look into how to better exploit different search strategies when scaling the number of workers.

Acknowledgments. We would like to thank to Frederik Boenneland, Jakob Dyhr, Mads Johannsen and Torsten Liebke for their help with running LoLA experiments. The work was funded by Sino-Danish Basic Research Center IDEA4CPS, Innovation Fund Denmark center DiCyPS and ERC Advanced Grant LASSO. The last author is partially affiliated with FI MU in Brno.

References

1. Barnat J. et al.: DiVinE 3.0 – an explicit-state model checker for multithreaded C & C++ programs. In: Sharygina N., Veith H. (eds) CAV 2013. LNCS, vol 8044, pp. 863–868. Springer, Heidelberg (2013)
2. Bellettini, C., Camilli, M., Capra, L., Monga, M.: Distributed CTL model checking in the cloud. arXiv preprint arXiv:1310.6670 (2013)
3. Bollig, B., Leucker, M., Weber, M.: Local parallel model checking for the alternation-free μ-calculus. In: Bošnački, D., Leue, S. (eds.) SPIN 2002. LNCS, vol. 2318, pp. 128–147. Springer, Heidelberg (2002). doi:10.1007/3-540-46017-9_11
4. Brim, L., Crhova, J., Yorav, K.: Using assumptions to distribute CTL model checking. ENTCS **68**(4), 559–574 (2002)

5. Cassez, F., David, A., Fleury, E., Larsen, K.G., Lime, D.: Efficient on-the-fly algorithms for the analysis of timed games. In: Abadi, M., Alfaro, L. (eds.) CONCUR 2005. LNCS, vol. 3653, pp. 66–80. Springer, Heidelberg (2005). doi:10.1007/11539452_9

6. Christoffersen, P., Hansen, M., Mariegaard, A., Ringsmose, J.T., Larsen, K.G., Mardare, R.: Parametric verification of weighted systems. In: SynCoP 2015, vol. 44, pp. 77–90. OASIcs, Schloss Dagstuhl-Leibniz-Zentrum fuer Informatik (2015)

7. Clarke, E., Grumberg, O., Jha, S., Lu, Y., Veith, H.: Progress on the state explosion problem in model checking. In: Wilhelm, R. (ed.) Informatics. LNCS, vol. 2000, pp. 176–194. Springer, Heidelberg (2001). doi:10.1007/3-540-44577-3_12

8. Clarke, E.M., Emerson, E.A.: Design and synthesis of synchronization skeletons using branching time temporal logic. In: Kozen, D. (ed.) Logic of Programs 1981. LNCS, vol. 131, pp. 52–71. Springer, Heidelberg (1982). doi:10.1007/BFb0025774

9. Clarke, E.M., Emerson, E.A., Sifakis, J.: Model checking: algorithmic verification and debugging. Commun. ACM 52(11), 74–84 (2009)

10. Dalsgaard, A.E., Enevoldsen, S., Larsen, K.G., Srba, J.: Distributed computation of fixed points on dependency graphs. In: Fränzle, M., Kapur, D., Zhan, N. (eds.) SETTA 2016. LNCS, vol. 9984, pp. 197–212. Springer, Cham (2016). doi:10.1007/978-3-319-47677-3_13

11. David, A., Jacobsen, L., Jacobsen, M., Jørgensen, K.Y., Møller, M.H., Srba, J.: TAPAAL 2.0: integrated development environment for timed-arc Petri nets. In: Flanagan, C., König, B. (eds.) TACAS 2012. LNCS, vol. 7214, pp. 492–497. Springer, Heidelberg (2012). doi:10.1007/978-3-642-28756-5_36

12. Esparza, J.: Decidability of model checking for infinite-state concurrent systems. Acta Informatica 34(2), 85–107 (1997)

13. Garavel, H., Lang, F., Mateescu, R., Serwe, W.: CADP 2011: a toolbox for the construction and analysis of distributed processes. STTT 15(2), 89–107 (2013)

14. Gibson-Robinson, T., Armstrong, P., Boulgakov, A., Roscoe, A.W.: FDR3 — a modern refinement checker for CSP. In: Ábrahám, E., Havelund, K. (eds.) TACAS 2014. LNCS, vol. 8413, pp. 187–201. Springer, Heidelberg (2014). doi:10.1007/978-3-642-54862-8_13

15. Greenlaw, R., Hoover, H.J., Ruzzo, W.L.: Limits to Parallel Computation: P-Completeness Theory, vol. 200. Oxford University Press Inc, New York (1995)

16. Groote, J., Mousavi, M.: Modeling and Analysis of Communicating Systems. The MIT Press, Cambridge (2014)

17. Grumberg, O., Heyman, T., Schuster, A.: Distributed symbolic model checking for μ-calculus. Formal Methods Syst. Des. 26(2), 197–219 (2005)

18. Heiner, M., Rohr, C., Schwarick, M.: MARCIE – model checking and reachability analysis done efficiently. In: Colom, J.-M., Desel, J. (eds.) PETRI NETS 2013. LNCS, vol. 7927, pp. 389–399. Springer, Heidelberg (2013). doi:10.1007/978-3-642-38697-8_21

19. Holzmann, G.: Spin Model Checker, the: Primer and Reference Manual. Addison-Wesley Professional, Boston (2003)

20. Jensen, J., Larsen, K., Srba, J., Oestergaard, L.: Efficient model checking of weighted CTL with upper-bound constraints. STTT 18(4), 409–426 (2016)

21. Jensen, J.F., Nielsen, T., Oestergaard, L.K., Srba, J.: TAPAAL and reachability analysis of P/T nets. In: Koutny, M., Desel, J., Kleijn, J. (eds.) Transactions on Petri Nets and Other Models of Concurrency XI. LNCS, vol. 9930, pp. 307–318. Springer, Heidelberg (2016). doi:10.1007/978-3-662-53401-4_16

22. Joubert, C., Mateescu, R.: Distributed on-the-fly model checking and test case generation. In: Valmari, A. (ed.) SPIN 2006. LNCS, vol. 3925, pp. 126–145. Springer, Heidelberg (2006). doi:10.1007/11691617_8

23. Kant, G., Laarman, A., Meijer, J., Pol, J., Blom, S., Dijk, T.: LTSmin: high-performance language-independent model checking. In: Baier, C., Tinelli, C. (eds.) TACAS 2015. LNCS, vol. 9035, pp. 692–707. Springer, Heidelberg (2015). doi:10.1007/978-3-662-46681-0_61

24. Keinänen, M.: Techniques for solving boolean equation systems. Research Report A105, Doctoral dissertation, Laboratory for Theoretical Computer Science, Helsinki University of Technology, pp. xii+95 (2006)

25. Keiren, J.J.A.: Advanced reduction techniques for model checking. Ph.D. thesis, Eindhoven University of Technology (2013)

26. Kordon, F., Garavel, H., Hillah, L.M., Hulin-Hubard, F., Chiardo, G., Hamez, A., Jezequel, L., Miner, A., Meijer, J., Paviot-Adet, E., Racordon, D., Rodriguez, C., Rohr, C., Srba, J., Thierry-Mieg, Y., Trinh, G., Wolf, K.: Complete results for the 2016th edition of the model checking contest. http://mcc.lip6.fr/2016/results.php

27. Kordon, F., Garavel, H., Hillah, L.M., Hulin-Hubard, F., Linard, A., Beccuti, M., Hamez, A., Lopez-Bobeda, E., Jezequel, L., Meijer, J., Paviot-Adet, E., Rodriguez, C., Rohr, C., Srba, J., Thierry-Mieg, Y., Wolf, K.: Complete results for the 2015th edition of the model checking contest (2015)

28. Kozen, D.: Results on the propositional μ-calculus. In: Nielsen, M., Schmidt, E.M. (eds.) ICALP 1982. LNCS, vol. 140, pp. 348–359. Springer, Heidelberg (1982). doi:10.1007/BFb0012782

29. Liu, X., Smolka, S.A.: Simple linear-time algorithms for minimal fixed points. In: ICALP 1998. LNCS, vol. 1443, pp. 53–66. Springer, Heidelberg (1998)

30. Tan, L., Cleaveland, R.: Evidence-based model checking. In: Brinksma, E., Larsen, K.G. (eds.) CAV 2002. LNCS, vol. 2404, pp. 455–470. Springer, Heidelberg (2002). doi:10.1007/3-540-45657-0_37

31. Wolf, K.: Running LoLA 2.0 in a model checking competition. In: Koutny, M., Desel, J., Kleijn, J. (eds.) Transactions on Petri Nets and Other Models of Concurrency XI. LNCS, vol. 9930, pp. 274–285. Springer, Heidelberg (2016). doi:10.1007/978-3-662-53401-4_13

Model Checking Concurrency and Causality

Karsten Wolf[(✉)]

Institut Für Informatik, Universität Rostock, 18051 Rostock, Germany
`karsten.wolf@uni-rostock.de`

Abstract. We consider a spectrum of properties proposed in [14], that is related to causality and concurrency between a pair of given transitions in a place/transition net. For each of these properties, we ask whether it can be verified using an ordinary, interleaving based, model checker. With a systematic approach based on two constructions, we reduce 75% of the properties in the spectrum to a reachability problem. We have to leave the remaining 25% as open problems.

1 Introduction

Concurrency and causality are the most fundamental concepts in Petri net theory, distinguishing Petri nets and related formalisms from automata based system models [1–3,5,12,13]. Based on the non-sequential behaviour of Petri nets that makes concurrency and causality explicit, model checking algorithms and tools have been designed [4,6,10,11,15]. In application areas such as business process modelling, studying relations based on causality and concurrency can be used for understanding and comparing processes [18], or for querying process repositories [16].

Concurrency and causality are defined on processes (partially ordered runs) of a Petri net. Given a process, event e_1 causally precedes event e_2 ($e_1 \rightarrow e_2$) if $[e_1, e_2]$ is in the transitive closure of the causality relation of the process, and they are concurrent ($e_1 \parallel e_2$) if they are not (in either order). When we want to study related questions on the Petri net itself, we need to acknowledge that a net can have several processes, and its transitions may be related to several events in a process. [14] proposed to lift causality and concurrency from the level of processes to the level of nets by quantifying the involved ingredients. Given a Petri net N and two transitions x and y, queries can be formulated using the following pattern:

$$Q_1 \pi Q_2 e_x Q_3 e_y : e_x R e_y.$$

Here, $Q_1, Q_2, Q_3 \in \{\exists, \forall\}$, $R \in \{\leftarrow, \rightarrow, \parallel\}$, the domain of π is the set of processes of N, the domain of e_x is the set of all events related to transition x, and the domain of e_y is the set of all events related to transition y. Ruling out obvious equivalences, this pattern yields a spectrum of 20 distinct net properties that is a substantial part of what [14] describes as the *4C spectrum* (from concurrency, causality, co-occurrence, conflict), with application in business process management. Conflict and co-occurrence can be easily traced back

© Springer International Publishing AG 2017
W. van der Aalst and E. Best (Eds.): PETRI NETS 2017, LNCS 10258, pp. 159–178, 2017.
DOI: 10.1007/978-3-319-57861-3_11

to reachability problems. In contrast, [14] left most of the properties related to concurrency and causality open. Consequently, we shall call each of the concurrency/causality related properties stated above a *2C-property*, collectively forming the *2C-spectrum*.

To name just one potential application, we can enhance a Petri net model of a business process with a matrix that records, for every pair of activities, a list of satisfied 2C (or 4C)-properties. In a large database of processes, retrieving a model with certain properties can then be done significantly faster. Properties referring to causality or concurrency between activities are quite common for legal requirements. Their satisfaction is commonly referred to as *compliance* and is a major research field in business process management.

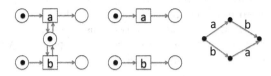

Fig. 1. Two Petri nets with same reachability graph

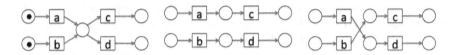

Fig. 2. A Petri net with two of its processes

In this paper, we shall succeed in reducing many 2C-properties to a reachability problem. This way, we can use ordinary model checkers (those that construct the reachability graph either explicitly [8,20] or symbolically [7,17], to name a few) as well as tools based on Petri net structure theory [19] for computer aided investigation. The reduction is not completely straight-forward since the reachability graph of the given net N in general does not preserve full information about concurrency and causality, see Fig. 1. The two nets (left and center) have precisely the same reachability graph (right). However, in the net (left), a and b are not concurrent while they are concurrent in the net (center). In Fig. 2, the net (left) has two processes (center and right) with completely different causalities. Both processes correspond, among others, to the sequence $abcd$. To make causality and concurrency visible in the sequential behaviour, our approach for verifying a 2C-property ϕ in a net N is to construct a net N' and a reachability query ϕ' such that $N \models \phi$ if and only if $N' \models \phi'$. For 75% of the queries, we propose such a construction. We did not find a solution so far for the remaining properties.

We do not consider the somewhat obvious additional capabilities, that model checkers based on non-sequential processes such as [6,10,15] might have for solving 2C-properties. These tools are based on complete prefixes of the processes of the given net. In their data structures, the relevant information may be present much more explicitly than in interleaving based model checkers. However, the sheer number and the level of sophistication of existing interleaving based model checkers justifies the investigation of *their* capability of analysing 2C-properties.

We first fix the basic notations for Petri nets and their processes. Then we introduce the principles of our transformation. It is based on introducing colours to the given net. Consequently, we introduce Coloured Petri net and their relations to place transitions nets and their partially ordered runs. We continue with introducing the actual constructions that we are going to systematically employ. Then, we show how to combine these constructions for solving the individual 2C-properties. We close with a discussion on open cases and complexity.

2   Place/Transition Nets and Partially Ordered Runs

Let $\mathbb{N}$ be the set of natural numbers, including 0. We consider place/transition nets using the following notation:

Definition 1 (Place/transition net). *A place/transition net* $[P, T, F, W, m_0, \text{final}]$ *consists of two finite, nonempty, and disjoint sets* P *(places) and* T *(transitions), a flow relation* $F \subseteq (P \times T) \cup (T \times P)$; *a weight function* $W : (P \times T) \cup (T \times P) \longrightarrow \mathbb{N}$ *such that* $W(x, y) = 0$ *if and only if* $[x, y] \notin F$, *and an initial marking* m_0. *A marking is a mapping* $m : P \longrightarrow \mathbb{N}$. *For a node* $x \in P \cup T$, $\bullet x = \{y \mid [y, x] \in F\}$ *and* $x \bullet = \{y \mid [x, y] \in F\}$ *are its pre-resp. post-set. Transition* t *is enabled in marking* m *iff, for all places* p, $m(p) \geq W(p, t)$. *Firing* t *in* m *yields marking* m' $(m \xrightarrow{t} m')$, *if* t *is enabled in* m *and, for all places* p, $m'(p) = m(p) - W(p, t) + W(t, p)$. *final is a Boolean predicate on the set of all markings. Lifting the notion of firing a transition to transition sequences* σ *in the usual way, we define the sequential semantics as the set of all sequences that start in the initial marking and end in some marking satisfying the* final *predicate:* $\text{SEQ}(N) = \{\sigma \mid \exists m : m_0 \xrightarrow{\sigma} m \wedge \text{final}(m)\}$.

For convenience, we shall restrict all our subsequent considerations to nets where every transition has at least one pre-place and at least one post-place. The concurrent behaviour of a Petri net is based on causal nets.

Definition 2 (Causal net, partially ordered process). *A causal net* $O = [B, E, C]$ *consists of two finite, nonempty, and disjoint sets* B *(conditions) and* E *(events), and a causality relation* $C \subseteq (B \times E) \cup (E \times B)$ *such that*

– *the transitive closure* C^* *of* C *in* $(B \cup E) \times (B \cup E)$ *is irreflexive,*
– *every condition* b *has at most one event* e *with* $[e, b] \in C$, *and at most one event* e' *with* $[b, e'] \in C$,
– *every event* e *has at least one condition* b *with* $[b, e] \in C$, *and at least one* b' *with* $[e, b'] \in C$.

For any $x, y \in (B \cup E)$, we say that x causally precedes y (or y causally follows x), denoted $x \rightarrow y$, iff $[x, y] \in C^*$ or $x = y$. If neither $x \rightarrow y$ nor $y \rightarrow x$, we say that x and y are concurrent (denoted $x \parallel y$). A partial cut of O is a set of pairwise concurrent conditions in O. A partial cut is a cut if it is not a proper subset of any other partial cut. Every causal net O has two distinct cuts $\text{MIN}(O) = \{b \mid b \in B, \neg \exists e : [e, b] \in C\}$ and $\text{MAX}(O) = \{b \mid b \in B, \neg \exists e : [b, e] \in C\}$.

The partial order semantics of a Petri net N is defined by aligning elements of causal nets with elements of N.

Definition 3 (Process). *A labeling of a causal net $O = [B, E, C]$ w.r.t. a Petri net $N = [P, T, F, W, m_0, \text{final}]$ is a mapping $\lambda : (B \cup E) \longrightarrow (P \cup T)$ that*

- *respects the node type, i.e. $\lambda(B) \subseteq P$ and $\lambda(E) \subseteq T$,*
- *respects the environment of transitions, i.e. for all events e and places p, q with $[p, \lambda(e)] \in F$, and $[\lambda(e), q] \in F$, it holds $\text{card}(\{b \mid [b, e] \in C, \lambda(b) = p\}) = W(p, \lambda(e))$, and $\text{card}(\{b \mid [e, b] \in C, \lambda(b) = q\}) = W(\lambda(e), q)$.*

Given a labeling λ w.r.t. N, every cut K of O defines a marking $\lambda(K)$ where, for all places p of N, $\lambda(K)(p) = \text{card}(\{b \mid b \in K, \lambda(b) = p\})$. A process $[B, E, C, \lambda]$ of a net N is a causal net $O = [B, E, C]$ with a labelling λ w.r.t. N such that $\lambda(\text{MIN}(O)) = m_0$ and $\text{final}(\lambda(\text{MAX}(O)))$ holds. The process semantics $\text{PAR}(N)$ of N is defined as the set of its processes.

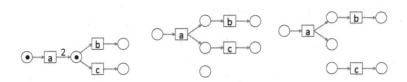

Fig. 3. A Petri net with two of its processes

Figure 3 shows a net (left) and two of its processes (center and right), assuming that final = *two tokens in post-set of b plus c*. Every process π corresponds to a set $\text{SEQ}(\pi)$ of firing sequences. Sequence σ is in $\text{SEQ}(\pi)$ if and only if each transition occurs in σ as frequent as it is used as a label in π, and the order of occurrences is compatible with (i.e. includes) the partial order defined by the (transitive closure of the) causality relation of π. This set is $\{abc, acb\}$ for the process in Fig. 3 (center) and $\{abc, acb, cab\}$ for the process in Fig. 3 (right).

Accordingly, every firing sequence σ corresponds to the set $\text{PAR}(\sigma) = \{\pi \mid \sigma \in \text{SEQ}(\pi)\}$. For the net in Fig. 3 (left), the process (right) is the only one contained in $\text{PAR}(cab)$. For safe Petri nets, $\text{PAR}(\sigma)$ is always singleton. This is not necessarily the case for unsafe Petri nets. For every process π and all $\sigma \in \text{SEQ}(\pi)$, as well as for every sequence σ and all $\pi \in \text{PAR}(\sigma)$ there exist (not necessarily unique) bijective mappings between the events in the process and the positions in the sequence. In the sequel, whenever we consider a corresponding pair of process and sequence, we shall silently assume such a mapping to be given and fixed. This way, we will feel free to state the occurrence of event e of π in the sequence σ meaning the occurrence of transition $\lambda(e)$ at the unique position given by the assumed labelling. Likewise, whenever we consider all $\pi \in \mathrm{PAR}(\sigma)$, or all $\sigma \in \mathrm{SEQ}(\pi)$, we actually mean all such π or σ with all such mappings.

3   Coloured Petri Nets

In Coloured Petri nets [9], tokens on a place can be distinguished if they have different colours. The firing rule establishes a relation between colours of consumed and produced tokens. In our approach, we shall just "mark" tokens using colours. We shall need at most four distinct colours. Hence, we fix this set to be $\mathrm{COL} = \{\mathrm{black, dark, light, white}\}$ throughout the remainder of this article. With MCOL, we denote the set of all multi-sets on COL. We propose a very simple version of coloured Petri nets.

Definition 4 (Coloured Petri net). *A Coloured Petri net $N =$ $[P, T, F, W, G, m_0, \mathrm{final}]$ consists of two disjoint, nonempty, and finite sets P (places), T (transitions), an arc relation $F \subseteq (P \times T) \cup (T \times P)$, and a weight function W that assigns a set of variables to each $f \in F$ such that all variable sets are pairwise disjoint. For each t, let $\mathrm{IN}(t) = \bigcup_{f \in P \times \{t\}} W(f)$ and $\mathrm{OUT}(t) = \bigcup_{f \in \{t\} \times P} W(f)$. Let $\mathrm{VAR}(t) = \mathrm{IN}(t) \cup \mathrm{OUT}(t)$. Then N further consists of a guard function G that assigns a Boolean predicate to each transition t that ranges over $\mathrm{VAR}(t)$, and an initial marking m_0. A marking m is a mapping from P to MCOL. final is a predicate that ranges over the set of all markings.*

A firing mode of transition t is an assignment $a : \mathrm{VAR}(t) \longrightarrow \mathrm{COL}$. Transition t is enabled in firing mode a in marking m iff $G(t)(a)$ is true and, for all $[p, t] \in F$, $m(p) \geq \sum_{v \in W([p,t])} a(v)$. Here, the sum symbol is to be interpreted as multiset summation of the singleton multisets given by the values of the individual variables. A firing sequence of a coloured net is a sequence of pairs of transition and firing mode. Otherwise, firing sequences accord to those of place/transition nets. A process of a coloured Petri net can be defined similarly to a process of a place/transition net. The only difference is that λ maps events to pairs of transition and firing mode, and conditions to pairs of place and colour. Hence, we do not need to separately define $\mathrm{SEQ}(N)$ and $\mathrm{PAR}(N)$ for coloured nets.

A coloured Petri net $N = [P, T, F, W, G, m_0, \mathrm{final}]$ naturally corresponds to two place/transition nets. The first one is called its *unfolding*. In the unfolding, the set of places is $P \times \mathrm{COL}$, and transitions are those pairs $[t, a]$ where $t \in T$ and a is a firing mode of t with $G(t)(a)$ being true. The other elements of the unfolding are defined such that N and its unfolding behave equivalently. We consider this construction to be well known and skip the details. A coloured net N and its unfolding basically have the same sequential and process semantics. We shall use the unfolding of N for actual verification, and for illustrating coloured nets in figures.

Definition 5 (Unfolding of a coloured Petri net). *The* unfolding *of coloured net* $N = [P, T, F, W, G, m_0, \text{final}]$ *is the place/transition net* $N' = [P', T', F', W', m_0', \text{final}']$ *where* $P' = P \times \text{COL}$, $T' = \{[t, a] \mid t \in T, G(a) \text{ is true }\}$, $W([[p, c], [t, a]]) = \text{card}(\{x \mid x \in W([p, t]), a(x) = c\})$, $W([[t, a], [p, c]]) = \text{card}(\{x \mid x \in W([t, p]), a(x) = c\})$, $F' = \{[x, y] \in (P' \times T') \cup (T' \times P') \mid W'([x, y]) \neq 0\}$, $m_0'([p, c]) = m_0(p)(c)$, and $\text{final}'(m')$ holds if and only if $\text{final}(m)$ holds for the marking m where, for all places p and all colours c, $m(p)(c) = m'([p, c])$.

The other place/transition net we can naturally assign to a coloured net $N = [P, T, F, W, G, m_0, \text{final}]$, is its *skeleton*. The skeleton of N basically uses the same net structure as N, but ignores the colours of tokens. Hence, $N' = [P, T, F, W', m_0', \text{final}']$ is the skeleton of N iff, for all $f \in F$, $W'(f) = \text{card}(W(f))$, and, for all p, $m_0'(p) = \sum_{c \in \text{COL}} m_0(p)(c)$. $\text{final}'(m)$ is true iff there exists an m^* such that, for all p, $m(p) = \sum_{c \in \text{COL}} m^*(p)(c)$, and $\text{final}(m^*)$ is true.

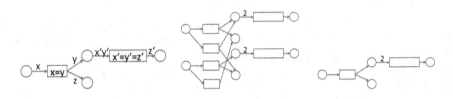

Fig. 4. A coloured net, its unfolding, and its skeleton

Figure 4 shows a coloured net, its unfolding (assuming that we have only two distinct colours), and its skeleton. Subsequently, we shall transform a given place/transition net N and a 2C-property ϕ into a coloured net N' and a reachability problem for N' such that N is the skeleton of N'. Hence it is worth to establish a few relations between the sequential and process semantics of a coloured net and its skeleton.

Proposition 1. *If* $[t_1, a_1] \ldots [t_n, a_n]$ *is a firing sequence in a coloured net* N, *then* $t_1 \ldots t_n$ *is a firing sequence in its skeleton. If* $[B, E, C, \lambda]$ *is a process of* N, *then* $[B, E, C, \lambda']$ *is a process of its unfolding where* $\lambda(e) = [t, a]$ *implies* $\lambda'(e) = t$ *and* $\lambda(b) = [p, c]$ *implies* $\lambda'(b) = p$, *for all events* e *and conditions* b.

This follows immediately from the construction of the skeleton. For a reverse correspondence, we introduce the concept of an *input-total* guard.

Definition 6 (input-total). *For a transition t of a coloured net N, its guard is* input-total *if for each assignment to* $\text{IN}(t)$ *there exists an assignment to* $\text{OUT}(t)$ *such that the resulting firing mode a satisfies* $G(t)$.

Proposition 2. *Assume that N is a coloured net where, for all t, $G(t)$ is input-total. Then*

(1) *for every firing sequence $t_1 \ldots t_n$ of the skeleton of N, there exist $a_1, \ldots, a_n$
    such that $[t_1, a_1] \ldots [t_n, a_n]$ is a firing sequence of N, and*
(2) *for every process $[B, E, C, \lambda]$ of the skeleton there is a process $[B, E, C, \lambda']$
    of N such that, for all events e and conditions b, and arbitrary places p,
    transitions t, firing modes a, and colours c, $\lambda'(e) = [t, a]$ implies $\lambda(e) = t$,
    and $\lambda'(b) = [p, c]$ implies $\lambda(b) = p$.*

This proposition can be proven by induction on the (partial) order of occurrences of places and transition. In each step, regardless of the colours of the
current marking or cut, the input-total guard yields at least one enabled firing
mode which defines the colours of produced tokens or post-conditions. That is,
a coloured Petri net and its skeleton have roughly (that is, up to colouring) the
same sequential and process semantics as long as the guards are input-total.

4   Building Blocks of Our Constructions

The basic idea of our constructions is to transform the given place/transition net
N into a coloured net N' with input-total guards such that N is the skeleton of
N'. We use the colours of N' for passing information about causality. Initially,
we start with a net having only black tokens in the initial marking. In N', every
arc f gets $W(f)$ variables. Hence, N is the skeleton of N'.
    We distinguish a causal cone and a causal throw/catch.

4.1   Causal Cone

In a process $[B, E, C, \lambda]$, a *causal cone* starting at a set of nodes X, is the set
$\{y \mid y \in B \cup E, \exists x \in X : [x, y] \in C^*\}$ of all conditions and events that causally
follow any node in X. We aim at making such a cone visible in the sequential
semantics of the coloured net N' by assigning a different colour to all tokens
that correspond to conditions in the cone. X, the starting point of the cone,
is the set of events that correspond to a set of transitions in N. We call these
transitions the *initiator* transitions of the cone. The initiators produce tokens in
another colour c (different from black). For taking care of transitive causality,
all transitions produce tokens in colour c as soon as they have at least one input
token of colour c. This way, every token that causally depends on an initiator
has colour c. Events causally depend on at least one initiator if they consume a
token of colour c.

Definition 7 (Causal cone construction). *Let N be a place/transition net
and N' a coloured net such that N is its skeleton (in particular, sharing the same
sets of places and transitions) and let all initial tokens in N' be black. Let X
be a set of transitions. Let $c \in \{\text{dark}, \text{white}\}$. Then the causal cone construction
with colour c for initiators X assigns guards to the transitions in N' as follows:*

- *for all $t \in X$, $g(t)$ is true in firing mode a if and only if, $a(\text{OUT}(t)) = \{c\}$;*
- *for all $t \notin X$, $g(t)$ is true in firing mode a if and only if either $a(\text{VAR}(t)) = \{\text{black}\}$, or $(c \in a(\text{IN}(t))$ and $a(\text{OUT}(t)) = \{c\})$.*

Figure 5 shows an example for the construction, assuming the presence of only two colours. As long as only black and c-coloured tokens flow in N', the construction is input-total. We can establish the following relations.

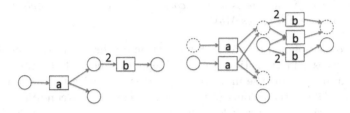

Fig. 5. Cone construction (right) in unfolded view for the net (left) with initiator a, assuming only two colors black (solid) and white (dashed).

Lemma 1. *Let π be a process and σ a sequence, both of N', such that $\pi \in$ PAR(σ) or $\sigma \in$ SEQ(π). Let e be an arbitrary event of π. Then there is some e_x with $\lambda(e_x) \in X$ and $e_x \to e$ if and only if the transition occurrence of e in σ consumes at least one token of colour c.*

Proof. Let π be a process of N' and consider the causal cone starting in the set $\lambda^{-1}(X)$ of events. Every event in the cone is an initiator, or has at least one input condition in the cone and all output conditions in the cone. By our construction, all conditions in the cone correspond to c-coloured tokens. Let $\sigma = t_1 \ldots t_n \in$ SEQ(π) and consider the transition occurrence t_i in σ that corresponds to event e. Let m be the marking with $m_0 \xrightarrow{t_1 \ldots t_{i-1}} m$. As $\sigma \in$ SEQ(π) and t_i is fired in m, there is a cut K in π that includes all input conditions of t_i and $m = \lambda(K)$. Hence, if e is in the causal cone of an initiator, m contains at least one c-coloured token and, if e is not in the causal cone of an initiator, m does not contain any c-coloured token.

Let σ be a sequence of N' and consider any process of N', $\pi \in$ PAR(σ). Consider an occurrence of some transition t in σ and the related event e_t in π. If the considered occurrence of t consumes a c-coloured token, our construction ensures that the unique event in the pre-set of c is either an initiator or an event that has again a c-coloured token in its pre-set. Continuing this argument along the reverse causality relation, we must arrive at an initiator, since the argument would otherwise end at a condition of MIN(N) which, however, does not contain c-coloured tokens. By construction of the guard condition, the producer of this token is either an initiator, or consumes a c-coloured token itself. Hence, there is a path in C from an initiator e_x to e_t proving $e_x \to e_t$. If t does not consume any c-coloured token, none of its predecessor events does. Hence, the complete backward cone starting from e_t cannot contain initiators proving that there is no initiator e_x with $e_x \to e_t$. $\square$

With Propositions 1 and 2, we may conclude:

Corollary 1. *Let X be a set of transitions.*

(1) If π is a process of N and e an event of π such that there exists an event e_x of π with $\lambda(e_x) \in X$ and $e_x \to e$, then there exists a firing sequence σ in N' that includes an occurrence of $\lambda(e)$ in a firing mode where it consumes at least one c-coloured token.

(2) If π is a process of N and e an event of π such that, for all events e_x of π with $\lambda(e_x) \in X$, we have not $e_x \to e$, then there exists a firing sequence σ in N' that includes an occurrence of $\lambda(e)$ in a firing mode where it consumes only black tokens.

(3) If σ is a firing sequence of N' and t a transition occurrence that consumes at least one c-coloured token, then there is a process π of N and events e_x and e in π such that $\lambda(e_x) \in X$, $\lambda(e) = t$, and $e_x \to e$.

(4) If σ is a firing sequence of N' and t a transition occurrence that consumes only black tokens, then there is a process π of N and events e_x and e in π such that $\lambda(e_x) \in X$, $\lambda(e) = t$, and not $e_x \to e$.

4.2   Causal Throw/Catch

In this construction, we use two distinguished transitions. We call them *thrower* and *catcher*, respectively. We want to see whether it is possible that every event related to the thrower causally precedes some event related to the catcher. To this end, the thrower issues a token of some colour c different from black. The catch transition consumes this token. Other transitions may consume the token but produce another token of colour c. If finally all c-tokens disappeared, all of them must have been eaten by a catcher. The paths of the c-coloured tokens mark the causality between thrower and catcher.

Definition 8 (Causal throw/catch construction). *Let N be a place/transition net and N' a coloured net such that N is its skeleton (in particular, sharing the same sets of places and transitions) and let all initial tokens in N' be black. Let X and Y be disjoint sets of transitions. Let $c \in \{\text{dark}, \text{white}\}$. Then the causal throw/catch construction with colour c for throwers X and catchers Y assigns guards to the transitions in N' as follows:*

- *for all $t \in X$, $g(t)$ is true in firing mode a if and only if, there is a $v^* \in \text{OUT}(t)$ with $a(v^*) = c$ and $a(\text{OUT}(t) \setminus \{v^*\}) = \{\text{black}\}$;*
- *for all $t \in Y$, $g(t)$ is true in firing mode a if and only if $a(\text{OUT}(t)) = \{\text{black}\}$;*
- *for all $t \notin X \cup Y$, $g(t)$ is true in firing mode a if and only if either $a(\text{VAR}(t)) = \{\text{black}\}$ or $(c \in a(\text{IN}(t))$, there is a $v^* \in \text{OUT}(t)$ with $a(v^*) = c$, and $a(\text{OUT}(t) \setminus \{v^*\}) = \{\text{black}\})$.*

The single output token of colour c is put nondeterministically on any post-place of t. Figure 6 shows an example of the throw/catch construction. With the causal throw/catch construction, we can capture the following relation between throwers and catcher.

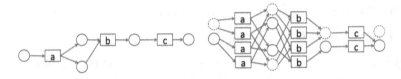

Fig. 6. Throw/catch construction (right) in unfolded view for the net (left) with thrower a and catcher c, assuming only two colors black (solid) and white (dashed).

Lemma 2. *The following statements are equivalent:*

(1) There is a process in $\mathrm{PAR}(N)$ *where, for every event* e_x *with* $\lambda(e_x) \in X$, *there is an event* e_y *with* $\lambda(e_y) \in Y$ *such that* $e_x \to e_y$.

(2) There exists a firing sequence in $\mathrm{SEQ}(N')$ *where, in the final marking, no tokens of colour* c *appear.*

Proof. Let π be a process as assumed in (1) and consider an arbitrary e_x with $\lambda(e_x) \in X$. Since there is an e_y with $e_x \to e_y$, there exists a path through π that starts at e_x and ends in e_y. Choosing such a path for every e_x with $\lambda(e_x) \in X$, yields a set Z of all nodes of π that occur on any of the chosen paths. Consider, among all possibilities to choose paths as described above, one where Z becomes minimal w.r.t. set inclusion. In this case, Z cannot contain any event e with more than one output condition since, if there is a path from e via condition b_1 to some e_y, any other path continuing through another condition b_2 would be redundant and contradict the assumed minimality of Z. Now every cut of π can be related to a marking such that conditions in Z correspond to c-coloured tokens while conditions in $B \setminus Z$ correspond to black tokens. Using this mapping, π can be transformed into firing sequence of N' that obeys the coloured firing rule defined in the causal throw/catch construction. Since the events e_y with $\lambda(e_y) \in Y$ are the maximal events in Z, the final marking contains only black tokens.

Let σ be a firing sequence as assumed in (2) and any process of N', $\pi \in \mathrm{PAR}(\sigma)$. Let e_x be an event with $\lambda(e_x) \in X$. Consider the path that starts in e_x, continues with the unique c-coloured token, then with the unique output event of the reached condition, and so forth. This path cannot end in a final condition as this contains only black tokens. So it ends in an e_y with $\lambda(e_y) \in Y$ since these are the only events without producing c-coloured tokens. The identified path proves $e_x \to e_y$. □

4.3 Interferences Between Several Cone and Throw/Catch Constructions

For some 2C-properties, we shall jointly apply two of the above constructions, for instance two cones or one cone and one throw/catch. In such cases, the two constructions may interfere, that is, one construction may require a token to have colour c_1 while the other construction requires it to have colour c_2. For this purpose, we use the remaining color light. Tokens of colour light are treated as if they carry both colours dark and white. This way, we can manage overlapping cones. As we believe that this idea is straight-forward, we skip the formal details. Instead, we just give an example of how the guard of an ordinary transition t (neither initiator, nor thrower, nor catcher) looks like if we apply a cone in dark and a throw/catch in white:

- if $IN(t) = \{black\}$ then $OUT(t) = \{black\}$, else
- if $\{dark, white\} \subseteq IN(t)$ or light $\in IN(t)$ then $OUT(t) \subseteq \{dark, light\}$ and $card(v \mid v \in OUT(t), a(v) = light\}) = 1$, else
- if dark $\in IN(t)$ then $OUT(t) = \{dark\}$, else
- (remaining case: white $\in IN(t)$) $OUT(t) \subseteq \{black, white\}$ and $card(v \mid v \in OUT(t), a(v) = white\}) = 1$,

Accordingly, the lemmas need to be rephrased such that every mentioning of c is replaced by "c or light". This way, all results established so far carry over to the joint application of two constructions.

4.4   All Occurrences Versus One Occurrence

Above, we have introduced transitions as initiators, throwers, and catchers of constructions. In a process, these transitions correspond to *all* events labeled with that transition. In some cases, we want to have a single event related to a transition t as initiator, thrower, or catcher. To this end, we split t into two parallel transitions (transitions with same pre- and post-set) t_1 and t_2 and modify their guards. The guard of t_1 is defined according to the requirements of being an initiator, thrower, or catcher, whatever applies, while the guard of t_2 is defined as for an ordinary transition. To make sure that t_1 fires only once, we insert an additional pre-place for t_1, initially carrying one token. Figure 7 illustrates the construction.

For every process of the resulting net, a process of the original net can be obtained by renaming t_1 and t_2 to t, and removing the condition related to the additional pre-place. The other way round, every process of the original net corresponds to a process of the resulting net by renaming all but one occurrence of t to t_2, and the remaining one to t_1 (with an additional condition to be inserted). Hence, this modification leaves the process semantics unchanged but restricts cone and throw/catch constructions to a single event related to the original transition t.

Using this construction, there will be firing sequences and processes where t_1 is not fired at all. This will be taken care of in the reachability property to be checked.

4.5   Reachability Queries

Given a net N and a 2C-property ϕ, we want to create a net N' using the constructions above, and a reachability problem ϕ'. ϕ' will either state that a

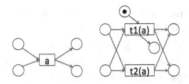

Fig. 7. Separating a single occurrence $t1$ of a (right) for the transition a (left)

marking with a certain property ψ is reachable (then we will formulate ϕ' as $EF\ \psi$) or that all reachable markings satisfy ψ (and we will formulate it as $AG\ \psi$), These notations accord to usual syntax of temporal logics. The latter property is in fact a reachability problem, too, as $AG\ \psi$ is equivalent to $\neg EF\ \neg\psi$.

In the state predicate ψ, we shall use the following properties as atomic propositions:

- the final predicate of the net N under investigation;
- a predicate formulated as $c = 0$, for some colour c; It is true of a marking m if there is no token of colour c on any place in m;
- a predicate formulated as fired(t); It is true if, in at least one firing sequence from m_0 to m, t has occurred.

The predicate fired(t) may have additional attributes such as "fired as initiator/thrower/catcher" or "fired with at least one input token of colour c". To capture such properties, we introduce one last construction. We split t into three parallel transitions t_1, t_2, and t_3. The guards of t_1 and t_2 are restricted to those firing modes that accord with the given attributes. The guard of t_3 is restricted to the firing modes where the given attribute is false. We add two fresh places p_1 and p_2. p_1 is initially marked and gets an arc to t_1. p_2 is initially unmarked and gets an arc from t_1, and arc from t_2, and an arc to t_2. All added arcs get multiplicity 1. This way, the occurrences of t in the original net are distributed over the new transitions as follows:

- Every occurrence of t in a mode not satisfying the attribute of the fired predicate is represented by t_3;
- The first occurrence of t in a mode satisfying the attribute is represented by t_1;
- Every other occurrence of t in a mode satisfying the attribute is represented by t_2.

Figure 8 illustrates the construction. It is easy to see that t has occurred in the original firing sequence in a mode satisfying the attribute if and only if p_2 is marked. This way, a model checker can recognise a fired predicate by just inspecting the reached marking.

5   Verifying Causality

At this point, we can get through the list of individual 2C-properties. We start with the properties related to causality.

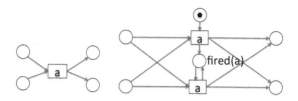

Fig. 8. Transforming transition a (left) such that "a has fired" is replaced by "fired(a) is marked".

5.1 $\exists \pi\ \exists e_x\ \exists e_y : e_x \to e_y$

Throughout the list of 2C-properties, we shall use the notation in the heading as a shorthand for (given net N and distinct transitions x and y):

$$\exists \pi \in \mathrm{PAR}(N)\ \exists e_x \in \lambda^{-1}(x)\ \exists e_y \in \lambda^{-1}(y) : e_x \to e_y.$$

Construction: Apply a causal cone in colour white initiated by (the whole) transition x.

Check: EF (final $\wedge$ fired(y with at least one white input token)).

Theorem 1. *N satisfies* $\exists \pi\ \exists e_x\ \exists e_y : e_x \to e_y$ *if and only if the net N' obtained through the mentioned construction satisfies the stated reachability property.*

Proof. Apply Items (1) and (3) of Corollary 1 with $X = \{x\}$.   □

5.2 $\exists \pi\ \exists e_x\ \forall e_y : e_x \to e_y$

Construction: Apply a causal cone in colour white initiated by a single occurrence t_1 of transition x.

Check: EF (final $\wedge$ fired(t_1) $\wedge \neg$ fired(y without white input token)).

Theorem 2. *N satisfies* $\exists \pi\ \exists e_x\ \forall e_y : e_x \to e_y$ *if and only if the net N' obtained through the mentioned construction satisfies the stated reachability property.*

Proof. Apply Items (2) and (4) of Corollary 1 with $X = \{t_1\}$.   □

Note that x must indeed have occurred once as initiator unless y has not occurred at all. Without occurrence as initiator, no white tokens would be in the system.

5.3 $\exists \pi\ \forall e_x\ \exists e_y : e_x \to e_y$

Construction: Apply a causal throw/catch in colour white with (all occurrences of) x as thrower and (all occurrences of) y as catcher.

Check: EF (final $\wedge$ card(white) $= 0$).

Theorem 3. *N satisfies* $\exists \pi\ \forall e_x\ \exists e_y : e_x \to e_y$ *if and only if the net N' obtained through the mentioned construction satisfies the stated reachability property.*

Proof. This is an immediate consequence of Lemma 2.   □

5.4 $\forall \pi \; \exists e_x \; \exists e_y : e_x \rightarrow e_y$

Construction: Apply a causal cone in colour white with (all occurrences of) x as initiator.

   Check: AG (final $\implies$ fired(y with white input token)).

Theorem 4. *N satisfies* $\forall \pi \; \exists e_x \; \exists e_y : e_x \rightarrow e_y$ *if and only if the net N' obtained through the mentioned construction satisfies the stated reachability property.*

Proof. Apply Items (1) and (3) of Corollary 1. $\square$

5.5 $\forall \pi \; \forall e_x \; \exists e_y : e_x \rightarrow e_y$

Construction: Apply a causal cone in colour white with a single occurrence t_1 of x as initiator.

   Check: AG (final $\land$ fired(t_1) $\implies$ fired(y with white input token)).

Theorem 5. *N satisfies* $\forall \pi \; \forall e_x \; \exists e_y : e_x \rightarrow e_y$ *if and only if the net N' obtained through the mentioned construction satisfies the stated reachability property.*

Proof. Apply Items (1) and (3) of Corollary 1. $\square$

5.6 $\forall \pi \; \forall e_x \; \forall e_y : e_x \rightarrow e_y$

Construction: Apply a causal cone in colour white with a single occurrence t_1 of x as initiator.

   Check: AG (final $\land$ fired(t_1) $\implies$ $\neg$ fired(y without white input token)).

Theorem 6. *N satisfies* $\forall \pi \; \forall e_x \; \forall e_y : e_x \rightarrow e_y$ *if and only if the net N' obtained through the mentioned construction satisfies the stated reachability property.*

Proof. Apply Items (2) and (4) of Corollary 1. $\square$

Remark. There is an alternative approach to this property proposed in [14].

6   Verifying Concurrency

For checking concurrent occurrence of two events, one may be tempted to operate with merging transitions x and y to a single (synchronised) transition. However, this idea seems not to work very well for two reasons. First, it assumes a one-to-one relation between x-events and y-events that is not required in the properties. Second, we cannot conclude very much from the fact that a synchronised transition did *not* fire. Hence, we shall tackle concurrency mainly as absence of causality.

6.1 $\exists \pi \, \exists e_x \, \exists e_y : e_x \parallel e_y$

Construction: Apply a causal cone in colour white with a single occurrence t_1 of x as initiator and a causal cone in colour dark with a single occurrence t_1' of y as initiator.

   Check: EF (final $\wedge$ fired(t_1 with only black tokens) $\wedge$ fired(t_1' with only black tokens)).

Theorem 7. *N satisfies $\exists \pi \, \exists e_x \, \exists e_y : e_x \parallel e_y$ if and only if the net N' obtained through the mentioned construction satisfies the stated reachability property.*

Proof. By Items (1) and (3) of Corollary 1, together with the considerations in Subsect. 4.3, we obtain $\neg e_x \rightarrow e_y$ and $\neg e_y \rightarrow e_x$, for the unique events e_x and e_y with $\lambda(e_x) = t_1$ and $\lambda(e_y) = t_1'$.   □

Remark. This is the only property where inserting a synchronised transition would actually help [14]. It would even be a simpler construction. We have included our cone-based solution just to stay in the systematics of our constructions.

6.2 $\exists \pi \, \exists e_x \, \forall e_y : e_x \parallel e_y$

Construction: Apply a causal cone in colour white with a single occurrence t_1 of x as initiator and a causal cone in colour dark with (all occurrences of) y as initiator.

   Check: EF (final $\wedge$ fired(t_1 with only black tokens) $\wedge \neg$ fired(y with any white or light token)).

Theorem 8. *N satisfies $\exists \pi \, \exists e_x \, \forall e_y : e_x \parallel e_y$ if and only if the net N' obtained through the mentioned construction satisfies the stated reachability property.*

Proof. By Corollary 1, together with the considerations in Subsect. 4.3, we obtain $\neg e_x \rightarrow e_y$ and $\neg e_y \rightarrow e_x$, for the unique event e_x with $\lambda(e_x) = t_1$ and any event e_y with $\lambda(e_y) = y$.   □

6.3 $\exists \pi \, \forall e_x \, \forall e_y : e_x \parallel e_y$

Construction: Apply a causal cone in colour white with (all occurrences of) x as initiator and a causal cone in colour dark with (all occurrences of) y as initiator.

   Check: EF (final $\wedge \neg$ fired(x with any dark or light token) $\wedge$ $\neg$ fired(y with any white or light token)).

Theorem 9. *N satisfies $\exists \pi \, \forall e_x \, \forall e_y : e_x \parallel e_y$ if and only if the net N' obtained through the mentioned construction satisfies the stated reachability property.*

Proof. By Corollary 1, together with the considerations in Subsect. 4.3, we obtain $\neg e_x \rightarrow e_y$ and $\neg e_y \rightarrow e_x$, for any event e_x with $\lambda(e_x) = t_1$ and any event e_y with $\lambda(e_y) = y$.   □

6.4 $\forall \pi \; \forall e_x \; \forall e_y : e_x \parallel e_y$

This property is equivalent to

$$\neg \exists \pi \; \exists e_x \; \exists e_y : e_x \to e_y \land \neg \exists \pi \; \exists e_x \; \exists e_y : e_y \to e_y.$$

These two properties can be checked separately using cone constructions.

6.5 $\forall \pi \; \forall e_x \; \exists e_y : e_x \parallel e_y$

Construction: Apply a causal cone in colour white with a single occurrence t_1 of x as initiator and a causal throw/catch in colour dark with (all occurrences of) y that consume only black or dark tokens as throwers and t_1 as catcher.
   Check: $\neg EF$ (final $\land$ fired(t_1) $\land$ card(dark) + card(light) = 0).

Theorem 10. *N satisfies* $\forall \pi \; \forall e_x \; \exists e_y : e_x \parallel e_y$ *if and only if the net* N' *obtained through the mentioned construction satisfies the stated reachability property.*

Proof. The investigated property is false if and only if $\exists \pi \; \exists e_x \; \forall e_y : (e_x \to e_y \lor e_y \to e_x)$. Fix e_x as the occurrence of t_1. Then, by Corollary 1, the events e_y with $e_x \to e_y$ are precisely those where y consumes a white or light token. For the remaining y-events, the throw/catch construction and Lemma 2 assert $e_y \to e_x$. Hence, the investigated property is false if and only if

$$EF \text{ (final} \land \text{fired}(t_1) \land \text{card(dark)} + \text{card(light)} = 0)$$

holds.   □

6.6 $\forall \pi \; \exists e_x \; \forall e_y : e_x \parallel e_y$

Construction: Apply a causal cone in colour dark with (all occurrences of) y as initiator and a causal throw/catch in colour white with (all occurrences of) x that consume only black or white tokens as throwers and (all occurrences of) y as catcher.
   Check: $\neg EF$ (final $\land$ card(white) + card(light) = 0).

Theorem 11. *N satisfies* $\forall \pi \; \exists e_x \; \forall e_y : e_x \parallel e_y$ *if and only if the net* N' *obtained through the mentioned construction satisfies the stated reachability property.*

Proof. The investigated property is false if and only if $\exists \pi \; \forall e_x \; \exists e_y : (e_x \to e_y \lor e_y \to e_x)$. By Corollary 1, the events e_x with $\lambda(e_x) = x$ and $e_y \to e_y$, for some e_y with $\lambda(e_y) = y$ are precisely those where x consumes a dark or light token. For the remaining x-events, the throw/catch construction and Lemma 2 assert $e_x \to e_y$, for some e_y with $\lambda(e_y) = y$. Hence, the investigated property is false if and only if

$$EF \text{ (final} \land \text{card(white)} + \text{card(light)} = 0)$$

holds.   □

7 Verifying Reverse Causality

The cases $\exists \pi \, \exists e_x \, \exists e_y : e_y \to e_x$, $\forall \pi \, \exists e_x \, \exists e_y : e_y \to e_x$, and $\forall \pi \, \forall e_x \, \forall e_y : e_y \to e_x$ can be traced back to the corresponding (forward) causality problems by just swapping x and y. For the remaining cases, x and y cannot be easily swapped as either the corresponding case has not been solved, or the quantifiers for e_x and e_y are different and thus the swapped version is not equivalent.

7.1 $\exists \pi \, \exists e_x \, \forall e_y : e_y \to e_x$

Construction: Apply a causal throw/catch in colour white with (all occurrences of) y as thrower and a single occurrence t_1 of x as catcher.

Check: EF (final $\land$ card(white) $= 0$).

Theorem 12. *N satisfies* $\exists \pi \, \exists e_x \, \forall e_y : e_y \to e_x$ *if and only if the net N' obtained through the mentioned construction satisfies the stated reachability property.*

Proof. Let the event e_x assumed to exist be the one corresponding to t_1 and apply Lemma 2. □

7.2 $\exists \pi \, \forall e_x \, \exists e_y : e_y \to e_x$

Construction: Apply a causal cone in colour white with (all occurrences of) y as initiator.

Check: EF (final $\land \neg$ fired(x with only black input tokens)).

Theorem 13. *N satisfies* $\exists \pi \, \forall e_x \, \exists e_y : e_y \to e_x$ *if and only if the net N' obtained through the mentioned construction satisfies the stated reachability property.*

Proof. Apply Items (1) and (3) of Corollary 1. □

7.3 $\forall \pi \, \forall e_x \, \exists e_y : e_y \to e_x$

Construction: Apply a causal cone in colour white with (all occurrences of) y as initiator.

Check: AG (final $\implies \neg$ fired(x with only black input tokens)).

Theorem 14. *N satisfies* $\forall \pi \, \forall e_x \, \exists e_y : e_y \to e_x$ *if and only if the net N' obtained through the mentioned construction satisfies the stated reachability property.*

Proof. Apply Items (1) and (3) of Corollary 1. □

8   Discussion

8.1   Summary and Unsolved Cases

Table 1 gives an overview on the achieved results. A plus sign means that we have a solution for the property, the minus sign means that we could not find a solution using causal cones and/or throw catch constructions. In all of the open cases, we have the impression that, based on the idea of passing information between x-events and y-events, a limited number of colours may not be sufficient.

Table 1. Results for the 2C-spectrum.

		$e_x \rightarrow e_y$		$e_x \parallel e_y$		$e_y \rightarrow e_x$	
		$\exists e_y$	$\forall e_y$	$\exists e_y$	$\forall e_y$	$\exists e_y$	$\forall e_y$
$\exists \pi$	$\exists e_x$	+	+	+	+	+	+
	$\forall e_x$	+	−	−	+	+	−
$\forall \pi$	$\exists e_x$	+	−	−	+	+	−
	$\forall e_x$	+	+	+	+	+	+

Consider, for example, the open property $\exists \pi \forall e_x \forall e_y : e_x \rightarrow e_y$. We have to make sure that every e_y is in the causal cone of every e_x. This appears to require different colours for every occurrence of x. Since the number of occurrences of x is not limited, and reachability for coloured nets with infinitely many colours may be undecidable even if the skeleton is bounded, this idea is not effective. At this point, it would be too early to state that the open cases cannot be handled by interleaving-based model checkers at all. It could well be that there is another idea for a construction, different from cone and throw/catch.

The unsolved cases have in common that π and e_x have different quantifiers. This quantifier alternation seems to complicate the experiments we have implemented in our constructions. There are, of course, solved cases where π and e_x have different quantifiers, too. In these cases, however, the information to be passed between x and y could be coarsened such that knowledge about the individual events e_x could be omitted.

8.2   Complexity

Our constructions transformed a place/transition net N into a coloured net N' with same skeleton, but up to four colours. Most available tools would verify a coloured net by unfolding it back to a place/transition net N^* that is larger than N. The number of places of N^* is two or four times the number of places of N. For every transition t of N, N^* would contain as many transitions as it has firing modes with satisfied guard. In worst case, this is 4^k where k is the number of variables in the vicinity of t in N', that is, the sum of all multiplicities of arcs from and to t. Observing a few regularities concerning the occurrence of multiple variables at a single arc, this number can be reduced but remains exponential in the number of arcs from and to t.

However, the growth of N^* only depends on the in/out degree of transitions and not on the overall number of transitions. For instance, if p_n is the size of an n philosophers net, and p'_n is the size of the resulting net to be verified, there is a linear factor c with $p'_n \leq c \cdot p_n$, for all n, since the in/out degree of nodes in the philosophers nets do not depend on n. That is, for nets with limited in/out degree of transitions, our constructions do not explode.

8.3 Conclusion

We studied problems related to causality and concurrency of events related to pairs of net transitions. Reducing them to plain reachability problems, we made interleaving based model checkers applicable for verifying these properties. This way, existing applications, e.g. in the world of business processes, get substantial tool support. Obviously, future work includes work on the unsolved cases. Additionally, we believe that complexity can be reduced if additional assumptions (e.g. restrictions of the covered class of nets) apply. Finally, there are patterns in the distribution of solved and unsolved cases as well as the use of the basic constructions. Their investigation might yield new insights into the nature of concurrency and causality as such.

References

1. Best, E., Devillers, R.: Sequential and concurrent behaviour in Petri net theory. Theoret. Comput. Sci. **55**(1), 87–136 (1987)
2. Best, E., Fernandez, C.: Nonsequential Processes: A Petri Net View. EATCS Monographs on Theoretical Computer Science. Springer, Heidelberg (1988)
3. Brauer, W., Reisig, W.: Carl adam Petri and "Petri nets". Fundam. Concepts Comput. Sci. **3**, 129–139 (2009)
4. Esparza, J., Heljanko, K.: Unfoldings - A Partial-Order Approach to Model Checking. EATCS Monographs in Theoretical Computer Science. Springer, Heidelberg (2008)
5. Goltz, U., Reisig, W.: The non-sequential behaviour of Petri nets. Inf. Control **57**(2/3), 125–147 (1983)
6. Grahlmann, B.: The PEP tool. In: Grumberg, O. (ed.) CAV 1997. LNCS, vol. 1254, pp. 440–443. Springer, Heidelberg (1997). doi:10.1007/3-540-63166-6_43
7. Heiner, M., Rohr, C., Schwarick, M., Tovchigrechko, A.A.: MARCIE's secrets of efficient model checking. In: Koutny, M., Desel, J., Kleijn, J. (eds.) Transactions on Petri Nets and Other Models of Concurrency XI. LNCS, vol. 9930, pp. 286–296. Springer, Heidelberg (2016). doi:10.1007/978-3-662-53401-4_14
8. Jensen, J.F., Nielsen, T., Oestergaard, L.K., Srba, J.: TAPAAL and reachability analysis of P/T nets. In: Koutny, M., Desel, J., Kleijn, J. (eds.) Transactions on Petri Nets and Other Models of Concurrency XI. LNCS, vol. 9930, pp. 307–318. Springer, Heidelberg (2016). doi:10.1007/978-3-662-53401-4_16

9. Jensen, K.: Coloured Petri Nets - Basic Concepts, Analysis Methods and Practical Use - EATCS Monographs in Theoretical Computer Science, vol. 1, 2nd edn. Springer, Heidelberg (1996)
10. Khomenko, V.: PUNF–Petri net unfolder. http://homepages.cs.ncl.ac.uk/victor.khomenko/tools/
11. McMillan, K.L.: A technique of state space search based on unfolding. Formal Methods Syst. Des. 6(1), 45–65 (1995)
12. Nielsens, M., Plotkin, G.D., Winskel, G.: Petri nets, event structures and domains. Theoret. Comput. Sci. 13(1), 85–108 (1981)
13. Petri, C.A.: Kommunikation mit Automaten. Dissertation, Schriften des IIM 2, Rheinisch-Westfälisches Institut für Instrumentelle Mathematik an der Universität Bonn, Bonn (1962)
14. Polyvyanyy, A., Weidlich, M., Conforti, R., Rosa, M., Hofstede, A.H.M.: The 4C spectrum of fundamental behavioral relations for concurrent systems. In: Ciardo, G., Kindler, E. (eds.) PETRI NETS 2014. LNCS, vol. 8489, pp. 210–232. Springer, Cham (2014). doi:10.1007/978-3-319-07734-5_12
15. Schwoon, S.: Mole–a Petri net unfolder. http://www.lsv.ens-cachan.fr/~schwoon/tools/mole/
16. Hofstede, A.H.M., Ouyang, C., Rosa, M., Song, L., Wang, J., Polyvyanyy, A.: APQL: a process-model query language. In: Song, M., Wynn, M.T., Liu, J. (eds.) AP-BPM 2013. LNBIP, vol. 159, pp. 23–38. Springer, Cham (2013). doi:10.1007/978-3-319-02922-1_2
17. Thierry-Mieg, Y.: Symbolic model-checking using ITS-tools. In: Baier, C., Tinelli, C. (eds.) TACAS 2015. LNCS, vol. 9035, pp. 231–237. Springer, Heidelberg (2015). doi:10.1007/978-3-662-46681-0_20
18. M. Weidlich. Behavioural profiles: a relational approach to behaviour consistency. Ph.D. thesis, University of Potsdam (2011)
19. Wimmel, H., Wolf, K.: Applying CEGAR to the Petri net state equation. In: Abdulla, P.A., Leino, K.R.M. (eds.) TACAS 2011. LNCS, vol. 6605, pp. 224–238. Springer, Heidelberg (2011). doi:10.1007/978-3-642-19835-9_19
20. Wolf, K.: Generating Petri net state spaces. In: Kleijn, J., Yakovlev, A. (eds.) ICATPN 2007. LNCS, vol. 4546, pp. 29–42. Springer, Heidelberg (2007). doi:10.1007/978-3-540-73094-1_5

Liveness and Opacity

Weak Observable Liveness and Infinite Games on Finite Graphs

Luca Bernardinello, Görkem Kılınç$^{(\boxtimes)}$, and Lucia Pomello

Dipartimento di Informatica, Sistemistica e Comunicazione,
Università degli Studi di Milano-Bicocca, Milan, Italy
`gorkem.kilinc@disco.unimib.it`

Abstract. The notion of observable liveness was introduced in the literature for 1-safe Petri net systems in which transitions are either observable or unobservable by a user and, among the observable ones, some are controllable, in the sense that they correspond to interactions with the user and cannot autonomously occur. An observable transition is observably live if a user can, from any reachable marking, force it to occur infinitely often by using controllable transitions. Here, we introduce a weaker version of this notion by considering the capability of the user, by means of controllable transitions, to force the considered observable transition to fire infinitely often, starting from the initial marking instead of considering each reachable marking. The main result of this paper is a method for checking weak observable liveness in state machine decomposable 1-safe nets whose transitions are observable. The introduced method is based on infinite games that are played on finite graphs. We transform the problem of weak observable liveness into a game between a system and a user, and we prove that a transition is weakly observably live if and only if the user has a winning strategy for the game.

1 Introduction

Observable liveness, introduced in [5] and further studied in [6,11], expresses serviceability of a partially observable and partially controllable distributed system. An example of such a serviceable system could be a server with some hidden actions and interacting with a user via observable and controllable actions. The user expects to get some services modeled by observable actions by choosing and performing the "right" controllable actions. Observable liveness guarantees that the user can always force the server to provide the requested service.

In this paper, we consider Petri nets with transitions that can be observable or unobservable (silent), and can be controllable or not. These nets are inspired by Petri net applications in control theory [4,8,15].

Observable liveness considers that a user can decide at any reachable marking to fire an observable transition t infinitely often in the future, thus we have to consider the possibility of forcing the system to fire t from each reachable marking. However, it can be the case that the user knows at the beginning that he/she wants to fire t infinitely often. So, given a net N and $t \in O$, the user

© Springer International Publishing AG 2017
W. van der Aalst and E. Best (Eds.): PETRI NETS 2017, LNCS 10258, pp. 181–199, 2017.
DOI: 10.1007/978-3-319-57861-3_12

decides to fire t at the initial marking, and whenever the user can make a choice he/she makes the right choice in order to eventually fire t infinitely often. Thus, with this assumption, we do not have to consider each reachable marking as we do for deciding observable liveness of t. In Sect. 3, we formally introduce *weak observable liveness* which relaxes observable liveness following the above idea.

Section 4 discusses a game theoretic method for checking weak observable liveness for 1-safe nets that are decomposable into sequential components. We consider the case in which all the transitions are observable and all the controllable transitions are in one sequential component. With these restrictions, we can transform the problem of checking if a transition is weakly observably live into an infinite game that is played on a finite graph with two players. This kind of games is described in [7,13,18]. A particular class of games is *Streett game* which is based on the *Streett acceptance condition* defined in [16]. We define a construction of a Streett game between a user and a system in order to check weak observable liveness of a transition. We prove that a given transition is weakly observably live in a given net if and only if the user has a winning strategy for the game that is constructed on the basis of the net and the transition.

2 Preliminary Definitions and Notations

A *net* is a triple (P, T, F) consisting of a set P of *places*, graphically represented as circles, a set T of *transitions*, graphically represented as boxes, with $P \neq \emptyset$, $T \neq \emptyset$, $P \cap T = \emptyset$, and $F \subseteq (P \times T) \cup (T \times P)$, such that $dom(F) \cup cod(F) = P \cup T$, the *flow relation*, represented by arcs connecting the related elements. For $x \in P \cup T$, ${}^\bullet x = \{y \in P \cup T | (y, x) \in F\}$ and $x^\bullet = \{y \in P \cup T | (x, y) \in F\}$ are the *preset* and the *postset* of x, respectively. For $X \subseteq P \cup T$, ${}^\bullet X = \bigcup_{x \in X} {}^\bullet x$ and $X^\bullet = \bigcup_{x \in X} x^\bullet$. A net is *finite* if the sets of places and of transitions are finite. A net is *pure* if there are no self-loops, i.e., if for any $t \in T$, ${}^\bullet t \cap t^\bullet = \emptyset$. A net is *simple* if for $x, y \in P \cup T$, whenever ${}^\bullet x = {}^\bullet y$ and $x^\bullet = y^\bullet$ then $x = y$. A net (P, T, F) is a *state machine* if for any $t \in T$, $|{}^\bullet t| = |t^\bullet| = 1$. A net (P, T, F) is *state machine decomposable* (SMD, for short) if there exists $k \geq 1$ such that $P = P_1 \cup \cdots \cup P_k$, where the sets $P_1, \ldots, P_k$ are not necessarily disjoint, and such that the subnets generated by P_i, i.e.: the nets $N_i = (P_i, T_i, F_i)$, where $T_i = {}^\bullet P_i \cup P_i^\bullet$ and $F_i = F|_{(P_i \times T_i) \cup (T_i \times P_i)}$ are state machines, $1 \leq i \leq k$.

A *marking* is a map $m : P \to \mathbb{N}$. A marking m is safe if $m(p) \in \{0, 1\}$ for all $p \in P$. Markings represent global states.

An (ordinary) Petri net $N = (P, T, F, m_0)$ is defined by a net (P, T, F), and an initial marking $m_0 : P \to \mathbb{N}$.

A transition t is *enabled* at a marking m, denoted $m[t\rangle$, if for each $p \in {}^\bullet t$, $m(p) > 0$. A transition t enabled at a marking m can *fire*, producing a new marking m', denoted $m[t\rangle m'$ where m' is defined as follows:

$$m'(p) = \begin{cases} m(p) - 1 & \text{for all } p \in {}^\bullet t \setminus t^\bullet \\ m(p) + 1 & \text{for all } p \in t^\bullet \setminus {}^\bullet t \\ m(p) & \text{in all other cases} \end{cases}$$

If $m_1[t_1\rangle m_2[t_2\rangle m_3[t_3\rangle m_4\cdots$, then $\tau = t_1\, t_2\, t_3\, t_4 \ldots$ is called *transition sequence*, enabled at the marking m_1. If a transition sequence τ is finite, i.e., $\tau = t_1 \ldots t_n$, then we write $m_1[\tau\rangle m_{n+1}$ and call m_{n+1} *reachable* from m_1. This includes the case $n = 0$, i.e., each marking is reachable from itself.

A *maximal transition sequence* is either infinite or it reaches a marking which does not enable any transition.

The set of markings reachable from m will be denoted by $[m\rangle$. The set of *reachable markings of the Petri net N* is the set of markings reachable from its initial marking m_0. If all the markings reachable from m_0 are safe, then $N = (P, T, F, m_0)$ is said to be *1-safe* (or, shortly, safe). N is *1-live* iff $\forall t \in T$ $\exists m \in [m_0\rangle$ such that $m[t\rangle$. A Petri net is *live* if, for each reachable marking m and each transition t, there exists a marking m' reachable from m that enables t. Equivalently, it is live if and only if, for each transition t and each finite transition sequence τ enabled at the initial marking m_0, there exists a transition sequence τ' containing an occurrence of t such that $\tau\tau'$ is a transition sequence enabled at m_0. Notice that in order to append two sequences, the left hand one is supposed to be finite; when writing $\tau\tau'$ we implicitly express that τ is finite.

Two transitions t_1 and t_2 of a Petri net are in *structural conflict* if they share an input place, i.e., if ${}^\bullet t_1 \cap {}^\bullet t_2 \neq \emptyset$. t_1 and t_2 are in *behavioral conflict* for a given marking $m \in [m_0\rangle$, if they are both enabled at marking m and the firing of one disables the other. In other words, t_1 and t_2 are in behavioral conflict if they are in structural conflict and $\exists m \in [m_0\rangle$ such that $m[t_1\rangle$ and $m[t_2\rangle$.

The non sequential behaviour of a system net is modelled by labelled causal nets, which record the partial order of the event occurrences together with all conditions (local states) involved in these events. A *causal net* $N' = (B, E, F')$ is a possibly infinite net such that: for any $b \in B$, $|{}^\bullet b| \leq 1$ and $|b^\bullet| \leq 1$, F'^* (the reflexive and transitive closure of F') is acyclic, and such that isolated B-elements are allowed. To a causal net $N' = (B, E, F')$ a partial order $(X = B \cup E, F'^+)$ can be associated, where F'^+ is the transitive closure of F'. A set of elements of a causal net $Y \subseteq X$ is a *coset* iff for any pair $x, y \in Y$, $(x, y) \notin F'^+$ and $(y, x) \notin F'^+$. A maximal coset is called *cut* and, if it contains only B-elements, it is called *B-cut*. In the following, we consider finite systems modelled by 1-safe finite Petri nets. Let $N = (P, T, F, m_0)$ be a 1-safe finite Petri net, a *non-sequential process* (shortly *process*) of N is a pair (N', ϕ), where $N' = (B, E, F')$ is a causal net and ϕ is a map: $B \cup E \to P \cup T$ such that it satisfies the following conditions:

(1) $\phi(B) \subseteq P$, $\phi(E) \subseteq T$
(2) $\forall x_1, x_2 \in B \cup E :$ $\phi(x_1) = \phi(x_2) \Rightarrow (x_1 F'^+ x_2)$ or $(x_2 F'^+ x_1)$
(3) $\forall e \in E :$ $\phi({}^\bullet e) = {}^\bullet\phi(e)$ and $\phi(e^\bullet) = \phi(e)^\bullet$
(4) $\phi(Min(N')) = m_0$,

where $Min(N') = \{x \in B \cup E \mid \nexists y : (y, x) \in F'\}$.

Any B-cut of a process corresponds to a reachable marking, i.e.: if (N', ϕ) is a process of $N = (P, T, F, m_0)$ and Y is a B-cut of N', then $\phi(Y) = m \in [m_0\rangle$.

For the class of 1-safe finite Petri nets, any transition sequence τ of N uniquely determines a process (N', ϕ) such that τ is a possible sequential execution of it; on the other way round, to a process (N', ϕ) of N it is possible to associate a non empty set of transition sequences of N which correspond to possible sequential executions of the process itself [1].

3   Weak Observable Liveness

We consider Petri net models in which users can interact with a system through an interface. Some transitions are observable by the users whereas others are hidden internal actions of the system. Among the observable transitions, some are controllable by the users. Controllable transitions are drawn as black squares, observable transitions as thick squares and unobservable ones as thin squares.

Intuitively, a transition is *weakly observably live* (WOL) if it can be forced to eventually fire infinitely often by choosing and performing the right controllable actions on the basis of the observed behavior.

Let $N = (P, T, F, m_0)$ be a 1-safe Petri net, such that $O \subseteq T$ is the set of observable transitions and $C \subseteq O$ is the set of controllable transitions. The strategy of a user in order to force t to eventually occur infinitely often is formalized by a *response function*, $\varphi : O^* \to 2^C$. Based on the observed actions, the response function gives a subset of controllable transitions.

Let τ be a transition sequence; $\overline{\tau}$ is the projection of τ on O; $\underline{\tau}$ is the projection on C.

Definition 1. *Let* $\tau = t_0 t_1 \ldots t_i \ldots$ *be an infinite sequence of transitions, enabled at* m_0, *with* $m_0[t_0\rangle m_1[t_1\rangle \ldots m_i[t_i\rangle \ldots$. *Let* t' *be a transition.*

We say that t' *is* finally postponed *in* τ *if, from some point on, it is always enabled, but never fires:*

$$\exists j \geq 0 : \forall k \geq j : m_k[t'\rangle \text{ and } t_k \neq t'.$$

Let $\tau_k = t_0 t_1 \ldots t_k$ *be the finite prefix of* τ *of length* $k + 1$.
We say that $c \in C$ *is* finally eligible *in* τ *if*

$$\exists j \geq 0 : \forall k \geq j : c \in \varphi(\overline{\tau_k}).$$

Definition 2. *Let* $t \in T$ *and let* τ *be an infinite transition sequence enabled at* m_0. τ *is* weakly fair *with respect to* t *iff* t *is not finally postponed in* τ.
A finite transition sequence is weakly fair with respect to any transition.

Definition 3. *A transition sequence* τ *is* consistent with *a response function* φ *if it satisfies the three following clauses:*

1. τ *is weakly fair with respect to* $T \setminus C$,
2. *for each prefix* $\tau_k t$ *of* τ, *if* $t \in C$, *then* $t \in \varphi(\overline{\tau_k})$,
3. *if* $\underline{\tau}$ *is finite, then no controllable* t *is both finally postponed and finally eligible in* τ.

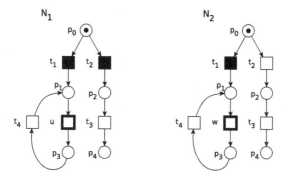

Fig. 1. u is WOL, whereas w is not WOL.

Definition 4. *An observable transition $t \in O$, called* target, *is weakly observably live (*WOL *for short) iff there exists a response function φ such that in each maximal transition sequence that is consistent with φ, t occurs infinitely often. If φ is such a function, we say that t is* WOL *by φ.*

Example 1. In Fig. 1, transition u in N_1 is WOL. Let ϵ be the empty transition sequence. Consider a response function φ such that $\varphi(\epsilon) = \{t_1\}$; in each maximal transition sequence that is consistent with it u occurs infinitely often. In fact, in this example there is only one such sequence: $t_1(ut_4)^\omega$. However, u is not observably live since there is a reachable marking, e.g. $\{p_2\}$, from which the user has no way to force the occurrence of u. The difference between observable liveness and WOL is based on the fact that, deciding the target transition at the beginning, the user can avoid to reach such marking. In N_2, t_2 is neither controllable nor observable. Here, t_2t_3 is a maximal transition sequence consistent with any response function; hence w is not WOL.

4 Checking Weak Observable Liveness

In this section, we describe an application of infinite games on finite graphs for checking weak observable liveness. The method only applies to a restricted class of Petri nets (described in Sect. 4.2) which is closer to the setting of two-players infinite games.

4.1 Infinite Games on Finite Graphs

Infinite games on finite graphs [7,13,18] are based on finite ω-automata [2,3,14,17]. There are several types of ω-automata with different acceptance conditions. Here we use Streett games based on the Streett acceptance condition [16]. The following definitions are adapted from [7].

A game consists of an *arena* and a *winning set* which is determined by the winning condition.

Definition 5. *An* arena *is a triple* $A = (V_0, V_1, E)$, *where* $V_0 \cap V_1 = \emptyset$. *Elements of* V_0 *are called* 0-vertices *and elements of* V_1 *are called* 1-vertices. $V = V_0 \cup V_1$. *Edges represent possible moves: such that* $E \subseteq V \times V$. *The set of successors of* $v \in V$ *is defined by* $E(v) = \{v' \in V : (v, v') \in E\}$.

In general, an arena can be infinite. In this paper, we consider infinite games that are played by two players on a finite arena. We will refer to the two players as *Player* 0 and *Player* 1. The set of vertices V_0 and V_1 belong to Player 0 and Player 1, respectively.

Definition 6. *A* play *on arena* A *is a maximal sequence of vertices of the arena which is either an infinite path* $\sigma = v_0 v_1 v_2 ... \in V^\omega$ *with* $v_{i+1} \in E(v_i)$ *for all* $i \in \mathbb{N}$ *or a finite path* $\sigma = v_0 v_1 v_2 ... v_l \in V^+$ *with* $v_{i+1} \in E(v_i)$ *for all* $i < l$, *and* $E(v_l) = \emptyset$.

A play on the arena is played in the following way. Let $x \in \{0, 1\}$

- A token is placed on a vertex $v \in V$.
- Let v be a x-vertex and the token be on v,
  1. Player x moves the token from v to $v' \in E(v)$
  2. Repeat step 1
     - either infinitely often
     - or until a dead end is reached (v is a dead end if $E(v) = \emptyset$)

The same player can make several (even infinite) consecutive moves.

Definition 7. *A* game *is a pair* $G = (A, Win)$, *where* A *is the arena and* $Win \subseteq V^\omega$ *is the* winning set.
   A game with a fixed vertex where all plays should start is called an initialized game *and denoted as* $\Gamma = (A, Win, v_0)$ *where* $v_0 \in V$.
   Player 0 *is the* winner *of a play* σ *in the game* G *iff* σ *is a finite play* $\sigma = v_0 v_1 ... v_l \in V^+$ *and* v_l *is a* 1-vertex *where Player* 1 *can't move anymore, or* σ *is an infinite play and* $\sigma \in Win$. *Player* 1 *wins* σ *if Player* 0 *does not win.*

Let σ be a play. i.e., a maximal sequence of vertices of an arena. $\text{Inf}(\sigma)$ is the set of infinitely often visited vertices during the play σ. *Streett winning condition* is defined as:

Definition 8. *A* Streett winning condition *is* $S = \{(K_1, L_1), ..., (K_m, L_m)\}$ *where* $K_i, L_i \subseteq V$ *for* $1 \leq i \leq m$.
   A play σ *satisfies* Streett winning condition S *iff* $\forall k, 1 \leq k \leq m$, $\text{Inf}(\sigma) \cap L_k \neq \emptyset \implies \text{Inf}(\sigma) \cap K_k \neq \emptyset$.
   $Win(S) = \{\sigma \in V^\omega | \sigma \text{ satisfies } S\}$ *is called* Streett winning set.
   A game with Streett winning condition is called Streett game.

Definition 9. *Let* A *be an arena,* $x \in \{0, 1\}$ *and* $f_x : V^* V_x \to V$ *a partial function. A prefix* $v_0 v_1 ... v_l$ *of a play is said to be* conform *with* f_x *if* $\forall i$ *such that* $0 \leq i < l$ *and* $v_i \in V_x$, *the function* f_x *is defined at* $v_0 v_1 ... v_i$ *and we have* $v_{i+1} = f_x(v_0 v_1 ... v_i)$. *This implies* $v_{i+1} \in E(v_i)$.
   A play is conform with f_x *if each of its prefixes is conform with* f_x.

Definition 10. *Let A be an arena, $x \in \{0,1\}$ and $f_x : V^* V_x \rightarrow V$ a partial function. f_x is a strategy for Player x on $U \subseteq V$ if it is defined for every prefix of a play which is conform with it, starts in a vertex from U, and does not end in a dead end of Player x.*

Definition 11. *Let $G = (A, \text{Win})$ be a game, and f_x a strategy for Player x on U. The strategy f_x is said to be a winning strategy for Player x on U if all plays which are conform with f_x and start in a vertex from U are won by Player x.*

Definition 12. *Given a game G, the winning region for Player x, denoted $U_x(G)$, is the set of all vertices v such that Player x wins G on $\{v\}$.*

Definition 13. *A game is determined if the winning regions for the two players partition the set of vertices [7, 12].*

Example 2. Figure 2 shows an arena and the winning condition for Player 0. Let 0 be the initial vertex. $0(12314)^\omega$ is a play won by Player 0. In fact, Player 0 has a winning strategy: never choose 0 at vertex 1, always choose 3 at vertex 2.

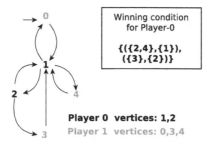

Fig. 2. An example of Streett game

4.2 Weak Observable Liveness as a Streett Game

Here, we propose a method for transforming a weak observable liveness problem into a Streett game. We choose Streett games because they give us the possibility to encode the weak observable liveness requirements after applying some transformations on the marking graph of the net and building a proper arena.

Let $N = (P, T, F, m_0)$ be a 1-safe, pure and simple SMD net where $O = T$, i.e., all transitions are observable, $C \subseteq O$ is the set of controllable transitions and all controllable transitions belong to just one state machine component, i.e., to User (Player 1), and, if $m[t_1\rangle$ and $m[t_2\rangle$ for a reachable marking m, and $t_1 \in C$ and $t_2 \in T \setminus C$ then ${}^\bullet t_1 \cap {}^\bullet t_2 = \emptyset$ (t_1 and t_2 are concurrently enabled). We do not consider the cases in which a controllable and an uncontrollable transition are in conflict because of the fact that the user's strategy cannot depend on being faster than the system.

$MG(N) = ([m_0\rangle, T, \alpha, m_0)$ is the *marking graph* of N, i.e., a labelled transition system where $[m_0\rangle$ is the set of all reachable markings in N, T is the set of transitions of N, $\alpha = \{(m,t,m')\mid\ m,m' \in [m_0\rangle\ \wedge\ m[t\rangle m'\}$ is the set of labelled arcs and m_0 is the initial marking of N. Since N is 1-safe, $MG(N)$ is finite. Given an arc $a = (m,t,m') \in \alpha$, its *label* is t (denoted $l(a) = t$, where $l : \alpha \longrightarrow T$ is a labelling function).

A game consists of an arena together with a winning set. The arena of the Streett game for checking the weak observable liveness of a transition t (called *target*) in N, denoted $Arena(N) = (V_0, V_1, E)$, is obtained from $MG(N)$. The set of vertices $V = V_0 \cup V_1$ contains all reachable markings plus a set of new vertices. Let $M_1 = \{m \in [m_0\rangle \mid \forall t \in T: m[t\rangle, t \in C\}$ be the set of markings at which only controllable transitions are enabled. Let $M_1' = \{m \in [m_0\rangle \mid \nexists\, t \in T: m[t\rangle\}$ be the set of dead markings and let $M = \{m \in [m_0\rangle \mid \exists t_1 \in C, \exists t_2 \in T\setminus C: m[t_1\rangle \wedge m[t_2\rangle\}$ be the set of reachable markings in which at least a controllable and an uncontrollable transition are concurrently enabled. $V_1 = M_1 \cup M_1' \cup M$. The remaining reachable markings are those in which only uncontrollable transitions are enabled: $M_0 = \{m \in [m_0\rangle \mid \exists\, t \in T: m[t\rangle \wedge \forall t \in T: m[t\rangle, t \notin C\}$. Additional vertices are obtained by duplicating the elements of M: $M^d = \{m^d \mid m \in M\}$. Finally, new vertices are added by splitting any arc of α in $MG(N)$. The set of vertices assigned to Player 0 is $V_0 = \alpha \cup M_0 \cup M^d$.

The set α encodes into the arena information about transition labels.

The set of the edges of $Arena(N)$ is then defined as:
$E = \{(m,a),(a,m') \mid a = (m,t,m') \in \alpha \wedge m \notin M\} \cup \{(m,a),(a,m') \mid a = (m,t,m') \in \alpha \wedge m \in M \wedge\ t \in C\} \cup \{(m^d,a),(a,m') \mid a = (m,t,m') \in \alpha \wedge m \in M \wedge t \in T\setminus C\} \cup \{(m,m^d) \mid m \in M\}$. The edges (m, m^d) are called *delay* edges.

Fixing the initial vertex as m_0, we get an initialized game from $G(N)$ and we call it $\Gamma(N)$. We now encode the winning set as a set of Streett conditions. Streett condition is also known as "fairness condition" which is suitable for expressing our weak fairness requirement for the uncontrollable transitions. Hence, we write the winning conditions for System (Player 0). Since Streett games are determined, only System or User has a winning strategy for $\Gamma(N)$, i.e., User has a winning strategy iff System does not have any winning strategy.

The winning set Win_t is determined by two kinds of winning conditions: one condition for not visiting a vertex, corresponding to an occurrence of the target, infinitely often, and other conditions to guarantee weak fairness for uncontrollable transitions.

Let $t \in T$ be the target transition to be checked; the first condition can be expressed as: $(\emptyset, \{a \in \alpha \mid l(a) = t\})$.

To ensure the weak fairness assumption, we look for strongly connected components in $MG(N)$, containing at least an arc labelled by an uncontrollable transition and such that there is another uncontrollable transition u enabled in each marking of the component and leaving the component. Any infinite path within such a component violates weak fairness for the uncontrollable transition u. For any maximal such component, we add a winning condition: $(\{x_1, \ldots, x_n\}, \{w_1, \ldots, w_k\})$, where $w_1, \ldots, w_k$ are the arcs of the component and $x_1, \ldots, x_n$ are all the outgoing arcs from the component.

The delay transitions let User wait until a concurrent uncontrollable transition occurs so that User can choose what to do after observing the uncontrollable one(s). In some cases, the user has to choose not to fire a controllable transition in order to force the system to fire the target transition.

The target transition is WOL in N iff System does not have a winning strategy for $\Gamma(N)$. This means that User has a winning strategy. Let f be a winning strategy for User, each f-conform play has the target transition infinitely often.

Example 3. Figure 3 illustrates a Streett game derived from the Petri net N in order to check weak observable liveness of transition c. The initial vertex, corresponding to the initial marking of N, is 1. Vertices 4 and 5 belong to Player 1 (User) since the only transitions that are enabled in the corresponding markings are controllable. Vertices 6 and 9 belong to Player 1 as well because they are dead. If a play ends in these markings, Player 1 loses. In the marking corresponding to vertex 1, both controllable and uncontrollable transitions are enabled concurrently; hence, we duplicate it so that Player 1 can choose to observe the choice by Player 0. In this way, Player 1, who aims to fire c, can escape from the deadlocks corresponding to vertices 6 and 9.

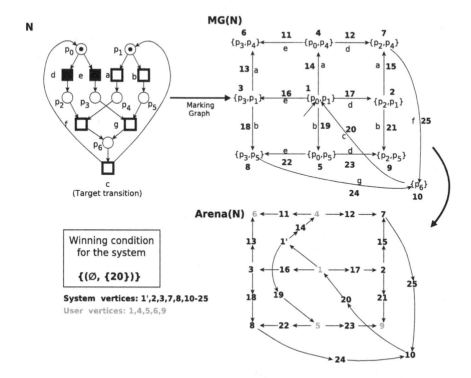

Fig. 3. Streett game for checking weak observable liveness of transition c

In order to represent the winning conditions easily, we label the arcs and markings of the MG(N) with numbers, which are also used for referring to the corresponding vertices of Arena(N). In this game the aim of Player 0 is to prevent Player 1 from firing the transition c infinitely often, which can be represented as one winning condition: $\{(\emptyset, \{20\})\}$.

In this game, User has a winning strategy to force System to visit 20 infinitely often, which is to choose 12 at 4 and to choose 22 at 5. So the game verifies that c is WOL.

Notice that following the right strategy from the initial marking, some markings like $\{p_2, p_5\}$ or $\{p_3, p_4\}$ are not reached. Indeed these markings represent deadlock in the system net and occurrence of c cannot be forced from them. So although c is WOL, it is not observably live.

Example 4. Figure 4 illustrates how we encode weak fairness as a winning condition. Transition f is persistently enabled and there is no transition in conflict to disable it. Weak fairness requires that f must fire. However, in the MG(N) we can find infinite paths in which f never appears. Obviously this is expected since we pass from a concurrent system to its sequential simulation. Although concurrency is not explicit, we can still recover it if we examine MG(N) with respect to some properties.

For example, in the illustrated fragment of MG(N) we see that f is enabled at each marking, and it is possible to go in between these markings forever without firing f. If we examine this structure we find three strongly connected components that consist of uncontrollable transitions. At each node of these components f is enabled and f does not appear inside the components. To be able to represent the components and winning conditions, we label the markings and arcs of the MG(N) with numbers, which are also used for referring to the corresponding vertices of Arena(N). The transitions belonging to the maximal of the set of strongly connected components in which f remains enabled are $8, 12, 9, 10, 6$. We encode the weak fairness requirement as a winning condition and add the condition that is given in Fig. 4 in the generated game.

In this specific example, firing f is the only way of going out from the strongly connected component. However, in general, in the left part of the condition, we write all the vertices that represent transitions whose firing means going out from the component. This is because we could also go out of this component with a transition which is in conflict with f or another transition which is concurrent with f. In the first case, f becomes disabled whereas in the second case, we will find another component in which f remains enabled and so there will be another winning condition for that too.

Remark. The weak fairness is required for the uncontrollable transitions so that we encode them as a winning condition of Player 0 (System).

4.3 Correspondence between Streett Games and WOL

We have to prove that the weak observable liveness problem really corresponds to the given Streett game construction. We have to show that given N and t,

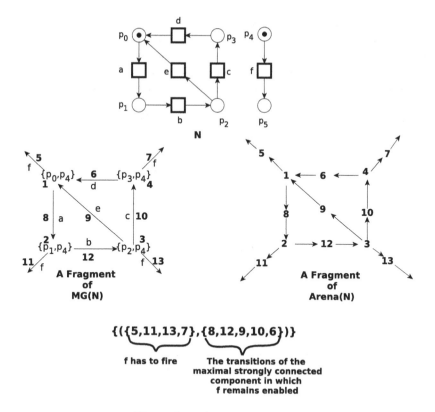

Fig. 4. Encoding weak fairness

as described in the previous section, t is WOL iff Player 1 (User) has a winning strategy in the constructed initialized game $\Gamma(N)$ which will be done step by step.

To start with, we fix some notations and definitions. Let N be a net, $MG(N)$ be its marking graph and $Arena(N)$ be the arena constructed from the net N as in the previous section, where in particular each vertex of $Arena(N)$ corresponds to either a reachable marking or an arc of $MG(N)$. We define a function $\mu : V \rightarrow [m_0\rangle \cup \alpha$, which gives the corresponding marking or arc of $MG(N)$ to a given vertex, i.e.: such that, for all $v \in V$, if $v = m^d$, $m^d \in M^d$, then $\mu(v) = m$, else $\mu(v) = v$.

A *path on MG(N)* is an infinite or a finite sequence of markings, $\pi = m_1 m_2 \ldots m_k \ldots$, such that for all $m_i, m_{i+1} \in \pi$ where $i \geq 1$, $m_i, m_{i+1} \in [m_0\rangle$ and $(m_i, t, m_{i+1}) \in \alpha$. The transitions along each path π of MG(N) are uniquely determined, since the net is simple, pure, and 1-safe. Moreover, for the same reason, two consecutive markings are always different.

A *path on Arena(N)* is an infinite or a finite sequence of vertices, $\sigma = v_1 v_2 \ldots v_n \ldots$. A play on $Arena(N)$ is a maximal path on it. If $\mu(v_i) \in [m_0\rangle$ then either $\mu(v_{i+1}) = \mu(v_i)$, or $(\mu(v_{i+1}) \in \alpha \wedge \mu(v_{i+2}) \in [m_0\rangle)$. In the first case, when two consecutive vertices correspond to the same reachable marking, it means that the two vertices are connected via a delay.

Here we define three functions. The first one transforms a play on $Arena(N)$ into the corresponding transition sequence. The concatenation of the other two functions transforms a play into the corresponding path on $MG(N)$.

Let $v \in V$ and $\sigma \in V^\omega$, $\sigma = v_1 \ldots v_i \ldots$ such that, for all $i \geq 1$, $(v_i, v_{i+1}) \in E$.

We define a function $\xi : V^\omega \rightarrow T^\omega$ which deletes the vertices corresponding to markings and extracts the transitions from σ.

$$\xi(v) = \begin{cases} l(\mu(v)), & \text{if } \mu(v) = a \in \alpha \\ \epsilon, & \text{if } \mu(v) \in [m_0\rangle \end{cases}$$

$$\xi(\epsilon) = \epsilon, \quad \xi(v\sigma) = \xi(v)\xi(\sigma)$$

Analogously, we now define a function $\rho : V^\omega \rightarrow [m_0\rangle^\omega$ as follows.

$$\rho(v) = \begin{cases} \epsilon, & \text{if } v \in \alpha \\ \mu(v), & \text{if } \mu(v) \in [m_0\rangle \end{cases}$$

$$\rho(\epsilon) = \epsilon, \quad \rho(v\sigma) = \rho(v)\rho(\sigma)$$

In this way we have deleted from σ the vertices corresponding to arcs. Now, in order to delete the duplicated markings due to delays, we define the following function $\Pi : [m_0\rangle^\omega \rightarrow [m_0\rangle^\omega$ to be applied to sequences of markings $\gamma = \rho(\sigma) = m_1 \ldots m_i \ldots$ that are by construction such that, for all $i \geq 1$, if $m_i = m_{i+1}$ then $m_i \neq m_{i-1}$ and $m_{i+1} \neq m_{i+2}$,

$$\Pi(m_1 m_2 \gamma) = \begin{cases} m_1 \Pi(\gamma), & \text{if } m_1 = m_2 \\ m_1 \Pi(m_2 \gamma), & \text{otherwise} \end{cases}$$

$$\Pi(m) = m, \quad \Pi(\epsilon) = \epsilon$$

Given a path σ on $Arena(N)$ by applying ξ we get the corresponding transition sequence in N, by applying the composition of the two functions ρ and Π we get the corresponding path $\Pi(\rho(\sigma))$ on $MG(N)$. On the other way around, given a transition sequence τ in N or a path π on $MG(N)$, a play σ on $Arena(N)$ is uniquely determined by τ or π such that $\xi(\sigma) = \tau$ and $\Pi(\rho(\sigma)) = \pi$. This is due to the construction of $Arena(N)$ and to the definitions of the functions ξ, ρ and Π. In the following, we exploit the fact that $O = T$ (all transitions are observable).

Given a response function φ, we define a corresponding strategy for User, f^φ.

Definition 14. *Let $\varphi : T^* \rightarrow 2^C$ be a response function. Let $v_1 \cdots v_k$ be a path in $Arena(N)$, with $v_k \in V_1$. Let $t_1 t_2 \cdots t_h = \xi(v_1 \cdots v_k)$ be the (unique) corresponding transition sequence in N. To φ associate a partial function $f^\varphi : V^* V_1 \rightarrow V$ as follows.*

If $\varphi(t_1 t_2 \cdots t_h) = J \neq \emptyset$, choose an element in J, and define $f^\varphi(v_1 \cdots v_k) = a$, where $l(a) \in J$.

If $\varphi(t_1 t_2 \cdots t_h) = \emptyset$ and $\mu(v_k) \in M$ (i.e. $\mu(v_k)$ is a marking enabling both controllable and uncontrollable transitions) then define $f^\varphi(v_1 \cdots v_k) = v_k^d$.

If $\varphi(t_1 t_2 \cdots t_h) = \emptyset$ and $\mu(v_k) \in M_1'$ (i.e. $\mu(v_k)$ is a dead marking) then define $f^\varphi(v_1 \cdots v_k) = undefined$.

Given a strategy f for User, we define a corresponding response function φ^f.

Definition 15. Let $f : V^* V_1 \to V$ be a strategy for User, and $m_0[e_1 e_2 \cdots e_K\rangle m$ be a transition sequence in N. Consider the unique corresponding path in $Arena(N)$ ending at m such that $m \notin M^d$.

1. If m is in V_1, then there are two cases: f chooses either m^d or a node a such that $l(a) = t \in T$; in the former case, define $\varphi^f(e_1 e_2 \cdots e_K) = \emptyset$; in the latter case, define $\varphi^f(e_1 e_2 \cdots e_K) = \{t\}$.
2. If m is in V_0, define $\varphi^f(e_1 e_2 \cdots e_K) = \emptyset$.

Theorem 1. Let t be WOL in N by φ. Then, User has a winning strategy in $\Gamma(N)$.

Proof. If t is WOL by φ, this means that for each φ-consistent sequence τ, t occurs infinitely often.

We derive a strategy f^φ for User from φ as it is described in Definition 14. Each f^φ-conform play σ corresponds to a unique transition sequence $\xi(\sigma)$ that is fireable in N. The sequence $\xi(\sigma)$ is infinite since t is WOL. Even if there is a deadlock in the system, following the response function φ, User can avoid it. And since the strategy is derived from φ, f^φ-conform plays are infinite.

The sequence $\xi(\sigma)$ can be either φ-consistent or not. Let us assume that $\xi(\sigma)$ is φ-consistent. Since t is WOL, t occurs infinitely often in each φ-consistent sequence. Clearly σ is won by User. If $\xi(\sigma)$ is not φ-consistent, at least one clause of Definition 3 is not satisfied. (2) is satisfied by definition. Since the strategy is derived from φ, all choices with respect to the controllable transitions in the game are based on the response function. (3) is also satisfied because if there was a controllable transition that is finally postponed and finally eligible, this would mean that User does not follow the strategy. And so σ cannot be an f^φ-conform play. If $\xi(\sigma)$ is not φ-consistent, this means that (1) is not satisfied. Namely, $\xi(\sigma)$ is not weakly fair with respect to all uncontrollable transitions. And in this case, since all weak fairness requirements are encoded in the game as winning conditions, σ does not satisfy at least one of the winning conditions concerning the weak fairness. So, again, σ is won by User.

The derived strategy f^φ is a winning strategy for User. □

Now we prove the other direction, given a winning strategy for User, the corresponding response function witnesses that the target is WOL in the net. Let f be a winning strategy for User and φ^f be the corresponding response function that is constructed from f, as in Definition 15. We will show that each maximal transition sequence that is consistent with φ^f has the target t infinitely often.

Let τ be a φ^f-consistent transition sequence. It is by definition weakly fair with respect to $T \setminus C$. The corresponding play σ such that $\xi(\sigma) = \tau$, is not f-conform in general. This is due to the uncontrollable events that are concurrent with the controllable events and do not change the choice of User. This happens when both kinds of transitions are enabled and the strategy of User is not to wait but to fire a controllable transition because the occurrence of the uncontrollable one does not change the choice of User. So, if in τ the uncontrollable transition occurs before the controllable one, the corresponding σ will not be f-conform. However, there is another transition sequence among the possible executions of the same process identified by τ such that the corresponding play is f-conform. And this new play does not violate any weak-fairness conditions of the game and so it is won by User because it contains the target infinitely often.

In the following, we give the construction of an f-conform play σ from a φ^f-consistent transition sequence τ. For this we use the notion of *configuration*.

Definition 16. *Let τ be a transition sequence of N and (N', ϕ) be the unique process identified by τ. A configuration is a 4-tuple (β, v, r, σ) where β is a B-cut of N', v is a vertex in $Arena(N)$ such that it corresponds to either $\phi(\beta)$ or $\phi(\beta)^d$, r is a residue of τ, and $\sigma \in V^*$.*

We construct the play σ inductively by subsequent configurations. Let (β, v, r, σ) be a configuration, the next configuration $(\beta', v', r', \sigma')$ is obtained as follows. Consider two cases:

- v is a Player 0 (System) vertex. Let u be the first transition in r (which is uncontrollable in this case). Then β' is obtained by simulating the occurrence of u from β in (N', ϕ). v' is $\phi(\beta')$. r' is obtained by deleting the first occurrence of u from r. And finally, σ' equals $\sigma(v, u, v')v'$.
- v is a Player 1 (User) vertex. We have two subcases.
  - f chooses delay. The new configuration is $(\beta, v^d, r, \sigma v^d)$. The marking remains the same but now we pass to a System vertex in $Arena(N)$.
  - f chooses to fire a controllable transition c. Then β' is obtained by simulating the occurrence of c from β. v' is $\phi(\beta')$. r' is obtained by deleting the first occurrence of c from r. And finally, σ' equals $\sigma(v, c, v')v'$.

The base case is when $\beta = Min(N')$ and v corresponds to the initial marking, $r = \tau$ and $\sigma = \epsilon$. This construction defines an f-conform play starting from an φ^f-consistent transition sequence.

Theorem 2. *Let f be a winning strategy for Player 1 in $\Gamma(N)$. Then t is WOL in N by φ^f.*

Proof. Let τ be a φ^f-consistent transition sequence. Assume that τ has only a finite number of occurrences of the target t. Because it is φ^f-consistent, τ is weakly fair with respect to $T \setminus C$. By the construction given above, σ is an f-conform play. Since τ is weakly fair with respect to all uncontrollable transitions, and in the construction, every time a System vertex is reached the play respects the firing of the uncontrollable transitions in τ. Thus, this play satisfies all the weak-fairness conditions of the game. Since f is a winning strategy for User, σ not having t infinitely often is a contradiction. This proves that each φ^f-consistent transition sequence has t infinitely often meaning that t is WOL in N.   □

Example 5. Consider the net N in Fig. 5, where c_1 is the only controllable transition, and u_3 is the target. In this very simple example, it is clear that the target is WOL. The corresponding arena, shown in the figure, contains two nodes labeled u_3, namely 1 and 7. The first winning condition for System requires that none of them be visited infinitely often. The other winning conditions encode the weak fairness requirement for uncontrollable transitions: System cannot indefinitely postpone u_1, u_2 or u_3 when they are enabled. A winning strategy f for User is easily found: for any sequence ending in m_2, choose node m_2', corresponding to postponing c_1; similarly, for sequences ending in m_3, choose node m_3'. This strategy forces the system to fire the uncontrollable transitions u_1 and u_3 by blocking c_1.

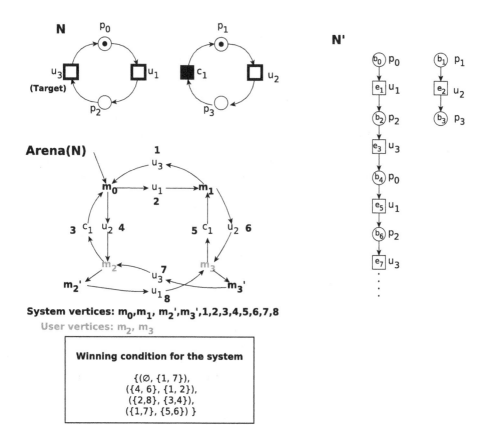

Fig. 5. From a winning strategy to a witnessing response function

Any f-conform play will pass infinitely often either through node 1 or through node 7 (or both), thus violating the first winning condition of System. The response function corresponding to f, φ^f is very simple: it returns the empty set for any transition sequence. The maximal φ^f-consistent transition sequences are, in this case, all the interleavings of $\tau_1 = (u_1 u_3)^\omega$ and $\tau_2 = u_2$. Let us take, for instance, $\tau = u_1 u_2 (u_3 u_1)^\omega$. The corresponding f-conform play σ is constructed as follows, according to Definition 16. The initial configuration is $(\{b_0, b_1\}, m_0, \tau, \epsilon)$. The current vertex, m_0, is a System vertex, so we apply the first clause of Definition 16. The first transition is u_1. By deleting its first occurrence from N', we reach $\{b_2, b_1\}$ which corresponds to the marking $\{p_2, p_1\}$. The corresponding moves on the arena lead to vertex m_1. The new configuration is:

$$\text{CON}_1 = (\{b_2, b_1\}, m_1, u_2(u_3 u_1)^\omega, m_0 \; 2 \; m_1).$$

The current vertex is again a System vertex. By applying the same rule we reach the following configuration:

$$\text{CON}_2 = (\{b_2, b_3\}, m_3, (u_3 u_1)^\omega, m_0 \; 2 \; m_1 \; 6 \; m_3).$$

The winning strategy at m_3 chooses m_3', where System is forced to choose 7 and then m_2. The strategy at m_2 chooses m_2' forcing the System to go through 8 and reach m_3. From here the play will cycle forever.

The resulting play is f-conform and does not violate any of the weak-fairness conditions of the game, while violating the target condition.

In this simple case, any φ^f-consistent sequence corresponds to an f-conform play. In the next example we will see that this is not always true.

Example 6. Consider now the net in Fig. 6, and the corresponding arena and winning condition for System. In this case, there is no need for weak fairness winning conditions, since each strongly connected component, persistently enabling an uncontrollable transition, contains only controllable transitions.

A winning strategy for User can be defined as follows. Let $\sigma \in V^*$; then

$$f(\sigma m_0) = 2 \quad f(\sigma m_1) = 1 \quad f(\sigma m_2) = 8 \quad f(\sigma m_3) = 7$$

The only f-conform play starting from m_0 repeatedly cycles around states $m_0, 2, m_1$, and 1.

Let us define the corresponding response function. A transition sequence τ in N is any finite prefix of an interleaving of $\tau_1 = (c_2 c_1)^\omega$ and $\tau_2 = (u_2 u_1)^\omega$. Then, $\varphi^f(\tau) = \{c_1\}$ if the last controllable transition in τ is c_2, and $\varphi^f(\tau) = \{c_2\}$ otherwise. Consider, for example, the φ^f-consistent transition sequence $\tau = u_2 u_1 c_2 u_2 c_1 (u_1 u_2 c_2 c_1)^\omega$. In order to construct the corresponding f-conform play, we start from the initial configuration

$$(\{b_0, b_1\}, m_0, \tau, \epsilon).$$

The initial vertex, m_0, belongs to User, and f prescribes to choose 2 as next vertex, corresponding to firing c_2. But c_2 is not the next transition in τ (this is

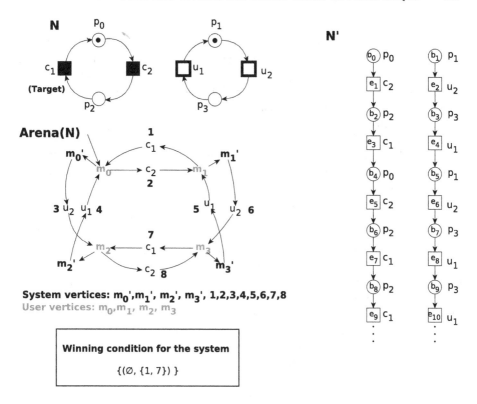

Fig. 6. From a winning strategy to a witnessing response function

the reason why in general τ does not directly correspond to an f-conform play). This next transition (u_2) is uncontrollable and concurrent with c_2. Changing the order of these concurrent transitions will not prevent the infinite occurrence of the target in general. The next move leads to m_1, and to the configuration

$$(\{b_2, b_1\}, m_1, u_2 u_1 u_2 c_1 (u_1 u_2 c_2 c_1)^\omega, m_0 \, 2 \, m_1)$$

We can continue like this, by always postponing the uncontrollable transitions, thus constructing the (unique in this case) f-conform play, which is won by User.

5   Conclusion

In this paper we have studied the observable liveness notion which was already introduced in the Petri net literature, see [5,6,11]. Observable liveness is defined on Petri nets in which transitions are either observable or unobservable by a user. Among the observable ones, some are controllable by the user whereas others are uncontrollable, meaning that they occur autonomously. Intuitively, an observable transition is observably live if the user can always, from each reachable marking, force it to fire infinitely often via controllable transitions. This paper weakens the notion by removing the requirement "from each reachable marking". The intuition is that when the user knows the target at the initial marking, he/she will follow the right strategy from the beginning. In this paper, we have proposed a method for checking weak observable liveness of a restricted class of nets, namely 1-safe, pure and simple SMD nets such that all transitions are observable and all controllable transitions are in one state machine component. The proposed method is on the basis of infinite games that are played on finite graphs (arenas), namely Streett games which are well studied in the literature (e.g., [7,13,18]). Streett games are two player infinite games which are based on Streett automata, i.e., ω-automata with Streett acceptance condition which is also known as fairness condition.

Given a net and a target transition, we translate the weak observable liveness problem into an initialized Streett game between the system and the user. We define a game construction such that the arena and the conditions for ensuring weak fairness are only based on the net system whereas the winning condition for the target is based on both the net system and the target together. Once the arena is constructed, the winning conditions can be rewritten on the same arena for checking weak observable liveness of different transitions of the same net. We write the winning conditions for the system because of the weak fairness requirement for the uncontrollable transitions. The system must behave weakly fair as well as not letting the user visit a vertex which corresponds to the firing of the target transition infinitely often. The winning set is determined by two types of Streett conditions: one condition for not firing the target infinitely often, and a condition for each strongly connected component in which an uncontrollable transition remains enabled (if such component exists) to enforce weak fairness. Then, the target transition is WOL iff the system does not have a winning strategy for the constructed game, dually the user has a winning strategy.

Observable liveness of a transition can be expressed in terms of weak observable liveness by considering on the same arena with the same winning conditions different games starting from different initial vertices, one for each reachable marking. The target is observably live iff the user has a winning strategy for all.

In [7] it is shown that every Streett game can be translated into a parity game. Deciding the winner of an initialized parity game is proven to be in UP ∩ co-UP in [9,10]. In [7] it is shown that computing the winning regions of parity games on finite graphs and the corresponding memoryless winning strategies can be carried out in time $O(m \times l^n)$, where m is the number of edges, l is the number of vertices and $n \leq l$ is the maximum priority in the game.

In this work, we have successfully adapted a well-known game to our problem of checking weak observable liveness. However, this method has two main drawbacks: the high complexity, and the restriction on the class of Petri nets. In order to cope with these drawbacks, we are currently working on another method for checking weak observable liveness based on unfoldings of Petri nets. Since the issues we face are related to the interleaving nature of the construction, we are now also considering the use of concurrent games.

Acknowledgements. This work is partially supported by MIUR.

References

1. Best, E., Devillers, R.: Sequential and concurrent behaviour in Petri net theory. Theoret. Comput. Sci. **55**(1), 87–136 (1987)
2. Richard Büchi, J.: Weak second-order arithmetic and finite automata. Z. Math. Logik Grundlagen Math. **6**, 66–92 (1960)
3. Richard Büchi, J.: On a decision method in restricted second order arithmetic. In: Proceedings of the 1960 International Congress Logic, Methodology and Philosophy of Science, pp. 1–11. Stanford University Press, Stanford (1962)
4. Cassandras, C.G., Lafortune, S.: Introduction to Discrete Event Systems. Springer, New York (2006)
5. Desel, J., Kılınç, G.: Observable liveness. In: Moldt, D., Rölke, H. (eds.) International Workshop on Petri Nets and Software Engineering (PNSE 2014). CEUR Workshop Proceedings, Aachen, vol. 1160, pp. 143–163. CEUR-WS.org. (2014). http://ceur-ws.org/Vol-1160/
6. Desel, J., Kılınç, G.: Observable liveness of Petri nets. Acta Inf. **52**(2–3), 153–174 (2015)
7. Grädel, E., Thomas, W., Wilke, T. (eds.): Automata Logics, and Infinite Games: A Guide to Current Research. Springer, New York (2002)
8. Holloway, L.E., Krogh, B.H., Giua, A.: A survey of Petri net methods for controlled discrete event systems. Discrete Event Dyn. Syst. **7**(2), 151–190 (1997)
9. Jurdzinski, M.: Deciding the winner in parity games is in UP ∩ co-up. Inf. Process. Lett. **68**(3), 119–124 (1998)
10. Jurdziński, M.: Small progress measures for solving parity games. In: Reichel, H., Tison, S. (eds.) STACS 2000. LNCS, vol. 1770, pp. 290–301. Springer, Heidelberg (2000). doi:10.1007/3-540-46541-3_24
11. Kılınç, G.: Formal Notions of Non-interference and Liveness for Distributed Systems. Ph.D thesis in computer science, Universitá Degli Studi di Milano-Bicocca, Dipartimento di Informatica, Sistemistica e Comunicazione (2016)
12. Martin, D.A.: Borel determinacy. Ann. Math. **102**, 363–371 (1975)
13. McNaughton, R.: Infinite games played on finite graphs. Ann. Pure Appl. Logic **65**(2), 149–184 (1993)
14. Muller, D.E.: Infinite sequences and finite machines. In: Proceedings of the 4th Annual Symposium on Switching Circuit Theory and Logical Design, Chicago, Illinois, USA, pp. 3–16, 28–30 October 1963
15. Silva, M.: Half a century after Carl Adam Petri's Ph.D. thesis: A perspective on the field. Ann. Rev. Control **37**(2), 191–219 (2013)
16. Streett, R.S.: Propositional dynamic logic of looping and converse. In: Proceedings of the Thirteenth Annual ACM Symposium on Theory of Computing, STOC 1981, pp. 375–383. ACM, New York, NY, USA (1981)
17. Thomas, W.: Automata on infinite objects. In: Van Leeuwen, J. (ed.) Formal Models and Semantics, Handbook of Theoretical Computer Science, pp. 133–191. Elsevier, Amsterdam (1990)
18. Thomas, W.: On the synthesis of strategies in infinite games. In: Mayr, E.W., Puech, C. (eds.) STACS 1995. LNCS, vol. 900, pp. 1–13. Springer, Heidelberg (1995). doi:10.1007/3-540-59042-0_57

The Complexity of Diagnosability and Opacity Verification for Petri Nets

Béatrice Bérard[1,2], Stefan Haar[2], Sylvain Schmitz[2(✉)], and Stefan Schwoon[2]

[1] Sorbonne Universités, UPMC University Paris 06, LIP6, Paris, France
beatrice.berard@lip6.fr

[2] INRIA and LSV, CNRS and ENS Cachan, Université Paris-Saclay, Cachan, France
stefan.haar@inria.fr, {schmitz,schwoon}@lsv.fr

Abstract. *Diagnosability* and *opacity* are two well-studied problems in discrete-event systems. We revisit these two problems with respect to expressiveness and complexity issues.

We first relate different notions of diagnosability and opacity. We consider in particular fairness issues and extend the definition of Germanos et al. [ACM TECS, 2015] of weakly fair diagnosability for safe Petri nets to general Petri nets and to opacity questions.

Second, we provide a global picture of complexity results for the verification of diagnosability and opacity. We show that diagnosability is NL-complete for finite state systems, PSPACE-complete for safe Petri nets (even with fairness), and EXPSPACE-complete for general Petri nets without fairness, while non diagnosability is inter-reducible with reachability when fault events are not weakly fair. Opacity is ESPACE-complete for safe Petri nets (even with fairness) and undecidable for general Petri nets already without fairness.

1 Introduction

Diagnosability and opacity are two aspects of partially observable discrete-event systems that have each received considerable attention. Although they are usually considered separately, they form a dual pair of tasks: an observer watches the current execution of a known system, where only some events are visible. As this execution evolves, the observer continually attempts to deduce whether the execution satisfies some property: in diagnosis, the observer strives to detect the occurrence of some *fault* event, while in opacity the observer may be hostile, and one requires to prevent her from being certain that a *secret* has occurred. These deductions are made on the basis of a finite prefix of the current execution; we will refer to this as the *Finite-Observation Property*.

Diagnosability. A system is *diagnosable* if, after the occurrence of a fault (which itself is invisible), it is always possible to deduce that a fault has happened after a sufficiently long observation. A formal-language framework for both diagnosis and the analysis of diagnosability was introduced by Sampath et al. [23] in the context of finite automata, for which diagnosability can be checked in polynomial time in the number of reachable states [16, 27].

© Springer International Publishing AG 2017
W. van der Aalst and E. Best (Eds.): PETRI NETS 2017, LNCS 10258, pp. 200–220, 2017.
DOI: 10.1007/978-3-319-57861-3_13

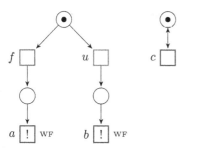 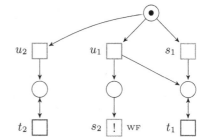

(a) Petri net that is not diagnosable but WF-disagnosable.

(b) Petri net that is opaque but not WF-opaque.

Fig. 1. Examples for diagnosis and opacity in weakly fair Petri nets.

Weak Fairness. The diagnosability framework from [23] is suitable for *sequential* but not for concurrent systems. Consider for instance the Petri net (PN) shown in Fig. 1(a), inspired by an example from [7]. It consists of two entirely independent components. We assume that an outside observer can see the actions a, b, c but not f, u, where f is a fault. If the system is eager to progress, then it is intuitively diagnosable because f will lead to the observation a, which is not possible otherwise. However, if one naively translates the Petri net into a labelled transition system (LTS) and applies the methods from [23], the net will be declared non-diagnosable because the two executions fc^ω and uc^ω are observationally equivalent. If the component on the right-hand side is removed, the system becomes diagnosable. In other words, the presence of the right-hand side component fully determines whether the system is diagnosable or not, although it is not related in any way to the faulty behaviour.

Such effects have motivated the study of diagnosability notions suitable for concurrent systems [7–11]. We focus in this paper on the *weakly fair* (WF) behaviours of the system in the sense of Vogler [26]: In a weakly fair run, no WF transition t that becomes enabled will remain idle indefinitely; either t itself eventually fires, or some conflicting transition does, thus (momentarily) disabling t. This notion of weak fairness is slightly weaker than the one studied by Jančar [14], but has the advantage that for safe Petri nets, the maximal partially ordered runs are exactly those generated by WF runs; and conversely, interleavings of such partially ordered runs yield WF firing sequences.

Under WF semantics, a fault can be diagnosed when the observations made so far can no longer be those of any fault-free WF execution. Then a net is WF-diagnosable if every infinite WF faulty execution has a prefix allowing the fault to be diagnosed. Under this characterisation, the net in Fig. 1(a) is considered WF-diagnosable. In [7,11], WF-diagnosability was shown decidable for safe PNs.

Opacity was introduced for general transition systems in [2]. The system has a secret subset of executions which is *opaque* if for any secret execution, there is a non-secret one with the same observation: an observer can never be sure whether

Table 1. Complexity results for diagnosability and opacity.

Model	Diagnosability	Opacity
Finite LTS	NL-c	PSPACE-c. [4]
Safe (WF-)PN	PSPACE-c	ESPACE-c.
PN	EXPSPACE-c	Undecidable
Strict WF-PN	PNReach $\leq_m^P$ ¬Diag $\leq_m^{EXP}$ PNReach	

the current execution is secret or not. State-based variants (where the observation of an execution is the associated sequence of states) were later studied for instance in [4,25] and shown in [4] to be PSPACE-complete for finite transition systems. Other language-based variants were also studied in [1,19]. Our focus here is on secret executions defined by the occurrence of some secret *transition*.

As for diagnosability, the notions of opacity developed for LTSs are not necessarily suitable for concurrent systems. Consider the net $\mathcal{W}_1$ in Fig. 1(b) and suppose that transitions s_1 and s_2 are secret, t_1 and t_2 visible for an attacker, and u_1 and u_2 invisible. Then an observation of t_2 shows that no secret has occurred, but observing occurrences of t_1 does not suffice to prove that s_1 or s_2 have occurred; therefore, according to traditional definitions, the Petri net $\mathcal{W}_1$ would be considered opaque. However, assuming that s_2 behaves in a *weakly fair* way, then, on observing t_1, the attacker can deduce with certainty that either s_1 has already fired, or s_2 will inevitably do so (or already has). We introduce a notion of *WF-opacity* that takes this into account and declares $\mathcal{W}_1$ non-opaque.

Contributions. We establish the relationships between several notions of diagnosability in the general setting of transition systems (Sect. 2). For concurrent systems, we extend in Sect. 3.3 the notion of WF-diagnosability from [7] to general Petri nets and define and study a refinement of opacity with weak fairness.

Moreover, we provide an almost complete picture of the complexity for diagnosability and opacity analysis for Petri nets with general and weakly fair semantics; see Table 1. For a start, we complete the picture for finite LTSs and show that diagnosability is complete for non-deterministic logarithmic space, while opacity had already been shown PSPACE-complete in [4]. For Petri nets, the outcome is roughly consistent with the 'rules of thumb' in Esparza's survey [5] when viewing diagnosability as a linear-time property and opacity as an inclusion problem. The salient points are as follows:

- As an auxiliary result for our lower bounds in Sect. 4, we re-discovered that trace inclusion in safe Petri nets was actually ESPACE-complete (Proposition 4.3), where ESPACE is the class of problems that can be solved in deterministic space $2^{O(n)}$. An ESPACE-complete problem is also EXPSPACE-complete—i.e., for deterministic space $2^{poly(n)}$—but the converse is not necessarily true.
- The upper bounds for safe Petri nets in Sect. 5.1 also hold for the weakly fair variants of diagnosability and opacity. Our PSPACE upper bound for

WF-diagnosability might thus come as a surprise, as this is a branching-time property (see Definition 3.3), which cannot be expressed in CTL due to its fairness aspect, while CTL* model-checking would yield an EXP upper bound. We analyse the complexity of the algorithm of Germanos et al. [7] for WF-diagnosability and give an algorithm in ESPACE for WF-opacity.

– For general Petri nets, we leave the decidability of WF-diagnosability open, but nevertheless show two positive results in Sect. 5.2 in restricted settings.

The first one is a tight EXPSPACE upper bound for diagnosability—a considerable improvement over the original algorithm of Cabasino et al. [3], which constructed coverability graphs with worst-case Ackermann size.

The second one is an algorithm checking for non WF-diagnosability when fault transitions are not weakly fair, i.e., when a fault is a *possible* outcome in the system but not one that is *required* to happen. We call such systems *strict*, and as illustrated in [7, Sect. 5], this is a reasonable assumption in practice. Our complexity analysis relies on a fragment of LTL studied by Jančar [14] and shares its complexity: at least as hard as reachability (noted 'PNReach' in Table 1), and at most exponentially harder; recall that the complexity of reachability in general Petri nets is a major open problem [24], with a gigantic gap between a forty years old EXPSPACE lower bound [20] and a cubic Ackermann upper bound obtained recently in [18].

Due to space constraints, several proofs are omitted, but they can be found in the full paper available from https://hal.inria.fr/hal-01484476.

2   Opacity and Diagnosability for Transition Systems

In this section, we recall and compare several notions of opacity and diagnosability for labelled transition systems (LTS), and we revisit the complexity of diagnosability for finite LTSs.

2.1   Transition Systems

Given a finite alphabet Σ, we denote by Σ^* the set of finite words over Σ, with ε the empty word, and by Σ^ω the set of infinite words over Σ. For a finite word $\sigma \in \Sigma^*$, $|\sigma|$ is its length. The (strict) *prefix ordering* is defined for two words $\sigma_1 \in \Sigma^*$ and $\sigma_2 \in \Sigma^* \cup \Sigma^\omega$ by $\sigma_1 < \sigma_2$ if there exists a non empty word σ such that $\sigma_2 = \sigma_1 \sigma$; we note $Pref(L) \stackrel{\text{def}}{=} \{\hat{\sigma} \in \Sigma^* \mid \exists \sigma \in L : \hat{\sigma} \leq \sigma\}$ for the set of finite prefixes of a language $L \subseteq \Sigma^* \cup \Sigma^\omega$; this defines a tree sharing common prefixes.

Labelled Transition System. A *labelled transition system* (LTS) is a tuple $\mathcal{A} = \langle Q, q_0, \Sigma, \Delta \rangle$ where Q is a set of states with $q_0 \in Q$ the initial state, Σ is a finite alphabet, and $\Delta \subseteq Q \times \Sigma \times Q$ is the set of transitions. We note $q \xrightarrow{a} q'$ for $\langle q, a, q' \rangle \in \Delta$; this transition is then said to be *enabled* in q.

An infinite *run* over the word $\sigma = a_1 a_2 \cdots \in \Sigma^\omega$ is a sequence of states $(q_i)_{i \geq 0}$ such that $q_i \xrightarrow{a_{i+1}} q_{i+1}$ for all $i \geq 0$, and we write $q_0 \stackrel{\sigma}{\Rightarrow}$ if such a run exists. A finite run over $\sigma \in \Sigma^*$ is defined analogously, and we write $q \xrightarrow{\sigma} q'$ if such a run ends at state q'. A state q is *reachable* if there exists a run $q_0 \xrightarrow{\sigma} q$ for some finite σ. An LTS $\mathcal{A}$ is *live* (aka deadlock-free) if for any reachable state there exists a transition enabled in that state.

Traces. The *finite trace language* $Trace^*(\mathcal{A}) \subseteq \Sigma^*$ of $\mathcal{A}$ and the *infinite trace language* $Trace^\omega(\mathcal{A}) \subseteq \Sigma^\omega$ of $\mathcal{A}$ are defined by:

$$Trace^*(\mathcal{A}) \stackrel{\text{def}}{=} \{ \sigma \in \Sigma^* \mid \exists q : q_0 \xrightarrow{\sigma} q \}, \qquad Trace^\omega(\mathcal{A}) \stackrel{\text{def}}{=} \{ \sigma \in \Sigma^\omega \mid q_0 \xrightarrow{\sigma} \}.$$

Note that for a live LTS $\mathcal{A}$, $Pref(Trace^\omega(\mathcal{A})) = Trace^*(\mathcal{A}) = Pref(Trace^*(\mathcal{A}))$. Also recall that a prefix-closed language $L = Pref(L)$ is *regular* if there exists a finite transition system $\mathcal{A}$ such that $L = Trace^*(\mathcal{A})$.

2.2   Observations

In order to formalise diagnosability and opacity, we introduce an observation mask $\mathcal{O}$. Given an LTS $\mathcal{A} = \langle Q, q_0, \Sigma, \Delta \rangle$, $\mathcal{O}$ is a mapping from Σ to $E \cup \{\varepsilon\}$, where E is a finite set of observable *events*: letters of Σ mapped to E correspond to events visible to an external observer, whereas letters mapped to ε remain invisible. We lift $\mathcal{O}$ to a homomorphism and to languages in the usual way.

When σ is an infinite trace, its observation $\mathcal{O}(\sigma)$ can be either finite or infinite; an LTS $\mathcal{A}$ is *convergent* (with respect to $\mathcal{O}$) if we forbid the former, i.e., if there is no infinite sequence of unobservable events from any reachable state. Note that it is the case in particular if $\mathcal{O}$ is *non erasing*, i.e., if $\mathcal{O}(\Sigma) \subseteq E$. Convergence and liveness are often assumed in diagnosability and opacity scenarii.

Both diagnosability and opacity fix a particular subset M of a set of executions L. Writing $\overline{M} \stackrel{\text{def}}{=} L \setminus M$, diagnosability requires $\mathcal{O}(M) \cap \mathcal{O}(\overline{M}) = \emptyset$, while opacity requires $\mathcal{O}(M) \subseteq \mathcal{O}(\overline{M})$. Observation sequences in $\mathcal{O}(M) \cap \mathcal{O}(\overline{M})$ are called 'ambiguous'; for opacity, all sequences in $\mathcal{O}(M)$ must be ambiguous. The negation of diagnosability can then be seen as a weak form of opacity, as defined in [19], requiring only the existence of ambiguous sequences in $\mathcal{O}(M) \cap \mathcal{O}(\overline{M})$.

2.3   Diagnosability

For diagnosability, we distinguish a special set F of *fault* letters such that $\mathcal{O}(f) = \varepsilon$ for $f \in F$. A finite (resp. infinite) sequence σ is *faulty* if it belongs to $\Sigma^* F \Sigma^*$ (resp. $\Sigma^* F \Sigma^\omega$). Otherwise σ is called *correct*. For an LTS $\mathcal{A}$, we define $Faulty^*(\mathcal{A}) \stackrel{\text{def}}{=} Trace^*(\mathcal{A}) \cap \Sigma^* F \Sigma^*$ for the subset of finite faulty traces and $Faulty^\omega(\mathcal{A}) \stackrel{\text{def}}{=} Trace^\omega(\mathcal{A}) \cap \Sigma^* F \Sigma^\omega$ for the set of infinite faulty traces. Dually, let $Correct^*(\mathcal{A}) \stackrel{\text{def}}{=} Trace^*(\mathcal{A}) \cap (\Sigma \setminus F)^*$ and $Correct^\omega(\mathcal{A}) \stackrel{\text{def}}{=} Trace^\omega(\mathcal{A}) \cap (\Sigma \setminus F)^\omega$ denote the correct traces.

We adopt the following language-based notion of diagnosability due to [21]. Although it is based on languages of infinite words, we shall see that it respects the Finite Observation Principle for all convergent LTS.

Definition 2.1 (Diagnosability [21]). *Given a set of faults F, an LTS $\mathcal{A}$ is diagnosable if*

$$\mathcal{O}(\mathit{Faulty}^\omega(\mathcal{A})) \cap \mathcal{O}(\mathit{Correct}^\omega(\mathcal{A})) = \emptyset.$$

Then $\mathcal{A}$ is *not diagnosable* if and only if there are two infinite traces σ and ρ in $\mathit{Trace}^\omega(\mathcal{A})$ such that σ is faulty, ρ is correct and $\mathcal{O}(\sigma) = \mathcal{O}(\rho)$. We first explain how this definition relates to other notions.

Dynamic and Finite Diagnosability. Various other notions of diagnosability were studied and discussed in [3,23]. The strongest is the notion of K-*diagnosability*: for a natural number K (that may depend on the LTS $\mathcal{A}$), it requires the faulty transition to be detected after at most K steps: for any faulty trace $\sigma f \in \mathit{Faulty}^*(\mathcal{A})$, and any suffix σ' with $|\sigma'| \geq K$ and $\sigma f \sigma' \in \mathit{Trace}^*(\mathcal{A})$, any trace $\rho \in \mathit{Trace}^*(\mathcal{A})$ such that $\mathcal{O}(\rho) = \mathcal{O}(\sigma f \sigma')$ is also faulty.

We use the term *dynamic diagnosability* for a less stringent notion studied in [3], which simply requires detection after a non-uniform finite number of steps $K_{\sigma f}$ that may depend on σf. Dynamic diagnosability and K-diagnosability for some K coincide if $\mathit{Trace}^*(\mathcal{A})$ is regular, but differ in general [3, Remark 5.5].

As we want to consider diagnosability in conjunction with fairness constraints, we shall need yet another notion of diagnosability able to take infinite runs into account while demanding that the observer diagnoses the occurrence of a fault in finite time. We say that an LTS $\mathcal{A}$ is *finitely diagnosable* if, for all $\sigma \in \mathit{Faulty}^\omega(\mathcal{A})$, there exists a finite prefix $\hat{\sigma} < \sigma$ such that every $\rho \in \mathit{Trace}^\omega(\mathcal{A})$ with $\mathcal{O}(\hat{\sigma}) < \mathcal{O}(\rho)$ is also faulty. We argue that this notion captures the Finite Observation Property. The restriction of finite diagnosability to weakly fair runs (recalled later in Definition 3.3) is exactly the definition used in [7].

The next proposition establishes the links between these various notions in the absence of fairness constraints (and includes the result mentioned above for completeness); its proof in the full paper relies mainly on König's Lemma.

Lemma 2.2 (Comparison of Diagnosability Notions). *Let $\mathcal{A}$ be an LTS. Then we have the implications $1 \Rightarrow 2 \Rightarrow 3 \Rightarrow 4$ where:*

1. $\mathcal{A}$ *is K-diagnosable for some $K \in \mathbb{N}$;*
2. $\mathcal{A}$ *is dynamically diagnosable;*
3. $\mathcal{A}$ *is finitely diagnosable;*
4. $\mathcal{A}$ *is diagnosable.*

Moreover, 1 and 2 are equivalent if $\mathit{Trace}^*(\mathcal{A})$ is regular [3, Proposition 5.3], 2 and 3 are equivalent if $\mathcal{A}$ is finitely branching and convergent, and 3 and 4 are equivalent if $\mathcal{A}$ is convergent.

Remark 2.3 (Counter-examples). Fig. 2(a) and (b) show that $\mathcal{A}$ must be both finitely branching and convergent for the equivalence $3 \Leftrightarrow 2$ to hold in Lemma 2.2. The system in Fig. 2(a) is diagnosable since $\mathcal{O}(ua^\omega) \neq \mathcal{O}(fu^n b^\omega)$ for all n, and as it is convergent it is also finitely diagnosable, but it is not dynamically diagnosable because the faulty prefix f may require an arbitrarily long finite delay

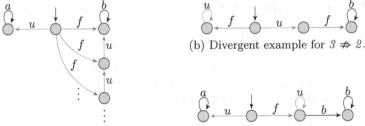

(a) Infinitely branching example for $3 \not\Rightarrow 2$.   (c) Divergent example for $4 \not\Rightarrow 3$.

Fig. 2. Counter-examples for Lemma 2.2, with $\mathcal{O}(u) = \mathcal{O}(f) = \varepsilon$, $\mathcal{O}(a) = a$, and $\mathcal{O}(b) = b$.

K before being diagnosed by $u^K b$. In contrast, the system in Fig. 2(b) is finitely branching but divergent; it is finitely diagnosable for the trivial reason that there is no infinite correct run. (We remark that there exist other examples without this particular property.) The system is not dynamically diagnosable because for the prefix f we have $\mathcal{O}(fu^K) = \mathcal{O}(u)$ for all K.

Figure 2(c) shows that $\mathcal{A}$ must be convergent for the equivalence $4 \Leftrightarrow 3$ to hold in Lemma 2.2. The system is diagnosable, as $\mathcal{O}(fe^\omega) \neq \mathcal{O}(ua^\omega) \neq \mathcal{O}(fe^n b^\omega)$ for all n, but is not finitely diagnosable because all the finite prefixes of the faulty fe^ω have the same observation $\varepsilon < \mathcal{O}(ua^\omega)$.

Complexity of Diagnosability for Finite LTSs. In the case of finite-state LTSs, and assuming an explicit representation with $|\mathcal{A}| \stackrel{\text{def}}{=} |\Delta| + |Q| + |\Sigma|$, it is easy to show that checking diagnosability takes quadratic time w.r.t. $|\mathcal{A}|$ [16,27]. This instantiates the classical squaring construction for ambiguity detection [6]. In fact, the same argument serves to show a tight complexity-theoretic upper bound (see the full paper for details). Note that under the conditions named in the following proposition all four diagnosability notions coincide.

Proposition 2.4. *Verifying diagnosability for finite-state, live and convergent LTSs is* NL-*complete.*

2.4   Opacity

The classical notion of opacity, as defined in [2], deals with finite traces only. For our purpose, we distinguish a subset S of Σ containing special *secret* letters such that $\mathcal{O}(s) = \varepsilon$ for all $s \in S$. We consider as secret any sequence containing some $s \in S$, hence the set of finite secrets in an LTS $\mathcal{A}$ is $Sec^*(\mathcal{A}) \stackrel{\text{def}}{=} Trace^*(\mathcal{A}) \cap \Sigma^* S \Sigma^*$, while the set of infinite secrets is $Sec^\omega(\mathcal{A}) \stackrel{\text{def}}{=} Trace^\omega(\mathcal{A}) \cap \Sigma^* S \Sigma^\omega$; dually, the set of finite non-secret traces is $Pub^*(\mathcal{A}) \stackrel{\text{def}}{=} Trace^*(\mathcal{A}) \cap (\Sigma \setminus S)^*$ and the set of infinite non-secret ones is $Pub^\omega(\mathcal{A}) \stackrel{\text{def}}{=} Trace^\omega(\mathcal{A}) \cap (\Sigma \setminus S)^\omega$.

Definition 2.5 (Opacity [2]). *The secret S in an LTS $\mathcal{A}$ is opaque if*

$$\mathcal{O}(Sec^*(\mathcal{A})) \subseteq \mathcal{O}(Pub^*(\mathcal{A})).$$

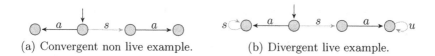

(a) Convergent non live example.   (b) Divergent live example.

Fig. 3. Counter-examples for Lemma 2.6, with $\mathcal{O}(u) = \mathcal{O}(s) = \varepsilon$ and $\mathcal{O}(a) = a$.

The problem of checking opacity was proven PSPACE-complete for finite LTSs [4] for a state-based variant, and this is easily seen to hold for Definition 2.5 as well.

Finite Opacity. As with diagnosability, we shall need a notion of opacity able to consider infinite runs, which we will then refine in Definition 3.5 for weakly fair opacity: we say that the secret in a LTS $\mathcal{A}$ is *finitely opaque* if, for all $\hat{\sigma} \in Sec^*(\mathcal{A})$, there exists an infinite non-secret trace $\rho \in Pub^\omega(\mathcal{A})$ such that $\mathcal{O}(\hat{\sigma}) \leq \mathcal{O}(\rho)$. By Kőnig's Lemma and arguments similar to those used for Lemma 2.2, we show that this notion coincides with opacity on live convergent LTSs in the full paper.

Lemma 2.6 (Comparison of Opacity Notions). *Let $\mathcal{A}$ be a live convergent LTS. Then the secret in $\mathcal{A}$ is opaque if and only if it is finitely opaque.*

Remark 2.7 (Counter-examples). Figure 3 shows that $\mathcal{A}$ must be live and convergent for the equivalence between opacity and finite opacity to hold in Lemma 2.6. In both Fig. 3(a) and (b) the system is opaque since $\mathcal{O}(Sec^*(\mathcal{A})) = \{\varepsilon, a\} = \mathcal{O}(Pub^*(\mathcal{A}))$, but is not finitely opaque because there exists a finite secret trace $s \in Sec^*(\mathcal{A})$ but there does not exist any infinite non-secret trace: $Pub^\omega(\mathcal{A}) = \emptyset$.

3   Opacity and Diagnosability for Petri Nets

After some reminders on Petri nets, we devote this section to the definitions of weakly fair Petri nets in Sect. 3.2 and of suitable variants of diagnosability and opacity in Sect. 3.3. We finally consider the case of weakly fair diagnosability when no faults are fair in Sect. 3.4.

3.1   Petri Nets

Syntax. A *Petri Net* (PN) is a tuple $\mathcal{N} = \langle P, T, w, m_0 \rangle$ where P and T are finite sets of *places* and *transitions* respectively, $w: (P \times T) \cup (T \times P) \to \mathbb{N}$ is the *flow mapping*, and $m_0 \in \mathbb{N}^P$ is the *initial marking*.

A *marking* is a mapping $m \in \mathbb{N}^P$. As usual, in figures, transitions are represented as rectangles and places as circles. If $m(p) \geq 1$, the corresponding number of black tokens are drawn in p. For a transition t, we denote its *preset* by $^\bullet t \overset{\text{def}}{=} \{p \in P \mid w(p, t) > 0\}$ and its *postset* by $t^\bullet \overset{\text{def}}{=} \{p \in P \mid w(t, p) > 0\}$.

Semantics. The operational semantics of a PN $\mathcal{N} = \langle P, T, w, \boldsymbol{m}_0 \rangle$ is an LTS $\mathcal{A}_\mathcal{N} = \langle \mathbb{N}^P, \boldsymbol{m}_0, T, \Delta \rangle$, whose states are the markings of $\mathcal{N}$, and whose transitions are labelled by T, where $\langle \boldsymbol{m}, t, \boldsymbol{m}' \rangle \in \Delta$ if and only if for each $p \in P$ we have $\boldsymbol{m}(p) \geq w(p, t)$, and $\boldsymbol{m}'(p) = \boldsymbol{m}(p) - w(p, t) + w(t, p)$ for all $p \in P$. Note that $\mathcal{A}_\mathcal{N}$ is 'deterministic' as no two different runs produce the same trace.

Note that adding an observation mask to a Petri net $\mathcal{N}$ results in what is usually called a 'labelled Petri net'. Then diagnosability with respect to a subset $F \subseteq T$ of fault transitions corresponds to diagnosability of the transition system $\mathcal{A}_\mathcal{N}$. As mentioned in the introduction, this notion declares the net from Fig. 1(a) to be non-diagnosable. Similarly, a Petri net $\mathcal{N}$ is opaque in the sense of Definition 2.5 with respect to a subset $S \subseteq T$ of secret transitions if $\mathcal{A}_\mathcal{N}$ is opaque. We shall abuse notations and write '$Trace^*(\mathcal{N})$' (resp. '$Trace^\omega(\mathcal{N})$', etc.) instead of '$Trace^*(\mathcal{A}_\mathcal{N})$' (resp. '$Trace^\omega(\mathcal{A}_\mathcal{N})$', etc.).

Safe Petri Nets. A Petri net $\mathcal{N}$ is *safe* if the reachable states form a subset of $\{0, 1\}^P$; as a result $\mathcal{A}_\mathcal{N}$ is finite, and $Trace^*(\mathcal{N})$ is regular. Note however that safe Petri nets are *implicit* descriptions of $\mathcal{A}_\mathcal{N}$: the latter can be of (at most) exponential size in terms of $|\mathcal{N}|$. This immediately entails that, in safe Petri nets, diagnosis is in PSPACE by Proposition 2.4 and opacity in EXPSPACE by [4]; we shall generalise and refine these upper bounds in Sect. 5 to take weak fairness into account.

3.2 Weak Fairness

We shall employ the following generalisation of weak fairness as defined in [7,11]:

Definition 3.1 (Weak Fairness). *A Petri net with weak fairness (WF-PN) is a tuple $\mathcal{W} = \langle \mathcal{N}, W \rangle$, where $\mathcal{N}$ is a Petri net and $W \subseteq T$ a set of transitions called* weakly fair.

Let $\sigma = (t_i)_{i \geq 1} \in T^\omega$ be an infinite trace, and $(\boldsymbol{m}_i)_{i \geq 0}$ the (uniquely determined) infinite run of $\mathcal{A}_\mathcal{N}$ over σ. Then σ is weakly fair *if for every $t \in W$,*

WF.1 *there are infinitely many i with $t_i = t$,* **or**
WF.2 *there are infinitely many i where t_i conflicts with t with respect to $\boldsymbol{m}_{i-1}$, i.e. there exists $p \in P$ s.t. $\boldsymbol{m}_{i-1}(p) < w(p, t_i) + w(p, t)$.*

Note that (WF.2) also covers the case where t is simply disabled. Informally, in a weakly fair sequence σ, each weakly fair transition t that is enabled either fires eventually, or some other transition that competes for a preset place with t fires. As shown by Jančar [14], it is decidable whether a WF-PN has at least one weakly fair trace.[1]

In drawings, we shall denote weakly fair transitions by the annotation 'WF' and a bang. For instance, in the net from Fig. 1(b), s_2 is a weakly fair transition,

---

[1] In Jančar's definition, (WF.2) uses the simpler condition $\boldsymbol{m}_{i-1}(p) < w(p, t)$. We could easily adapt our treatment of weak fairness to work with that definition, but we preferred to remain compatible with [7,11].

and $u_1 t_1^\omega$ is not weakly fair since s_2 is continuously enabled and never fires. (In this case, no other transition conflicts with s_2.) We shall use 'WF' subscripts to denote the restriction of a set of infinite traces to weakly fair ones, as in '$Trace_{WF}^\omega(\mathcal{N})$' or '$Faulty_{WF}^\omega(\mathcal{N})$'.

When $\mathcal{N}$ is safe, Definition 3.1 coincides with the definition employed in [7,11,26]; see the full paper for details.

Proposition 3.2 (Weak Fairness in Safe PNs). *Let $\mathcal{W} = \langle \mathcal{N}, W \rangle$ be a safe WF-PN. An infinite trace $\sigma = (t_i)_{i \geq 1}$ with run $(m_i)_{i \geq 0}$ is weakly fair if and only if, for every $i > 0$ and every $t \in W$ enabled in m_{i-1}, there exists some $j \geq i$ such that $\bullet t \cap \bullet t_j \neq \emptyset$.*

3.3 Diagnosability and Opacity with Weak Fairness

In the context of Petri nets with weak fairness, the definitions of both notions must take into account the set of weakly fair transitions while maintaining the Finite Observation Property.

Weakly Fair Diagnosability. We restrict finite diagnosability to the set of weakly fair runs, as is done in [7], but with a generalised notion of weak fairness.

Definition 3.3 (Weakly Fair Diagnosability). *A WF-PN $\mathcal{W} = \langle \mathcal{N}, W \rangle$ is said to be WF-diagnosable if every infinite, weakly fair, faulty trace $\sigma \in Faulty_{WF}^\omega(\mathcal{N})$ has a finite prefix $\hat{\sigma}$ such that every infinite weakly fair trace $\rho \in Trace_{WF}^\omega(\mathcal{N})$ satisfying $\mathcal{O}(\hat{\sigma}) < \mathcal{O}(\rho)$ is faulty.*

Consider again the net from Fig. 1(a) and assume that transition a is WF. Then this net is WF-diagnosable since a weakly fair trace that contains f also eventually contains a, and a is only possible after f. Note that, as shown in [7], this definition is not equivalent to simply restricting diagnosability according to Definition 2.1 to weakly fair traces. The precise relation of WF-diagnosability with other notions was not examined in [7]; however, by Lemma 2.2, we obtain:

Lemma 3.4. *Let $\mathcal{W} = \langle \mathcal{N}, W \rangle$ be a convergent WF-PN such that $W = \emptyset$. Then $\mathcal{W}$ is WF-diagnosable if and only if $\mathcal{N}$ is diagnosable.*

Weakly Fair Opacity. We now turn to opacity and provide a definition of weakly fair opacity that also respects the Finite Observation Property, again by restricting finite opacity to weakly fair runs. Informally, Definition 3.5 means that any finite observation prefix can be extended in a way compatible with a weakly fair non-secret run, hence making the occurrence of a secret uncertain for the observer.

Definition 3.5 (Weakly Fair Opacity). *The secret in a WF-PN $\mathcal{W} = \langle \mathcal{N}, W \rangle$ is said to be WF-opaque if, for any trace $\hat{\sigma}$ in $Sec^*(\mathcal{N})$, there exists an infinite, weakly fair, non-secret trace $\rho \in Pub_{WF}^\omega(\mathcal{N})$ such that $\mathcal{O}(\hat{\sigma}) \leq \mathcal{O}(\rho)$.*

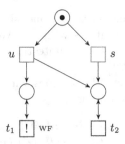

Fig. 4. WF-PN $\mathcal{W}_2$ with t_1 weakly fair, s secret and u unobservable.

Example 3.6. The WF-PN $\mathcal{W}_1 = \langle \mathcal{N}_1, \{s_2\} \rangle$ depicted in Fig. 1(b) shows that weakly fair opacity is more discriminating that standard opacity. We consider the observation mask $\mathcal{O}$ defined by $\mathcal{O}(u_1) = \mathcal{O}(u_2) = \mathcal{O}(s_1) = \mathcal{O}(s_2) = \varepsilon$, for two secret transitions s_1 and s_2, $\mathcal{O}(t_1) = a$ and $\mathcal{O}(t_2) = b$.

The net $\mathcal{N}_1$ is opaque according to Definition 2.5 because the finite secret is observed as $\mathcal{O}(Sec^*(\mathcal{N}_1)) = a^*$, while the non-secret executions are observed as $a^* \cup b^*$, and the former is a subset of the latter.

On the other hand, the secret is not WF-opaque in $\mathcal{W}_1$ according to Definition 3.5. Let $\hat{\sigma} = s_1 t_1 \in Sec^*(\mathcal{N}_1)$. Then $\mathcal{O}(\hat{\sigma}) = a$, and the set of infinite, weakly fair traces ρ such that $\mathcal{O}(\hat{\sigma}) < \mathcal{O}(\rho)$ is $s_1 t_1^\omega \cup u_1 t_1^* s_2 t_1^\omega$, and all of these executions contain a secret transition.

As with Lemma 3.4, we obtain from Lemma 2.6 that WF-opacity and opacity coincide when no transition is weakly fair, thus Definition 3.5 is a proper generalisation of Definition 2.5.

Lemma 3.7. *Let $\mathcal{W} = \langle \mathcal{N}, W \rangle$ be a live convergent WF-PN such that $W = \emptyset$. Then the secret is WF-opaque in $\mathcal{W}$ if and only if it is opaque in $\mathcal{W}$.*

Comparing Definitions 2.5 and 3.5, we see that the formulation of WF-opacity is considerably more complex than the simple inclusion required by standard opacity. It is tempting to 'simplify' Definition 3.5 by mimicking Definition 2.5, but restricting to weakly fair executions, i.e., to demand that $\mathcal{O}(Sec^\omega_{WF}(\mathcal{N})) \subseteq \mathcal{O}(Pub^\omega_{WF}(\mathcal{N}))$. However such a definition would not respect the Finite Observation Property.

Example 3.8. For the WF-PN $\mathcal{W}_2 = \langle \mathcal{N}_2, \{t_1\} \rangle$ depicted in Fig. 4, we consider the observation mask $\mathcal{O}$ defined by $\mathcal{O}(u) = \mathcal{O}(s) = \varepsilon$, $\mathcal{O}(t_1) = a$ and $\mathcal{O}(t_2) = b$.

In $\mathcal{W}_2$, the system can either fire the secret transition s and then infinitely often t_2, or it can fire u and then arbitrarily often a and b, where the weak fairness condition requires to fire a infinitely often. Thus, $\mathcal{O}(Sec^\omega_{WF}(\mathcal{N}_2)) = b^\omega$, and $\mathcal{O}(Pub^\omega_{WF}(\mathcal{N}_2)) = (b^*a)^\omega$; since the first set is not included in the second, a definition based on the above inclusion would declare $\mathcal{W}_2$ non-opaque. However, even when s is fired, no *finite* observation is sufficient to determine that this was the case; indeed an observation b^n, for any $n \geq 0$, could also be the consequence of firing u first. Definition 3.5 captures this fact: for any $\hat{\sigma} = st_2^n \in Sec^*(\mathcal{N}_2)$ there exists an infinite WF trace without secret, e.g. $\rho = ut_2^n t_1^\omega$ satisfying $\mathcal{O}(\hat{\sigma}) < \mathcal{O}(\rho)$, thus $\mathcal{W}_2$ is WF-opaque.

3.4   No Weakly Fair Faults: The Strict Case

We finally investigate the special case where fault transitions are not weakly fair, i.e., a fault is a *possible* outcome in the system but not one that is *required* to happen: we call *strict WF-PN* a WF-PN $\mathcal{W} = \langle \mathcal{N}, W \rangle$ where $W \cap F = \emptyset$. Under this assumption, weakly fair diagnosability has a simple characterisation, reminiscent of Definition 2.1, which generalises [7, Lemma 3.4 and 3.5] to general Petri nets. Note that this also provides an alternative proof of Lemma 3.4.

Lemma 3.9. *Let $\mathcal{W} = \langle \mathcal{N}, W \rangle$ be a strict convergent WF-PN. Then $\mathcal{W}$ is WF-diagnosable if and only if $\mathcal{O}(Faulty_{WF}^\omega(\mathcal{N})) \cap \mathcal{O}(Correct^\omega(\mathcal{N})) = \emptyset$.*

Proof. For the 'only if' part, assume there exists $\sigma \in Faulty_{WF}^\omega(\mathcal{N})$ and $\rho \in Correct^\omega(\mathcal{N})$ such that $\mathcal{O}(\sigma) = \mathcal{O}(\rho)$. If ρ is weakly fair, then $\mathcal{W}$ is not WF-diagnosable. Otherwise, consider some prefix $\hat{\sigma} < \sigma$ and let us build a suitable $\rho_{\hat{\sigma}} \in Correct_{WF}^\omega(\mathcal{N})$. Let $j \in \mathbb{N}$ be an index such that $\mathcal{O}(\hat{\sigma}) \leq \mathcal{O}(\hat{\rho})$ for the prefix $\hat{\rho}$ of length j of ρ.

Since ρ is not weakly fair, it must violate (WF.2) for some $t \in W$: writing $m_0 \xrightarrow{t_1} m_1 \xrightarrow{t_2} \cdots$ for its underlying run, this means that there are infinitely many indices i such that $m_i(p) \geq w(p, t_{i+1}) + w(p, t)$ for all $p \in P$. Thus for infinitely many i, $m_i(p) - w(p, t) + w(t, p) \geq w(p, t_{i+1})$ for all $p \in P$. Since $t \notin F$, this means that we can insert a transition by t in all those indices $i > j$ and still obtain a trace in $Correct^\omega(\mathcal{N})$; however this trace now satisfies (WF.1) for t. Applying this to all the $t \in W$ for which ρ was not weakly fair yields a weakly fair trace $\rho_{\hat{\sigma}} \in Correct_{WF}^\omega(\mathcal{N})$. Furthermore, since we inserted those occurrences of t (which might be observable) after the index j, $\mathcal{O}(\hat{\sigma}) \leq \mathcal{O}(\hat{\rho}) < \mathcal{O}(\rho_{\hat{\sigma}})$. Hence $\mathcal{W}$ is not WF-diagnosable.

Conversely, for the 'if' part, assume that $\mathcal{W}$ is not WF-diagnosable: there exists $\sigma \in Faulty_{WF}^\omega(\mathcal{N})$ such that for every prefix $\hat{\sigma} < \sigma$, there exists $\rho_{\hat{\sigma}} \in Correct_{WF}^\omega(\mathcal{N})$ with $\mathcal{O}(\hat{\sigma}) < \mathcal{O}(\rho_{\hat{\sigma}})$. Define the tree

$$\mathcal{T} \stackrel{\text{def}}{=} Pref(\{\hat{\rho} \mid \exists \hat{\sigma} < \sigma, \mathcal{O}(\hat{\rho}) = \mathcal{O}(\hat{\sigma}) \text{ and } \hat{\rho} < \rho_{\hat{\sigma}}\}). \tag{1}$$

Since Σ is finite, $\mathcal{T}$ has finite degree. Since $\mathcal{N}$ is assumed to be convergent, $\{\mathcal{O}(\hat{\sigma}) \mid \hat{\sigma} < \sigma\}$ is infinite, and therefore $\mathcal{T}$ is infinite as well. By Kőnig's Lemma, it has an infinite branch $\rho \in \Sigma^\omega$ such that every finite prefix $\hat{\rho} < \rho$ satisfies

- $\hat{\rho} < \rho_{\hat{\sigma}}$ thus $\hat{\rho} \in Correct^*(\mathcal{N})$ and therefore $\rho \in Correct^\omega(\mathcal{N})$, and
- $\mathcal{O}(\hat{\rho}) \leq \mathcal{O}(\hat{\sigma}) < \mathcal{O}(\sigma)$ and therefore $\mathcal{O}(\sigma) = \mathcal{O}(\rho)$.

Thus $\mathcal{W}$ satisfies $\mathcal{O}(Faulty_{WF}^\omega(\mathcal{N})) \cap \mathcal{O}(Correct^\omega(\mathcal{N})) \neq \emptyset$. $\square$

4   Lower Bounds

In this section, we give reductions that yield lower bounds for the problems of diagnosability and opacity. Notice that we first study the problem variants *without* weak fairness. Thanks to Lemmas 3.4 and 3.7, these lower bounds also apply to the WF variants of both problems: checking diagnosability/opacity for the special case of a WF-PN $\langle \mathcal{N}, \emptyset \rangle$ is equivalent to checking WF-diagnosability/WF-opacity for a PN $\mathcal{N}$. For the hardness of WF-diagnosability, we show a reduction from the reachability problem for PNs.

Live and Convergent Nets. As we saw in Lemmas 2.2 and 2.6, in the absence of weak fairness constraints, (most of) the various definitions of diagnosability and opacity turn out to be equivalent when the transition systems under consideration are finitely branching, live, and convergent. As we wish our results to have the widest possible applicability, we shall require these properties of all the systems we study in lower bound proofs—but not necessarily in upper bound proofs. Because Petri nets yield finitely branching LTSs, we only need our nets to be live and convergent.

Remark 4.1. A Petri net can always be made live by adding an observable 'clock tick' transition connected back-and-forth to a single, initially marked place (like the transition c in Fig. 1(a)). Intuitively, such a transition can be understood as modelling the passage of time marked by an observer when nothing else happens in the system. Importantly, the addition of a 'clock tick' transition does not change the properties of diagnosability and opacity in our constructions.

4.1   Diagnosability

For diagnosability, we reduce from the *coverability problem*: Given a PN $\mathcal{N}$ and a place p, is there a reachable marking $\boldsymbol{m}$ such that $\boldsymbol{m}(p) \geq 1$?

Proposition 4.2 (Hardness of Diagnosability). *Diagnosability is* PSPACE-*hard for safe Petri nets and* EXPSPACE-*hard in general, already for live convergent nets.*

Proof. We exhibit a polynomial time reduction from the coverability problem to non diagnosability. The coverability problem is known to be PSPACE-complete for safe Petri nets [17] and EXPSPACE-hard in general [20]. The statement follows because these two complexity classes are closed under complement.

Let $\mathcal{N} = \langle P, T, w, \boldsymbol{m}_0 \rangle$ be a PN and let $p \in P$. We construct a live and convergent PN $\mathcal{N}'$ and an observation $\mathcal{O}$ such that a marking $\boldsymbol{m}$ with $\boldsymbol{m}(p) \geq 1$ can be reached in $\mathcal{N}$ if and only if $\mathcal{N}'$ is not diagnosable; furthermore $\mathcal{N}'$ is safe whenever $\mathcal{N}$ is safe.

The construction consists in adding to $\mathcal{N}$ a single new place $q \notin P$, initially marked, and a single unobservable faulty transition $f \notin T$ taking one token from p and q to fire and putting the token back into p afterwards (see left part

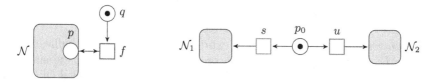

Fig. 5. Constructions for the nets $\mathcal{N}'$ in Proposition 4.2 (left) and Proposition 4.4 (right).

of Fig. 5). Thus $\mathcal{N}' \stackrel{\text{def}}{=} \langle P', T', w', m_0 \rangle$ with $P' \stackrel{\text{def}}{=} P \cup \{q\}$, $T' \stackrel{\text{def}}{=} T \cup \{f\}$ and w' coincides with w on $P \times T \cup T \times P$, with $w'(q, f) = w'(p, f) = w'(f, p) = 1$ in addition. For the observation mask $\mathcal{O}$, we let $E \stackrel{\text{def}}{=} T$ and all transitions from T are observable with $\mathcal{O}(t) \stackrel{\text{def}}{=} t$ and $\mathcal{O}(f) \stackrel{\text{def}}{=} \varepsilon$. The faulty transition f can fire once in $\mathcal{N}'$ if and only if there is a reachable marking m in $\mathcal{N}$ with $m(p) \geq 1$. In this case, all the infinite runs in $\mathcal{N}'$ reaching m have ambiguous observations.

The construction ensures that if $\mathcal{N}$ is safe then it is also the case for $\mathcal{N}'$. Since f can fire only once and no transition from $\mathcal{N}$ is erased, $\mathcal{N}'$ is convergent. It is not necessarily live since $\mathcal{N}$ may contain a deadlock; however, $\mathcal{N}'$ can be made live by adding a 'clock tick' transition (cf. Remark 4.1) without affecting the validity of the reduction. $\qquad\square$

4.2 Opacity

For the opacity problem, we prove our hardness results by reducing from the *trace inclusion problem* for Petri nets: Given two PNs $\mathcal{N}_1$ and $\mathcal{N}_2$ with associated observation masks $\mathcal{O}_1$ and $\mathcal{O}_2$ into the same E, is $\mathcal{O}_1(Trace^*(\mathcal{N}_1)) \subseteq \mathcal{O}_2(Trace^*(\mathcal{N}_2))$? This problem is well-known to be undecidable for general Petri nets and EXPSPACE-complete for safe Petri nets [5].

However, because we insist on our systems being convergent, some additional care is required: in our main reduction (c.f. Proposition 4.4), we need the two PNs $\mathcal{N}_1$ and $\mathcal{N}_2$ to be convergent, hence we need to show that the trace inclusion problem remains hard even for convergent instances. Along the way, we re-discovered that its complexity in the safe case can be refined and shown to be ESPACE-complete (see Proposition 4.3), based on a reduction from the universality problem for shuffle expressions (SE) studied by Mayer and Stockmeyer [22].

Shuffle Expressions. Recall that the *shuffle* of two words σ and ρ in E^* is the language $\sigma \sqcup\!\sqcup \rho \stackrel{\text{def}}{=} \{\sigma_1 \rho_1 \sigma_2 \rho_2 \cdots \sigma_n \rho_n \mid n \in \mathbb{N}, \sigma_1 \cdots \sigma_n = \sigma, \rho_1 \cdots \rho_n = \rho\}$ (σ_i and ρ_i are words in E^*); this is lifted to $L \sqcup\!\sqcup M \stackrel{\text{def}}{=} \bigcup_{\sigma \in L, \rho \in M} \sigma \sqcup\!\sqcup \rho$ for two languages L and M.

Shuffle expressions in SE are built according to the abstract syntax

$$e := \varepsilon \mid a \mid e + e \mid e \cdot e \mid e \sqcup\!\sqcup e \mid e^*,$$

where a ranges over some alphabet E. The language of an expression in SE is defined inductively by $L(\varepsilon) \stackrel{\text{def}}{=} \{\varepsilon\}$, $L(a) \stackrel{\text{def}}{=} \{a\}$ for all $a \in E$, $L(e_1 + e_2) \stackrel{\text{def}}{=}$

$L(e_1) \cup L(e_2)$, $L(e_1 \cdot e_2) \overset{\text{def}}{=} L(e_1) \cdot L(e_2)$, $L(e_1 \shuffle e_2) \overset{\text{def}}{=} L(e_1) \shuffle L(e_2)$, and $L(e^*) \overset{\text{def}}{=} L(e)^*$, where e_1 and e_2 are two expressions.

The *universality* problem for shuffle expressions asks, given e a shuffle expression over E, whether $E^* \subseteq L(e)$. This problem is ESPACE-complete since its complement is ESPACE-complete [22, Theorem 7.1, where it is called NEC] and since ESPACE is closed under complement.

We provide in the full paper an inductive construction of a safe PN $\mathcal{N}(e)$ with coverability language $L(e)$ for e in SE. This is basically Thompson's inductive construction of a finite-state automaton from a regular expression with an extra case for shuffles, but some additional care is required in order to ensure that $\mathcal{N}(e)$ is convergent. One last pitfall is that we work with trace languages instead of coverability languages; this is handled using an additional endmarker symbol.

Proposition 4.3. *The trace inclusion problem is* ESPACE-*complete for safe convergent Petri nets.*

Reduction from the Trace Inclusion Problem. We wrap-up our lower bound proof using a reduction from the trace inclusion problem in convergent nets to the opacity problem.

Proposition 4.4 (Hardness of Opacity). *Opacity is* ESPACE-*hard for safe Petri nets, and undecidable in general, already for live convergent nets.*

Proof. We exhibit a polynomial time reduction from the trace inclusion problem for convergent PNs to the opacity problem, which preserves safety. As seen in Proposition 4.3, the trace inclusion problem is ESPACE-hard for safe convergent Petri nets. In the general case, it is undecidable by the generic proof of Jančar [15] for equivalence and preorder problems in Petri nets: given a 2-counter machine, his proof builds two Petri nets $\mathcal{N}_1$ and $\mathcal{N}_2$ with non erasing observation functions $\mathcal{O}_1$ and $\mathcal{O}_2$—thus those nets are convergent—, such that the machine halts if and only if $\mathcal{O}_1(\mathit{Trace}^*(\mathcal{N}_1)) \neq \mathcal{O}_2(\mathit{Trace}^*(\mathcal{N}_2))$.

For the reduction, let $\mathcal{N}_1 = \langle P_1, T_1, w_1, \boldsymbol{m}_{0,1} \rangle$ and $\mathcal{N}_2 = \langle P_2, T_2, w_2, \boldsymbol{m}_{0,2} \rangle$ be two convergent PNs, with observation masks $\mathcal{O}_1$ and $\mathcal{O}_2$ into the same alphabet E; without loss of generality they have disjoint sets of places and transitions.

We first build a convergent PN $\mathcal{N}'$ by adding a new place $p_0 \notin P_1 \cup P_2$, initially marked, and two new transitions s and u not in $T_1 \cup T_2$. The observation mask $\mathcal{O}'$ of $\mathcal{N}'$ extends $\mathcal{O}_1$ and $\mathcal{O}_2$ by $\mathcal{O}'(s) = \mathcal{O}'(u) = \varepsilon$. The construction (see right part of Fig. 5) consists in linking p_0 to $\mathcal{N}_1$ and $\mathcal{N}_2$ through the transitions s and u respectively, making them produce the initial markings of $\mathcal{N}_1$ and $\mathcal{N}_2$. The convergence of $\mathcal{N}'$ results from that of $\mathcal{N}_1$ and $\mathcal{N}_2$. The construction ensures that if $\mathcal{N}_1$ and $\mathcal{N}_2$ are safe, so is $\mathcal{N}'$. Now the set of secret words in $\mathcal{N}'$ is observed as $\mathcal{O}_1(\mathit{Trace}^*(\mathcal{N}_1))$ while the set of non-secret words is observed as $\mathcal{O}_2(\mathit{Trace}^*(\mathcal{N}_2))$. Thus, the secret is opaque in $\mathcal{N}'$ if and only if the inclusion $\mathcal{O}_1(\mathit{Trace}^*(\mathcal{N}_1)) \subseteq \mathcal{O}_2(\mathit{Trace}^*(\mathcal{N}_2))$ holds.

Finally, adding a 'clock tick' as in Remark 4.1 to $\mathcal{N}'$ with a fresh observation $\flat \notin E$ yields the desired $\mathcal{N}$ and $\mathcal{O}$. Indeed, $\mathcal{O}(\mathit{Sec}^*(\mathcal{N})) = \mathcal{O}'(\mathit{Sec}^*(\mathcal{N}')) \shuffle \{\flat^n \mid n \in \mathbb{N}\}$ and $\mathcal{O}(\mathit{Pub}^*(\mathcal{N})) = \mathcal{O}'(\mathit{Pub}^*(\mathcal{N}')) \shuffle \{\flat^n \mid n \in \mathbb{N}\}$, and inclusion holds between these two languages if and only if $\mathcal{O}'(\mathit{Sec}^*(\mathcal{N}')) \subseteq \mathcal{O}'(\mathit{Pub}^*(\mathcal{N}'))$. $\square$

4.3 Weakly Fair Diagnosability

We prove that WF-diagnosability is at least as hard as reachability—and thus EXPSPACE-hard [20]. The reduction itself is inspired by a hardness proof by Howell et al. [13, Theorem 4.9] for deciding the existence of a weakly fair run.

Proposition 4.5 (Hardness of WF-Diagnosability). *There is a polynomial time reduction from the reachability problem in Petri nets to non WF-diagnosability, which outputs live convergent nets with $W \cap F = \emptyset$.*

Proof. Consider an instance $\langle \mathcal{N}, \boldsymbol{m} \rangle$ of the reachability problem where $\mathcal{N} = \langle P, T, w, \boldsymbol{m}_0 \rangle$ and $\boldsymbol{m} \in \mathbb{N}^P$. Define $n_0 \stackrel{\text{def}}{=} 1 + \sum_{p \in P} \boldsymbol{m}_0(p)$ and $n \stackrel{\text{def}}{=} 1 + \sum_{p \in P} \boldsymbol{m}(p)$.

We start by constructing a net $\mathcal{N}' \stackrel{\text{def}}{=} \langle P \uplus \{sum, active\}, T, w', \boldsymbol{m}_0' \rangle$ that extends $\mathcal{N}$ with a 'checksum' place sum and a control place $active$. The initial marking $\boldsymbol{m}_0'$ extends $\boldsymbol{m}_0$ with $\boldsymbol{m}_0'(sum) \stackrel{\text{def}}{=} n_0$ and $\boldsymbol{m}_0'(active) \stackrel{\text{def}}{=} 1$. The flow w' is defined as w extended for all $t \in T$ with

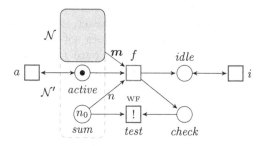

Fig. 6. The Petri net $\mathcal{N}''$ in the proof of Proposition 4.5.

– $w(sum, t) \stackrel{\text{def}}{=} \sum_{p \in P} w(p, t)$ and $w(t, sum) \stackrel{\text{def}}{=} \sum_{p \in P} w(t, p)$, which ensures that, in any reachable marking $\boldsymbol{m}'$ of $\mathcal{N}'$, $\boldsymbol{m}'(sum) = 1 + \sum_{p \in P} \boldsymbol{m}'(p)$;
– $w(active, t) \stackrel{\text{def}}{=} w(t, active) \stackrel{\text{def}}{=} 1$, which ensures that the original transitions in T can only be fired if $active$ is marked; we call such markings 'active'.

We now construct $\mathcal{N}''$ extending $\mathcal{N}'$ as shown in Fig. 6. It features:

– a fault transition f that can be fired at most once, from an active marking $\boldsymbol{m}'$ that covers $\boldsymbol{m}$, and the projection of $\boldsymbol{m}'$ to P was equal to $\boldsymbol{m}$ if and only if sum is empty as a result of firing f;
– a weakly fair transition $test$ that can be fired at most once, necessarily at some point after f was fired, and whose purpose is to test whether sum is empty;
– two transitions a and i, idling respectively when $active$ or $idle$ is marked.

We define $E \stackrel{\text{def}}{=} \{a, e\}$ and let our observation mask $\mathcal{O}$ map every transition to a, except for $\mathcal{O}(test) \stackrel{\text{def}}{=} e$ and $\mathcal{O}(f) \stackrel{\text{def}}{=} \varepsilon$; we set $W \stackrel{\text{def}}{=} \{test\}$ and $F \stackrel{\text{def}}{=} \{f\}$. Observe that $\mathcal{N}''$ is live and convergent with $W \cap F = \emptyset$.

Claim. The marking m is reachable in $\mathcal{N}$ if and only if $\mathcal{N}''$ is not WF-diagnosable.

Since $W \cap F = \emptyset$, by Lemma 3.9, $\mathcal{N}''$ is not WF-diagnosable if and only if there exist $\sigma \in Faulty_{WF}^{\omega}(\mathcal{N}'')$ and $\rho \in Correct^{\omega}(\mathcal{N}'')$ such that $\mathcal{O}(\sigma) = \mathcal{O}(\rho)$.

For the 'only if' direction, assume $m_0 \overset{\hat{\sigma}}{\Rightarrow} m$ in $\mathcal{N}$. Then the same transition sequence $\hat{\sigma}$ leads in $\mathcal{N}''$ to an active marking equal to m over P, with n tokens in sum. Then $\sigma \overset{\text{def}}{=} \hat{\sigma} f i^{\omega}$ can be fired in $\mathcal{N}''$, and is weakly fair because sum becomes empty once f has fired. Defining $\rho \overset{\text{def}}{=} a^{\omega}$, we get $\mathcal{O}(\sigma) = a^{\omega} = \mathcal{O}(\rho)$ and $\mathcal{N}''$ is therefore not WF-diagnosable.

For the 'if' direction, let us first consider any $\rho \in Correct^{\omega}(\mathcal{N})$: as *check* cannot be marked in any correct run, *test* cannot be fired, and $\mathcal{O}(\rho) = a^{\omega}$. Turning our attention to $\sigma \in Faulty_{WF}^{\omega}(\mathcal{N}'')$, since it is faulty, f has been fired, hence the run on σ is of the form $m_0'' \overset{\hat{\sigma}}{\Rightarrow} m' \overset{f}{\Rightarrow} m'' \overset{\sigma'}{\Rightarrow}$ in $\mathcal{N}''$. We know that $m'(p) \geq m(p)$ for all $p \in P$ because f could be fired from m'. Assume for the sake of contradiction that $m'(p) > m(p)$ for some $p \in P$, and let us show that it implies that σ is not weakly fair; this will prove that m was reachable in $\mathcal{N}$.

By the invariant on sum, $m'(p) > m(p)$ for some $p \in P$ entails $m''(sum) > 0$ and therefore that *test* is enabled in m''. However, if *test* were fired in σ', this would entail $\mathcal{O}(\sigma) \in a^* e a^{\omega} \neq \mathcal{O}(\rho)$ (thus σ does not satisfy (WF.1)). Furthermore, σ does not satisfy (WF.2) either, since, once f has fired, *test* is the only fireable transition with either sum or *check* in its preset. □

5   Upper Bounds

In this section, we give upper complexity bounds in Sect. 5.1 for safe WF-PNs, that match the lower bounds of the previous section. For general Petri nets in Sect. 5.2, since opacity is undecidable, we only consider diagnosability and show that the problem is EXPSPACE-complete in the absence of weak fairness. We also consider strict WF-PNs and show an exponential time reduction to the reachability problem in this case. The general case of WF-PN remains open.

5.1   Safe Petri Nets

In the case of safe Petri nets, our upper complexity bounds for checking diagnosability and opacity *with weak fairness* match the lower bounds of Sect. 4 for the variants without weak fairness. From this viewpoint, weak fairness can be included 'for free' in diagnosability and opacity checking for concurrent systems.

WF-Diagnosability. Germanos et al. [7] show that, given a convergent WF-PN $\mathcal{W} = \langle \mathcal{N}, W \rangle$, one can construct in polynomial time a PN $\mathcal{N}'$ and a state-based LTL formula φ, such that $\mathcal{W}$ is WF-diagnosable if and only if $\mathcal{N}'$ has an infinite run satisfying φ. Since LTL model-checking of safe PNs is in PSPACE [5], the same upper bound applies to WF-diagnosis, which shows that the lower bound in Proposition 4.2 is tight.

Proposition 5.1. *WF-diagnosability is in* PSPACE *for safe convergent Petri nets.*

Weakly Fair Opacity. In the case of WF-opacity, we argue directly that there is an ESPACE algorithm for safe Petri nets, matching the lower bound from Proposition 4.4.

Proposition 5.2. *WF-opacity is in* ESPACE *for safe Petri nets.*

Proof (sketch). Let $\mathcal{W}$ be a safe WF-PN with n places. We sketch a nondeterministic algorithm $\mathcal{M}$ working in space $2^{O(n)}$ that checks for the negation of Definition 3.5 in $\mathcal{W}$. The result then follows from Savitch's Theorem showing NESPACE=ESPACE and the fact that ESPACE is deterministic.

We must look for a finite prefix $\hat{\sigma}$ of a run that uses a secret transition, and such that there exists no infinite WF trace $\rho \in Pub^\omega_{WF}(\mathcal{W})$ satisfying that $\mathcal{O}(\hat{\sigma}) < \mathcal{O}(\rho)$. The algorithm works in two phases:

1. the first phase nondeterministically picks a suitable prefix $\hat{\sigma}$ 'on the fly', along with the set $M \subseteq 2^n$ of possible markings reachable by some $\hat{\rho} \in Pub^*(\mathcal{W})$ with $\mathcal{O}(\hat{\sigma}) = \mathcal{O}(\hat{\rho})$—this can be carried in space $2^{O(n)}$—and
2. the second phase checks whether any marking $\boldsymbol{m} \in M$ can start a weakly fair infinite run; this can be verified by a model-checking algorithm for LTL—in PSPACE [5]. □

5.2   General Petri Nets

Because opacity is undecidable for general Petri nets by Proposition 4.4, we shall focus on (WF-)diagnosability. We rely for our results on decidable fragments of LTL on Petri net executions. The first step in the following reductions is to build (in polynomial time) a suitable *verifier net* $\mathcal{V}(\mathcal{W})$ from the input WF-PN $\mathcal{W}$; this consists simply in synchronising two copies $\mathcal{W}_1$ and $\mathcal{W}_2$ of $\mathcal{W}$ on their observations while letting unobservable transitions run asynchronously, and discarding fault transitions from the second copy—see the full paper for the precise construction, variants were used for instance in [3,7,21]. Then $\mathcal{W}$ is not diagnosable according to Definition 2.1 (thus ignoring weak fairness constraints for the moment) if and only if there exists an infinite run σ in $\mathcal{V}(\mathcal{W})$ that eventually visits some fault transition $f \in F$ (thus in the first copy):

$$\exists \sigma \in \mathit{Trace}^\omega(\mathcal{V}(\mathcal{W})), \exists i \in \mathbb{N} : \bigvee_{f \in F_1} \sigma(i) = f \, ; \tag{2}$$

here the '$_1$' subscript denotes the fact that we are looking for a transition from the first copy $\mathcal{W}_1$ of $\mathcal{W}$.

Diagnosability. The characterisation of non diagnosability in (2) translates immediately into the existence of an infinite trace of $\mathcal{V}(\mathcal{W})$ satisfying the *action-based* LTL formula

$$\Diamond(\bigvee_{f \in F_1} f). \tag{3}$$

Model-checking of action-based LTL formulæ in general Petri nets can be performed in EXPSPACE [12], hence in the absence of weakly fair transitions the lower bound from Proposition 4.2 is tight. This result dramatically improves the procedure proposed in [3], which relies on the construction of the coverability graph for the verifier net, producing an Ackermannian complexity.

Proposition 5.3. *Diagnosability for Petri nets is in* EXPSPACE.

Strict Case. By Lemma 3.9, if no fault is weakly fair in a WF-PN, then non WF-diagnosability is equivalent to the existence of a run satisfying (2) and whose projection on transitions from the first copy is weakly fair. In order to check those conditions, we are going to use another fragment of LTL proven decidable over Petri nets by Jančar [14]. The fragment LTL($\square\Diamond$) can use both actions and states in its atomic propositions, but only allows positive Boolean combinations of 'infinitely often' $\square\Diamond$ formulæ at top-level.

As LTL($\square\Diamond$) does not feature $\square$ on its own, we cannot use (3) directly, and we first modify $\mathcal{V}(\mathcal{W})$ so that all the fault transitions add a token to a new place *fault*, which is initially empty; once *fault* is marked, it remains so forever. Then non WF-diagnosability is equivalent to the existence of an infinite run of $\mathcal{V}(\mathcal{W})$ satisfying

$$\square\Diamond(\mathit{fault} > 0) \wedge \bigwedge_{t \in W_1} ((\square\Diamond t) \vee (\square\Diamond \bigvee_{t' \in T_1} \bigvee_{p \in P_1} t' \wedge (p < w(t, p) + w(t', p)))). \tag{4}$$

Because Jančar [14] proved existential LTL($\square\Diamond$) model checking of Petri nets to reduce in exponential time to the reachability problem, by Proposition 4.5 we get an equivalence between non WF-diagnosability when $W \cap F = \emptyset$ and reachability, modulo exponential-time many-one reductions.

Proposition 5.4. *There is an exponential time reduction from non WF-diagnosability in strict convergent WF-PNs to the reachability problem.*

6   Concluding Remarks

We have revisited the problems of diagnosability and opacity with a focus on expressivity for concurrent systems, and introduced a new notion of opacity for Petri nets under weakly fair semantics.

We have conducted a comparative study of complexity for both diagnosability and opacity analysis. Not surprisingly, opacity is always harder than diagnosability, and complexity also increases when moving from automata to safe Petri nets to general Petri nets, i.e., from the sequential to the concurrent to the infinite.

Safe Petri Nets. Note that the price to pay in safe Petri nets for the extra precision of analysis under *weak fairness*—which allows to capture indirect dependencies, as seen above and in [9,11]—is not higher than for the corresponding analyses with ordinary semantics. We therefore argue that the refined notions of WF-diagnosability from [7,11], and of WF-opacity that we have introduced in this paper, are valid and important contributions to the design and monitoring of concurrent systems. Future work should investigate efficient algorithms for the analysis of partially observed Petri nets.

General Petri Nets. For strict WF-PNs, Proposition 4.5 leaves an exponential complexity gap with our upper bound in Proposition 5.4. It might be worth investigating whether this gap could be filled by considering a reduction from reachability in *succinctly* presented Petri nets. In the general case, the main difficulty is that Definition 3.3 is essentially a branching-time property, which are generally undecidable in Petri nets. It is however quite a specific property, as can be seen in the case of safe Petri nets where it can be reduced to a linear-time property [7, Lemma 3.4]—unfortunately this reduction does not hold in general Petri nets—, and this might explain why we could not prove it undecidable either.

References

1. Badouel, E., Bednarczyk, M.A., Borzyszkowski, A.M., Caillaud, B., Darondeau, P.: Concurrent secrets. Discrete Event Dyn. Syst. **17**(4), 425–446 (2007)
2. Bryans, J., Koutny, M., Mazaré, L., Ryan, P.Y.A.: Opacity generalised to transition systems. Int. J. Inf. Secur. **7**(6), 421–435 (2008)
3. Cabasino, M.P., Giua, A., Lafortune, S., Seatzu, C.: A new approach for diagnosability analysis of Petri nets using verifier nets. IEEE Trans. Autom. Control **57**(12), 3104–3117 (2012)
4. Cassez, F., Dubreil, J., Marchand, H.: Dynamic observers for the synthesis of opaque systems. In: Liu, Z., Ravn, A.P. (eds.) ATVA 2009. LNCS, vol. 5799, pp. 352–367. Springer, Heidelberg (2009). doi:10.1007/978-3-642-04761-9_26
5. Esparza, J.: Decidability and complexity of Petri net problems — an introduction. In: Reisig, W., Rozenberg, G. (eds.) ACPN 1996. LNCS, vol. 1491, pp. 374–428. Springer, Heidelberg (1998). doi:10.1007/3-540-65306-6_20
6. Even, S.: On information lossless automata of finite order. IEEE Trans. Elec. Comput. **EC-14**(4), 561–569 (1965)
7. Germanos, V., Haar, S., Khomenko, V., Schwoon, S.: Diagnosability under weak fairness. ACM Trans. Embed. Comput. Syst. **14**(4:69), 132–141 (2015)
8. Haar, S.: Qualitative diagnosability of labeled Petri nets revisited. In: Proceedings of CDC 2009 and CCC 2009, pp. 1248–1253. IEEE (2009)
9. Haar, S.: Types of asynchronous diagnosability and the reveals-relation in occurrence nets. IEEE Trans. Autom. Control **55**(10), 2310–2320 (2010)
10. Haar, S.: What topology tells us about diagnosability in partial order semantics. Discrete Event Dyn. Syst. **22**(4), 383–402 (2012)
11. Haar, S., Rodríguez, C., Schwoon, S.: Reveal your faults: it's only fair! In: Proceedings of ACSD 2013, pp. 120–129. IEEE (2013)

12. Habermehl, P.: On the complexity of the linear-time μ-calculus for Petri Nets. In: Azéma, P., Balbo, G. (eds.) ICATPN 1997. LNCS, vol. 1248, pp. 102–116. Springer, Heidelberg (1997). doi:10.1007/3-540-63139-9_32
13. Howell, R.R., Rosier, L.E., Yen, H.C.: A taxonomy of fairness and temporal logic problems for Petri nets. Theor. Comput. Sci. **82**(2), 341–372 (1991)
14. Jančar, P.: Decidability of a temporal logic problem for Petri nets. Theor. Comput. Sci. **74**(1), 71–93 (1990)
15. Jančar, P.: Nonprimitive recursive complexity and undecidability for Petri net equivalences. Theor. Comput. Sci. **256**(1–2), 23–30 (2001)
16. Jiang, S., Huang, Z., Chandra, V., Kumar, R.: A polynomial algorithm for testing diagnosability of discrete event systems. IEEE Trans. Autom. Control **46**(8), 1318–1321 (2001)
17. Jones, N.D., Landweber, L.H., Lien, Y.E.: Complexity of some problems in Petri nets. Theor. Comput. Sci. **4**(3), 277–299 (1977)
18. Leroux, J., Schmitz, S.: Demystifying reachability in vector addition systems. In: Proceedings of LICS 2015, pp. 56–67. IEEE (2015)
19. Lin, F.: Opacity of discrete event systems and its applications. Automatica **47**(3), 496–503 (2011)
20. Lipton, R.: The reachability problem requires exponential space. Technical report 62. Yale University (1976)
21. Madalinski, A., Khomenko, V.: Diagnosability verification with parallel LTL-X model checking based on Petri net unfoldings. In: Proceedings of SysTol 2010, pp. 398–403. IEEE (2010)
22. Mayer, A.J., Stockmeyer, L.J.: The complexity of word problems–this time with interleaving. Inf. Comput. **115**(2), 293–311 (1994)
23. Sampath, M., Sengupta, R., Lafortune, S., Sinnamohideen, K., Teneketzis, D.: Diagnosability of discrete-event systems. IEEE Trans. Autom. Control **40**(9), 1555–1575 (1995)
24. Schmitz, S.: Automata column: the complexity of reachability in vector addition systems. ACM SIGLOG News **3**(1), 3–21 (2016)
25. Tong, Y., Li, Z., Seatzu, C., Giua, A.: Verification of initial-state opacity in Petri nets. In: Proceedings of CDC 2015, pp. 344–349. IEEE (2015)
26. Vogler, W.: Fairness and partial order semantics. Inf. Process. Lett. **55**(1), 33–39 (1995)
27. Yoo, T.S., Lafortune, S.: Polynomial-time verification of diagnosability of partially observed discrete event systems. IEEE Trans. Autom. Control **47**(9), 1491–1495 (2002)

Stochastic Petri Nets

Getting the Priorities Right: Saturation for Prioritised Petri Nets

Kristóf Marussy[1], Vince Molnár[1,2(✉)], András Vörös[1,2], and István Majzik[1]

[1] Department of Measurement and Information Systems,
Budapest University of Technology and Economics, Budapest, Hungary
[2] MTA-BME Lendület Cyber-Physical Systems Research Group,
Budapest, Hungary
{molnarv,vori}@mit.bme.hu

Abstract. Prioritised Petri net is a powerful modelling language that often constitutes the core of even more expressive modelling languages such as GSPNs (Generalized Stochastic Petri nets). The saturation state space traversal algorithm has proved to be efficient for non-prioritised concurrent models. Previous works showed that priorities may be encoded into the transition relation, but doing so defeats the main idea of saturation by spoiling the locality of transitions. This paper presents an extension of saturation to natively handle priorities by considering the priority-related enabledness of transitions separately, adopting the idea of constrained saturation. To encode the highest priority of enabled transitions in every state we introduce edge-valued interval decision diagrams. We show that in case of Petri nets, this data structure can be constructed offline. According to preliminary measurements, the proposed solution scales better than previously known matrix decision diagram-based approaches, paving the way towards efficient stochastic analysis of GSPNs and the model checking of prioritised models.

Keywords: Saturation · Priority · Prioritised Petri net · Petri net · Decision diagram · edge-valued interval decision diagram · GSPN

1 Introduction

Priorities in Petri nets provide a convenient way to represent dependencies between transitions, making them useful in the modelling of complex problems. One particularly important subset of prioritised Petri nets is Generalized Stochastic Petri nets (GSPN, [1]). To analyse the stochastic behaviour of a GSPN, the model must not express any nondeterminism. One way to guarantee this is to assign priorities to the transitions [12]. While explicit (graph-based) model checking algorithms naturally handle priorities, symbolic model checkers often have trouble representing the resulting complex transition relations compactly.

Saturation is one of the most efficient symbolic algorithms when it comes to concurrent, asynchronous systems [4]. It works on a decision diagram representation of the state space and its iteration strategy follows the structure

© Springer International Publishing AG 2017
W. van der Aalst and E. Best (Eds.): PETRI NETS 2017, LNCS 10258, pp. 223–242, 2017.
DOI: 10.1007/978-3-319-57861-3_14

of the diagram. The original algorithm required the transition relation to be Kroenecker-consistent, which was later overcome by the introduction of more flexible representations, e.g. matrix decision diagrams [8].

Exploiting the ability to encode arbitrary relations, [8] also introduced a way to encode priorities into the transition relations of Petri nets by removing elements where the source state enables a higher-priority transition. Although doing so spoils the locality property of concurrent systems (i.e. transitions become dependent on additional components), [8] presents a method to factor the relations such that saturation can still exploit some of the original locality.

The motivation of our work comes from the intuition that any alteration to the transition relations (without priorities) that affects locality will hurt the efficiency of saturation more than what is absolutely necessary. Therefore we devised a solution that, with the modification of the saturation algorithm (inspired by constrained saturation [15]), uses the transition relations as is and handles the priority-related enabledness separately, encoded in a new kind of decision diagram called edge-valued interval decision diagram (EVIDD). We show that for Petri nets, such a diagram can be constructed offline.

We expect our approach to yield smaller intermediate decision diagrams and thus result in better performance for the state space generation of prioritised models. Our preliminary experiments comparing our results to that of [8] seems to confirm this expectation, demonstrating that the presented algorithm scales better with the size of benchmark models than previous implementations.

The paper is structured as follows. The rest of this section recalls the relevant details about prioritised Petri nets and GSPNs, introduces our notations for multivalued decision diagrams and briefly presents saturation. In Sect. 2, we provide the details of our approach, including the definition and operations of EVIDDs, the encoding of priority-related enabledness and the modified saturation algorithm. The results of preliminary evaluation are presented in Sect. 3, while Sect. 4 provides concluding remarks and our plans for future work.

1.1 Petri Nets with Priority

Petri nets are a well-known and widespread modelling language mainly used to describe and study concurrent, asynchronous and nondeterministic systems. Here we present the notion of prioritised Petri nets, an extension of the traditional formalism with priorities. The following definition also includes inhibitor arcs.

Definition 1 (Prioritised Petri nets). *A prioritised Petri net is a tuple $PN = \langle P, T, W, M_0, \pi \rangle$ where:*

- *P is the set of places (defining state variables);*
- *T is the set of transitions (defining behaviour) such that $P \cap T = \emptyset$;*
- *$W = W^- \cup W^+ \cup W^\circ$ is a multiset of three types of arcs (the weight function), where $W^-, W^\circ : P \times T \to \mathbb{N}$ and $W^+ : T \times P \to \mathbb{N}$ are the set of input arcs, inhibitor arcs and output arcs, respectively;*
- *$M_0 : P \to \mathbb{N}$ is the initial marking, i.e. the number of tokens on each place;*
- *$\pi : T \to \mathbb{N}$ assigns priorities to transitions.*

The three types of weight functions describe the structure of the Petri net: there is an input or output arc between a place p and a transition t iff $W^-(p,t) > 0$ and $W^+(t,p) > 0$, respectively, and there is an inhibitor arc iff $W^\circ(p,t) < \infty$.

The state of a Petri net is defined by the current marking $M : P \to \mathbb{N}$. The dynamic behaviour of a prioritised Petri net is described as follows. A transition t is *enabled* iff $\forall p \in P : M(p) \in [W^-(p,t), W^\circ(p,t))$. An enabled transition is *fireable* iff there is no other enabled transition t' such that $\pi(t) < \pi(t')$. Upon firing transition t, the new marking M' of the Petri net will be as follows: $\forall p \in P : M'(p) = M(p) - W^-(p,t) + W^+(t,p)$. The firing of fireable transitions is nondeterministic. We denote the firing of transition t in marking M resulting in M' with $M \xrightarrow{t} M'$. A marking M_i is *reachable* from the initial marking if there exists a sequence of markings such that $M_0 \xrightarrow{t_1} M_1 \xrightarrow{t_2} \cdots \xrightarrow{t_i} M_i$. The set of reachable markings (i.e. the *state space* of the Petri net) is denoted by $\mathcal{S}_r$. This work assumes $\mathcal{S}_r$ to be finite.

Generalized Stochastic Petri Nets. Stochastic Petri nets (SPN) extend Petri nets with timed behaviours, where transitions are equipped with exponentially distributed firing delay random variables. Timed semantics of SPNs are defined by continuous-time Markov chains. Generalized Stochastic Petri nets (GSPN) further extend modelling capabilities to support both timed and instantaneous behaviours [1]. In GSPNs, transitions with zero priority (called *timed*) have exponentially distributed firing delays, while transitions with $\pi(t) \geq 1$ are *immediate*.

A Prioritised Petri net marking M where no transition t with $\pi(t) \geq 1$ is enabled is called *tangible*, while markings with an enabled transition with $\pi(t) \geq 1$ are called *vanishing*. We write $M \in \mathcal{T}$ if $M \in \mathcal{S}_r$ is a reachable tangible marking and $M \in \mathcal{V}$ if M is a reachable vanishing marking. In tangible markings, the timed semantics of Stochastic Petri nets apply to GSPNs. In contrast, immediate transitions are fired in vanishing markings while no time elapses. Conflicts between immediate transitions may yield nondeterministic behaviours. To ensure that probability distribution of GSPN markings evolve deterministically in time, conflicts must be resolved by assigning *probability weights* and priorities [1]. Conflict resolution may yield Prioritised Petri nets with many priority levels [12].

1.2 Multivalued Decision Diagrams

Multivalued decision diagrams (MDD, [7]) can be regarded as the extensions of binary decision diagrams. Symbolic model checking uses MDDs to compactly represent the reachability set. Assuming the states are given as integer tuples (each integer representing the state of a component, e.g. a place in a Petri net), the state space can be encoded by a function $f : \mathbb{N}^K \to \mathbb{B}$, where the value of f is $\top$ if the given state is part of the set and $\bot$ otherwise.

Definition 2 (Multivalued Decision Diagram). *An ordered quasi-reduced multivalued decision diagram over K variables is a tuple $\langle K, V, r, lvl, children, val \rangle$ such that:*

- $V = \bigsqcup_{i=0}^{K} V_i$ is the set of nodes, where items of V_0 are terminal nodes, the rest $(V_{>0} = V \setminus V_0)$ are internal nodes;
- $lvl : V \rightarrow \{0, 1, \ldots, K\}$ assigns non-negative level numbers to each node, associating them with variables $(V_i = \{n \in V \mid lvl(n) = i\})$;
- $r \in V$ is the root node of the MDD $(lvl(r) = K)$;
- $val : V_0 \rightarrow \{\bot, \top\}$ assigns a binary value to each terminal node (therefore $V_0 = \{0, 1\}$, where 0 is the terminal zero node $(val(0) = \bot)$ and 1 is the terminal one node $(val(1) = \top)$;
- children: $V_{>0} \times \mathbb{N} \rightarrow V$ defines edges between nodes labelled with elements of $\mathbb{N}$, denoted by $n[i]$ (i.e. $children(n, i) = n[i]$, $n[i]$ is left-associative), such that for each node $n \in V_{>0}$ and value $i \in \mathbb{N} : lvl(n) = lvl(n[i]) + 1$ or $n[i] = 0$;
- for every pair of nodes $n, m \in V_{>0}$, if for all $i \in \mathbb{N} : n[i] = m[i]$, then $n = m$.

Note that in this form (contrary to the literature), the representation is not finite due to the definition of children. In practice, we assume that $n[i] = 0$ for any node n and value i for which children is not defined explicitly and the explicit definition will be finite at any point in the algorithms.

Definition 3 (Semantics of MDD). The function encoded by an MDD rooted in node r is $f(\mathbf{v}) = f(v_1, \ldots, v_K) = val(r[v_K][v_{K-1}] \cdots [v_1])$, where $v_i \in \mathbb{N}$. The set of tuples encoded by r is therefore $\mathcal{S}(r) = \{\mathbf{v} \mid f(\mathbf{v}) = \top\}$.

Common set operations such as union and intersection can be efficiently implemented directly over MDDs with recursive functions and caching [7].

1.3 Saturation

Saturation is a state space traversal strategy specifically tailored to work on decision diagram representations [4]. The problem of state space generation is the computation of the set of system states reachable from one or more initial states $\mathcal{I}$. This can be done by computing the reflexive transitive closure of the next-state function $\mathcal{N}$ and applying it on the initial state, i.e. by computing the least fixed point of $\mathcal{N}$ including $\mathcal{I}$. One way of computing this fixed point is to compute the series $S_i = S_{i-1} \cup \mathcal{N}(S_{i-1})$ (with $S_0 = \mathcal{I}$) until two consecutive sets are equal. This approach essentially implements a breadth-first search strategy (BFS). Although the disadvantages of explicit graph-based BFS do not apply in a symbolic setting, a huge disadvantage is that decision diagrams representing the intermediate sets tend to be much larger than the final result. To do better, saturation uses additional information from the high-level model.

Definition 4 (Component-based model). Given a system with K components, saturation requires the models to be given as a 4-tuple $\langle \mathcal{S}, \mathcal{I}, \mathcal{E}, \mathcal{N} \rangle$, where:

- $\mathcal{S} = \mathcal{S}_1 \times \cdots \times \mathcal{S}_K$ is the set of potential global states with $\mathcal{S}_k$ being the set of possible local states of the kth component;
- $\mathcal{I} \subseteq \mathcal{S}$ is the set of initial states;
- $\mathcal{E}$ is the set of high-level events, i.e. the building blocks of behaviour;

– $\mathcal{N} \subseteq \mathcal{S} \times \mathcal{S}$ is the *next-state relation*, also defined for every event $\varepsilon \in \mathcal{E}$: $\mathcal{N} = \bigcup_{\varepsilon \in \mathcal{E}} \mathcal{N}_\varepsilon$.

The next-state relation in Definition 4 is equivalent to the next-state function used before, $\mathcal{N}(S)$ meaning the relational product $S \circ \mathcal{N}$. The reflexive transitive closure of the next-state relation is denoted by $\mathcal{N}^*$.

For example, in case of (non-prioritised) Petri nets, usually every transition is considered a separate event and places are assigned to components. In the common case when every place is considered as a separate component, a single state is a tuple defined by the marking (assigning a local state to every place).

Saturation for MDDs uses an MDD representation to encode and handle the set of reachable states $\mathcal{S}_r$. The encoding requires a total ordering of the system components, i.e. the assignment of local state variables to decision diagram levels. Based on this indexing, we can also partition the events of the model.

Definition 5 (Partitioning of the next-state relation). *An event $\varepsilon \in \mathcal{E}$ is* independent *from component k if 1) its firing does not change the state of the component and 2) it is enabled independently of the state of the component (i.e. the projection of $\mathcal{N}_\varepsilon$ to component k is an identity relation). Other components are said to be in the support of ε: $k \in supp(\varepsilon)$. Let $Top(\varepsilon) = max(supp(\varepsilon))$ denote the supporting component of ε with the highest index. Along the value of Top, events can be grouped: $\mathcal{E}_k = \{\varepsilon \in \mathcal{E} \mid Top(\varepsilon) = k\}$. The partitioning of the next-state relation is then defined based on this notion of levelling: $\mathcal{N}_k = \bigcup_{\varepsilon \in \mathcal{E}_k} \mathcal{N}_\varepsilon$.*

The defined partitioning aims to exploit a common feature of concurrent models: *locality*. Due to locality, events in such systems tend to depend on only a small number of components. Saturation exploits this by applying the next-state functions on the lowest level possible (i.e. on level Top), iterating through them in a bottom-up fashion. In addition, at every level k, the algorithm applies $\mathcal{N}_k$ exhaustively until a local fixed point is reached, recursively processing lower levels again if necessary. Hence the definition of a *saturated MDD node*: node n on level k is saturated if all of its child nodes are saturated and $\mathcal{S}(n)$ is a fixed point of $\mathcal{N}_k$. Saturating the root node r of an MDD representing the initial states therefore means that $\mathcal{S}(r) = \mathcal{N}^*(\mathcal{I})$ will hold.

Another benefit of considering locality is the reduced size of the next-state function representation. By the introduction of Top and the similarly defined $Bot(\varepsilon) = min(supp(\varepsilon))$, most variants of the saturation algorithm consider the next-state function only between these levels.

2   State Space Exploration with Priorities

In this chapter, we investigate the problem of state space generation for models with priorities. Our goal is to efficiently build the handling of priorities into saturation–which in its original form does not consider priorities directly.

Previous works has addressed this problem by encoding the effect of priorities into the transition relations. In [8], the author had two main goals. Firstly,

Boolean matrix decision diagrams have been introduced to encode the transition relations, thus relaxing the requirement of having to use Kroenecker-consistent next-state relations. This was necessary because the modification of the relations to exclude states in which a higher-priority transition is enabled almost always spoils Kroenecker-consistency. Although it is possible to decompose such a relation into Kroenecker-consistent relations, this was deemed inefficient.

Secondly, [8] has also pointed out that the modified next-state relations lose the property of locality. With regard to saturation, this means a drastic raise in the *Top* values of events, degrading saturation to the previously described BFS strategy. This problem has been alleviated by slicing the relations to extract the part which really depends on the additional components and keeping the rest lower. This way they have managed to preserve locality as much as possible without modifying the saturation algorithm.

On the contrary, we chose to extend saturation and use every next-state relation as is in the hopes of achieving better scalability. Assuming the priorities are given as integers (contrary to [8] but in accordance with [12]), the highest priority among enabled transitions $\pi_{\max}$ is encoded into a separate data structure. This information is passed along with recursive calls in a modified saturation algorithm and used to decide whether a transition can be fired, similarly to the passing of constraints in constrained saturation [15].

The highest priority of enabled transitions $\pi_{\max}(M)$ depends on the current marking M of the Petri net. Thus the encoding must be suitable to compute $\pi_{\max}$ for any marking M encountered by saturation, in one of the following ways.

Firstly, an overapproximation $\hat{\mathcal{S}}_r$ of the prioritised model's reachable state space $\mathcal{S}_r$ can be calculated. As saturation only encounters reachable markings $M \in \mathcal{S}_r$, it is sufficient to encode $\pi_{\max}(M)$ for the elements for $\hat{\mathcal{S}}_r$. The approximation may come from knowing bounds of places *a priori*, deriving bounds from P-invariants or exploring the state space of the unprioritised version of the model. However, this calculation may not always be possible, e.g. due to lack of known place bounds or the unprioritised model being unbounded. Moreover, poor overapproximations may produce unneccessarily large encodings.

Secondly, the encoding of $\pi_{\max}(M)$ may be calculated on the fly. When saturation encounters a new local state, the data structure can be updated accordingly. We aim to explore this approach in future work.

Thirdly, a specialized data structure may be introduced that can encode $\pi_{\max}$ for any reachable or unreachable marking and compiled before saturation. To this end, we introduce edge-valued interval decision diagrams (EVIDD) to encode for each state the maximum of the priorities of enabled transitions (Sect. 2.1). We show that in case of Petri nets this information can be compiled offline (Sect. 2.3). The extended saturation algorithm and a more detailed comparison of our approach and that of [8] will be discussed in Sect. 2.4.

2.1   Edge-Valued Interval Decision Diagrams

This section introduces edge-valued interval decision diagrams, a hybrid between edge-valued decision diagrams [11] and interval decision diagrams [13].

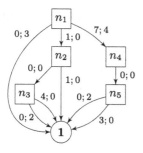

x_3	x_2	x_1	$g_{\langle 0,n_1\rangle}(\mathbf{x})$
$[0,1)$	$[0,\infty)$	$[0,\infty)$	3
$[1,7)$	$[0,1)$	$[0,4)$	2
$\ldots$	$\ldots$	$[4,\infty)$	0
$\ldots$	$[1,\infty)$	$[0,\infty)$	0
$[7,\infty)$	$[0,\infty)$	$[0,3)$	6
$\ldots$	$\ldots$	$[3,\infty)$	4

Fig. 1. Example quasi-reduced and ordered EVIDD. Nodes are denoted by squares and the terminal node by a circle. The edges are represented by the labels $lb_i; v_i$ of the directed arcs. The table shows the semantics of a 0-valued root handle $\langle 0, n_1 \rangle$ (columns encode the relevant intervals of input variables and the corresponding function value $g_{\langle 0,n_1\rangle}(\mathbf{x})$ for each row).

Definition 6 (Edge-valued interval decision diagram). *An (ordered) edge-valued interval decision diagram (EVIDD) over K variables is a tuple $\langle K, V, H, r, r_h, lvl, edges \rangle$ such that:*

- *$V = \bigsqcup_{i=0}^{K} V_i$ is the set of nodes with $V_0 = \{1\}$ (the single terminal node) and $V_{\geq 1} = V \setminus V_0$ being the set of internal nodes;*
- *$H = \bigsqcup_{i=0}^{K} H_i$ is the set of handles where $H_i = \mathbb{N} \times (V_i \cup \{1\})$, i.e. every handle is a pair of a value and a node;*
- *$lvl : (V \cup H) \to \{0, 1, \ldots, K\}$ assigns non-negative level numbers to each node and handle, associating them with the variables ($V_i = \{n \in V \mid lvl(n) = i\}$ and $H_i = \{h \in H \mid lvl(h) = i\}$);*
- *The root node r is the single node on level K ($V_K = \{r\}$) and $r_h = \langle v, r \rangle$ is the root handle with value v, representing the encoded function;*
- *$edges : V_{\geq 1} \to (\mathbb{N} \times H)^*$ assigns an edge list (a sequence of edges) to internal nodes, i.e. for any node $n \in V_{\geq 1}$, $edges(n) = (\langle lb_1, h_1 \rangle, \ldots, \langle lb_c, h_c \rangle)$, c denoting the number of edges of n. Each edge consists of a lower bound lb_j and a handle h_j such that $h_j \in H_{i-1}$. We require that $lb_1 = 0$ and for all $1 < j \leq c : lb_{j-1} < lb_j$, i.e. the lower bounds form an increasing sequence.*

An EVIDD may be represented by a directed graph (see Fig. 1 for an example). Internal nodes of the EVIDD have several outgoing edges. Each edge $\langle lb_j, h_j \rangle \in edges(n)$ is labelled with a lower bound lb_j and value v of the handle $h_j = \langle v, m \rangle$, connecting n to m. The terminal node **1** has no outgoing edge.

If $\langle v, n \rangle$ is a handle and $w \in \mathbb{N}$, let $\langle v, n \rangle + w$ and $\langle v, n \rangle - w$ denote $\langle v + w, n \rangle$, $\langle v - w, n \rangle$, respectively. The latter is defined only when $w \leq v$.

The edge lower bounds lb_j of some internal EVIDD node n partition $\mathbb{N}$ into disjoint intervals $[lb_1 = 0, lb_2), [lb_2, lb_3), \ldots, [lb_{c-1}, lb_c), [lb_c, \infty)$. For convenience we will write $lb_{c+1} = \infty$. For any $x \in \mathbb{N}$ there is a unique highest index j of $edges(n)$ such that $lb_j \leq x$, which corresponds to the interval $[lb_j, lb_{j+1})$ containing x. Let $\langle v, n \rangle[x] = h_j + v$, where $\langle lb_j, h_j \rangle \in edges(n)$ and j is the index defined above. Moreover, let $\langle v, \mathbf{1} \rangle[x] = \langle v, \mathbf{1} \rangle$ for any x.

Definition 7 (Semantics of EVIDD). *An EVIDD rooted in handle h encodes the function $g_h \colon \mathbb{N}^K \to \mathbb{N}$ such that $g_h(\mathbf{x}) = g_h(x_K, \ldots, x_1) = w$, iff $\langle w, 1 \rangle = h[\mathbf{x}] = h[x_K][x_{K-1}] \cdots [x_1]$, where $\mathbf{x} \in \mathbb{N}^K$.*

Since $h[x] \in H_{i-1}$ for all $h \in H_i$, the result of K-fold indexing is always defined for root handles and it always returns a handle of the form $\langle w, 1 \rangle$.

Lemma 1. *For every suffix $\mathbf{x}_{\geq k} = (x_k, x_{k+1}, \ldots, x_K)$ of $\mathbf{x}$, $g_h(\mathbf{x}_{\geq k}) \leq g_h(\mathbf{x})$.*

Proof. Due to nonnegative edge values, $h[\mathbf{x}_{\geq k}] = \langle z, m \rangle$ implies $g_h(\mathbf{y}) \geq z$ for all $\mathbf{y} = (y_1, y_2, \ldots, y_{k-1}, \mathbf{x}_{\geq k})$. Note that if $h[\mathbf{x}_{\geq k}] = \langle z, 1 \rangle$, then $g_h(y) = z$.

Definition 8. *An internal EVIDD node $n \in V_{\geq 1}$ is canonical if 1) for all adjacent edges $(\langle lb_i, h_i \rangle, \langle lb_{i+1}, h_{i+1} \rangle) \subseteq edges(n)$, $h_i \neq h_{i+1}$ and 2) there is an edge $\langle lb_i, \langle v_i, m_i \rangle \rangle \in edges(n)$ such that $v_i = 0$; The terminal EVIDD node 1 is canonical. An (ordered) EVIDD is quasi-reduced if 1) all nodes are canonical, 2) no two internal nodes have equal edge lists and 3) if the following holds: ifedges(n) = $((0, \langle v_1, m_1 \rangle))$ for some internal node n, then $m_1 \neq 1$.*

In the rest of this paper we assume all EVIDDs to be quasi-reduced and ordered.

The following lemma shows that the handle h uniquely represents g_h, which means caching may be used to speed up operations with functions g_h.

Lemma 2. *Let $h = \langle v, n \rangle$ and $q = \langle w, m \rangle$ be handles of nodes in a quasi-reduced ordered EVIDD such that $h, q \in H_i$. If $g_h(\mathbf{x}) = g_q(\mathbf{x})$ for all $\mathbf{x} \in \mathbb{N}^i$, then $h = q$.*

Proof. We proceed by induction by increasing i. If $i = 0$, the claim is trivial.

In the inductive case, we need to consider handles $h \in H_i \setminus H_0$. Thanks to the induction hypothesis, it suffices to show that $h[x] = q[x]$ for all $x \in \mathbb{N}$ implies $h = q$. Let x be such that v' is minimized in $h[x] = q[x] = \langle v', n' \rangle$. Then $v' = v + \min(v_j) = w + \min(w_j)$, where v_j and w_j range over the edge values of n and m, respectively. For canonical n and m, $\min(v_j) = \min(w_j) = 0$, thus $v = w$.

Now we show that $edges(n) = edges(m)$, which implies $n = m$. Consider some $y \in \mathbb{N}$ such that $h[y - 1] \neq h[y]$. Then $\langle y, h[y] - v \rangle$ must appear in $edges(m)$. Conversely, if $h[y - 1] = h[y]$ and m is canonical, no edge with lower bound y may appear in $edges(m)$. Finally, note that the first element of $edges(m)$ is $\langle 0, h[0] - v \rangle$, which is also the first element on $edges(m)$.

2.2 EVIDD Operations

Building Canonical EVIDDs. Fig. 2a shows the procedure EVIDDCHECKIN that creates a canonical EVIDD node from a list of edges. Callers must ensure that the edge list contains no invalid level skipping, i.e. all child nodes are located on the same level or are the terminal node 1. Adjacent edges with equal values and child nodes are removed in lines 4–6. If only a single edge to 1 remains, a handle to the terminal node is returned instead of a new node in line 8. Otherwise, the edge list is brought into canonical form in lines 9–10 by subtracting $offset = \min(v_i)$ from the edge values so that a zero valued edge appears.

Input: edges $E = (\langle lb_i, \langle v_i, m_i \rangle \rangle)_{i=1}^c$
Output: checked in EVIDD handle
1 **if** $lb_1 \neq 0$ **then fail**
2 **for** $i \leftarrow 2$ **to** c **do**
3   **if** $lb_{i-1} \geq lb_i$ **then fail**
4   **if** $v_i = v_{i-1}$ and $m_i = m_{i-1}$ **then**
5   drop $\langle lb_i, \langle v_i, m_i \rangle \rangle$ from E
6         $i \leftarrow i - 1, c \leftarrow c - 1$

7 **if** $c = 1$ and $m_1 = 1$ **then**
8   **return** $\langle v, 1 \rangle$

9 $\textit{offset} \leftarrow \min_{i=1,2,\ldots,c} v_i$
10 $\textbf{for } i \leftarrow 1 \textbf{ to } c \textbf{ do } v_i \leftarrow v_i - \textit{offset}$
11 $n \leftarrow \text{EVIDDNODE}(E)$
12 **if** $\neg\text{UNIQUETABLEGET}(n)$ **then**
13    $\text{UNIQUETABLEPUT}(n)$

14 **return** $\langle \textit{offset}, n \rangle$

(a) Procedure EVIDDCHECKIN.

Input: $a = \langle v, n \rangle, b = \langle w, m \rangle \in H_\ell$
Output: $\max\{a, b\}$
1 **if** $n = 1$ and $m = 1$ **then**
2   **return** $\langle \max\{v, w\}, 1 \rangle$

3 $\textit{offset} \leftarrow \min\{v, w\}$
4 $a \leftarrow a - \textit{offset}$
5 $b \leftarrow b - \textit{offset}$
6 **if** $\neg\text{MAXCACHEGET}(\{a, b\}, h)$ **then**
7   **if** $n = 1$ **then**
8         $h \leftarrow \text{MERGECONSTANT}(b, v)$
9   **else if** $m = 1$ **then**
10        $h \leftarrow \text{MERGECONSTANT}(a, w)$
11   **else**
12        $h \leftarrow \text{MERGE}(a, b)$
13    $\text{MAXCACHEPUT}(\{a, b\}, h)$

14 **return** $h + \textit{offset}$

(b) Procedure MAXIMUM.

Fig. 2. Basic EVIDD operations.

Lines 11–13 depend on three other routines to produce a node object in memory. The constructor EVIDDNODE(E) creates a new node object from a canonical list of edges E. As in other decision diagram implementations, space is conserved and comparisons of nodes are made more efficient by the use of a unique table. If the unique table contains a node with the same edges as n, UNIQUETABLEGET(n) disposes of the object pointed by n, replaces n with a reference to the equivalent node from the unique table and returns **true**. Otherwise **false** is returned and UNIQUETABLEPUT(n) is used to add n to the unique table. Finally, *offset* is recovered as the value of the returned handle $\langle \textit{offset}, n \rangle$.

Elementwise Maximum

Definition 9. *The* elementwise maximum *of the EVIDD handles* $a, b \in H_\ell$ *is the handle* $h = \max\{a, b\}$, *such that* $\max\{g_a(\mathbf{x}), g_b(\mathbf{x})\} = g_h(\mathbf{x})$ *for all* $\mathbf{x} \in \mathbb{N}^\ell$.

The semantics of EVIDDs together with the definition of $\max\{a, b\}$ imply that $\max\{g_a(\mathbf{x}), g_b(\mathbf{x})\} = \max\{g_{a[x_\ell]}(\mathbf{x}_{\leq \ell-1}), g_{b[x_\ell]}(\mathbf{x}_{\leq \ell-1})\}$. Therefore $\max\{a, b\}[x] = \max\{a[x], b[x]\}$ for all $x \in \mathbb{N}$, which allows recursive calculation of $\max\{a, b\}$. The operation has two further properties which will be exploited in our implementation to facilitate caching. Firstly, the operation is symmetric: $\max\{a, b\} = \max\{b, a\}$. Secondly, because $q = h + w$ implies $g_q(\mathbf{x}) = g_h(\mathbf{x}) + w$ for all $\mathbf{x}$, the elementwise maximum is *offset invariant*. If $h = \max\{a, b\}$, we have $h + w = \max\{a + w, b + w\}$ and $h - w = \max\{a - w, b - w\}$.

Figure 2b shows the implementation MAXIMUM of the elementwise maximum operation. The algorithm is divided into four cases based on whether the handles

Input: $a = \langle v, n \rangle$ and $w \in \mathbb{N}$
Output: $\max\{a, \langle w, 1 \rangle\}$
1 $E \leftarrow ()$
2 **for each** $\langle lb_i, h_i \rangle \in edges(n)$ **do** $E \leftarrow E +\!\!+ (\langle lb_i, \text{MAXIMUM}(h_i + v, \langle w, 1 \rangle) \rangle)$
3 **return** $\text{EVIDDCHECKIN}(E)$

(a) Procedure MERGECONSTANT.

Input: $a = \langle v, n \rangle, b = \langle w, m \rangle \in H_\ell$
Output: $\max\{a, b\}$
1 $c \leftarrow |edges(n)|$, $c' \leftarrow |edges(m)|$, $i \leftarrow 1$, $j \leftarrow 1$, $E \leftarrow ()$, $lb_{\text{out}} \leftarrow 0$
2 let us denote $edges(n)$ by $(\langle lb_k, h_k \rangle)_{k=1}^{c}$ and $edges(n)$ by $(\langle lb'_k, h'_k \rangle)_{k=1}^{c'}$
3 **while** $i \leq c$ and $j \leq c'$ **do**
4 $\quad E \leftarrow E +\!\!+ (\langle lb_{\text{out}}, \text{MAXIMUM}(h_i + v, h'_j + w) \rangle)$
5 $\quad$ **if** $i = c$ **then** $nextA \leftarrow \infty$ **else** $nextA \leftarrow lb_{i+1}$
6 $\quad$ **if** $j = c'$ **then** $nextB \leftarrow \infty$ **else** $nextB \leftarrow lb'_{j+1}$
7 $\quad lb_{\text{out}} \leftarrow \max\{nextA, nextB\}$
8 $\quad$ **if** $nextA = lb_{\text{out}}$ **then** $i \leftarrow i + 1$
9 $\quad$ **if** $nextB = lb_{\text{out}}$ **then** $j \leftarrow j + 1$
10 **return** $\text{EVIDDCHECKIN}(E)$

(b) Procedure MERGE.

Fig. 3. Subroutines for the MAXIMUM operation ($+\!\!+$ denotes concatenation).

a and b point to terminal or internal EVIDD nodes. If a and b are both handles of the terminal node **1** (line 1), the functions g_a and g_b are constant. This base case is processed directly without caching. The remaining recursive cases make use of caching. MAXIMUM depends on the routines MAXCACHEGET and MAXCACHEPUT to manage the cache. MAXCACHEGET($\{a, b\}, h$) takes an unordered caching key $\{a, b\}$ and sets the reference h to the cached result $\max\{a, b\}$. Successful retrievals are indicated by returning **true**, while **false** is returned on cache misses. MAXCACHEGET($\{a, b\}, h$) associates the result h with the key $\{a, b\}$.

To increase the number of potential cache hits, lines 3–5 subtract the minimum of their values from the handles $a = \langle v, n \rangle$ and $b = \langle w, m \rangle$, so that at least one of v and w is 0. After possibly retrieving $\max\{a, b\}$ from the cache, this *offset* is added back to the result in line 14.

The function MERGECONSTANT in Fig. 3a processes the two cases when one of a and b is a handle to **1**, while the other references an internal node. Due to symmetry, we may assume that $a = \langle v, n \rangle \in H_\ell$ and $b = \langle w, 1 \rangle \in H_\ell$. Because $\langle w, 1 \rangle[x] = \langle w, 1 \rangle$, $\max\{a, b\}[x]$ must be set to $\min\{a[x], \langle w, 1 \rangle\}$ for all $x \in \mathbb{N}$. This is accomplished by replacing all edges $\langle lb_i, h_i \rangle$ of n with $\max\{a[lb_i], \langle w, 1 \rangle\}$.

The most interesting case, when the handles $a = \langle v, n \rangle$, $b = \langle w, m \rangle$ both refer to internal nodes $n, m \in V_\ell$ is processed by MERGE in Fig. 3b. The difficulty arises from the edge lists $edges(n) = (\langle lb_k, h_k \rangle)_{k=1}^{c}$ and $edges(m) = (\langle lb'_k, h'_k \rangle)_{k=1}^{c'}$ having possibly different lower bound sequences lb_i and lb'_j. Therefore a new edge list E with a new sequence of lower bounds $\{lb_i\} \cup \{lb'_j\}$ must be constructed.

Input: transition t
Output: priority EVIDD handle
1   if $\pi(t) = 0$ **then return** $\langle 0, 1 \rangle$
2   $h^{(0)} \leftarrow \langle \pi(t), 1 \rangle$
3   **for** $i \leftarrow 1$ **to** K **do**
4   $\quad$ **if** $W^-(t, p_i) > W^\circ(t, p_i)$ **then**
5   $\quad\quad$ **return** $\langle 0, 1 \rangle$
6   $\quad$ **if** $W^-(t, p_i) > 0$ **then**
7   $\quad\quad E \leftarrow (\langle 0, \langle 0, 1 \rangle \rangle,$
    $\quad\quad\quad\quad \langle W^-(t, p_i), h^{(i-1)} \rangle)$
8   $\quad$ **else** $E \leftarrow (\langle 0, \langle 0, h^{(i-1)} \rangle \rangle)$
9   $\quad$ **if** $W^\circ(t, p_i) < \infty$ **then**
10 $\quad\quad E \leftarrow E \# (\langle W^\circ(t, p_i), \langle 0, 1 \rangle \rangle)$
11 $\quad h^{(i)} \leftarrow$ EVIDDCHECKIN(E)
12 **return** $h^{(k)}$

(a) Procedure TRANSITIONHANDLE.

Input: set of all transitions T
Output: EVIDD handle encoding
$\quad\quad$ the highesty priority of
$\quad\quad$ enabled transitions
1   $h \leftarrow \langle 0, 1 \rangle$
2   order T by $Top(t)$ nondecreasing
3   **for each** $t \in T$ **do**
4   $\quad q \leftarrow$ TRANSITIONHANDLE(t)
5   $\quad h \leftarrow$ MAXIMUM(h, q)
6   **return** h

(b) Procedure HIGHESTPRIORITY.

Fig. 4. Encoding the highest priority of enabled transitions.

Since $lb_1 = lb'_1 = 0$, the first edge of the new edge list is $\langle 0, \max\{a[0], b[0]\} \rangle = \langle 0, \max\{h_1 + v, h'_1 + w\} \rangle$. The loop in lines 3–9 of MERGE traverses the lower bounds lb_i and lb'_j with the indices i and j. Lines 5 and 6 peek at the next elements $nextA = lb_{i+1}$ and $nextB = lb'_{j+1}$ of the lower bound sequences. We follow the convention that $lb_{c+1} = lb'_{c'+1} = \infty$. The lower bound lb_{out} of the next edge to be created is equal to the smaller of the two next elements. Thus an intersection of the interval partitions of $\mathbb{N}$ induced by $edges(n)$ and $edges(m)$ is built. If both edge lists are exhausted, $lb_{out} = nextA = nextB = \infty$, which causes both i and j to be incremented beyond their limits and the loop to terminate.

2.3   Encoding the Highest Priority of Enabled Transitions

In this section we construct an EVIDD and a handle h that encodes the highest priority of enabled transitions of a prioritised Petri net for any state. We will have $g_h(M(p_k), M(p_{k-1}), \ldots, M(p_1)) = \pi_{\max}(M)$ for a marking M of the Petri net if a transition with priority π has the highest priority among all enabled transitions in M. If there are no enabled transitions in M, we set $\pi_{\max}(M) = 0$.

TRANSITIONHANDLE(t), which is shown in Fig. 4a, associates an EVIDD handle h to a prioritised Petri net transition t. The handle encodes the function

$$g_h(M(p_k), M(p_{k-1}), \ldots, M(p_1)) = \begin{cases} \pi(t), & \text{if } M \in En(t), \\ 0, & \text{if } M \notin En(t), \end{cases}$$

where $En(t)$ is the set of markings in which t is enabled:

$$En(t) = \prod_{i=1}^{k} [W^-(t, p_i), W^\circ(t, p_i)) \cap \mathbb{N}^k,$$

i.e. $En(t)$ is the set of integer vectors where the component corresponding to the place p_i lies in the interval $[W^-(t, p_i), W^\circ(t, p_i))$. Recall that if there are no inhibitor edges between t and the place p_i, then $W^\circ(t, p_i) = \infty$. If $\pi(t) = 0$ or $En(t) = \emptyset$, g_h is constant and h is $\langle 0, 1 \rangle$.

These intervals are encoded by the loop in lines 3–11 from the lowest to the top level of the EVIDD. If t is never enabled due to an empty interval, a zero handle is returned in line 5. The function checks in handles $h^{(i)} \in H_i$ such that $g_{h^{(i)}}(\mathbf{x}_{\leq i}) = \pi(t)$ for all $\mathbf{x}_{\leq i} \in \prod_{j=1}^{i}[W^-(t, p_j), W^\circ(t, p_j)) \cap \mathbb{N}^i$, otherwise 0. For all $i < Bot(t)$, $h^{(i)} = \langle \pi(t), 1 \rangle$ due to the reduction of zero nodes in EVIDDCHECKIN. Moreover, for all $i > Top(t)$, $h^{(i)} = \langle \pi(t), n \rangle$, where $edges(n) = (\langle 0, h^{(i-1)} \rangle)$ and the EVIDD is a single path, because $W^-(t, p_i) = 0$ and $W^\circ(t, p_i) = \infty$.

HIGHESTPRIORITY in Fig. 4b encodes $\pi_{\max}$ as an EVIDD handle. For each transition t the EVIDD handle describing the enabling states $En(t)$ and the priority $\pi(t)$ is constructed by TRANSITIONHANDLE. The MAXIMUM operation is used to merge the transition handles into a single handle. Analogously to a heuristic in constraint programming with MDDs [10], MAXIMUM is called for the transition handles ordered by $Top(t)$ nondecreasing. Hence upper levels of the EVIDD are left as a single path for as long as possible, which we have found to improve performance.

2.4   Saturation with Priority Constraints

In the following paragraphs, we characterize an abstract form of next-state representation to use in the saturation algorithm, then our extension is discussed in detail. We also give some remarks about its advantages over previous approaches.

Encoding the Next-State Function. Saturation has been designed with various next-state representations, including Kroenecker matrices [3], MDDs with $2K$ levels [6] or matrix-decision diagrams [8]. For simple Petri nets (without priorities), transitions can be described by for each place an interval over the natural numbers (how many tokens can enable the transitions) and an offset (how the marking will change on the corresponding place), which is already encoded in the weight function W [13]. All of these approaches has been shown to work with saturation.

In the following definition, we characterize the minimum requirement towards a next-state representation to be "compatible" with saturation and, in particular, our extended version of it that is capable of handling priorities natively.

Definition 10 (Abstract next-state diagram). *An* abstract next-state diagram *is a tuple* $\langle \mathcal{D}, next, r, \mathbf{1}, \mathbf{0} \rangle$ *where:*

- $\mathcal{D}$ *is the set of* descriptors, *such that* $r \in \mathcal{D}$ *is the* root descriptor, $\mathbf{1} \in \mathcal{D}$ *is the* identity descriptor *and* $\mathbf{0} \in \mathcal{D}$ *is the* empty descriptor

- $next: \mathcal{D} \times \mathbb{N} \times \mathbb{N} \to \mathcal{D}$ *is the indexing function that given a descriptor and a pair returns another descriptor. Also denoted by* $d[x, x'] = d' \Leftrightarrow \langle d, x, x', d' \rangle \in next$ *(with* $d, d' \in \mathcal{D}$, $x, x' \in \mathbb{N}$) *and* $d[\mathbf{x}, \mathbf{x}'] = d[(x_1, \ldots, x_K), (x'_1, \ldots, x'_K)] = d[x_K, x'_K] \cdots [x_1, x'_1]$. *We require for any* $x, x', x'' \in \mathbb{N}$ *and* $x \neq x'$ *that* $\mathbf{1}[x, x] = \mathbf{1}$, $\mathbf{1}[x, x'] = \mathbf{0}$, *and* $\mathbf{0}[x, x''] = \mathbf{0}$.

The abstract next-state diagram rooted in r *encodes the relation* $\mathcal{R} \subseteq \mathbb{N}^K \times \mathbb{N}^K$ *iff for all* $\mathbf{x}, \mathbf{x}' \in \mathbb{N}^K$ *the following holds:*

$$(\langle \mathbf{x}, \mathbf{x}' \rangle \in \mathcal{R} \Leftrightarrow r[\mathbf{x}, \mathbf{x}'] = \mathbf{1}) \wedge (\langle \mathbf{x}, \mathbf{x}' \rangle \notin \mathcal{R} \Leftrightarrow r[\mathbf{x}, \mathbf{x}'] = \mathbf{0})$$

Decision diagram-based representations such as MDDs with $2K$ levels or matrix decision diagrams naturally implement abstract next-state diagrams–descriptors are nodes of the diagram, the identity descriptor is the terminal one node $(\mathbf{1})$, the empty descriptor is the terminal zero node $(\mathbf{0})$ and the indexing is the same (in case of MDDs with $2K$ levels $d[x, x']$ is implemented by $d[x][x']$).

In our work, we use the simplest encoding for Petri nets: the structure of the model itself. We can do so, because we encode the priority-related enabledness separately in an EVIDD and it is not possible nor necessary to split or combine the relations any further in order to lower the *Top* values as done in [8]. Thus, given a Petri net with $K = |P|$ places each constituting a separate component (p_k denoting the single place belonging to the kth component), our implementation of the abstract next-state diagram for every transition $t \in T$ is as follows.

- The set of descriptors is $\mathcal{D} = (\{t\} \times \{Bot(t), \ldots, Top(t)\}) \cup \{\mathbf{1}, \mathbf{0}\}$, i.e. pairs of the transition and a level number.
- The root descriptor is $r = \langle t, Top(t) \rangle$.
- The *next* function (assuming that the local state of a place is its marking) is

$$\langle t, k \rangle [x, x'] = \begin{cases} lower(t, k), & \text{if } x \in [W^-(p_k, t), W^\circ(p_k, t)) \\ & \quad \text{and } x' = x - W^-(p_k, t) + W^+(p_k, t), \\ \mathbf{0}, & \text{otherwise,} \end{cases}$$

where

$$lower(t, k) = \begin{cases} \langle t, k - 1 \rangle, & \text{if } k > Bot(t), \\ \mathbf{1}, & \text{if } k = Bot(t). \end{cases}$$

Note that in this case, a descriptor is identified by the transition and the level number, i.e. two descriptors will be equal only if both the transition and the level number is the same. This is somewhat weaker than the equality of decision diagram nodes in the sense that it will sometimes fail to recognize equal constructs. This could occur, for example, when two descriptors belonging to the same level but different transitions have the same weight functions on the lower levels. Because the transitions are not the same, our definition will say that the descriptors are not equal, even though they actually have the same meaning. There is no minimal requirement for the strength of equality of descriptors, but stronger equality relations make caching more efficient.

Details of the Algorithm. Given the EVIDD notation and the operations defined so far, as well as the abstract next-state diagram notation, Fig. 5 presents the pseudocode of the extended saturation algorithm capable of handling prioritised models natively. The pseudocode uses $\mathcal{E}_k^\pi = \{\varepsilon \in \mathcal{E}_k \mid \pi(\varepsilon) = \pi\}$ to denote the set of events "belonging" to level k (as defined in Definition 5) and having priority π, as well as the self-explanatory $\mathcal{E}_k^{\pi \geq v}$ (v is a given priority level). The abstract next-state diagram descriptor corresponding to event ε and therefore encoding $\mathcal{N}_\varepsilon$ without priority considerations is denoted by $d(\varepsilon)$.

The procedure SATURATE (Fig. 5a) takes an MDD node n and an EVIDD handle h–which are initially the root of the MDD representing the set of initial states ($\mathcal{I}$ in Definition 4) and the root handle of the EVIDD as returned by HIGHESTPRIORITY (Fig. 4b)–and saturates n. Recall that when the root node gets saturated, it represents the set of reachable states $\mathcal{S}_r = \mathcal{N}^*(\mathcal{I})$. The procedure first recursively saturates every child node (lines 3–5). The constructor MDDNODE creates a new node on the current level which will hold the new (saturated) children. Similarly to EVIDDCHECKIN, CHECKIN in line 6 ensures that the resulting node n' is unique (i.e. the MDD currently being processed is quasi-reduced). Lines 7–12 perform the fixed point computation with the next-state functions corresponding to $\mathcal{E}_{lvl(n)}^{\pi \geq v}$, i.e. those events that "belong" to the current level and have a priority of at least v, the value of handle h. Note that v is indeed a lower bound of the priority of any fireable transition, as shown by Lemma 1. Terminal nodes are returned immediately.

The procedure SATFIRE computes the image of $\mathcal{N}_\varepsilon$ on $\mathcal{S}(n)$. RELPRODSAT is used to compute the image recursively for every component, also saturating new nodes during the process (line 9 of Fig. 5c). Due to this, both procedures return a saturated (and also quasi-reduced) node. SATFIRE uses the priority and the descriptor belonging to event ε to evaluate base cases. If $\mathcal{S}(n)$ is empty or the value of the priority handle h is higher than $\pi(t)$ (i.e. there is at least one enabled transition with a higher priority), the terminal zero node is returned immediately. On the other hand, if the descriptor d is the identity descriptor and the node of the handle is the terminal EVIDD node, we expect that the priority of the current transition will be v and then we can return n as is (because of the identity relation). If v is lower than the current priority, then either the descriptor or the priority EVIDD is invalid, since the event ε is enabled and has higher priority than any enabled transition (including itself), which is an obvious contradiction. Lines 5–8 recursively compute the image of $\mathcal{N}_\varepsilon$. RELPRODSAT does essentially the same, but it also saturates the resulting node before returning it (line 9 of Fig. 5c). Note, however, that in RELPRODSAT we consider two EVIDD handles–one for the source state (h) and one for the target state (h'). The former is used to evaluate the enabledness of the transition currently being fired, while the latter will be used to saturate the resulting node.

To exploit the structure of decision diagrams (i.e. the same node may be reached on multiple paths), SATURATE and RELPRODSAT use caches to store previously computed results (lines 2, 14 of Fig. 5a and lines 4, 9 of Fig. 5c).

Input: MDD node n,
        EVIDD handle $h = \langle v, m \rangle$
Output: saturated MDD node n'

1 **if** $n = 0$ or $n = 1$ **then return** n
2 **if** $\neg\textsc{SatCacheGet}(n, h, n')$ **then**
3      $n' \leftarrow \textsc{MddNode}(lvl(n))$
4   **for each** x **where** $n[x] \neq 0$ **do**
5         $n'[x] \leftarrow \textsc{Saturate}(n[x], h[x])$
6      $\textsc{CheckIn}(n')$
7   **repeat**
8         $changed \leftarrow$ **false**
9   **for each** $\varepsilon \in \mathcal{E}_{lvl(n)}^{\pi \geq v}$ **do**
10            $n'' \leftarrow \textsc{SatFire}(\varepsilon, n, h)$
11   **if** $n' \neq n''$ **then**
12               $n' \leftarrow n''$, $changed \leftarrow$ **true**
13   **until** $\neg changed$
14      $\textsc{SatCachePut}(n, h, n')$
15 **return** n'

(a) Procedure $\textsc{Saturate}$.

Input: event ε, MDD node n,
        EVIDD handle $h = \langle v, m \rangle$
Output: the result of firing d from
      the states n with the
      children saturated

1 $\pi \leftarrow \pi(\varepsilon)$, $d \leftarrow d(\varepsilon)$
2 **if** $n = 0$ or $\pi < v$ **then return** 0
3 **if** $d = 1$ and $m = 1$ **then**
4   **if** $\pi = v$ **then return** n
      else fail "invalid descriptor"
5 $n' \leftarrow \textsc{MddNode}(lvl(n))$
6 **for each** x, y **where** $d[x, y] \neq 0$ **do**
7      $s \leftarrow \textsc{RelProdSat}(\pi, d[x, y], n[x],$
                            $h[x], h[y])$
8      $n'[y] \leftarrow \textsc{Union}(n'[y], s)$
9 $\textsc{CheckIn}(n')$
10 **return** n'

(b) Procedure $\textsc{SatFire}$.

Input: priority π, descriptor d, MDD node n, EVIDD handles $h = \langle v, m \rangle$, h'
Output: saturated MDD node n'', which is the result of firing d from n

1 **if** $n = 0$ or $\pi < v$ **then return** 0
2 **if** $d = 1$ and $m = 1$ **then**
3   **if** $\pi = v$ **then return** n **else fail** "invalid descriptor"
4 **if** $\neg\textsc{RelProdCacheGet}(\pi, d, n, h, h', n'')$ **then**
5      $n' \leftarrow \textsc{MddNode}(lvl(n))$
6   **for each** x, y **where** $d[x, y] \neq 0$ **do**
7         $s \leftarrow \textsc{RelProdSat}(\pi, d[x, y], n[x], h[x], h'[y])$
8         $n'[y] \leftarrow \textsc{Union}(n'[y], s)$
9      $\textsc{CheckIn}(n')$, $n'' \leftarrow \textsc{Saturate}(n', h')$, $\textsc{RelProdCachePut}(\pi, d, n, h, h', n'')$
10 **return** n''

(c) Procedure $\textsc{RelProdSat}$.

Fig. 5. Saturation with EVIDDs for prioritised models.

Discussion. The correctness of the presented algorithm can be proved along the following (schematic) considerations. Suppose that we decompose the next-state relation into $\mathcal{N}_\varepsilon = \widehat{\mathcal{N}}_\varepsilon \setminus E_\varepsilon$ such that $\widehat{\mathcal{N}}_\varepsilon$ is the next-state relation without considering priorities (which is by definition a superset of $\mathcal{N}_\varepsilon$) and $E_\varepsilon = En^{\pi > \pi(\varepsilon)} \times \mathcal{S}$ where $En^{\pi > \pi(\varepsilon)} = \bigcup_{\varepsilon' \in \mathcal{E}^{\pi > \pi(\varepsilon)}} En(\varepsilon')$, i.e. the Cartesian product of the states in which an event with higher priority is enabled and the state space. The root descriptor of ε encodes $\widehat{\mathcal{N}}_\varepsilon$. To encode $En^{\pi > \pi(\varepsilon)}$, we use the EVIDD built by $\textsc{HighestPriority}$: by selecting only the paths to which the EVIDD assigns a value larger than $\pi(\varepsilon)$, we can exactly compute $En^{\pi > \pi(\varepsilon)}$.

It is easy to see that the modified saturation algorithm performs the selection whenever π is compared to the value of a handle and also computes $\mathcal{N}_\varepsilon = \widehat{\mathcal{N}}_\varepsilon \setminus E_\varepsilon$ on the fly. Edge-labelling therefore enables the compact representation of a series of sets $En^{\pi > i}$, where every set is the superset of the previous one. Handling of intervals instead of values, on the other hand, enables us to encode the highest priority offline in case of Petri nets.

Compared to the matrix decision diagram-based solution of [8], we expect to build more compact decision diagrams in the intermediate steps. This assumption is based on the intuition that the efficiency of saturation comes from the ability to saturate nodes as low as possible, minimizing the size of the diagram before moving to the next level. Although the firing of an event is similar in the two approaches both in terms of computing the image and caching (where [8] has more matrix decision diagram nodes we have more EVIDD nodes to spoil the cache), the significant difference comes from the iteration order of the whole saturation algorithm. Because our approach keeps the events as is (as opposed to modifying them and raising their *Top* values), it can process more transitions when saturating a node, potentially yielding a smaller (denser) diagram after every SATURATE call. The confirmation of this hypothesis would require a thorough analysis of the algorithms or the observation of how the state space MDD evolves in each case. At this stage of the work, we can provide empirical measurements that seem to confirm our expectations.

Application: Stochastic Petri Nets. Tangible state space generation of Generalized Stochastic Petri nets can be performed efficiently by the proposed saturation method. First, the EVIDD encoding the highest priority of enabled transitions $\pi_{\max}$ is constructed by HIGHESTPRIORITY (Fig. 4b). The EVIDD will encode a nonzero value for each vanishing marking. Then SATURATE (Fig. 5a) is called on the MDD with the initial marking to explore the reachable state of the GSPN. Finally, tangible states are extracted into a new MDD by simultaneously traversing the saturated MDD and the EVIDD. This approach is similar to the "elimination after generation" in [8].

3   Evaluation

A prototype implementation[1] of our algorithm has been written in the Scala programming language. Measurements were run on a 2.50 GHz Intel® Xeon® L5420 processor and 32 GB memory under Ubuntu Linux 14.04. Heap space for the Java 1.8 virtual machine was maximized in 25 GB. Concurrent mark-and-sweep garbage collection was enabled in the JVM. However, no additional garbage collection routines were implemented to reclaim unique table and cache entries during saturation, i.e. MDD node collection was LAZY [3].

---

[1] See https://inf.mit.bme.hu/en/pn2017 for more details about the measurements.

3.1 Benchmark Models

We used several scalable families of GSPN models from the literature as benchmarks. As only the state space of the models are explored, transition timings were ignored and only transition priorities were kept. *Phils* is the modified version of the dining philosophers model from [8], where the action of picking up a fork is an immediate transition. The prioritised versions of the *Kanban*, *FMS* and *Poll* models were also taken from [8]. In particular, the *FMS* model was modified from its original version in [5] by setting marking-dependent arc weights to constant. *Courier* describes Courier protocol software from [14]. We follow [9] by setting $N = M$.

Phils is grown structurally, i.e. by repeating submodels, for increasing values of N. *Poll* is grown both structurally and by increasing initial token counts, while the rest of the model families grow only by initial marking.

No further modifications were needed to analyze the models. We decompose the models into single places such than the highest priority of enabled transitions can be encoded as an EVIDD.

3.2 Comparison with Matrix Diagram Methods

Table 1 shows the number of decision diagram nodes and the running times of our algorithm when applied to generate the tangible state space $\mathcal{T}$ as described in paragraph *Application: Stochastic Petri Nets* of Sect. 2.4. Unfortunately, we were unable to directly compare our algorithm to matrix diagram based approaches [8, 9] implemented in SMART [2], as the currently available version of SMART does not support prioritised models. We instead compare to the results published in [8,9]. For *Courier*, we compare with the best-scaling approach from [8], OTF. For the other models, we compare with "elimination after generation" (EAG) from [9]. To account for differences between the hardware used, the semi-log plots in the Scaling column show normalized running times. The running times for each algorithm and model family were divided by the running time of the algorithm on the smallest model of the family before plotting. For example, the running time of EAG on *Phils* was divided by 1.3 s, while the running time of our algorithm was divided by 0.216 s.

Our preliminary measurements indicate that our EVIDD-based modified saturation approach scales better than matrix diagram based approaches that handle priorities by changing the next-state relations. Scaling is especially good with the structurally grown *Phils* family. However, further measurements are needed to obtain a more accurate comparison.

Table 2 shows the number of decision diagram nodes required for representing the highest priority of enabled transitions $\pi_{\max}$, the reachable states $\mathcal{S}_r$ and the tangible states $\mathcal{T}$, as well as the unique table and cache utilizations on the *Courier* model family. When comparing with the utilizations of OTF published in [8], it is apparent that–in accordance with our expectations–prioritised saturation with EVIDDs requires the creation of less temporary MDD nodes and therefore reduces the size of the cache as well (even though using pairs as keys would obviously lead to worse cache coherence in itself).

Table 1. Comparison with matrix diagram based methods.

| | N | $|\mathcal{T}|$ | DD nodes | | | Comparison | | |
			Final	Peak	Time	Alg.	Time	Scaling
Phils	16	4.87×10^6	1188	10 662	0.216 s		1.3 s	
	30	3.46×10^{12}	2364	26 086	0.390 s	EAG [9]	10.1 s	
	60	1.20×10^{25}	4884	75 449	0.930 s		69.2 s	
	90	4.15×10^{37}	7404	147 772	1.420 s		204.4 s	
	120	1.44×10^{50}	9924	238 976	2.261 s		—	
Kanban	8	4.23×10^7	280	1800	0.045 s		0.5 s	
	30	2.36×10^{12}	1985	21 259	0.638 s	EAG [9]	67.0 s	
	40	2.86×10^{13}	3240	41 464	1.151 s		280.0 s	
	50	2.01×10^{14}	4795	71 569	2.252 s		979.0 s	
FMS	8	4.46×10^7	280	5972	0.186 s		0.2 s	
	20	8.83×10^9	3646	45 031	1.407 s	EAG [9]	2.5 s	EVIDD
	40	4.97×10^{12}	13 276	232 061	7.413 s		29.0 s	
	80	3.71×10^{15}	50 536	1 352 121	52.009 s		477.0 s	
Poll	5	5.91×10^6	279	2806	0.056 s		0.4 s	
	10	9.34×10^{16}	1604	30 602	0.726 s	EAG [9]	13.0 s	
	15	2.28×10^{28}	4729	135 267	3.867 s		113.1 s	EAG
	20	3.20×10^{40}	10 404	398 512	11.831 s		540.1 s	
Courier	10	4.25×10^9	1433	17 703	0.626 s		14 s	
	20	2.26×10^{12}	4193	55 458	2.666 s	OTF [8]	82 s	
	40	2.18×10^{15}	13 913	191 268	14.789 s		668 s	OTF
	60	1.44×10^{17}	29 233	407 478	42.847 s		—	

Table 2. Unique table and cache utilization for the *Courier* model.

| | N | EVIDD | | | MDD | | | | OTF [8] | |
		π_{max}	Peak	Cache	$\mathcal{S}_r$	$\mathcal{T}$	Peak	Cache	Peak	Cache
Courier	10	69	538	424	3236	1433	17165	85414	71735	304612
	20	69	538	424	9346	4193	54920	264639	227230	857572
	40	69	538	424	30566	13913	190730	891589	801920	2656692
	60	69	538	424	63786	29233	406940	1876539	—	—

3.3 Models with Many Priority Levels

To study the effects of more complicated priority structures, we created three additional modifications of the *Phils* model family where we assign multiple priority levels to transitions. In these models, the picking up of a fork is an immediate event with $\pi \geq 0$, while the rest of the behaviours are timed with $\pi = 0$. In *PhilsRight*, picking up the left fork has priority 1, while picking the right fork has priority 2. In *PhilsBH* and *PhilsTH*, picking up the two forks have equal priorities. However, in *PhilsBH*, philosophers have sequentially increasing

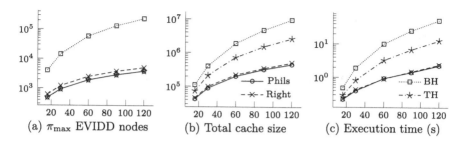

Fig. 6. Measurements with many priority levels.

priority from the top to the bottom of the EVIDD and MDD variable order. In *PhilsTH* the order is reversed. All models have the same tangible states. Moreover, *PhilsBH* and *PhilsTH* have isomorphic reachable state spaces, albeit with different variable ordering.

Figure 6 shows the number of EVIDD nodes required to encode π_{max}, the total number of cache entries created, and the execution time of the tangible state space generation. Adding another priority level in *PhilsRight* increased only the number of EVIDD nodes by a constant factor. The effects of assigning sequential priorities to philosophers heavily depended on the order of priorities. EVIDDs could encode priorities increasing from bottom to top in *PhilsTH* with the same number of nodes as *Phils*; however, the reversed order in *PhilsBH* increased node count substantially.

While *PhilsRight* only increased cache usage moderately compared to *Phils*, the more complicated effective next-state relations of *PhilsTH* and *PhilsBH* required much more cache entries in saturation. This problem is further amplified by the large number of EVIDD nodes that appear in cache keys in *PhilsBH*. This effect also manifests in the running times, which were found to be strongly correlated ($R = 0.999$) with the number of cache entries.

4   Summary and Future Work

In this work we have introduced a modified saturation algorithm capable of natively handling prioritised models. To this end, we introduced edge-valued interval decision diagrams which can efficiently encode the priority-related enabledness of transitions and can be constructed before state space generation in case of Petri nets. We have described the new algorithm in detail and also defined abstract next-state diagrams as an abstraction of next-state representations compatible with saturation. The results of our empirical experiments have been compared to the results of [8], demonstrating that handling priorities separately can indeed yield smaller intermediate diagrams and better performance.

As the direct follow-up of this work, we plan to define a full workflow to efficiently analyse the stochastic behaviour of large GSPNs, also supporting phase-type distributions and marking-based behaviour.

Acknowledgement. This work was partially supported by the ARTEMIS JU and the Hungarian National Research, Development and Innovation Fund in the frame of the R5-COP project and the ÚNKP-16-2-I. New National Excellence Program of the Ministry of Human Capacities.

Special thanks to Andrew S. Miner for sharing his benchmark models.

References

1. Chiola, G., Ajmone, M.M., Balbo, G., Conte, G.: Generalized stochastic Petri nets: a definition at the net level and its implications. IEEE Trans. Softw. Eng. **19**(2), 89–107 (1993)
2. Ciardo, G., Jones, R.L., Miner, A.S., Siminiceanu, R.I.: Logic and stochastic modeling with SMART. Perform. Eval. **63**(6), 578–608 (2006)
3. Ciardo, G., Lüttgen, G., Siminiceanu, R.: Saturation: an efficient iteration strategy for symbolic state—space generation. In: Margaria, T., Yi, W. (eds.) TACAS 2001. LNCS, vol. 2031, pp. 328–342. Springer, Heidelberg (2001). doi:10.1007/3-540-45319-9_23
4. Ciardo, G., Marmorstein, R., Siminiceanu, R.: The saturation algorithm for symbolic state-space exploration. Int. J. Softw. Tools Technol. Transf. **8**(1), 4–25 (2006)
5. Ciardo, G., Trivedi, K.S.: A decomposition approach for stochastic reward net models. Perform. Eval. **18**(1), 37–59 (1993)
6. Ciardo, G., Yu, A.J.: Saturation-based symbolic reachability analysis using conjunctive and disjunctive partitioning. In: Borrione, D., Paul, W. (eds.) CHARME 2005. LNCS, vol. 3725, pp. 146–161. Springer, Heidelberg (2005). doi:10.1007/11560548_13
7. Kam, T., Villa, T., Brayton, R., Sangiovanni-Vincentelli, A.: Multi-valued decision diagrams: theory and applications. Multiple-Valued Logic **4**(1), 9–62 (1998)
8. Miner, A.S.: Implicit GSPN reachability set generation using decision diagrams. Perform. Eval. **56**(1–4), 145–165 (2004)
9. Miner, A.S.: Saturation for a general class of models. IEEE Trans. Softw. Eng. **32**(8), 559–570 (2006)
10. Molnár, V., Majzik, I.: Constraint programming with multi-valued decision diagrams: a saturation approach. In: Proceedings of the 24th PhD Mini-Symposium of the Department of Measurement and Information Systems (2017) (in Preparation)
11. Roux, P., Siminiceanu, R.: Model checking with edge-valued decision diagrams. In: Proceedings of the 2nd NASA Formal Methods Symposium, pp. 222–226 (2010)
12. Teruel, E., Franceschinis, G., Pierro, M.D.: Well-defined generalized stochastic Petri nets: a net-level method to specify priorities. IEEE Trans. Softw. Eng. **29**(11), 962–973 (2003)
13. Tovchigrechko, A.A.: Efficient symbolic analysis of bounded Petri nets using interval decision diagrams. Ph.D. thesis. Brandenburg University of Technology, Cottbus-Senftenberg, Germany (2008)
14. Woodside, C.M., Li, Y.: Performance Petri net analysis of communications protocol software by delay-equivalent aggregation. In: Proceedings of the 4th International Workshop on Petri Nets and Performance Models, pp. 64–73 (1991)
15. Zhao, Y., Ciardo, G.: Symbolic CTL model checking of asynchronous systems using constrained saturation. In: Liu, Z., Ravn, A.P. (eds.) ATVA 2009. LNCS, vol. 5799, pp. 368–381. Springer, Heidelberg (2009). doi:10.1007/978-3-642-04761-9_27

Modelling and Evaluation
of a Control Room Application

Elvio Gilberto Amparore[1]([✉]), Susanna Donatelli[1], and Elisa Landini[2]

[1] Dipartimento di Informatica, Università di Torino, Torino, Italy
{amparore,donatelli}@di.unito.it
[2] RE:Lab S.r.l., Reggio Emilia, Italy
elisa.landini@re-lab.it

Abstract. This application paper describes the study of a control room system that has been performed inside the EU Artemis project HoliDes. The control room object of the study is for an Italian operator in gas energy distribution. Customers call the control room of the energy operator to signal malfunctioning of gas distribution and/or of gas apparatus. Upon a call the control room operators assign a technician delegated to physically reach the intervention site and make it, in first place, secure, and, in second place, back to normal operating condition. Because of the safety issues inherently associated with the gas distribution, the Italian Regulatory Authority for Electricity Gas and Water has set a service level agreement (SLA) requirement that states that an operator should reach the client site in less than 60 min in 95% of the times.

This paper describes the Petri net models that have been used to assess what is the load of calls that can be dealt with without violating the SLA, and what type of conditions make the system in a critical state. Petri nets considered are colored stochastic Petri Nets with and without deterministic and generally distributed transitions. In modelling terms the main issue that has been faced is that of adequately represents the geographical distribution of calls and technicians, while the main issue for the computation of the performance indicator has been the SLA assessment, that requires a passage-time computation, an index that is not widely available in Petri net tools.

1 Introduction

Energy network surveillance systems are important services for the maintenance of safety-critical infrastructures. In this paper we consider the case of a utility company operating in Italy which, among other businesses, controls a part of the gas distribution network. Problems in this network are treated with great urgency, since a gas leak could easily result in explosions and other dangerous outcomes. For this reason, the Italian Regulatory Authority for Electricity Gas and Water (AEEG) requires that company treating gas networks should have an Emergency Call Center (ECC) available h24 subject to the additional constraint that at least 95% of the time a client reports a problem, a company technician should be on site in less than 1 h. The company addresses this requirement by

© Springer International Publishing AG 2017
W. van der Aalst and E. Best (Eds.): PETRI NETS 2017, LNCS 10258, pp. 243–263, 2017.
DOI: 10.1007/978-3-319-57861-3_15

deploying an extensive network of company technicians distributed all over the service area, and keeps track of each intervention in a detailed log, for inspections and for planning the human resource allocation.

This cases study stems from our work with the utility company and RE:Lab inside the EU-funded Artemis project HoliDes. RE:Lab is an Italian SME, located in Reggio Emilia devoted to human and machine interfaces. The project main aim is to study adaptive behaviour of cooperative systems, and in the desire to make the assignment of technicians more adaptive to the environment. For the HoliDes project RE:Lab has developed a prototype interface for the management of the intervention list by the field technicians. Technicians are equipped with a hand-held device with a GPS sensor, which helps the control room in selecting the nearest (free) technician to intervene. We have worked with RE:Lab to understand and support their choice of the nearest technician, and to identify the critical load over which it is not possible to respect the AEEG constraint without calling additional technicians from other areas.

Modelling in control rooms: literature. We have found limited literature that address the problem of complying strict SLA requirement for emergency call centers. The work in [21] provides a good overview of the typical problematics that emergency control planning needs to address, and the amount of support a simulation tool can provide. The work in [17] addresses the problem of determine the critical load conditions of a emergency call center by using computer simulations, using a multi-agent system. The work in [24] considers the performance and availability measures for an emergency call center with a look at the cost optimization, but no need for strict SLA requirement is present.

In this paper we present a model for the evaluation of the AEEG SLA based on Generalized Stochastic Petri Nets (GSPN) [23] and Stochastic Well-formed Nets (SWN) [13]: GSPN are P/T Petri nets in which transition duration is either immediate or exponentially distributed, while SWN are their colored counterpart. We shall also use Deterministic Stochastic Petri nets (DSPN) [1] and the stochastic logic CSL^{TA} [16]. Often we shall use the non-Markovian extensions of GSPN and SWN in which distributions can assume any shape.

The paper is organized as follows: Sect. 2 states the problem being addressed: the control room functioning and the objective of this study; Sect. 3 discusses the modelling problems encountered and how they have been solved; Sect. 4 presents a first model of the control room, that is the basis for the definition, in Sect. 5, of the setting of the CSL computation. In Sect. 6 the SLA is studied using a model checker for the CSL^{TA} stochastic logic, while Sect. 7 addresses the problem of identifying the critical load conditions under which the system cannot guarantee the SLA, done using stochastic simulations. Section 8 concludes the paper.

Reproducibility. All models used for the analysis are available at www.di.unito. it/~amparore/ATPN17-models.zip. The data from the gas energy operator that have been used to set the timing of the models are instead not available as they contain sensible data.

2   The Control Room Problem

This paper presents an application case study centered around the problem of human resource allocation of an utility company. The company manages the gas distribution network, and has many logical units (*areas*) for each cluster of municipalities. The company further subdivides an area into *zones*. Each area has a dedicated control room that takes care of the incoming calls made by the customers, which mainly concern critical problems related to the gas network (malfunctions, leakages, gas odour in the air, etc.). Commercial assistance is done by a separate call center, to reduce the load. We mainly focus on the Reggio Emilia district, which groups together 42 municipalities, and has an area of 2291 km^2 and a population of 531K inhabitants. That area is subdivided into four zones: North, East, West and South.

Control room description. There are one or more operators in the control room that deal with incoming calls. Sometimes, calls are not related to gas problem, and are therefore diverted to the other call center. When a client calls the control room to report a gas problem, the control room operator opens a ticket and transmits the assistance request to a group of company technicians (mainly plumbers) to reach the client site and inspect the problem. Each area has an area supervisor (reference technician) that receives the control room transmission and either intervenes directly, or redirects the request to another company technician. Each task of dealing with the identified problem is split in two subtasks: a **securing subtask** followed by a **repairing subtask**. The first one consists in reaching the client site and removing the direct cause of the problem (like closing a valve to avoid a gas leakage). An idle technician assigned to a securing task has to reach the location, analyse the problem and make the site secure. Typically, the securing task is done quickly. The second task is the actual fixing, and may require longer times. The second one may be missing if there is no repair to be done, or if the repair can be postponed. Usually, if there are other urgent calls, the repair task is assigned to a separate technician, and is done later.

Service Level Agreement. The period of time from the instant in which the call is answered until a technician reaches the location for which the call has been placed is named *intervention time*. The Italian Regulatory Authority for Electricity Gas and Water requires that in 95% of the cases the intervention time is less than 1 h, otherwise the company will incur in a fine. The company takes detailed logs of each ticket, with timings from the client call to the closing of the intervention.

Task assignment policy. In the current assignment protocol, technicians are pre-assigned to zones (and we can speak of *his zone*), but they may occasionally intervene on problems in other zones. Therefore, a ticket of a problem in a zone is preferentially assigned to the zone technician. We call this *assignZone* policy. If the zone technician is already busy when a new call arrives, then the call is diverted to the area responsible that may decide to assign the ticket to a technician of another zone in the same area (but not outside the boundary of the area). The policy of calling a technician to intervene in a zone different from his zone is subject to a different consideration: When the travelling time is reasonable, we call the assignment policy *assignNextTo*, otherwise we call it *assignNonConvenient*. Since the area is quite large it is not always possible to ensure the 1 h requirement by allocating any technician to arbitrary calls. The policy has been modified recently by the company RE:Lab with to support of precise localization of the technicians using GPS-tracking hand-held devices. The devices cover the transmission protocol using a dedicated GUI.

The problem being verified. The goal of the studied system is to first define a model whose behaviour fits the empirical data provided by the company logs. Given the model, it is then of interest to determine how the system behaves in critical situations: what is the maximum load capacity of the system can support with a given, fixed amount, of technicians? What are the conditions that determine the possibility to respect the SLA?

We performed this analysis together with RE:Lab that was in charge of building the new technician GUIs over the smart phones. The data that we had available for model validation was limited (8 weeks of operations with recorded info like intervention site, time of arrival on the call, time of arrival on-site) and we did not have access to the record of the contracts, to know the geographical distribution of the Clients.

3   Modelling Issues

In this section we describe the model of the interventions planned by the control room. We use a continuous stochastic approach, with Generalized Stochastic Petri Nets (GSPN) [23]. In particular, we are interested in making distinctions between tokens of the net, i.e. we use Stochastic Well-formed Nets (SWN) [13] as the modeling formalism. All nets have been created and solved with the GreatSPN tool [3], unless otherwise indicated.

The system is decomposed into multiple logical blocks:

CG: calls' generation. A subsystem of the calls that reach the control room (calls distribution in time and in the geographical space)

CR: Control room. A subsystem of the control room operators, that receive the client calls and open new tickets.

TP: Technician assignment protocol. A subsystem of the protocol that assigns technicians to open tickets

TA: Technician activity. A subsystem modelling the activity of each technician, i.e. reaching the target site and securing the gas distribution network.

Since we have had assurance from RE:Lab colleagues that the control room is never a bottleneck of the system, the model of the **CR** subsystem is reduced to a minimum and we assume that all call lead to an assignment of a technician while in reality many calls are inappropriate and are discarded. Since the goal of the study is to compute the SLA satisfaction, and since SLA satisfaction is computed only for calls that lead to an intervention, assuming that all calls lead to a technician intervention is adequate. Considering the simplicity of the **CR** subsystem, its behaviour has been included into the model of the **CG** subsystem.

Modelling by subsystems is usually a good approach, but there are issues that are common to the whole model, in particular it is necessary to decide whether or not *to manage the identities* of the clients and of the technicians and how to manage the *physical locations* of the calls.

Modelling clients. In the SLA objective of the study there is no notion of specific client. An example of SLA of this type is instead: "calls within a week from the same client should be dealt with by the same technician". An identification of the clients may be needed to be able to compute the time of intervention, which is central in the notion of the considered SLA, but, although the model should be built taking into consideration the performance indicators we need to compute, changing the model to favour the computation of the performance indicators is delegated to a later stage (Sect. 5), as we believe it is important to distinguish the model from the model modified so as to favour the computation of the indices. The first model therefore will consider clients as black tokens. The only relevant information is the location of the intervention (site) required by a call, as discussed next.

Modelling the geographical aspects. Calls may come from any client in the area, and the issue is the level of abstraction at which to model the call sites. Since an area is split into zones a first model is to abstract the geographical coordinates of the call sites and to identify the call site with their zone. Another possibility is to consider municipalities. We shall discuss this issue in more details when describing the **CG** subsystem.

Modelling technicians. None of the objectives of the study involves the single technician, there is no requirement to make comparison among technicians, so technicians, as calls, should be identified by their position in the area, with the same level of details as that of the location sites.

Timing of the model. All times are expressed in minutes. Timings are based on distributions fitted from real data, as specified in Sect. 4.

4   A First Model

Figure 1 depicts two possible models for the **CG** subsystem. The Figure is a screenshot of the GreatSPN GUI [3] with which all the models used in this paper have been created and through which all numerical results have been obtained. In the model canvas there is a color class Z that represents the site locations (the location in which there is a failure that requires a technician intervention): the choice of the location sites is very coarse, and we use the 4 geographical zones, as discussed before, to model the geographical origin of the calls.

The simple model on the left generates the calls through the exponential transition *Simple_calls*, which is of single server type. Each generated call gets the color of a location site in a non deterministic manner, as, at each firing, a value for the variable r of color class Z is chosen and a token of that color is deposited in place *Simple_OpenRequests*. In the solution process this non-determinisms results in equal probability.

This model has three peculiarities: it has no explicit model of the control room operators (which is consistent with the information we had that the bottleneck of the system are the technicians and not the control room operators), it assumes an infinite population of calls (as transition *Simple_calls* has no input place) which may make the performance evaluation impractical, and there is no way to generate a load of calls that are not uniformly distributed over the four zones that represent our geographical space.

These limitations are lifted in the "Complete model" of Fig. 1. There is a pool of clients (place *Clients*) initialized with the parameter N, that arrive as soon as there is an operator available (place *Operators* initialized with Op operators) to answer the call (immediate transition *call*). As we shall see later when the full model will be composed, place *Clients* will be used to close the model and to generate a finite state space. Calls receive a geographical identity through the four immediate transitions that transform a generic call (neutral token in place *Dispatch*) into a call from a geographical zone. The weights associated to the four immediate transitions are what allows to model calls from certain geographical areas as being more probable than others: in the model a call from the *South* zone is almost three times less probable than a call from the other zones, as we shall later see. This difference indeed accounts for the actual difference in population in the four zones. Remember that in GSPN/SWN the modeller does not assigns probabilities to immediate transitions, but weights, that are then normalized to compute the probabilities of the choices out of the vanishing states of the reachability graph.

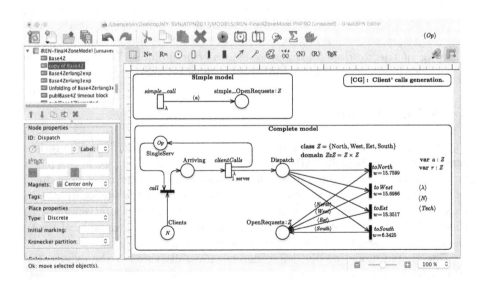

Fig. 1. The first model of the **CG** component.

Figure 2 depicts the model of the **TP** subsystem. The technicians (place *IdleTechs*) are identified upon their geographical location (class Z). The assignment protocol in use before the HoliDes project had one technician assigned to each geographical zone, which would lead to an initial marking of *All* for place *IdleTechs*, meaning that, in the initial state, there is one technician per zone.

Since the current protocol assigns to each call the closest available technician, a way to represent the position of each technicians is a model requirement. Should we have made a model that includes continuous variables so as to represent the distance of a technician from an intervention site? Or should we model the GPS coordinates of a technician and how these coordinates evolves while he/she is travelling? Since the law with which the coordinates change while travelling depends on many conditions that change from time to time (like traffic and weather conditions), we believe that a very detailed modelling approach will not help, since we would model very detailed aspects for which there is no available evolution law. We have therefore taken a discretization approach, in which we, again, consider only the zones, and we define which zones are close to each other and which ones are not. The distinction between convenient and non-convenient assignment is based on the travelling times, which will be explained later.

To define closeness we have checked the distance among the middle points of the four zones, as explained in the comment to Fig. 5 and we have observed that the only pair of zones that cannot be considered close one to the other are *North* and *South*, which lead to three levels of closeness: technician and site in the same zone, in a "next to" zone and in a "non convenient" zone, implemented, in Fig. 2 by the three immediate transitions *assignSameZone*, *assignNextTo*, and *assignNonConvenient*. The three transitions have decreasing priorities, so if there is a technician in the same zone as that of the call (tokens of the same color in places *IdleTechs* and *OpenRequests*) *assignSameZone* fires; if there are not, transition *assignNextTo*, which has the next smaller priority, fires. If even this transition is not enabled, transition *assignNonConvenient* fires. Note that the output places differ, since if the technician is assigned to the same zone the travelling time will be significantly smaller than that of the other two cases.

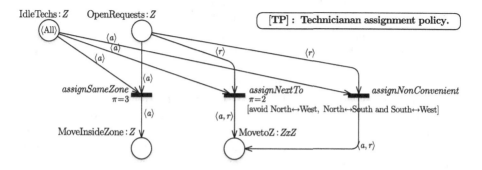

Fig. 2. The first model of the **TP** component.

Figure 3 depicts the model of the **TA** subsystem: from the time a call is assigned to a technician and he/she starts travelling, to the end of the intervention. The travelling time model consider two cases: travelling among zones, or travelling inside a single zone. The set of 6, mutually exclusive, exponential transitions on the right in the SWN of Fig. 3 models the time it takes to reach the target zone r from the current zone a of the technician. The rate of these transitions corresponds to the inverse of the average times reported in the tables contained in Fig. 5. Similarly, the set of four transitions $move\_*$ on the left model the traveling times inside a zone.

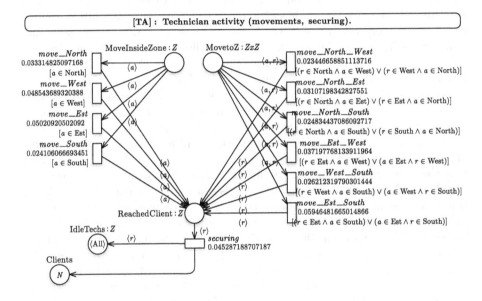

Fig. 3. The first model of the **TA** component.

Figure 4 depicts the composition of the three models by superposition over places of equal names. The composition is achieved by using the composition facility of GreatSPN (the Σ button in the GUI depicted in Fig. 1), which is a pairwise composition based on places and/or transition superposition, as described in [12]. The model has been then slightly modified by hand to make it easier to read.

In the composed model it is immediate to observe that there is a pool of N unidentified clients going around in the model. Closing the model to generate a finite state space is a rather standard technique in performance evaluation, but it is important to make sure that N is big enough. Since what we want to model is an arrival process with inter-arrival time equal to the inverse of λ, the value of N has to be large enough to guarantee that there is a very low probability that transition *clientCalls* is not enabled because of lack of tokens in the *Clients*. Moreover we have fixed $Op = 1$, therefore setting to 1 the initial marking of the *SingleServer* place. This choice is based on what has been reported by the

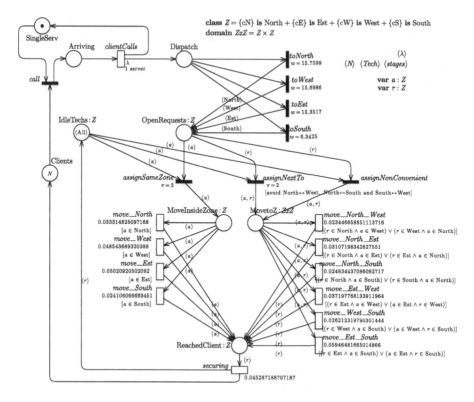

Fig. 4. The first model of the control room.

company (control room operators are never a bottleneck of the system), moreover the data that we have available to estimate the arrival rate do not distinguish the information flux of the different operators, but we can only observe the inter-arrival time of calls at the control room. Note that at this point the *Clients* place could have been directly connected to the single server transition *clientCalls*, but keeping place *SingleServ* does not increase the tangible state space and makes explicit the single server policy. This will be particularly useful in more detailed models in which clients are identified.

Another observation is that there is no specific queue associated to the calls that wait for an idle operator. This is the easiest choice since GSPN and SWN do not have queueing places, although extension in that sense have been defined [11]. By not keeping the queue, and due to the presence of priorities over the three immediate transitions in the SWN of Fig. 2, in the model we tend to assign "same zone" technicians more frequently than in reality.

Figure 5 shows the data that we have used to set the model's parameter. The zone considered is the area of Reggio Emilia. The main town, Reggio Emilia, concentrates around 1/3 of the population (531K inhabitants) in 1/10 of the area. The colour on the map reflects the aggregation of municipalities into zones, with the amount of population in each zone reported in the upper table.

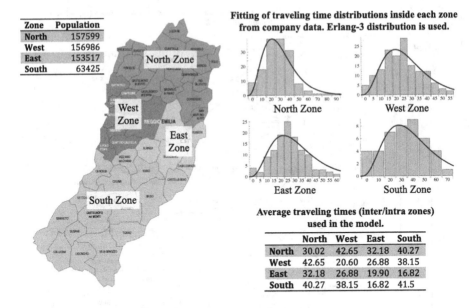

Zone	Population
North	157599
West	156986
East	153517
South	63425

Fitting of traveling time distributions inside each zone from company data. Erlang-3 distribution is used.

North Zone

West Zone

East Zone

South Zone

Average traveling times (inter/intra zones) used in the model.

	North	West	East	South
North	30.02	42.65	32.18	40.27
West	42.65	20.60	26.88	38.15
East	32.18	26.88	19.90	16.82
South	40.27	38.15	16.82	41.5

Fig. 5. Data for model parametrization.

These data have been used to set the weights of the immediate transitions of the subnet in Fig. 1: since we have no data on the amount of clients per municipality (which is considered a sensible information by the company not to be disclosed to third parties) we have assumed that the clients are spread in the zone proportionally to the number of inhabitants. The time to move inside an area has been computed as the time to move among two municipalities chosen among the most populated municipalities and among the pairs that where not at the extreme opposite points of the zone. The data have been computed through the Google Maps API, by using a script, so as to be able to try different choices. Another possibility would be to make an exhaustive search and do the weighted

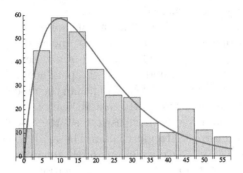

Fig. 6. Bar chart of the securing time obtained from company logs. (Color figure online)

sum (based on population) of the distance among any two pairs of municipalities. The average time taken for the travelling time inside a zone (intra-zone travel) is reported in the lower table. Times are expressed in minutes. To compute the travelling time among two zones a similar criteria has been applied but the pairs of municipalities considered have to be in different zones.

Figure 5 reports also the travelling time inside a zone computed from the available data. The records in the company logs report the indication of the destination of the travel (the intervention site), but not the location from which the technician started from. Not surprisingly the experimental data give a longer travelling time than the one computed using Google Maps, which assumes that the technician is already somewhere in the area. Of course estimating the average travelling time is not enough, as also the distribution (or at least the variance) of this value may have a significant impact. Figure 5 shows the four bar-charts of the travelling times computed on the available data, while the smooth curve is an Erlang-3 shape with average time equal to the one computed using Google Maps API.

Figure 6 shows the histogram of the securing times, obtained from the available 320 samples extracted again from the company logs. The overlayed red curve shows an Erlang distribution with 2 stages that fits the sampled data. The obtained distribution is used for the *securing* distribution in the model. All fittings have been done using the Mathematica tool.

5   SLA Computation

The *passage time distribution* is a specific type of performance index which is particularly useful when reasoning about properties related with SLA or safety requirements. For our SLA we do not need to have the full distribution, but simply the probability that passage time is greater than one hour, that is to say the probability that the system violates the SLA.

The definition of the SLA includes a passage time (60 min from when a call is received by the operator, until a technician arrives on-site), and the computation of a passage time requires to identify a start and an ending conditions: the passage time is accumulated from the time the start condition gets true until the ending condition gets true. In our system the SLA is based on the time it takes from the end of the call with control room application until a technician reaches the location, therefore the start and end conditions are respectively defined as the events: a client enters in place *OpenRequest* and the same client reaches place *StartSecuring*. In addition, we have to ensure that the time is taken *for the same client*.

A passage time measure specification for CTMC is usually based on the definition of entry, goal and forbidden states: the distribution of the time required to reach a goal state from any entry state without hitting any forbidden state can be computed with different methods and tools [15,22]. This typically requires the (automatic) manipulation of either the CTMC or of the high level model used to generate the CTMC, often through the synchronization with an automaton that specifies the behaviours to be taken into account, as for Extended Stochastic Probes (XSP [14], operating on PEPA models [19]) and Path Automata (PA, operating on Stochastic Activity Networks [20]).

Computing passage time of an entity in a Petri net requires to be able to identify that entity (typically called "a client") and its evolution in the net, and to measure the time required for the identified entity to go from one state to another of the net, or from one transition firing to another. In GSPN terms this often leads to the need to follow a specific token through the net. Since the identification of the flux of clients is trivial in our model, to distinguish one client from the other we can simply define a color class *Cli* with N distinguished colors c_i and change the color domain of all places that carry a client so as to account for the change (places *Clients, Arriving, Dispatch, OpenRequests, AssignedLocal, AssignedMove, StartSecuring*). The resulting net is shown in Fig. 7.

The passage time identification and computation is not trivial if the token to be followed may go through places containing other tokens, since they are indistinguishable and/or if the flux of tokens in the net is not clearly identifiable: this aspect has been tackled in the literature by introducing a formalism extension called Tagged GSPNs [8], for which a specific language for passage time specification has been later developed (Probe Automata [5]) to ease the task of defining the TGSPN conditions for entry, goal, and forbidden states. In Tagged GSPN the user specifies the initial and final condition of the "passage" and the system takes care of coloring the net so as to identify the client, and to associate to the client a subnet that represents the client evolution during the "passage", based on P-semiflows computation.

In our model, we do not need forbidden states (states that abort the computation of the passage time if a certain condition happen), and the notion of client is simple. Following the intuition behind tagged GSPN we can also simplify the definition of the color class *Cli*: If all clients behave the same, then it is enough to follow a generic one, so the color class *Cli* can be defined as having only two colors: anonymous client (cA) and one identified, tagged, client (cT). The net is then initialized with $N + 1$ clients, N anonymous and one tagged. Figure 7 shows the resulting net.

This allows, in the next subsections, to present two different approaches for the SLA computation. We recall that the SLA is satisfied if

[**SLA:**] 95% of the calls that require an intervention observe the intervention time (from client call to the arrival of a technician) in within 1 h.

which implies that the computation required is not a passage time distribution, but it is enough to compute the probability that the passage time is less than 60 min, although, as usual, the distribution is more informative. In the following we shall present two different approaches: in Sect. 6 the SLA is computed as a path property in the stochastic logic CSL^{TA}, while in Sect. 7 the net is modified and the SLA satisfaction is based on standard performance evaluation features (throughput of transitions) on the modified model.

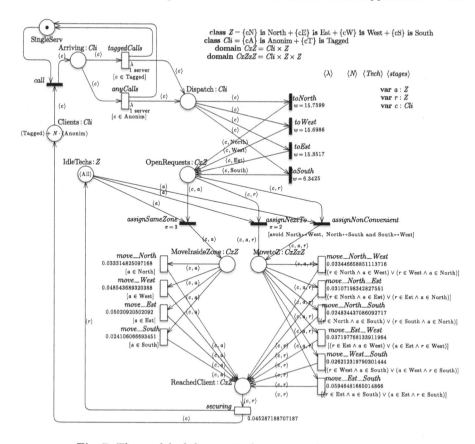

Fig. 7. The model of the system for passage time computation

6 Use of CSLTA for SLA Computation

Stochastic logics for CTMCs define formulas of the type $Prob_{\bowtie\alpha}(\varphi)$ that are satisfied by a CTMC if the probability of the set of executions of the CTMC that satisfy the constraints φ is $\bowtie \alpha$. The most well-known of the stochastic logics is CSL [7], that, in the desire to limit the cost of the model-checking, trades simplicity of φ for efficiency, resulting in a logic that is not adequate for passage time computation [4].

The CSL^{TA} [16] logics has been introduced to give more flexibility to the modeler, as formula takes the form of $Prob_{\bowtie\alpha}(\mathcal{A})$, where $\mathcal{A}$ is a one-clock timed-automaton. CSL^{TA} model-checker is part of the GreatSPN suite. The model-checking is based on numerical solution and requires the solution of a Markov Regenerative Process (MRP). An efficient solution algorithm for this type of MRPs has been developed [6].

The relationship between passage time and stochastic logics has been investigated in [4], in the context of HASL (Hybrid Automata Stochastic Logic) [10]. HASL allows very complicated properties to be expressed as $Prob_{\bowtie\alpha}(H)$, where

H is an Hybrid Automata. The complexity of the path specification makes the underlying stochastic process impossible to solve in numerical form, and simulation is the only viable option. Cosmos [9] is a simulation-based model-checker for HASL that operates on systems specified as Petri nets. Following the approach in [4] we use a stochastic logic to compute the passage times. We have used CSL^{TA}: the reason why CSL^{TA} has been preferred over HASL is that CSL^{TA} is part of the GreatSPN suite and *allows an exact numerical solution*, while HASL properties can only be checked through simulation.

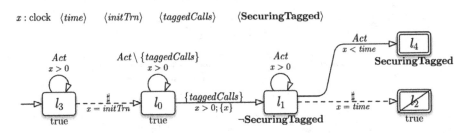

Fig. 8. The timed automata for the CSL^{TA} computation of passage time

Figure 8 shows the Timed Automaton used to compute the SLA: it consists of 5 locations, including the initial location l_3, a success final location l_4 and a failure final location l_2. Locations are labelled with atomic propositions, and edges are labelled with action sets. In GreatSPN the DTA is defined in parametric form; when the DTA is used to model check a CTMC generated by a GSPN, the DTA actions are instantiated on transitions names and the atomic proposition are instantiated on boolean formulas over the Petri net markings.

Following the ideas in [4] the DTA of Fig. 8 accepts, at the beginning (while in location l_3) all the GSPN behaviours (*Act* stays for "any transition firing", there is no constraint on the value of the clock x, and the atomic proposition associated to l_3 is *true*). When the DTA clock reaches *initTrn* the DTA keeps accepting anything until a tagged call takes place (action *taggedCalls*). At this point the clock is reset and the DTA moves to location l_4 and starts observing until the condition **SecuringTagged** does not hold. When the condition **SecuringTagged** becomes true before time *time*, the DTA moves to location l_4 and accepts the path. If instead the time boundary *time* is exceeded, the DTA is forced to move to the failure location l_2.

To check the SLA, we apply CSL^{TA} model-checking by binding the DTA parameters to the net elements. Note that the model we have defined is an SWN, while CSL^{TA} is defined for CTMCs, and the implementation in GreatSPN assumes that the CTMC is generated from a GSPN. Therefore the net of Fig. 7 has been unfolded[1] and the parameters of the DTA have been instantiated over

---

[1] The unfolding facility is available through the GUI (open box icon on the toolbar), a facility that has been implemented for the participation at the Petri net Model-Checking Contest, while the definition of the parameters in terms of GSPN elements is not automatically supported.

the marking of the GSPN resulting from the unfolding. It was shown in [4] that if the transient behaviour is long enough (and this depends on the value of $initTrn$) so that the CTMC is in steady state when the simulator reaches time $initTrn$, then the model checking of the DTA of Fig. 8 corresponds to verify the SLA in steady state.

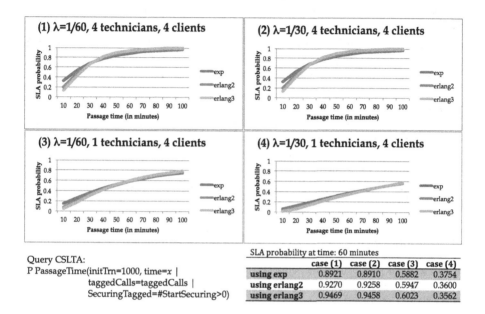

Query CSLTA:
P PassageTime(initTrn=1000, time=x |
            taggedCalls=taggedCalls |
            SecuringTagged=#StartSecuring>0)

SLA probability at time: 60 minutes

	case (1)	case (2)	case (3)	case (4)
using exp	0.8921	0.8910	0.5882	0.3754
using erlang2	0.9270	0.9258	0.5947	0.3600
using erlang3	0.9469	0.9458	0.6023	0.3562

Fig. 9. SLA computation with CSL^{TA}.

Figure 9 depicts the distribution of the passage time in four different situations: charts (1) and (2) consider four technician and a load of incoming call generated from a population of $N = 4$ clients and a duration of 60 (left chart) and 30 (right chart). Charts (3) and (4) depicts the same situations, but with a single technician. As from the data available from the company, the situation of (1) is considered the normal condition (4 technicians available, about 1 client call per area per hour). The lower charts show instead a situation of congestion, when the number of incoming calls cannot be handled by a single technician without breaking the SLA.

On each chart there are three passage time distributions for three models: the "exp" curves refer to the case where all SWN transitions are either immediate or exponential, the "Erlang-2" (Erlang-3) labelled curve are obtained by expanding the exponentially distributed transitions of travelling time and security activity in 2 (3) exponential stages twice (three times) as fast as the exponential transition they substitute. This approach, which is rather standard [2] allows to generate the CTMC while using distributions (like Erlang-2 and Erlang-3) that have a significantly lower variance than not exponential.

Note that, by not explicitly considering a FIFO queue, when N increases the probability of having one or more clients waiting in place *Dispatch* increases as well, which increases the probability that an idle technician gets immediately assigned to a new client and that the technician will find a client request for the same zone where he/she is currently located. This phenomenon tends to make a heavily loaded system to work a bit better than it should be.

The charts show also the impact of using Erlang-3 distributions (which actually fit quite well the experimental data) instead of using exponential transitions. Lower variance of the Erlang distribution makes the system closer to the SLA requirement.

The model-checking of CSL^{TA} allows to exactly compute the probability of exceeding the 60 min, but it suffers the standard limitation of state space explosion, worsened by the fact that the stochastic process to be solved is an MRP. The largest state space covered in this test were of about 1.7×10^6 states. Despite big improvements in memory and space on MRP solution [18], it is difficult to solve MRP's with more than a few million states, which in our case limits the exact solution at instances of the SWN of Fig. 7 with 4 clients, 4 technicians and the Erlang-3 expansion (that, obviously, significantly increases the state space).

6.1   Summary of CSL^{TA} Results and Lesson Learned

Lesson learned - case study. From the results of the analytical solution of CSL^{TA} we can observe that 4 technicians are a minimal number to sustain the load of calls.

Lesson learned – modelling and tools. Thanks to unfolding and stage expansion we have been able to model-check CSL^{TA} for an SPN that includes also non exponential transitions.

7   Use of Timeouts and DSPN for SLA Computation

Since the exact model checking of CSL^{TA} is limited to small systems, then the only viable solution for larger systems is simulation. In this context simulation can take two forms: use a model-checker based on simulation (what is now called "statistical model-checking") or modify the model so as to compute the SLA with a generic SWN simulator. We have previous experience in using Cosmos [9], the tool for statistical model-checking of the HASL logic, but the performance indicator for this case study does not require the power of a complex simulator like Cosmos, that has to take into account the full power of hybrid automata, moreover the use of another tool would have required to translate the net from the GreatSPN format to the Cosmos one.

We took the second approach: the net has been modified so that the SLA satisfaction can be computed based on transition throughputs. Since the SLA requires to compute the percentage of calls for which the time period from the time of the call until the time the technician reaches the site is less or equal to 60 min, it is enough to set a timeout of 60 min whenever a call enters the *OpenRequests* (which is the same time at which the transitions *anyCalls* and *taggedCalls* fire) and to check whether the associated technician reaches the site before or after the timeout has expired.

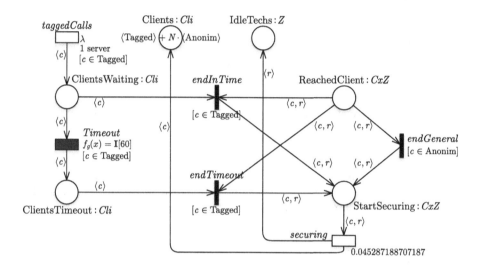

Fig. 10. The model of the system for passage time computation with DSPNs.

Figure 10 shows the modification to the model of Fig. 7. Note that a timeout is set only when transition *taggedCalls* fires, since, as already done for the CSL^{TA} solution, we know (from, for ex. [8] that observing a single selected client is enough for correctly computing the SLA. When the technician r associated to the tagged client c reaches the intervention site (a token of color $\langle c, Tagged\rangle$ reaches place *ReachedClient*) the net immediately fires either transition *endInTime* (if the deterministic transition *Timeout* has not fired yet) or transition *endTimeout* (if the deterministic transition *Timeout* has already fired, meaning that the deadline of 60 min was violated). The probability of the SLA is then computed as the ratio between the throughput of transition *endInTime* and the sum of the throughput of transitions *endInTime* and *endTimeout*.

Note that, since there is a single tagged client, in any one state there is at most a single deterministic transition enabled, therefore the model of Fig. 10, or, better, its unfolding, is a DSPN model [1]. Using the DSPN solver of GreatSPN we could check that the two techniques for SLA computation (CSL^{TA} formula or model modification to include a timeout) are equivalent or not.

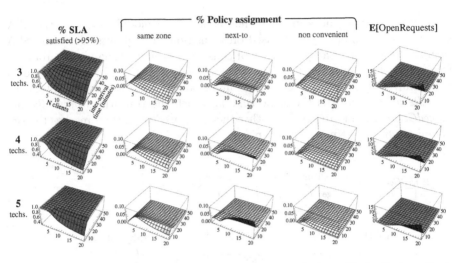

Fig. 11. Results space obtained by running multiple simulations. (Color figure online)

Figure 11 shows the result space of the model (for the Erlang-3 case). Since the solution technique is simulation we could introduce Erlang-3 as distribution for SWN transitions. The net was not unfolded, as the GreatSPN simulator for SWN was used, which already includes a number of common activity.

Each point in the charts corresponds to a simulation run of the SWN simulator. 600 separate simulations were run in batch to generate the result space. We have used a batch method with 95% confidence and 10% accuracy. Simulations end when all the default performance indicators (mean number of tokens in places and throughput of transitions) satisfy the confidence and accuracy requirements. Simulations are run on a standard laptop with a Core 2 Duo processor in single thread mode. It took about 5 h to compute all the samples. Each row of Fig. 11 shows the results for 3, 4 and 5 technicians in the system. Each 3D plot depicts the results for a varying number of clients in the system (1 to 20), and for different inter-arrival times of the client' calls (from 5 to 60 min). The first column is the probability of respecting the SLA requirement: the red zone stays below the 95% requirement, while the blue zone stays above. The second, third and fourth columns show the probability of each technicians to have to move between far zones (non-convenient), near zones (next-to) or to remain in the same zone when a new ticket is assigned. Finally, the last column shows the number of open requests in the system, which measures the system stability (high inter-arrival and not-enough technicians will end up in a divergent system).

Lessons learned – case study. The plot shows that for the average client call rate (about 1 call every hour), the system is well beyond the red zone of the SLA plot, i.e. it is expected to maintain the SLA requirement. The critical inter-arrival time (which may happen in a crisis situation) obviously depends on the number of available technicians. With 3, 4 and 5 technicians, it is about 26, 18 and 13 min of calls inter-arrival times, respectively. This information may be used to design a pro-active policy, where for instance if the last N client calls have arrived with a 20 min time delay, and the company has currently 4 technicians, it should start alerting another technician (not currently in service) to be ready for any incoming task.

Lessons learned – modelling and tools. The simulation proved quite effective, but the analysis would have greatly profited by the possibility of specifying different accuracies for different performance indicators and by the possibility of computing the accuracy of simple formulas (like the ratio among throughputs that we use to compute the SLA).

Another aspect that was important is the simulator ability to compute the throughput also of immediate transitions: this is a feature that is not always available but that is very convenient to have.

We have also observed that the availability of a DSPN numerical solver allowed to check whether the model in Fig. 10 and that in Fig. 7 lead to the same SLA computation (a comparison difficult to do if only simulation results are available). The DSPN solver was also used to check that the setting of the parameter *initTrn* of the timed automaton that defines the SLA, that identifies the time to reach steady state, is correctly set.

8   Conclusions and Perspectives

In this work we have developed a model of a utility company control room, based on real data provided by the company, aimed at studying the critical conditions that make the system in use unable to fulfil a required SLA. Two different actors were involved in this project, the utility company and RE:Lab company. RE:Lab was in charge of developing an application that, making use of geographical information, supports the control room operator in the task of assigning technicians to calls The modelling and the analysis performed allowed RE:Lab to develop an application that correctly takes into account the different behaviours identified through the model analysis, on the other side the utility company has taken advantage of the numerical results presented to set the limits at which it is necessary to increase the number of technicians assigned to an area.

This case study raised different interesting modelling questions, concerning the choice of the distributions for delays and the modelling of geographical positions.

Indeed using histograms of the available data recorded by the utility company, we observed that most quantities involved can be fitted accurately using Erlang distributions, thus making the model easy to specify using standard stochastic Petri nets.

The problem of addressing the high variability of the geographical positions is only considered in an approximate form, by considering a discretization based on only four zones. By using a different technique (using the actual map of the area and by modelling the actual municipalities and the distance among them) it would be possible to simulate the movement in a more accurate way. However, since we are mostly interested in the average behaviour, and since there is no available data on the geographical distribution of the utility users, an approximated average distribution of the travelling time, as used in this work, should provide measures which are adequately accurate.

An aspect that we have not considered is the modelling of assignment policies different from the one currently in use by the company. For instance, it is not clear if, under critical conditions, it is better not to move technicians out of their zone at all (since they would spend time travelling back, thus potentially missing the deadline of a local call). This is left to further investigations.

Acknowledgements. This research was supported by the Artemis EU project HoliDes (grant no. 332933). The goal of the HoliDes project is the improvement of adaptive systems where human and machines operate together to guarantee critical goals.

References

1. Ajmone Marsan, M., Chiola, G.: On Petri nets with deterministic and exponentially distributed firing times. In: Rozenberg, G. (ed.) APN 1986. LNCS, vol. 266, pp. 132–145. Springer, Heidelberg (1987). doi:10.1007/3-540-18086-9_23
2. Ajmone Marsan, M., Conte, G., Balbo, G.: A class of generalized stochastic Petri nets for the performance evaluation of multiprocessor systems. ACM Trans. Comput. Syst. **2**, 93–122 (1984). http://doi.acm.org/10.1145/190.191
3. Amparore, E.G.: A new greatSPN GUI for GSPN editing and CSL^{TA} model checking. In: Norman, G., Sanders, W. (eds.) QEST 2014. LNCS, vol. 8657, pp. 170–173. Springer, Cham (2014). doi:10.1007/978-3-319-10696-0_13
4. Amparore, E.G., Barbot, B., Beccuti, M., Donatelli, S., Franceschinis, G.: Simulation-based verification of hybrid automata stochastic logic formulas for stochastic symmetric nets. In: Proceedings of the 1st ACM SIGSIM Conference on Principles of Advanced Discrete Simulation, pp. 253–264. ACM (2013)
5. Amparore, E.G., Beccuti, M., Donatelli, S., Franceschinis, G.: Probe automata for passage time specification. In: Proceedings of the 2011 Eighth International Conference on Quantitative Evaluation of SysTems, QEST 2011, pp. 101–110. IEEE Computer Society, Washington, DC (2011)
6. Amparore, E.G., Donatelli, S.: Optimal aggregation of components for the solution of Markov Regenerative Processes. In: Agha, G., Houdt, B. (eds.) QEST 2016. LNCS, vol. 9826, pp. 19–34. Springer, Cham (2016). doi:10.1007/978-3-319-43425-4_2
7. Aziz, A., Sanwal, K., Singhal, V., Brayton, R.: Model-checking continuous-time Markov chains. ACM Trans. Comput. Logic **1**(1), 162–170 (2000)
8. Balbo, G., Beccuti, M., De Pierro, M., Franceschinis, G.: First passage time computation in tagged GSPNs with queue places. Comput. J. **54**, 653–673 (2010). First published online 22 July 2010
9. Ballarini, P., Djafri, H., Duflot, M., Haddad, S., Pekergin, N.: COSMOS: a statistical model checker for the hybrid automata stochastic logic. In: Proceedings of the 8th International Conference on Quantitative Evaluation of Systems (QEST 2011), pp. 143–144. IEEE Computer Society Press, Aachen, September 2011

10. Ballarini, P., Djafri, H., Duflot, M., Haddad, S., Pekergin, N.: HASL: an expressive language for statistical verification of stochastic models. In: Proceedings of the 5th International Conference on Performance Evaluation Methodologies and Tools (VALUETOOLS 2011), Cachan, France, pp. 306–315, May 2011

11. Bause, F., Buchholz, P.: Queueing Petri nets with product form solution. Perform. Eval. **32**(4), 265–299 (1998)

12. Bernardi, S., Donatelli, S., Horváth, A.: Implementing compositionality for stochastic Petri nets. Int. J. Softw. Tools Technol. Transf. (STTT) **3**(4), 417–430 (2001)

13. Chiola, G., Dutheillet, C., Franceschinis, G., Haddad, S.: Stochastic well-formed colored nets and symmetric modeling applications. IEEE Trans. Comput. **42**(11), 1343–1360 (1993)

14. Clark, A., Gilmore, S.: State-aware performance analysis with eXtended stochastic probes. In: Thomas, N., Juiz, C. (eds.) EPEW 2008. LNCS, vol. 5261, pp. 125–140. Springer, Heidelberg (2008). doi:10.1007/978-3-540-87412-6_10

15. Dingle, N.J., Harrison, P.G., Knottenbelt, W.J.: HYDRA: HYpergraph-based Distributed Response-time Analyser. In: International Conference on Parallel and Distributed Processing Techniques and Applications (PDPTA 2003), pp. 215–219, June 2003

16. Donatelli, S., Haddad, S., Sproston, J.: Model checking timed and stochastic properties with CSL^{TA}. IEEE Trans. Softw. Eng. **35**(2), 224–240 (2009)

17. Dugdale, J., Pavard, J., Soubie, B.: A pragmatic development of a computer simulation of an emergency call center. In: Designing Cooperative Systems: The Use of Theories and Models, pp. 241–256 (2000)

18. German, R.: Iterative analysis of Markov regenerative models. Perform. Eval. **44**, 51–72 (2001)

19. Hillston, J.: Compositional Markovian modelling using a process algebra. In: Stewart, W.J. (ed.) Computations with Markov Chains, pp. 177–196. Springer, Heidelberg (1995)

20. Ii, W.D.O., Sanders, W.H.: Measure-adaptive state-space construction. Perform. Eval. **44**(1–4), 237–258 (2001). http://dx.doi.org/10.1016/S0166-5316(00)00052-3

21. Jain, S., McLean, C.: Simulation for emergency response: a framework for modeling and simulation for emergency response. In: Proceedings of the 35th Conference on Winter Simulation: Driving Innovation, Winter Simulation Conference, pp. 1068–1076 (2003)

22. Kulkarni, V.G.: Modeling and Analysis of Stochastic Systems. Chapman & Hall Ltd., London (1995)

23. Marsan, M.A., Balbo, G., Conte, G., Donatelli, S., Franceschinis, G.: Modelling with Generalized Stochastic Petri Nets. Wiley, New York (1994)

24. de QV Lima, M.A., Maciel, P.R., Silva, B., Guimarães, A.P.: Performability evaluation of emergency call center. Perform. Eval. **80**, 27–42 (2014)

Specific Net Classes

On Liveness and Deadlockability in Subclasses of Weighted Petri Nets

Thomas Hujsa[1](✉) and Raymond Devillers[2]

[1] Department of Computing Science,
Carl von Ossietzky Universität Oldenburg, 26111 Oldenburg, Germany
thomas.hujsa@uni-oldenburg.de

[2] Département d'Informatique, Université Libre de Bruxelles, Brussels, Belgium
rdevil@ulb.ac.be

Abstract. Structural approaches have greatly simplified the analysis of intractable properties in Petri nets, notably liveness. In this paper, we further develop these structural methods in particular weighted subclasses of Petri nets to analyze liveness and deadlockability, the latter property being a strong form of non-liveness.

For homogeneous join-free nets, from the analysis of specific substructures, we provide the first polynomial-time characterizations of structural liveness and structural deadlockability, expressing respectively the existence of a live marking and the deadlockability of every marking.

For the join-free class, assuming structural boundedness and leaving out the homogeneity constraint, we show that liveness is not monotonic, meaning not always preserved upon any increase of a live marking.

Finally, we use this new material to correct a flaw in the proof of a previous characterization of monotonic liveness and boundedness for homogeneous asymmetric-choice nets, published in 2004 and left unnoticed.

Keywords: Structural analysis · Weighted Petri net · Deadlockability · Liveness · Boundedness · Monotonicity · Fork-attribution · Join-free · Communication-free · Synchronization-free · Asymmetric-choice

1 Introduction

Liveness is a behavioral property of Petri nets that is fundamental for many real world applications, notably embedded and flexible manufacturing systems. Such applications have to keep all their functions (transitions) active over time, a condition modeled by the liveness property. Deadlockability states the existence of a reachable deadlock (*i.e.* a dead marking, from which no transition is fireable) and is a particular case of non-liveness; its negation, deadlock-freeness, is often studied together with liveness.

Importance of weights. In this paper, we investigate weighted Petri nets, which are well suited to the modeling of real-life systems. In the domain of

© Springer International Publishing AG 2017
W. van der Aalst and E. Best (Eds.): PETRI NETS 2017, LNCS 10258, pp. 267–287, 2017.
DOI: 10.1007/978-3-319-57861-3_16

embedded systems, Synchronous Data Flow graphs [12] have been introduced to model the communications between a finite set of periodic processes. These graphs can be modeled by weighted T-nets, a Petri net subclass in which each place has at most one input and one output. In the domain of flexible manufacturing systems (FMS), the weights make possible the modeling of bulk consumption or production of resources [20]. In these cases, weights allow a compact representation of the volumes of data or resources exchanged.

Relationship with boundedness. Embedded applications have to use a limited amount of memory, a requirement formalized by the notion of boundedness in Petri nets. An objective is to extend the expressiveness of weighted T-nets so as to model more complex embedded applications while ensuring liveness and boundedness efficiently.

Analysis, subclasses and structure. Although decidable [6,7], the problems of checking liveness or boundedness are EXPSPACE-hard [4,7,13]. A common approach to alleviate this difficulty is to consider specific subclasses and to relate the structure of the net to its behavior.

Homogeneity of weights is a restriction that simplifies the study of weighted classes: a net is homogeneous if each place has all its outputs weights equal [11,22]. In this paper, we focus on join-free (JF) Petri nets, which forbid synchronizations, and homogeneous asymmetric-choice (HAC) nets, in which each pair p, p' of input places of any synchronization satisfies the following: all the outputs of p are also outputs of p', or conversely. HAC nets generalize weighted T-nets and homogeneous JF (HJF) nets.

Many efforts have been devoted to the structural analysis of Petri nets, yielding efficient checking methods in particular subclasses. Structural liveness states the existence of a live marking, while structural boundedness ensures boundedness for every initial marking. Polynomial-time characterizations of both properties are known for ordinary (unit-weighted) free-choice (OFC) nets (in which all conflicting transitions have equal enabling conditions), based on *decompositions* into specific subnets (e.g. *siphons* and *traps*) and inequalities on the rank of the incidence matrix of the net (*Rank theorems*) [2,5,18]. From such structural conditions, polynomial-time methods checking the liveness of an initial marking have been deduced for bounded OFC nets [5].

Similar techniques, sometimes in a weaker form, have been developed for other classes with weights, including JF and HAC nets [1,9,11,16,18,20,22].

Monotonic behavior. Another crucial criterion is the *monotonicity* of desired properties, meaning their preservation upon any increase of the initial marking. Embedded and manufacturing systems, among others, need their behavior to be maintained regardless of any addition of initial data items or resources. Liveness and boundedness are not monotonic in general, even when taken together, e.g. in HAC nets [8,18]. However, monotonic liveness (m-liveness) is fulfilled by OFC nets and some larger classes that contain HJF nets [1–3,5,16,22].

Several complex Petri net subclasses are decomposable into specific JF subnets induced by subsets of places. In the HAC class and its subclass of homogeneous (weighted) free-choice (HFC) nets, m-liveness has been expressed in terms of the m-liveness of such JF substructures [11,22]. Exploiting this fact in a bottom-up approach, polynomial-time sufficient conditions of m-liveness for bounded JF nets were shown to propagate to the decomposable, bounded HFC nets [10]. For the larger class of weighted free-choice nets, which contains HFC nets, there exist polynomial-time sufficient conditions of decomposability into structurally live and bounded JF nets [22].

Moreover, in any m-live system, every subsystem induced by any subset of places is necessarily m-live [3,8,11]. Hence, JF subnets form basic modules of major importance for the study of liveness in decomposable classes.

Contributions. For the structural liveness analysis of HJF nets, we highlight the importance of *sub-consistency*, which states the existence of a positive vector whose left-multiplication by the incidence matrix yields a non-null vector with no positive component. We use this algebraic notion to develop the first polynomial time characterizations of structural deadlockability (meaning deadlockability of every marking) and structural liveness for HJF nets, without the classical assumption of structural boundedness (or conservativeness) exploited in previous studies [5,18,22][1].

To achieve it, we first restrict our attention to *siphons, i.e.* subsets S of places satisfying the next property on their surrounding transitions: the input set of S is included in the output set of S. More precisely, in any HJF net whose set of places is its unique siphon, we show the following: sub-consistency is equivalent to structural deadlockability, and non-sub-consistency is equivalent to structural liveness. Since sub-consistency can be checked with a linear program, these conditions can be evaluated in polynomial-time. Also, we extend this result to the rest of the HJF class, using a decomposition into minimal siphons.

Then, leaving out homogeneity, we show that live, structurally bounded JF nets are not always m-live, in contrast with the homogeneous case [22].

Finally, we use this new material to correct an erroneous proof of a previous characterization of m-liveness-boundedness for HAC nets, published in 2004 in [11] and left unnoticed.

Organisation of the paper. We formalize in Sect. 2 the notions used in this paper. In Sect. 3, we present the polynomial-time conditions for the structural deadlockability and liveness of HJF nets. We show in Sect. 4 that m-liveness does not apply to all bounded JF nets. In Sect. 5, we correct the proof of the mentioned previous result on the m-liveness-boundedness of HAC nets. Finally, Sect. 6 presents our conclusion and perspectives.

2 Definitions, Notations and Properties

In this section, we present the main notions used in the paper.

---

[1] Moreover, the well-known necessary conditions of liveness based on siphons containing traps or based on the existence of a repetitive vector [3,5,18] do not help.

2.1   Weighted and Ordinary Nets

A *(weighted) net* is a triple $N = (P, T, W)$ where the sets P and T are finite and disjoint, P is the set of *places*, T is the set of *transitions*, and $W : (P \times T) \cup (T \times P) \to \mathbb{N}$ is a *weight function*. $P \cup T$ is the set of the nodes of the net. An arc leads from a place p to a transition t (respectively from a transition t to a place p) if $W(p, t) > 0$ (respectively $W(t, p) > 0$). An *ordinary* net is a net whose weight function W takes its values in $\{0, 1\}$.

The *incidence matrix* of a net (P, T, W) is a place-transition matrix $\mathcal{I}$ such that $\forall p \in P$, $\forall t \in T$, $\mathcal{I}[p, t] = W(t, p) - W(p, t)$, where the weight of a non-existing arc is 0. The *pre-set* of element x of $P \cup T$, denoted by ${}^{\bullet}x$, is the set $\{w | W(w, x) > 0\}$. By extension, for any subset E of P or T, ${}^{\bullet}E = \bigcup_{x \in E} {}^{\bullet}x$. The *post-set* of element x of $P \cup T$, denoted by $x^{\bullet}$, is the set $\{y | W(x, y) > 0\}$. Similarly, $E^{\bullet} = \bigcup_{x \in E} x^{\bullet}$.

A *join-transition* is a transition having at least two input places. Such a transition represents a *synchronization* on its input places. A *choice-place* is a place having at least two output transitions.

2.2   Markings, Systems, Firing Sequences and Reachability

A *marking* M of a net $N = (P, T, W)$ is a mapping $M : P \to \mathbb{N}$. The pair (N, M) defines a *system* whose initial marking is M. The system (N, M) *enables* a transition $t \in T$ if $\forall p \in {}^{\bullet}t, M(p) \geq W(p, t)$. The marking M' obtained from M by firing the enabled transition t, denoted by $M \xrightarrow{t} M'$, is defined as follows: $\forall p \in P$, $M'(p) = M(p) - W(p, t) + W(t, p)$.

A *firing sequence* σ of length $n \geq 1$ on the set of transitions T, denoted by $\sigma = t_{i_1} t_{i_2} \ldots t_{i_n}$ with $t_{i_1}, t_{i_2}, \ldots, t_{i_n} \in T$, is a mapping $\{1, \ldots, n\} \to T$. The firing sequence σ is *feasible* in (N, M_0) if the successive markings obtained, $M_0 \xrightarrow{t_{i_1}} M_1 \xrightarrow{t_{i_2}} M_2 \ldots \xrightarrow{t_{i_n}} M_n$, are such that M_{k-1} enables the transition t_{i_k} for each $k \in \{1, \ldots, n\}$. We denote $M_0 \xrightarrow{\sigma} M_n$.

The *Parikh vector* $\Psi(\sigma) : T \to \mathbb{N}$ associated with a finite sequence of transitions σ maps every transition t of T to the number of occurrences of t in σ.

A marking M' is said to be *reachable* from the marking M if there exists a firing sequence σ feasible in (N, M) such that $M \xrightarrow{\sigma} M'$. The set of markings reachable from M is denoted by $[M\rangle$.

2.3   Petri Net Properties

Main properties and monotonicity. Let $S = (N, M_0)$ be a system.

- A transition t is *dead* in S if no marking of $[M_0\rangle$ enables t. A *deadlock*, or *dead marking*, is a marking enabling no transition. S is *deadlock-free* if no deadlock belongs to $[M_0\rangle$; otherwise it is *deadlockable*. The net N is *structurally deadlockable* if, for every marking M, (N, M) is deadlockable.
- A transition t is *live* in S if for every marking M in $[M_0\rangle$, there is a marking M' in $[M\rangle$ enabling t. S is *live* if every transition is live in S. N is *structurally live* if a marking M exists such that (N, M) is live.

- S is *bounded* if an integer k exists such that: $\forall M \in [M_0\rangle$, for each place p, $M(p) \le k$. N is *structurally bounded* if (N, M) is bounded for each M.
- A behavioral property $\mathcal{P}$ is *monotonic* for S, or S is *monotonically* $\mathcal{P}$, or S is m-$\mathcal{P}$, if (N, M_0') satisfies $\mathcal{P}$ for every $M_0' \ge M_0$. A marking M is m-$\mathcal{P}$ if (N, M) is m-$\mathcal{P}$, where N is deduced from the context. We shall typically instantiate $\mathcal{P}$ with the liveness property.

Properties defined on nets extend to systems through their underlying net.

Vectors. The *support* of a vector V with index set $I(V)$, noted $\mathcal{S}(V)$, is the set $\{i \in I(V) | V[i] \ne 0\}$ of indices of nonnull components. We denote by $\mathbb{0}^n$ (respectively $\mathbb{1}^n$) the column vector of size n whose components are all equal to 0 (respectively 1). We may use the simpler notation $\mathbb{0}$ and $\mathbb{1}$ when n is deduced from the context.

Conservativeness, consistency and variants. Let $N = (P, T, W)$ be a net with incidence matrix $\mathcal{I}$.

- N is *conservative* if there exists a vector $X \ge \mathbb{1}$ such that $X^T \cdot \mathcal{I} = \mathbb{0}$.
- N is *consistent* (respectively *sur-consistent*, *sub-consistent*) if there exists a vector $Y \ge \mathbb{1}$ such that $\mathcal{I} \cdot Y = \mathbb{0}$ (respectively $\mathcal{I} \cdot Y \gneq \mathbb{0}$, $\mathcal{I} \cdot Y \lneq \mathbb{0}$). N is *weakly sur-consistent* (respectively *weakly sub-consistent*) if there exists a vector $Y \ge \mathbb{1}$ such that $\mathcal{I} \cdot Y \ge \mathbb{0}$ (respectively $\mathcal{I} \cdot Y \le \mathbb{0}$), *i.e.* if it is consistent or sur-consistent (respectively consistent or sub-consistent). Weak sur-consistency is also known as *structural repetitiveness*.
- N is *partially consistent* (respectively *partially sur-consistent*, *partially sub-consistent*) if there exists a vector $Y \gneq \mathbb{0}$ such that $\mathcal{I} \cdot Y = \mathbb{0}$ (respectively $\mathcal{I} \cdot Y \gneq \mathbb{0}$, $\mathcal{I} \cdot Y \lneq \mathbb{0}$).

2.4   Petri Nets Subclasses

A weighted net $N = (P, T, W)$ is:

- a *P-net* (or *S-net*) if $\forall t \in T : |{}^\bullet t| \le 1$ and $|t^\bullet| \le 1$.
- a *T-net* (or *generalized event graph*) if $\forall p \in P : |{}^\bullet p| \le 1$ and $|p^\bullet| \le 1$.
- *join-free* (JF) (or *generalized communication-free*, *synchronization-free*) if $\forall t \in T : |{}^\bullet t| \le 1$.
- *choice-free* (CF) (or *output-nonbranching*) if $\forall p \in P : |p^\bullet| \le 1$.
- *fork-attribution* (FA) if it is both JF and CF.
- *free-choice* (FC) (or *Topologically Extended Free Choice*) if $\forall p_1, p_2 \in P$, $p_1^\bullet \cap p_2^\bullet \ne \varnothing \Rightarrow p_1^\bullet = p_2^\bullet$. This class generalizes, with arbitrary weights, the ordinary *free-choice* nets (OFC) of the literature [5].
- *asymmetric-choice* (AC) if $\forall p_1, p_2 \in P$, $p_1^\bullet \cap p_2^\bullet \ne \emptyset \Rightarrow p_1^\bullet \subseteq p_2^\bullet$ or $p_2^\bullet \subseteq p_1^\bullet$. The class of AC nets contains the FA, CF, JF, and FC nets.
- *homogeneous* if, $\forall p \in P$, $\forall t, t' \in p^\bullet$, $W(p, t) = W(p, t')$. The homogeneous subclass of a class is obtained with an additional prefix letter H, e.g. HFC denoting the homogeneous FC nets.

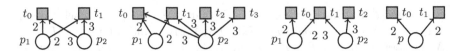

Fig. 1. The net on the left is HFC, the second one is HAC. The third net is homogeneous, non-AC since $^\bullet t_1 = \{p_1, p_2\}$, while $p_1{}^\bullet \not\subseteq p_2{}^\bullet$ and $p_2{}^\bullet \not\subseteq p_1{}^\bullet$. Since they have synchronizations, they are not JF. However, the fourth net is HJF.

Some illustrations for these classes are presented in Fig. 1.

2.5   Graph Structures

Subnets and subsystems. Let $N = (P, T, W)$ and $N' = (P', T', W')$ be two nets. N' is a *subnet* of N if P' is a subset of P, T' is a subset of T, and W' is the restriction of W to $(P' \times T') \cup (T' \times P')$. $S' = (N', M_0')$ is a *subsystem* of $S = (N, M_0)$ if N' is a subnet of N and its initial marking M_0' is the restriction of M_0 to P', i.e. $M_0' = M_0|_{P'}$.

N' is a *P-subnet* of N if N' is a subnet of N and $T' = {}^\bullet P' \cup P'^\bullet$, the pre- and post-sets being taken in N. $S' = (N', M_0')$ is a *P-subsystem* of $S = (N, M_0)$ if N' is a P-subnet of N and S' is a subsystem of S.

Similarly, N' is a *T-subnet* of N if N' is a subnet of N and $P' = {}^\bullet T' \cup T'^\bullet$, the pre- and post-sets being taken in N. $S' = (N', M_0')$ is a *T-subsystem* of $S = (N, M_0)$ if N' is a T-subnet of N and S' is a subsystem of S.

Notice that a T-subnet (respectively P-subnet) is not necessarily a T-net (respectively P-net).

Siphons and traps. Consider a net $N = (P, T, W)$. A non-empty subset $D \subseteq P$ of places is a *siphon* (sometimes also called a *deadlock*) if $^\bullet D \subseteq D^\bullet$. A non-empty subset $Q \subseteq P$ of places is a *trap* if $Q^\bullet \subseteq {}^\bullet Q$.

Reduced graphs. The *reduced graph* R of a net N is the directed graph $G = (V, A)$ obtained from N by contracting every maximal strongly connected component c of N into one single node $g_c \in V$. The set A of arcs represents the connections that remain after the contraction: for any two distinct nodes $g_u, g_{u'}$ of R that represent respectively the distinct components u, u' of N, we have an arc $(g_u, g_{u'})$ from g_u to $g_{u'}$ if $W(q, q') > 0$ in N for some $q \in u$ and $q' \in u'$. By definition, each reduced graph is acyclic. This is illustrated on Fig. 2.

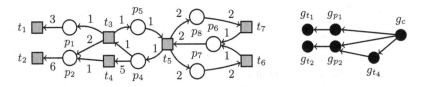

Fig. 2. On the right, the reduced graph represents the net on the left. The node g_c represents the subnet c defined by places p_4, p_5, p_6, p_7, p_8 and transitions t_3, t_5, t_6, t_7.

In what follows, without loss of generality, we consider connected nets that contain at least a place and a transition, unless otherwise specified.

3   Deadlockability and Liveness of Homogeneous JF Nets

Liveness, deadlockability and related properties have been studied previously in the (weighted) join-free class, notably under the conservativeness (*i.e.* structural boundedness) assumption [9,18,20,22] or in more restricted subclasses [14,15].

In this section, we show that the notion of *sub-consistency* is a fundamental algebraic property characterizing structural deadlockability in the HJF nets covered by a (unique) minimal siphon[2]. As a corollary, we obtain for the same nets that structural liveness is equivalent to non-sub-consistency. Since sub-consistency can be checked with linear programming, we deduce a polynomial-time method checking structural deadlockability or structural liveness. We then generalize these conditions to all HJF nets, by means of coverings with minimal siphons. These results are dedicated to the HJF structure and do not apply to inhomogeneous JF nets.

The characterization of structural deadlockability for the HJF nets covered by a unique (minimal) siphon arises from a series of intermediate results.

First, we study a general relationship between deadlockability, non-liveness and sub-consistency in the JF class.

Second, using previous results on the CF class, we show that strongly connected JF systems are covered by strongly connected FA T-subsystems that may either decrease, preserve or generate tokens in the JF system.

Third, we provide a variant of this classification, proving that sub-consistency is equivalent to structural deadlockability in strongly connected FA nets.

Fourth, we show that each strongly connected, sub-consistent JF net contains a strongly connected, sub-consistent (structurally deadlockable) FA T-subnet.

Finally, we prove by induction on the structure of the sub-consistent HJF nets covered by a unique siphon that every marking can reach a deadlock by directing tokens towards a sub-consistent, hence deadlockable, FA T-subsystem.

To simplify the development of these statements, we reveal and exploit the graph structures corresponding to minimal siphons in join-free nets (Lemma 1), namely *quasi strongly connected* nets, defined below.

Quasi-strong connectedness and siphons. A net is called *quasi strongly connected* if it is connected and becomes strongly connected once we omit the transitions with no output. We will use the next correspondence with siphons.

Lemma 1. *Let $N = (P, T, W)$ be a connected JF net. Then, P is the unique siphon of N if and only if N is quasi strongly connected.*

---

[2] In this paper, we study siphons that may contain traps, remarkably in JF nets. Hence, we cannot use the results of [3]. Also, our nets will often be structurally repetitive (weakly sur-consistent), which is another well-known necessary condition of structural liveness (Proposition 10 in [18]) that is not sufficient in the HJF class.

Proof. Assume that P is the unique siphon of N. If N is not quasi strongly connected, consider a maximal quasi strongly connected subnet N' without input node and containing a place (consider a node g without input in the reduced graph of N; since P is a non-empty siphon, g is not a single transition and contains a place, while the subnet induced by the union of g with its output transitions defines N'). Since N is not quasi strongly connected, the places of N' define a smaller siphon of N, a contradiction.

Conversely, if N is quasi strongly connected, then P is a siphon. Suppose that a smaller siphon P' exists. For any place $p \in P \setminus P'$, and any directed path from p to some place of P', every place of this path belongs to P' (by definition of siphons and by join-freeness). Since all places of a quasi strongly connected net belong to the same unique maximal strongly connected component of the net, $P' = P$, a contradiction. Hence, P is the unique siphon of N.   □

3.1 Relating Deadlockability to Non-liveness and Sub-consistency

We provide next a necessary condition for structural deadlockability in JF nets.

Lemma 2. *Let N be a JF net in which every place p has at least one output transition. If N is structurally deadlockable, it is sub-consistent.*

Proof. One can choose a sufficiently large marking M_0, with $M_0(p) \geq W(p,t)$ $\forall p \in P$, $\forall t \in p^\bullet$, that enables a sequence σ containing all transitions, leading to a marking M. A sequence σ' is feasible at M that leads to a deadlock M'. From join-freeness, for each place p and each output transition t of p, we have $M'(p) < W(p,t)$. Let us define $\tau = \sigma\sigma'$. The Parikh vector $\Psi(\tau)$ satisfies $\Psi(\tau) \geq \mathbb{1}$. Moreover, for every place p, $M'(p) < M_0(p)$, from which we deduce $\mathcal{I} \cdot \Psi(\tau) \leq -\mathbb{1}$, where $\mathcal{I}$ is the incidence matrix of N. Thus, N is sub-consistent.   □

The converse does not hold: the ordinary HJF net formed of two transitions t, t', a place p and two unit-weighted arcs such that t is the input of p and t' is its output, is sub-consistent (look at $\Psi(tt't')$) and live for every initial marking.

The next equivalence between liveness and deadlock-freeness is inspired from [21, 22], restricted to HJF nets but extended to possibly unbounded nets.

Lemma 3. *Let $S = (N, M_0)$ be a quasi strongly connected HJF system. S has a non-live transition if and only if it is deadlockable.*

Proof. As usual, we consider nets with $T \neq \emptyset$. It is clear that the reachability of a deadlock implies non-liveness. Now, if a transition t is dead in some reachable marking M, all transitions in $({}^\bullet t)^\bullet$ are also dead in M since the net is HJF, and since $|{}^\bullet t| = 1$ we deduce that each transition in ${}^{\bullet\bullet}t$ can be fired only a finite number of times from M, leading to a marking at which these transitions are dead. One can iterate this process on each directed path that reaches some dead transition, leading to a deadlock by quasi strong connectedness.   □

The next lemma relates structural deadlockability to non-structural liveness in the systems for which liveness is equivalent to deadlock-freeness.

Lemma 4. *Let N be a net such that, for every marking M of N, deadlock-freeness of (N, M) implies liveness of (N, M). Then, N is structurally deadlock-able if and only if it is not structurally live.*

Proof. Structural deadlockability obviously implies non-structural liveness for all Petri nets with $T \neq \emptyset$. For the converse, if N is not structurally live, every marking M is non-live for this net. Then, using the assumption that non-liveness of (N, M) implies deadlockability of (N, M), we deduce that a deadlock is reachable from every marking M, implying structural deadlockability of N. □

This result also applies to quasi strongly connected HJF nets by Lemma 3.

3.2 Previous Results Relating JF and CF Nets to Their FA Subclass

Basing on previous works on the FA and CF classes, we exhibit fundamental structural and behavioral properties of JF nets, expressed in terms of FA nets: strongly connected JF nets are covered by strongly connected FA T-subnets, the latter benefiting from a structural classification for liveness and boundedness. Roughly speaking, actions performed in such FA T-subnets may either decrease, preserve or generate tokens in the associated area of the JF system.

Reverse-duality and covering. Structural results may be obtained directly from known properties of the *reverse-dual* net, which is defined by reversing arcs and swapping places with transitions. This method has been used for CF nets, whose reverse-dual class is the JF class [20]. However, in general, the relationship between the structure of a net and its behavioral properties cannot be deduced from known properties of the reverse-dual net. Using reverse-duality, we obtain the next variation of Lemma 10 in [20], getting a first glimpse of the important role played by particular FA T-subnets in the behavior of JF nets since any sequence feasible in a T-subsystem is feasible in the system.

Lemma 5 (Reverse-dual of Lemma 10 in [20]). *Let N be a strongly connected JF net. For each transition t of N, there is a strongly connected FA T-subnet of N containing t.*

In the following, we link the structure of FA nets to their behavior.

Structural liveness of CF nets. We deduce from Corollary 4 in [20] the next characterization of structural liveness for CF nets, which generalize FA nets.

Lemma 6. *A CF net is structurally live if and only if it is weakly sur-consistent.*

A previous classification of strongly connected FA nets. Strongly connected FA nets have been previously studied, notably in [19,20] where they are presented as a natural generalization of weighted circuits. In the same studies (page 6 in [20] and Sect. 4.1 in [19]), it is explained that the class of strongly connected FA nets can be partitioned into three subclasses: "neutral", when the FA

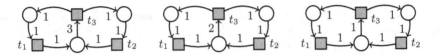

Fig. 3. From left to right: an absorbing, a neutral and a generating FA net.

$$t_1 \ 1 \ p \ 3 \ t_2 \qquad p \ [\text{-}1\,1]\begin{bmatrix} 2 \\ 1 \end{bmatrix} \lneqq [0] \qquad p \ [\text{-}1\,1]\begin{bmatrix} 1 \\ 1 \end{bmatrix} = [0] \qquad p \ [\text{-}1\,1]\begin{bmatrix} 1 \\ 2 \end{bmatrix} \gneqq [0]$$

Fig. 4. The inequalities on the right show the homogeneous P-net on the left to be jointly sub-consistent, consistent and sur-consistent. Hence, these three properties cannot be used alone to tri-partition the class of strongly connected homogeneous P-nets.

net is consistent and conservative; "absorbing", when the FA net is not weakly sur-consistent; or "generating", when the FA net is not structurally bounded. Figure 3 depicts an element of each class.

This partition does not apply to strongly connected JF nets, even if one tries to replace non-weak sur-consistency by sub-consistency and even for their subclass of homogeneous P-nets, as shown in Fig. 4.

Hence, this classification is tightly related to the FA structure. We will show in Lemma 12 that non-weak sur-consistency is equivalent to sub-consistency in strongly connected FA nets.

3.3   Small Nets in Petri Nets and Sub-consistency in JF Nets

We present below the notion of *small nets* and introduce associated results about decompositions into T-subnets. From this development, we express a variant of the previous classification of FA nets in terms of sub-consistency, and deduce the existence of a strongly connected sub-consistent FA T-subnet in every strongly connected sub-consistent JF net.

In the sequel, the general type $\mathcal{P}$ used in the next definition shall be specialized to consistency, sur-consistency or sub-consistency.

Definition 1 ([17]). *A net of type $\mathcal{P}$ is said to be small $\mathcal{P}$ if it does not contain any non-empty proper T-subnet of the same type $\mathcal{P}$.*

In strongly connected, partially sub-consistent JF nets, the strong connectedness of small sub-consistent T-subnets is revealed next.

Lemma 7. *Let N be a strongly connected, partially sub-consistent JF net. Then, every small sub-consistent T-subnet of N is strongly connected. Moreover, there exists such a (non-empty) strongly connected T-subnet in N.*

Proof. Denote by $\mathcal{I}$ the incidence matrix of N. By partial sub-consistency, there exists a vector $\pi \gneqq 0$ such that $\mathcal{I} \cdot \pi \leq 0$. Let us denote by J any small sub-consistent T-subnet of N. Such a subnet exists, since the T-subnet N_π of N

induced by the support of π is sub-consistent. We show that J is necessarily strongly connected. Suppose that J is not strongly connected. If J is not connected, it contains a proper sub-consistent T-subnet, contradicting the fact that J is small sub-consistent. Hence, J is connected.

Consider the *reduced graph* R of J. It is acyclic (so that it defines a partial order), connected (since so is J) and finite (so that there are maximal nodes). Let us consider any such maximal node g, meaning that g has some input in R (otherwise g would be R and J would be strongly connected) but no output in R. We show that the subgraph corresponding to g is a strongly connected T-subnet of N that contains at least a place and a transition. By definition, g contains a node and is strongly connected.

If g is a single place, then it has an input transition in J and no output in J, so that a sub-consistency vector μ_J for J cannot yield a null or negative value (when left-multiplied by the incidence matrix $\mathcal{I}_J$ of J) for this place, a contradiction. If g is a single transition, it has no output in J, hence no output in N since J is a T-subnet of N, contradicting the strong connectedness of N.

Thus, g contains at least a place and a transition. If g is not a T-subnet of J, this means that it contains a transition t lacking an input or an output. The transition t must have its (unique, since N is JF) input place in g, since g is strongly connected. It has all its outputs in g too, since g has no output in R (hence in $J \setminus g$) by the choice of g. We obtain a contradiction, implying that g is a T-subnet of J and N.

Now, we show that g is sub-consistent. Denote by $\mathcal{I}_J$ the sub-matrix of $\mathcal{I}$ restricted to J. Since J is sub-consistent, we have $\mathcal{I}_J \cdot \mu_J \lneq \mathbb{0}$ for some integer vector $\mu_J \geq \mathbb{1}$. Since g has some input node in R, it has some input node n in J, and since g is strongly connected while J is JF, n must be a transition. Because g is a maximal strongly connected component of J, any input transition of (a place of) g cannot have its input place in g. Denote by g' the union of the net represented by g and all its input transitions in J with the arcs going from these inputs to g. (Notice that g' is a P-subnet of J.) Denote by μ_g and μ'_g the restriction of μ_J to (the transitions of) g and g' (so that $\mu_g, \mu'_g \geq \mathbb{1}$) and by $\mathcal{I}_g$, $\mathcal{I}'_g$ the incidence matrices of g, g' respectively. Since g has no output in R (nor in J), hence in particular no output transition in J, we have $\mathcal{I}'_g \cdot \mu'_g \leq \mathbb{0}$ (we may have equality if the negative values correspond to places not in g). Let p be a place of g that is an output of n. Then, $(\mathcal{I}_g \cdot \mu_g)(p) < 0$, and g is sub-consistent.

J thus contains a proper T-subnet of the same type, *i.e.* a sub-consistent one, whereas J is small sub-consistent, a contradiction. We deduce that J is strongly connected, hence the claimed property. □

This result is tightly related to the JF structure and does not apply to Petri nets with synchronizations, as illustrated in Fig. 5.

The next result investigates small sub-consistent FA nets.

Lemma 8. *Let N be a strongly connected FA net. Then, N does not contain any non-empty proper strongly connected T-subnet. Moreover, if N has the property of sub-consistency it is small for this property.*

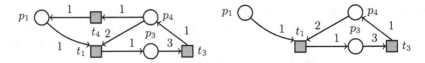

Fig. 5. The net on the left is strongly connected, sub-consistent and is not JF. On the right, its unique non-empty, small, sub-consistent T-subnet, is neither strongly connected nor JF.

Proof. Let us assume that N contains a non-empty proper strongly connected T-subnet F. Hence, there exists a node in $N \setminus F$. Since N is strongly connected, there exists a node n in $N \setminus F$ that is an output of a node n' in F. The node n' cannot be a place (since F is strongly connected and $n'^{\bullet} = \{n\}$, we should have that n' is the only node of F, but then F is not a T-subnet). Thus, n' is a transition and n is an output place of n' that is not in F, contradicting the fact that F is a T-subnet.

If N is sub-consistent, Lemma 7 applies, implying that every small sub-consistent T-subnet of N is strongly connected, and there is a non-empty one in N; from the first part of the claim, we deduce that N is small sub-consistent. □

It can be seen that the second part of the above result becomes false when sur-consistency is considered instead of sub-consistency.

Structural deadlockability and sub-consistency in FA nets. To characterize structural deadlockability in FA nets, we need the next technical result.

Lemma 9 (Propositions 16a, 18a in [17]). *If a net is small sur-consistent, then it does not contain any consistent or sub-consistent T-subnet (either proper or not). If a net is small sub-consistent, then it does not contain any consistent or sur-consistent T-subnet (either proper or not).*

We are now able to deduce the following necessary and sufficient condition.

Lemma 10. *Let N be any strongly connected FA net. N is structurally deadlockable if and only if it is sub-consistent.*

Proof. If N is sub-consistent, it is small sub-consistent (by Lemma 8). By Lemma 9 it is neither consistent nor sur-consistent, hence it is not weakly sur-consistent. By Lemma 6, it is not structurally live. By Lemma 4, it is structurally deadlockable. For the converse, suppose that N is structurally deadlockable. Then, Lemma 2 applies. □

A variant of the classification of strongly connected FA nets. By relating sub-consistency to structural deadlockability and non-weak sur-consistency, we obtain a variant of the classification of [19,20]. To achieve it, we need the next lemma.

Lemma 11. *Consider any net $N = (P, T, W)$ with incidence matrix $\mathcal{I}$ having a consistency vector π_1 and a vector $\pi \geq 0$ such that $\mathcal{I} \cdot \pi \leq 0$ or $\mathcal{I} \cdot \pi \geq 0$. Then, in both cases, N is sub-consistent and sur-consistent.*

Proof. Define $\pi' = \pi_1 + \pi$, so that $\pi' \geq 1$, and $\pi'' = k \cdot \pi_1 - \pi$, where k is any (sufficiently large) positive integer such that $\pi'' \geq 1$. If $\mathcal{I} \cdot \pi \leq 0$, then π' is a sub-consistency vector for N and π'' is a sur-consistency vector. Similarly, if $\mathcal{I} \cdot \pi \geq 0$, π' is a sur-consistency vector and π'' is a sub-consistency vector. $\quad\square$

Lemma 12. *Let N be a strongly connected FA net. N satisfies exactly one of the following properties: consistency, sub-consistency or sur-consistency.*

Proof. For this class, structural liveness is equivalent to weak sur-consistency (consistency or sur-consistency) (Lemma 6), while non-structural liveness is equivalent to structural deadlockability (Lemma 4) and sub-consistency (Lemma 10). We deduce that this class can be partitioned into two subclasses: the sub-consistent ones and the weakly sur-consistent ones. If N is both consistent and sur-consistent, it is also sub-consistent (by Lemma 11), a contradiction with the previous observation. We deduce the claim. $\quad\square$

Existence of strongly connected sub-consistent FA T-subnets. Using the new classification, the next refinement of Lemma 7 reveals the FA structure.

Lemma 13. *Let N be a strongly connected, partially sub-consistent JF net. Then, every small sub-consistent T-subnet of N is a strongly connected FA net. Moreover, N contains such a (non-empty) strongly connected FA T-subnet.*

Proof. Applying Lemma 7, every small sub-consistent T-subnet of N is strongly connected, and N contains such a non-empty T-subnet J. Suppose that J is not FA. By Lemma 5, we know that J is covered by strongly connected FA T-subnets. Since J is small sub-consistent, none of them is sub-consistent. Then, using the new classification (Lemma 12), each of them is either consistent or sur-consistent. By Lemma 9, J does not contain any consistent T-subnet nor any sur-consistent T-subnet. We obtain a contradiction, and J is FA. $\quad\square$

3.4   Polynomial-Time Intermediary Characterizations

In the following, we provide two characterizations of structural deadlockability and liveness for the HJF nets covered by a unique siphon, or equivalently quasi strongly connected HJF nets by Lemma 1.

The next theorem investigates structural deadlockability. The main step of the proof is illustrated in Fig. 6.

Theorem 1 (Structural deadlockability). *Consider any quasi strongly connected HJF net. It is sub-consistent if and only if it is structurally deadlockable.*

Proof. Structural deadlockability and Lemma 2 imply sub-consistency. We prove the other direction by induction on the number n of places with several outputs.

Base case: $n = 0$. If N does not contain any choice, it is either a sub-consistent strongly connected FA net, or a single output-free transition together with its unique input place. In the first case, Lemma 10 applies, from which we deduce structural deadlockability. We see easily that the second case also implies structural deadlockability.

Inductive case: $n > 0$. N contains choices: it is not an FA net. We suppose that the claim is true for every $n' < n$. If N is strongly connected, Lemma 13 applies, and N contains a sub-consistent, strongly connected FA T-subnet F. Otherwise, N contains an output-free transition, and we denote by F the T-subnet formed of this transition with its unique input place.

Let N' be the subnet of N obtained by deleting all the places of F and their outgoing transitions. If N' is empty, then all the places of N belong to F, in which case firing only in F leads to a deadlock (by Lemma 10 if F is strongly connected, trivially in the case of two nodes), since the net is homogeneous. Otherwise, in the rest of the proof, we suppose that N' is not empty.

Let $N_1, \ldots, N_k$ be all the maximal connected (not necessarily strongly connected) components of N'. In the following, we prove these components to be structurally deadlockable. Consider any such net N_i. It cannot contain a transition without input, since such transitions do not occur in N and all outputs of the deleted places were deleted. Thus, since it is not empty, it contains a place.

Since all places of N belong to a same unique maximal strongly connected component of N, there is in N a directed path from a place of F to any place in N_i, and reciprocally. Consequently, there is a deleted node u (not in N_i) input of some node in N_i. Since each transition of N_i has an input place in N_i, and N is JF, u is a transition. By definition of N', the input place of u, and each input place of every other transition of the same kind, are deleted places and cannot belong to N_i. Moreover, all the transitions of N that are outputs of places of N_i have not been deleted and belong to N_i, since otherwise their input would have been deleted. Let $\mathcal{I}$ be the incidence matrix of N and π be a sub-consistency vector for N. In the sequel, each *union* of a transition t with a subnet g of a net h is a net containing g, t and all arcs between t and g in h. We have two cases.

First case. Suppose that N_i is quasi strongly connected. A transition t exists in N that has been deleted and is an input of N_i, the input of t not being in N_i. Also recall that N_i has no output transition in $N \setminus N_i$. Denote by N_i' the union of N_i with its deleted input transitions (and the arcs from these transitions to N_i). If $\mathcal{I}_i'$ (respectively $\mathcal{I}_i$) is the incidence matrix of N_i' (respectively N_i), the projection π_i' of π to N_i' satisfies $\mathcal{I}_i' \cdot \pi_i' \leq 0$. Denoting by π_i the projection of π to N_i, we deduce that $\mathcal{I}_i \cdot \pi_i \lneq 0$: N_i is sub-consistent. Since it is quasi strongly connected and contains strictly fewer choices than N, the induction hypothesis applies, and N_i is structurally deadlockable.

Second case. Otherwise, suppose that N_i has a different structure; it is not strongly connected. Recall that N_i does not contain any transition having no input. Denote by R its reduced graph. Consider any node g of R that contains at least one place and one transition. If no such g exists in R, which is acyclic, it is clear that N_i is structurally deadlockable. We consider the next cases for g.

Case a. If g has no input in R, it has some output in R, because N_i is not strongly connected. g has necessarily a deleted input transition whose input has been deleted. Similarly to the "First case", the union of g with its deleted input transitions and its possible output transitions is a sub-consistent or consistent net. Thus, the union of g with its possible outgoing transitions is a sub-consistent subnet of N_i that is quasi strongly connected.

Case b. If g has some input transition and some output in R, similarly to the previous cases, the union of g with its possible output transitions satisfies sub-consistency and is quasi strongly connected.

Case c. If g has some input transition in R and no output in R, it may have only output places in N. Using similar arguments as before, g satisfies sub-consistency and is quasi strongly connected.

  In all cases, the induction hypothesis can be applied to the union of g with its possible output transitions, which all belong to N_i. We deduce that every such subnet of N_i is structurally deadlockable. By following the partial order defined by R on its directed paths, starting from the smallest nodes of R for this order (*i.e.* with no input in R), selecting arbitrary (homogeneous) choices if needed, every node of R can be successively deadlocked, finally deadlocking N_i.

  Thus, N_i is always structurally deadlockable. Its possible inputs in N are necessarily deleted transitions, while its possible outputs are necessarily deleted places. Since all deleted places belong to a structurally deadlockable T-subnet F of N, all the tokens produced in such places when deadlocking all N_j, $1 \leq j \leq k$, can be decreased by only firing transitions in F (since F is a T-subnet, and it is structurally deadlockable) until F deadlocks. Moreover, no deleted input transition of any N_i is a transition of F; thus, by homogeneity, one can fire in F while never firing such inputs of N_i, and new tokens will not be produced in any N_i in the process. We deduce that a firing sequence always exists that deadlocks all N_i's first, then deadlocks F, reaching a global deadlock.   □

Figure 6 depicts three quasi strongly connected HJF nets[3]. The first one is structurally live and not sub-consistent; the second and the third ones are sub-consistent, thus structurally deadlockable.

  We are now able to deduce the next corollary for structural liveness.

Corollary 1 (Structural liveness). *Consider a quasi strongly connected HJF net. It is structurally live if and only if it is not sub-consistent.*

Proof. If such a net is sub-consistent, then it is structurally deadlockable by Theorem 1, thus not structurally live. For the converse, if it is not structurally live, it is structurally deadlockable (Lemmas 3 and 4) and sub-consistent by Lemma 2.   □

---

[3] Each of them has traps and is weakly sur-consistent (*i.e.* structurally repetitive).

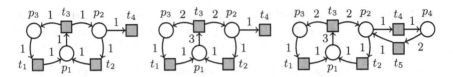

Fig. 6. Three quasi strongly connected HJF nets are pictured. On the left, it is not sub-consistent, hence it is structurally live (a token in p_1 yields liveness). The nets in the middle and on the right are sub-consistent. In both of them, there is a structurally deadlockable FA T subnet: the T-subnet F induced by t_4 in the middle, the T-subnet F' induced by $\{t_4, t_5\}$ on the right. In the proof, after the deletion of F and F' with their outgoing transitions, the cycle $t_1 p_1 t_3 p_3$ remains in both nets. This cycle is strongly connected and sub-consistent, thus it can deadlock; when firings in this cycle occur in the initial nets (before deletion), tokens are produced only in p_2, and t_2 shall never be fired. After the cycle deadlocks, F and F' deadlock, inducing a global deadlock.

Polynomial-time complexity. Checking the existence of a rational solution to $\mathcal{I} \cdot Y \leq 0, Y \geq 1$, and computing one when it exists, can be done in weakly polynomial time with linear programming. Multiplying this solution by an adequate rational number, we get an integer solution. Thus, Theorem 1 and Corollary 1 can be checked in polynomial time.

3.5   Generalization of the Conditions to All HJF Nets

A simple necessary condition for structural deadlockability is stated next.

Lemma 14. *If a net (P, T, W) is structurally deadlockable, then P is a siphon.*

Proof. If P is not a siphon, then $^\bullet P \not\subseteq P^\bullet$, meaning that some input transition of some place in P has no input place: such a transition is always fireable, contradicting deadlockability. Thus, P is a siphon.   □

In Theorem 1 and Corollary 1, the nets considered are quasi strongly connected. Their set of places is their unique siphon by Lemma 1. We generalize Theorem 1 and Corollary 1 through the two following corollaries.

Corollary 2 (Structural deadlockability). *Consider a connected HJF net $N = (P, T, W)$. Denote by C the set of all the maximal quasi strongly connected subnets of N that contain at least one place and one transition. N is structurally deadlockable if and only if P is a siphon and each element of C is sub-consistent.*

Proof. Assume that N is structurally deadlockable. P is a siphon by Lemma 14. Consider a non-sub-consistent element c of C. By Corollary 1, c is structurally live. In N, the outputs of nodes of c that do not belong to c may only be places while the inputs of nodes of c that do not belong to c may only be transitions: in the first case, each output transition belongs to c since c is a maximal quasi strongly connected subnet; in the second case, an input place would be the unique input of a transition t, such that t has no input in c, contradicting the definition of c. Thus, c remains structurally live in N, contradicting deadlockability.

Conversely, each element of c is sub-consistent, hence structurally deadlockable (Theorem 1). For each place p of N, either p has no output, or the maximal quasi strongly connected subnet containing p has a transition, belongs to C and is structurally deadlockable. Since P is a siphon, each transition of N has an input. Hence, for every marking M_0, (N, M_0) can be deadlocked by following the paths of the reduced graph R of N, since each node of R denotes either a place with no output or a subnet of an element of C.   □

Corollary 3 (Structural liveness). *Let $N = (P, T, W)$ be a connected HJF net. Let C be the set of maximal quasi strongly connected subnets of N with no input node in N and containing a place and a transition. Then, N is structurally live if and only if no element of C is sub-consistent.*

Proof. If an element of C is sub-consistent, it is structurally deadlockable (Theorem 1) with no input, hence N cannot be structurally live. Conversely, if no element of C is sub-consistent, each is structurally live (Corollary 1). Thus, there exists a marking for which all elements of C are live. Such live subsystems can generate an arbitrarily large number of tokens in their output places in N. There may also exist nodes without input, which are necessarily single transitions, hence also live subsystems. By join-freeness and homogeneity, an arbitrarily large number of tokens can reach each place of the system by following the directed paths in the reduced graph of N. We deduce liveness.   □

Polynomial-time complexity. The set of the maximal quasi strongly connected subnets of a join-free net forms a partition (or disjoint covering) of its nodes. Thus, the number of these subnets is linear in the size of the system. Determining these subnets and checking their sub-consistency are polynomial-time problems, and the conditions of Theorem 1 and Corollary 1 can be checked in polynomial-time.

4   Non-monotonic Liveness of Inhomogeneous JF Nets

Liveness is not always monotonic, as shown for a bounded HAC system in [8]. In HFC (hence also OFC and HJF) nets and in some other classes, liveness is known to be monotonic [5,16,22]. For the inhomogeneous join-free class, we present on the left of Fig. 7 a simple example of non-monotonic liveness under the strong connectedness assumption. On the right of the same figure, we provide, as far as we know, the first structurally bounded, live, non m-live join-free system.

5   Improvements on a Previous Work on HAC Nets

We focus here on results of [11]. First, we observe that the *pureness* assumption used in [11], which forbids nodes x such that $^\bullet x \cap x^\bullet \neq \emptyset$, is not necessary. Then,

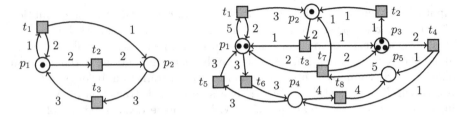

Fig. 7. The live and unbounded JF system on the left is not m-live, since adding a token to p_1 allows to fire t_2, leading to a deadlock. On the right, the JF system is strongly connected and live; however, it is not m-live, since adding a token to p_3 and firing two times t_4 leads to a deadlock.

we exhibit an incorrect argument of a proof in one of the central theorems of the same paper, which is based on quasi strongly connected HJF subnets. Finally, we correct this proof using Theorem 1.

Unnecessary pureness. The assumption of pureness, which forbids self-loops, is only exploited in the proof of the very first lemma of [11] (Lemma 3.1), which is used in various later occasions. By refining a bit the proof, one can get rid of this precondition.

An incorrect argument in a previous proof for HAC nets. Consider the next characterization of [11] for the m-live and bounded markings of HAC nets, where N_D denotes the P-subnet of N induced by the set D of places and M_0^D is the restriction $M_0|_D$.

Theorem 2 (Theorem 5.2 in [11]). *An HAC system (N, M_0) is monotonically live and bounded if and only if every place p is covered by a minimal siphon, and for every minimal siphon D, (N_D, M_0^D) is live and bounded.*

Let us exhibit the problem that appears in the proof of this theorem. The paper correctly shows the "if" part, *i.e.* that the liveness and boundedness of all the P-subsystems induced by all the minimal siphons, which cover all places, implies the monotonic liveness and boundedness of the entire HAC system. It also proves that if (N, M_0) is live and bounded, then every place is covered by a minimal siphon, and that if N is live from each marking $M \geq M_0$ then (N_D, M_0^D) is live for every minimal siphon D. However, to show that the existence of a minimal siphon D such that (N_D, M_0^D) is live and unbounded implies that (N, M_0) is not monotonically bounded, the authors use the next argument:

> If p is unbounded in (N_D, M_0^D), for each integer k there is a firing sequence σ_k such that $M_0^D[\sigma_k\rangle M_k$ in N_D with $M_k(p) > k$. Then there exist $M \geq M_0$ and M' such that, in N, $M[\sigma_k\rangle M'$ and $M'(p) = M_k(p) > k$, contradicting the boundedness of (N, M).

This argument is incorrect, since it considers that $\exists p \in S$, $\forall k \in \mathbb{N}$, $\exists M \geq M_0$, $\exists M' \in [M\rangle$: $M'(p) > k$ instead of the desired goal, which is: $\exists p \in S$, $\exists M \geq M_0$, $\forall k \in \mathbb{N}$, $\exists M' \in [M\rangle$: $M'(p) > k$. Actually, the authors do not use there the fact that D is a minimal siphon. However, we are going to show that the authors had a correct intuition and the property they claim is valid. Other properties of the literature for HAC nets, like [1,3], do not help.

From Theorem 3.2 in the same paper [11], we know that (N_D, M_0^D) is live. Let us now proceed by contradiction and assume that (N_D, M_0^D) is unbounded. Since it is known that live and bounded Petri nets are consistent [18], the net N is consistent. Hence, every P-subnet induced by any subset of places is also consistent. In particular, this is also the case for N_D. If a system is unbounded, the underlying net is not structurally bounded. We recall the next characterization for this property, which can be found in various studies, e.g. in [18].

Lemma 15 (Corollary 16 in [18]). *A net with incidence matrix $\mathcal{I}$ is not structurally bounded if and only if there exists a vector $X \gneq \mathbb{0}$ such that $\mathcal{I} \cdot X \gneq \mathbb{0}$.*

Applying Lemma 11, we get the sub-consistency and sur-consistency of N_D.

Each minimal siphon of an HAC net induces a quasi strongly connected HJF P-subnet (by [11] and Lemma 1). Applying Theorem 1, N_D is structurally deadlockable, contradicting the liveness of (N_D, M_0^D), which must thus be bounded. We deduce the validity of Theorem 5.2 in [11].

6   Conclusion and Perspectives

We examined a crucial substructure of several complex subclasses of Petri nets, the weighted join-free class. In the homogeneous case, we obtained polynomial-time characterizations of structural deadlockability and structural liveness that are not subsumed by previous known methods. They enrich the set of efficient structural analysis techniques for weighted Petri nets. In the inhomogeneous, structurally bounded join-free case, we showed the non-monotonicity of liveness. Finally, we used our new structural conditions on the homogeneous join-free class to correct a previous erroneous proof of a characterization of monotonic liveness and boundedness in the homogeneous asymmetric-choice class.

An important perspective is to find out, for the class of Petri net systems that are decomposable into monotonically live siphon-induced join-free P-subsystems, under which conditions such local behaviors propagate to the entire system. A complementary objective is to broaden the methods that check decomposability in polynomial-time and to deduce efficient sufficient conditions of monotonic liveness and boundedness for larger classes. Future applications of such methods encompass notably the design of embedded systems.

References

1. Barkaoui, K., Couvreur, J.-M., Klai, K.: On the equivalence between liveness and deadlock-freeness in Petri nets. In: Ciardo, G., Darondeau, P. (eds.) ICATPN 2005. LNCS, vol. 3536, pp. 90–107. Springer, Heidelberg (2005). doi:10.1007/11494744_7
2. Barkaoui, K., Minoux, M.: A polynomial-time graph algorithm to decide liveness of some basic classes of bounded Petri nets. In: Jensen, K. (ed.) ICATPN 1992. LNCS, vol. 616, pp. 62–75. Springer, Heidelberg (1992). doi:10.1007/3-540-55676-1_4
3. Barkaoui, K., Pradat-Peyre, J.-F.: On liveness and controlled siphons in Petri nets. In: Billington, J., Reisig, W. (eds.) ICATPN 1996. LNCS, vol. 1091, pp. 57–72. Springer, Heidelberg (1996). doi:10.1007/3-540-61363-3_4
4. Cheng, A., Esparza, J., Palsberg, J.: Complexity results for 1-safe nets. In: Shyamasundar, R.K. (ed.) FSTTCS 1993. LNCS, vol. 761, pp. 326–337. Springer, Heidelberg (1993). doi:10.1007/3-540-57529-4_66
5. Desel, J., Esparza, J.: Free Choice Petri Nets. Cambridge Tracts in Theoretical Computer Science, vol. 40. Cambridge University Press, New York (1995)
6. Esparza, J.: Decidability and complexity of Petri net problems – an introduction. In: Reisig, W., Rozenberg, G. (eds.) ACPN 1996. LNCS, vol. 1491, pp. 374–428. Springer, Heidelberg (1998). doi:10.1007/3-540-65306-6_20
7. Esparza, J., Nielsen, M.: Decidability issues for Petri nets–a survey. BRICS Rep. Ser. (8) (1994)
8. Heiner, M., Mahulea, C., Silva, M.: On the importance of the deadlock trap property for monotonic liveness. In: International Workshop on Biological Processes and Petri nets (BioPPN), A satellite event of Petri Nets 2010 (2010)
9. Hujsa, T., Delosme, J.M., Munier-Kordon, A.: Polynomial sufficient conditions of well-behavedness and home markings in subclasses of weighted Petri nets. Trans. Embed. Comput. Syst. **13**, 1–25 (2014)
10. Hujsa, T., Delosme, J.M., Munier-Kordon, A.: On liveness and reversibility of equal-conflict Petri nets. Fundam. Inf. **146**(1), 83–119 (2016)
11. Jiao, L., Cheung, T.Y., Lu, W.: On liveness and boundedness of asymmetric choice nets. Theor. Comput. Sci. **311**(1–3), 165–197 (2004)
12. Lee, E.A., Messerschmitt, D.G.: Synchronous data flow. Proc. IEEE **75**(9), 1235–1245 (1987)
13. Lipton, R.: The reachability problem requires exponential space. Technical report 62, Department of Computer Science, Yale University (1976)
14. Mayr, E.W., Weihmann, J.: Results on equivalence, boundedness, liveness, and covering problems of BPP-Petri nets. In: Colom, J.-M., Desel, J. (eds.) PETRI NETS 2013. LNCS, vol. 7927, pp. 70–89. Springer, Heidelberg (2013). doi:10.1007/978-3-642-38697-8_5
15. Mayr, E.W., Weihmann, J.: Complexity results for problems of communication-free Petri nets and related formalisms. Fundam. Inf. **137**(1), 61–86 (2015)
16. Recalde, L., Teruel, E., Silva, M.: Modeling and analysis of sequential processes that cooperate through buffers. IEEE Trans. Robot. Autom. **14**(2), 267–277 (1998)
17. Sifakis, J.: Structural properties of Petri nets. In: Winkowski, J. (ed.) MFCS 1978. LNCS, vol. 64, pp. 474–483. Springer, Heidelberg (1978). doi:10.1007/3-540-08921-7_95
18. Silva, M., Teruel, E., Colom, J.M.: Linear algebraic and linear programming techniques for the analysis of place/transition net systems. In: Reisig, W., Rozenberg, G. (eds.) ACPN 1996. LNCS, vol. 1491, pp. 309–373. Springer, Heidelberg (1998). doi:10.1007/3-540-65306-6_19

19. Teruel, E.: Structure Theory of Weighted Place/Transition Net Systems: The Equal Conflict Hiatus. Ph.D. thesis, DIEI. University of Zaragoza, Spain (1994)
20. Teruel, E., Colom, J.M., Silva, M.: Choice-free Petri nets: a model for deterministic concurrent systems with bulk services and arrivals. IEEE Trans. Syst. Man Cybern. Part A **27**(1), 73–83 (1997)
21. Teruel, E., Silva, M.: Liveness and home states in equal conflict systems. In: Ajmone Marsan, M. (ed.) ICATPN 1993. LNCS, vol. 691, pp. 415–432. Springer, Heidelberg (1993). doi:10.1007/3-540-56863-8_59
22. Teruel, E., Silva, M.: Structure theory of equal conflict systems. Theor. Comput. Sci. **153**(1&2), 271–300 (1996)

Restricting HORNETS
to Support Self-adaptive Systems

Michael Köhler-Bußmeier[(⊠)]

University of Applied Science Hamburg, Berliner Tor 7, 20099 Hamburg, Germany
michael.koehler-bussmeier@haw-hamburg.de

Abstract. Adaptivity plays a major role in the context of cyber physical systems (among them sensor networks, mobile adhoc networks, etc.), also known as the internet of things. Since the interaction of sensors and actors as well as their evolution plays a major role in this context, we concentrate on protocols and their adaption in this paper. Whenever we adapt protocols we typically have to modify more than one part of the interaction, i.e. adaptation becomes a *distributed* activity. As Petri nets are an established means to formalise distributed activities, we have chosen them for adaption-protocols as well.

Since our adaption-protocol nets operate on protocol nets, we obtain a recursive structure as manifested in the *nets-within-nets* paradigm proposed by Rüdiger Valk. In this paper we study self-adaptive systems in the formalism of HORNETS. HORNETS are algebraic Petri nets that have nets as tokens.

In previous work we have shown that the reachability problem for safe elementary HORNETS requires at least exponential space. To obtain a complexity that is feasible for run-time verification we study structural restrictions of elementary HORNETS. It turns out that reachability is in PSPACE again for the class of so called fan-bounded HORNETS, where the number of places in the pre- and postset is used as a parameter. This class includes – among others – the well known class of State Machines.

Keywords: Adaption · Hornets · Nets-within-nets · Reachability

1 Self-adaption: Petri Nets that Modify Petri Nets

Adaptivity plays a major role in the context of cyber physical systems, among them sensor networks, mobile adhoc networks, and other aspect – nowadays subsumed in the so-called internet of things (IoT) [1]. One way to capture adaptivity is to introduce additional model parameters that are varied via a feedback procedure, i.e. a learning process. But this approach has conceptual limitations: Sometimes these configuration parameters are visible at the same level where applicational parameters are used, which sometimes blurs the modeller's intention and – even worse – whenever interesting parameter clusters are learned at run-time then the adequate reaction is unknown at design time. Therefore, we advocate a model that allows *self-modification* of protocols at run-time, i.e. the modification of the system's structure itself.

© Springer International Publishing AG 2017
W. van der Aalst and E. Best (Eds.): PETRI NETS 2017, LNCS 10258, pp. 288–306, 2017.
DOI: 10.1007/978-3-319-57861-3_17

In this paper, we concentrate on (i) interaction between sensors, actors, and such alike within IoT scenarios and on (ii) the run-time adaption of these interactions. These kind of processes are typically structured by protocols and Petri nets are an established means to formalise those. This has the interesting consequence that whenever we have to adapt some protocol we have to adapt different sides of the interaction, i.e. adaptation becomes a *distributed* activity.

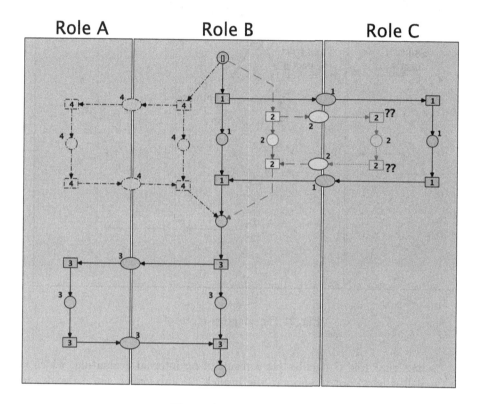

Fig. 1. A 3-party-protocol

Example 1. Figures 1 and 2 illustrate the relationship between normal and adaption protocols. In Fig. 1 the normal protocol is shown, which models the interaction between three parties, called *role A*, *role B*, and *role C*. The interaction is started by role *B*, which first calls *C*. There are two alternative branches, labelled with "1" and "2", respectively. Afterwards *B* calls *A* on the branch labelled with "3". (Ignore the branch labelled with "4" for the moment. It will be introduced as the result of an adaption process later on).

Each role "owns" the places and transitions within it boxed areas. Each role may modify its own nodes, as each role has access to the underlying code structures and associated resources, but it cannot access nodes belonging to other roles.

Role A   Role B   Role C

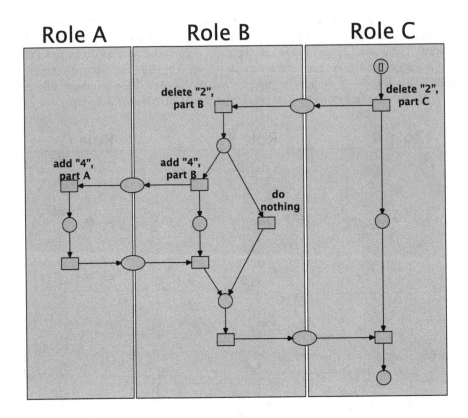

Fig. 2. The adaption-protocol

Assume that role C decides (as a result of an internal evaluation, which is not modelled here) not to support the branch "2" any longer, i.e. it decides to delete the nodes marked with "??" in Fig. 1. Of course, when this service is not provided any longer by C, role B, which owns the requesting side, has to delete its nodes marked with "2" also.

After all we have to check whether the modified protocol is still functional, i.e. whether it still has proper termination possibilities, which essentially is expressed by well-formedness for workflow nets. (Usually, one has to consider other non-functional properties, like performance, too). In our case it is, since B can still use "service 1" instead of the deleted "service 2". But assume furthermore that B knows that role A is capable of providing a substitute for "service 2" as indicated by the nodes labelled with "4". The choice, whether to rely on "service 1" only or to retain two options via shifting from "service 2" to the freshly instantiated "service 4" is up to the decision of role B.

This simple scenario can be easily captured as an self-adaptive workflow system. The adaption process therefore has the structure given in Fig. 2, where we use pseudo inscriptions for the modifying operations: First role C deletes its part of "service 2" by the transition named *delete "2", part C*. Then role B deletes its calling part by *delete "2", part B*. After this distributed deletion of "service 2" role B has two options: It can *do nothing*; or it can add a call to the new "service 4" by the transition *add "4", part B* and hands over to role A, which calls *add "4", part A* to finish the distributed creation of "service 4".

This example shows an essential aspect: These adaption-protocols reside on the meta-level, since they operate on "normal" protocols. It seems natural to formalise this kind of adaption-protocols again as Petri nets, which operate on normal protocol Petri nets. Therefore it seems natural to study protocol adaptivity in the context of *nets-within-nets* paradigm as proposed by Rüdiger Valk [2,3].

For most IoT contexts it is highly desirable that adaptivity takes place in an automated manner. Therefore, we demand for transformation processes where one can verify that the adaption (i) does not violate essential properties, i.e. invariants etc., and (ii) leads to improvement w.r.t. performance indicators etc. Therefore, we are interested in verification procedures that are possible at runtime. Hence, we are interested in feasible complexity.

In this paper we study adaption and self-modifying systems in the nets-within-nets formalisms of HORNETS [4]. We like to study the *complexity* that arises due the algebraic structure, since this feature expresses the modification of the net structure. Therefore, we restrict HORNETS in an appropriate way to guarantee that the system has a finite state space: First, we allow at most one token on each place, which results in the class of *safe* HORNETS. However, this restriction does not guarantee finite state spaces, since we have the nesting depth as a second source of unboundedness, leading to undecidability [5]. Second, we restrict the nesting depth and introduce the class of *elementary* HORNETS (EHORNETS), which have a two-levelled nesting structure. This is done in analogy to the class of *elementary object net systems* (EOS) [6], which are the two-level specialisation of general object nets [5,6]. Finally, we restrict the universe of object nets to finite sets to rule out another source of undecidability.

If we rule out these sources of complexity the remaining origin of complexity is the use of algebraic transformations, which are still allowed for safe, elementary HORNETS. As a result we obtain the class of safe, elementary HORNETS – in analogy to the class of *safe* EOS [7]. We have shown in [7–9] that most problems for *safe* EOS are PSPACE-complete. More precisely: All problems that are expressible in LTL or CTL, which include reachability and liveness, are PSPACE-complete. This means that with respect to these problems *safe* EOS are no more complex than p/t nets. In a previous publication [10] we have shown that *safe, elementary* HORNETS are beyond PSPACE. We have shown a lower bound, i.e. that "the reachability problem requires exponential space" for safe, elementary HORNETS – similarly to well known result for *bounded* p/t nets by Lipton [11]. In [12] we give an algorithm thats needs at most exponential space, which shows that lower and upper bound coincide.

In this paper we would like to study restrictions of Elementary HORNETS to obtain net classes where the reachability requires less than exponential space.

From [10] we know that the main source of complexity for EHORNETS is mainly due to the huge number of different net-tokens, which is double-exponential for safe EHORNETS. A closer look reveals that the number of net-token's marking is rather small – "only" single-exponential, while the number of different object nets is double-exponential. We conclude that restricting the net-tokens' marking beyond safeness would not improve complexity. Instead, we have to impose *structural* restrictions on the object-nets. Petri net theory offers several well known candidates for structural restrictions, like state machines, free-choice nets etc. Here, we restrict object-nets to a generalisation of state-machines, called fan-bounded nets, which is obtained by imposing a bound β to the number of places in the pre- and postset. This restriction is motivated from the observation that many net models use standard Petri net patters, i.e. operators like SEQ, AND, or OR, which have a fan-bound $\beta = 2$.

The paper has the following structure: Sect. 2 defines Elementary HORNETS. Since the reachability problem is known to be undecidable even for EOS, we restrict elementary HORNETS to safe ones, which have finite state spaces. In Sect. 3 we generalise the notion of State Machines, which have at most one place in the pre- and in the postset, in the way that the number of all places in pre- and postset of an object-net is below a given bound, called the fan-bound. So, we obtain the maximal synchronisation degree of the objects nets (i.e. the maximal pre- and postset size) as a fresh complexity parameter. Section 4 shows that the reachability problem is PSPACE-complete for this class. The work ends with a conclusion and outlook to further work.

2   Elementary Hornets (EHORNETS)

HORNETS are a generalisation of object nets [5,6], which follow the *nets-within-nets* paradigm as proposed by R. Valk [3].

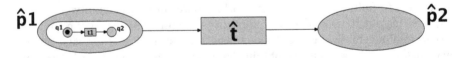

Fig. 3. An Elementary Object Net System (EOS)

With object nets we study Petri nets where the tokens are nets again, i.e. we have a nested marking. Events are also nested. We have three different kinds of events – as illustrated by the example given in Fig. 3:

1. System-autonomous: The system net transition $\hat{t}$ fires autonomously, which moves the net-token from $\hat{p}_1$ to $\hat{p}_2$ without changing its marking.
2. Object-autonomous: The object net fires transition t_1 "moving" the black token from q_1 to q_2. The object net remains at its location $\hat{p}_1$.

3. Synchronisation: Whenever we add matching synchronisation inscriptions at the system net transition $\hat{t}$ and the object net transition t_1, then both must fire synchronously: The object net is moved to $\hat{p}_2$ and the black token moves from q_1 to q_2 inside. Whenever synchronisation is specified, autonomous actions are forbidden.

Approaches adapting the nets-within-nets approach are nested nets [13], mobile predicate/transition nets [14], Reference nets [15], PN^2 [16], hypernets [17], Mobile Systems [18], and adaptive workflow nets [19]. Object Nets can be seen as the Petri net perspective on mobility, in contrast to the Ambient Calculus [20] or the π-calculus [21], which form the process algebra perspective.

For HORNETS we extend object-nets with algebraic concepts that allow to modify the structure of the net-tokens as a result of a transition firing. This is a generalisation of the approach of algebraic nets [22], where algebraic data types replace the anonymous black tokens.

Example 2. We consider a HORNET with two workflow nets N_1 and N_2 as tokens – cf. Fig. 4. To model a run-time adaption, we combine N_1 and N_2 resulting in the net $N_3 = (N_1 \| N_2)$. This modification is modelled by transition t of the HORNETS in Fig. 4. In a binding α with $x \mapsto N_1$ and $y \mapsto N_2$ the transition t is enabled. Assume that $(x\|y)$ evaluates to N_3 for α. If t fires it removes the two net-tokens from p and q and generates one new net-token on place r. The net-token on r has the structure of N_3 and its marking is obtained as a transfer from the token on v in N_1 and the token on s in N_2 into N_3. This transfer is possible since all the places of N_1 and N_2 are also places in N_3 and tokens can be transferred in the obvious way.

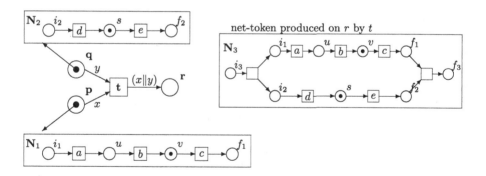

Fig. 4. Modification of the net-token's structure

It is not hard to prove that the general HORNET formalism is Turing-complete. In [4] we have proven that there are several possibilities to simulate counter programs: One could use the nesting to encode counters. Another possibility is to encode counters in the algebraic structure of the net operators.

The use of algebraic operations in HORNETS relates them to *algebraic higher-order (AHO) systems* [23], which are restricted to two-levelled systems but have a greater flexibility for the operations on net-tokens, since each net transformation is allowed. There is also a relationship to Nested Nets [24], which are used for adaptive systems, and to distributed graph transformations [25].

2.1   Formal Definition of Elementary Hornets (EHORNETS)

In the following we recall the definition of EHORNETS from [4,10]. A multiset $\mathbf{m}$ on the set D is a mapping $\mathbf{m} : D \to \mathbb{N}$. Multisets can also be represented as a formal sum in the form $\mathbf{m} = \sum_{i=1}^{n} x_i$, where $x_i \in D$.

Multiset addition is defined component-wise: $(\mathbf{m}_1 + \mathbf{m}_2)(d) := \mathbf{m}_1(d) + \mathbf{m}_2(d)$. The empty multiset $\mathbf{0}$ is defined as $\mathbf{0}(d) = 0$ for all $d \in D$. Multiset-difference $\mathbf{m}_1 - \mathbf{m}_2$ is defined by $(\mathbf{m}_1 - \mathbf{m}_2)(d) := \max(\mathbf{m}_1(d) - \mathbf{m}_2(d), 0)$.

The cardinality of a multiset is $|\mathbf{m}| := \sum_{d \in D} \mathbf{m}(d)$. A multiset $\mathbf{m}$ is finite if $|\mathbf{m}| < \infty$. The set of all finite multisets over the set D is denoted $MS(D)$.

Multiset notations are used for sets as well. The meaning will be apparent from its use.

Any mapping $f : D \to D'$ extends to a multiset-homomorphism $f^{\sharp} : MS(D) \to MS(D')$ by $f^{\sharp}(\sum_{i=1}^{n} x_i) = \sum_{i=1}^{n} f(x_i)$.

A *p/t net* N is a tuple $N = (P, T, \mathbf{pre}, \mathbf{post})$, such that P is a set of places, T is a set of transitions, with $P \cap T = \emptyset$, and $\mathbf{pre}, \mathbf{post} : T \to MS(P)$ are the pre- and post-condition functions. A marking of N is a multiset of places: $\mathbf{m} \in MS(P)$. We denote the enabling of t in marking $\mathbf{m}$ by $\mathbf{m} \xrightarrow{t}$. Firing of t is denoted by $\mathbf{m} \xrightarrow{t} \mathbf{m}'$.

Net-Algebras. We define the algebraic structure of object nets. For a general introduction of algebraic specifications cf. [26].

Let K be a set of net-types (kinds). A (many-sorted) *specification* (Σ, X, E) consists of a signature Σ, a family of variables $X = (X_k)_{k \in K}$, and a family of axioms $E = (E_k)_{k \in K}$.

A signature is a disjoint family $\Sigma = (\Sigma_{k_1 \cdots k_n, k})_{k_1, \cdots, k_n, k \in K}$ of operators. The set of terms of type k over a signature Σ and variables X is denoted $\mathbb{T}_{\Sigma}^{k}(X)$.

We use (many-sorted) predicate logic, where the terms are generated by a signature Σ and formulae are defined by a family of predicates $\Psi = (\Psi_n)_{n \in \mathbb{N}}$. The set of formulae is denoted PL_{Γ}, where $\Gamma = (\Sigma, X, E, \Psi)$ is the *logic structure*.

Let Σ be a signature over K. A *net-algebra* assigns to each type $k \in K$ a set $\mathcal{U}_k$ of object nets – the net universe. Each object $N \in \mathcal{U}_k, k \in K$ net is a p/t net $N = (P_N, T_N, \mathbf{pre}_N, \mathbf{post}_N)$. We identify $\mathcal{U}$ with $\bigcup_{k \in K} \mathcal{U}_k$ in the following. We assume the family $\mathcal{U} = (\mathcal{U}_k)_{k \in K}$ to be disjoint.

The nodes of the object nets in $\mathcal{U}_k$ are not disjoint, since the firing rule allows to transfer tokens between net tokens within the same set $\mathcal{U}_k$. Such a transfer is possible, if we assume that all nets $N \in \mathcal{U}_k$ have the same set of places P_k. P_k is the place universe for all object nets of kind k. In the example of Fig. 4 the object nets N_1, N_2, and N_3 must belong to the same type since otherwise it would be impossible to transfer the markings in N_1 and N_2 to the generated N_3.

In general, P_k is not finite. Since we like each object net to be finite in some sense, we require that the transitions T_N of each $N \in \mathcal{U}_k$ use only a finite subset of P_k, i.e. $\forall N \in \mathcal{U} : |{}^\bullet T_N \cup T_N{}^\bullet| < \infty$.

The family of object nets $\mathcal{U}$ is the universe of the algebra. A net-algebra $(\mathcal{U}, \mathcal{I})$ assigns to each constant $\sigma \in \Sigma_{\lambda,k}$ an object net $\sigma^{\mathcal{I}} \in \mathcal{U}_k$ and to each operator $\sigma \in \Sigma_{k_1 \cdots k_n, k}$ with $n > 0$ a mapping $\sigma^{\mathcal{I}} : (\mathcal{U}_{k_1} \times \cdots \times \mathcal{U}_{k_n}) \to \mathcal{U}_k$.

A net-algebra is called *finite* if P_k is a finite set for each $k \in K$.[1]

Since all nets $N \in \mathcal{U}_k$ have the same set of places P_k, which is finite for EHORNETS, there is an upper bound for the cardinality of $\mathcal{U}_k$.

Proposition 1 (Lemma 2.1 in [10]). *For each $k \in K$ the cardinality of each net universe $\mathcal{U}_k$ is bound as follows: $|\mathcal{U}_k| \leq 2^{\left(2^{4|P_k|}\right)}$.*

The main idea behind this bound is that the place set P_k allows $2^{2|P_k|}$ different transitions. Each transition carries its own synchronisation label. Since there are no more labels than transitions, this leads $\left(2^{2|P_k|}\right)^2 = 2^{4|P_k|}$ different synchronised transitions and this generates $2^{\left(2^{4|P_k|}\right)}$ different object nets (cf. also the discussion in Sect. 3).

A variable assignment $\alpha = (\alpha_k : X_k \to \mathcal{U}_k)_{k \in K}$ maps each variable onto an element of the algebra. For a variable assignment α the evaluation of a term $t \in \mathbb{T}_\Sigma^k(X)$ is uniquely defined and will be denoted as $\alpha(t)$.

A net-algebra, such that all axioms of (Σ, X, E) are valid, is called *net-theory*.

Nested Markings. A marking of an EHORNET assigns to each system net place one or many net-tokens. The places of the system net are typed by the function $k : \widehat{P} \to K$, meaning that a place $\widehat{p}$ contains net-tokens of kind $k(\widehat{p})$. Since the net-tokens are instances of object nets, a *marking* is a *nested* multiset of the form:

$$\mu = \sum_{i=1}^{n} \widehat{p}_i[N_i, M_i] \quad \text{where} \quad \widehat{p}_i \in \widehat{P}, N_i \in \mathcal{U}_{k(\widehat{p}_i)}, M_i \in MS(P_{N_i}), n \in \mathbb{N}$$

Each addend $\widehat{p}_i[N_i, M_i]$ denotes a net-token on the place $\widehat{p}_i$ that has the structure of the object net N_i and the marking $M_i \in MS(P_{N_i})$. The set of all nested multisets is denoted as $\mathcal{M}_H$. We define the partial order $\sqsubseteq$ on nested multisets by setting $\mu_1 \sqsubseteq \mu_2$ iff $\exists \mu : \mu_2 = \mu_1 + \mu$.

The projection $\Pi_N^{1,H}(\mu)$ is the multiset of all system-net places that contain the object-net N:[2]

$$\Pi_N^{1,H}\left(\sum_{i=1}^{n} \widehat{p}_i[N_i, M_i]\right) := \sum_{i=1}^{n} \mathbf{1}_N(N_i) \cdot \widehat{p}_i \tag{1}$$

---

[1] Of course, this has consequences for the possible modifications on net-tokens. E.g. an operator $\sigma^{\mathcal{I}}$ which appends a fresh place contradicts finiteness of P_k. Therefore, the boundary case where the net-token already contains all possible places has to be defined as an exception. From a practical perspective the possibility to generate net-tokens of unbounded size might also indicate a modelling problem.

[2] The superscript H indicates that the function is used for HORNETS.

where the indicator function $\mathbf{1}_N$ is defined as: $\mathbf{1}_N(N_i) = 1$ iff $N_i = N$.

Analogously, the projection $\Pi_N^{2,H}(\mu)$ is the multiset of all net-tokens' markings (that belong to the object-net N):

$$\Pi_N^{2,H}\left(\sum_{i=1}^n \widehat{p}_i[N_i, M_i]\right) := \sum_{i=1}^n \mathbf{1}_k(N_i) \cdot M_i \tag{2}$$

The projection $\Pi_k^{2,H}(\mu)$ is the sum of all net-tokens' markings belonging to the same type $k \in K$:

$$\Pi_k^{2,H}(\mu) := \sum_{N \in \mathcal{U}_k} \Pi_N^{2,H}(\mu) \tag{3}$$

Synchronisation. The transitions in a HORNET are labelled with synchronisation inscriptions. We assume a fixed set of channels $C = (C_k)_{k \in K}$.

– The function family $\widehat{l}_\alpha = (\widehat{l}_\alpha^k)_{k \in K}$ defines the synchronisation constraints. Each transition of the system net is labelled with a multiset $\widehat{l}^k(\widehat{t}) = (e_1, c_1) + \cdots + (e_n, c_n)$, where the expression $e_i \in \mathbb{T}_\Sigma^k(X)$ describes the called object net and $c_i \in C_k$ is a channel. The intention is that $\widehat{t}$ fires synchronously with a multiset of object net transitions with the same multiset of labels. Each variable assignment α generates the function $\widehat{l}_\alpha^k(\widehat{t})$ defined as:

$$\widehat{l}_\alpha^k(\widehat{t})(N) := \sum_{\substack{1 \le i \le n \\ \alpha(e_i) = N}} c_i \quad \text{for} \quad \widehat{l}^k(\widehat{t}) = \sum_{1 \le i \le n}(e_i, c_i) \tag{4}$$

Each function $\widehat{l}_\alpha^k(\widehat{t})$ assigns to each object net N a multiset of channels.
– For each $N \in \mathcal{U}_k$ the function l_N assigns to each transition $t \in T_N$ either a channel $c \in C_k$ or $\perp_k$, whenever t fires without synchronisation, i.e. autonomously.

System Net. Assume we have a fixed logic $\Gamma = (\Sigma, X, E, \Psi)$ and a net-theory $(\mathcal{U}, \mathcal{I})$. An *elementary higher-order object net* (EHORNET) is composed of a system net $\widehat{N}$ and the set of object nets $\mathcal{U}$. W.l.o.g. we assume $\widehat{N} \notin \mathcal{U}$. To guarantee finite algebras for EHORNETS, we require that the net-theory $(\mathcal{U}, \mathcal{I})$ is finite, i.e. each place universe P_k is finite.

The system net is a net $\widehat{N} = (\widehat{P}, \widehat{T}, \mathbf{pre}, \mathbf{post}, \widehat{G})$, where each arc is labelled with a multiset of terms: $\mathbf{pre}, \mathbf{post} : \widehat{T} \to (\widehat{P} \to MS(\mathbb{T}_\Sigma(X)))$. Each transition is labelled by a guard predicate $\widehat{G} : \widehat{T} \to PL_\Gamma$. The places of the system net are typed by the function $k : \widehat{P} \to K$. As a typing constraint we have that each arc inscription has to be a multiset of terms that are all of the kind that is assigned to the arc's place:

$$\mathbf{pre}(\widehat{t})(\widehat{p}), \quad \mathbf{post}(\widehat{t})(\widehat{p}) \quad \in \quad MS(\mathbb{T}_\Sigma^{k(\widehat{p})}(X)) \tag{5}$$

For each variable binding α we obtain the evaluated functions $\mathbf{pre}_\alpha, \mathbf{post}_\alpha : \widehat{T} \to (\widehat{P} \to MS(\mathcal{U}))$ in the obvious way.

Definition 1 (Elementary Hornet, EHORNET).   *Assume a fixed many-sorted predicate logic* $\Gamma = (\Sigma, X, E, \Psi)$.

An elementary HORNET *is a tuple* $EH = (\widehat{N}, \mathcal{U}, \mathcal{I}, k, l, \mu_0)$ *such that:*

1. $\widehat{N}$ *is an algebraic net, called the* system net.
2. $(\mathcal{U}, \mathcal{I})$ *is a finite net-theory for the logic* Γ.
3. $k : \widehat{P} \to K$ *is the typing of the system net places.*
4. $l = (\widehat{l}, l_N)_{N \in \mathcal{U}}$ *is the labelling.*
5. $\mu_0 \in \mathcal{M}_H$ *is the initial marking.*

Events. The synchronisation labelling generates the set of system events Θ. We have three kinds of events:

1. Synchronised firing: There is at least one object net that has to be synchronised, i.e. there is an object net N such that $\widehat{l}(\widehat{t})(N)$ is not empty.

   Such an event is a triple $\theta = \widehat{t}^{\alpha}[\vartheta]$, where $\widehat{t}$ is a system net transition, α is a variable binding, and ϑ is a function that maps each object net to a multiset of its transitions, i.e. $\vartheta(N) \in MS(T_N)$. It is required that $\widehat{t}$ and $\vartheta(N)$ have matching multisets of labels, i.e. $\widehat{l}(\widehat{t})(N) = l_N^{\sharp}(\vartheta(N))$ for all $N \in \mathcal{U}$.

   (Remember that $l_N^{\sharp}$ denotes the multiset extension of l_N.)
   The intended meaning is that $\widehat{t}$ fires synchronously with all the object net transitions $\vartheta(N), N \in \mathcal{U}$.
2. System-autonomous firing: The transition $\widehat{t}$ of the system net fires autonomously, whenever $\widehat{l}(\widehat{t})$ is the empty multiset $\mathbf{0}$.

   We consider system-autonomous firing as a special case of synchronised firing generated by the function ϑ_{id}, defined as $\vartheta_{id}(N) = \mathbf{0}$ for all $N \in \mathcal{U}$.
3. Object-autonomous firing: An object net transition t in N fires autonomously, whenever $l_N(t) = \perp_k$.

   Object-autonomous events are denoted as $id_{\widehat{p}, N}[\vartheta_t]$, where $\vartheta_t(N') = \{t\}$ if $N = N'$ and $\mathbf{0}$ otherwise. The meaning is that object net N fires t autonomously within the place $\widehat{p}$ of the system net $\widehat{N}$.

   For the sake of uniformity we define for an arbitrary binding α:

$$\mathbf{pre}_{\alpha}(id_{\widehat{p}, N})(\widehat{p}')(N') = \mathbf{post}_{\alpha}(id_{\widehat{p}, N})(\widehat{p}')(N') = \begin{cases} 1 & \text{if } \widehat{p}' = \widehat{p} \wedge N' = N \\ 0 & \text{otherwise.} \end{cases}$$

The set of all *events* generated by the labelling l is $\Theta_l := \Theta_1 \cup \Theta_2$, where Θ_1 contains synchronous events (including system-autonomous events as a special case) and Θ_2 contains the object-autonomous events:

$$\begin{aligned} \Theta_1 &:= \left\{ \widehat{t}^{\alpha}[\vartheta] \quad | \, \forall N \in \mathcal{U} : \widehat{l}_{\alpha}(\widehat{t})(N) = l_N^{\sharp}(\vartheta(N)) \right\} \\ \Theta_2 &:= \left\{ id_{\widehat{p}, N}[\vartheta_t] \mid \widehat{p} \in \widehat{P}, N \in \mathcal{U}_{k(\widehat{p})}, t \in T_N \right\} \end{aligned} \tag{6}$$

Firing Rule. A system event $\theta = \widehat{\tau}^\alpha[\vartheta]$ removes net-tokens together with their individual internal markings. Firing the event replaces a nested multiset $\lambda \in \mathcal{M}_H$ that is part of the current marking μ, i.e. $\lambda \sqsubseteq \mu$, by the nested multiset ρ. The enabling condition is expressed by the *enabling predicate* ϕ_{EH} (or just ϕ whenever EH is clear from the context):

$$
\begin{aligned}
\phi_{EH}(\widehat{\tau}^\alpha[\vartheta], \lambda, \rho) &\iff \forall k \in K : \\
&\forall \widehat{p} \in k^{-1}(k) : \forall N \in \mathcal{U}_k : \Pi_N^{1,H}(\lambda)(\widehat{p}) = \mathbf{pre}_\alpha(\widehat{\tau})(\widehat{p})(N) \wedge \\
&\forall \widehat{p} \in k^{-1}(k) : \forall N \in \mathcal{U}_k : \Pi_N^{1,H}(\rho)(\widehat{p}) = \mathbf{post}_\alpha(\widehat{\tau})(\widehat{p})(N) \wedge \quad (7) \\
&\Pi_k^{2,H}(\lambda) \geq \sum_{N \in \mathcal{U}_k} \mathbf{pre}_N^\sharp(\vartheta(N)) \wedge \\
&\Pi_k^{2,H}(\rho) = \Pi_k^{2,H}(\lambda) + \sum_{N \in \mathcal{U}_k} \mathbf{post}_N^\sharp(\vartheta(N)) - \mathbf{pre}_N^\sharp(\vartheta(N))
\end{aligned}
$$

The predicate ϕ_{EH} has the following meaning: Conjunct (1) states that the removed sub-marking λ contains on $\widehat{p}$ the right number of net-tokens, that are removed by $\widehat{\tau}$. Conjunct (2) states that generated sub-marking ρ contains on $\widehat{p}$ the right number of net-tokens, that are generated by $\widehat{\tau}$. Conjunct (3) states that the sub-marking λ enables all synchronised transitions $\vartheta(N)$ in the object N. Conjunct (4) states that the marking of each object net N is changed according to the firing of the synchronised transitions $\vartheta(N)$.

Note, that conjuncs (1) and (2) assure that only net-tokens relevant for the firing are included in λ and ρ. Conditions (3) and (4) allow for additional tokens in the net-tokens.

For system-autonomous events $\widehat{t}^\alpha[\vartheta_{id}]$ the enabling predicate ϕ_{EH} can be simplified further: Conjunct (3) is always true since $\mathbf{pre}_N(\vartheta_{id}(N)) = \mathbf{0}$. Conjunct (4) simplifies to $\Pi_k^{2,H}(\rho) = \Pi_k^{2,H}(\lambda)$, which means that no token of the object nets get lost when a system-autonomous events fires.

Analogously, for an object-autonomous event $\widehat{\tau}[\vartheta_t]$ we have an idle-transition $\widehat{\tau} = id_{\widehat{p},N}$ and $\vartheta = \vartheta_t$ for some t. Conjunct (1) and (2) simplify to $\Pi_{N'}^{1,H}(\lambda) = \widehat{p} = \Pi_{N'}^{1,H}(\rho)$ for $N' = N$ and to $\Pi_{N'}^{1,H}(\lambda) = \mathbf{0} = \Pi_{N'}^{1,H}(\rho)$ otherwise. This means that $\lambda = \widehat{p}[M]$, M enables t, and $\rho = \widehat{p}[M - \mathbf{pre}_N(\widehat{t}) + \mathbf{post}_N(\widehat{t})]$.

Definition 2 (Firing Rule). *Let EH be an* eHORNET *and* $\mu, \mu' \in \mathcal{M}_H$ *markings.*

- *The event* $\widehat{\tau}^\alpha[\vartheta]$ *is enabled in* μ *for the mode* $(\lambda, \rho) \in \mathcal{M}_H^2$ *iff* $\lambda \sqsubseteq \mu \wedge$ $\phi_{EH}(\widehat{\tau}[\vartheta], \lambda, \rho)$ *holds and the guard* $\widehat{G}(\widehat{t})$ *holds,*
  i.e. $E \models_{\mathcal{I}}^\alpha \widehat{G}(\widehat{\tau})$.
- *An event* $\widehat{\tau}^\alpha[\vartheta]$ *that is enabled in* μ *can fire – denoted* $\mu \xrightarrow[EH]{\widehat{\tau}^\alpha[\vartheta](\lambda,\rho)} \mu'$.
- *The resulting successor marking is defined as* $\mu' = \mu - \lambda + \rho$.

Note, that the firing rule has no a-priori decision on how to distribute the marking on the generated net-tokens. Therefore we need the mode (λ, ρ) to formulate the firing of $\widehat{\tau}^\alpha[\vartheta]$ in a functional way.

3   Fan-Bounded Safe, Elementary HORNETS

We know from [10, Lemma 3.1] that a safe EHORNET has a finite reachability set. More precisely: There are at most $\left(1 + U(m) \cdot 2^m\right)^{|\widehat{P}|}$ different markings, where m is the maximum of all $|P_k|$ and $U(m)$ is the number of object nets. In the general case we have $U(m) = 2^{\left(2^{4m}\right)}$, which dominates the bound. It is double-exponential, while the number of different marking within each net-token is 2^m, i.e. "only" single-exponential. The huge number of object nets is the source of the exponential space requirement for the reachability problem.

Therefore, if one wants to require less than exponential space one has to restrict the structure of possible object nets in $\mathcal{U}_k$. The huge number of object-nets in $\mathcal{U}_k$ arises since we allow object nets with any number of places in the preset or postset, i.e. unbounded joins or forks. Therefore it seems promising to restrict the synchronisation degree.

In the following we want to restrict the number of object-nets in $\mathcal{U}_k$: We forbid unbounded joins or forks. From a practical point of view this restriction seems to be a common one: In most Petri net models the number of places in the pre- or postset is rather small when compared to the total number of places. Many models use standard Petri net patters, i.e. operators like SEQ, AND, or OR, which have a fan-bound $\beta = 2$.

From a theoretical point of view we can take this into account with a parameterised complexity analysis. The parameter considered here is the maximal number of places in the pre- or postset, i.e. the maximal synchronisation at object-net level.

Definition 3. *An elementary* HORNET $EH = (\widehat{N}, \mathcal{U}, \mathcal{I}, k, l, \mu_0)$ *is called β-fan-bounded whenever all transitions of all object-nets have at most β places in the pre- and in the postset:*

$$\forall k \in K : \forall N \in \mathcal{U}_k : \forall t \in T_N : |{}^{\bullet}t| \leq \beta \wedge |t^{\bullet}| \leq \beta$$

The *fan-bound* of EH is defined as:

$$\beta(EH) := \max\left\{|{}^{\bullet}t|, |t^{\bullet}| \ : \ k \in K : N \in \mathcal{U}_k : t \in T_N\right\}$$

Note, that an elementary HORNET is always fan-bounded, since $P_N \subseteq P_k$ and P_k is always finite in the elementary case: $\beta(EH) \leq |P_k| \leq m := \max\{|P_k| : k \in K\} < \infty$ for each net-type $k \in K$.

Proposition 2. *For a safe, β-fan-bounded* EHORNET *the cardinality of each net universe $\mathcal{U}_k$ is bounded for each $k \in K$ as follows: $|\mathcal{U}_k| \leq 2^{O\left(n^{(4\beta)}\right)}$ where $n := |P_k|$.*

Proof. For a safe, *β-fan-bounded* EHORNET the number of possible objects is calculated as follows: Each possible transition t chooses a subset of P_k for the preset $^\bullet t$ and another subset for the postset $t^\bullet$ with the constraint that these subsets have a cardinality of at most β. The number of these subsets is:

$$\left| \bigcup_{i=0}^{\beta} \binom{P_k}{i} \right| = \sum_{i=0}^{\beta} \binom{|P_k|}{i} = \binom{|P_k|}{0} + \binom{|P_k|}{1} + \cdots + \binom{|P_k|}{\beta}$$

(Here $\binom{A}{i}$ denote the set of all subsets of A that have cardinality i).

We identify t with the pair $(^\bullet t, t^\bullet)$. The number of different transitions is:[3]

$$\begin{aligned}
|T_k| &= \left(\binom{|P_k|}{0} + \binom{|P_k|}{1} + \cdots + \binom{|P_k|}{\beta} \right)^2 \\
&\leq \left(1 + n + \frac{n \cdot (n-1)}{2!} \cdots + \frac{(n)_\beta}{\beta!} \right)^2 \\
&\leq \left(const \cdot \beta \cdot n^\beta \right)^2 \\
&= const \cdot \beta^2 \cdot n^{(2\beta)}
\end{aligned}$$

So, the number of different transitions is in $O\left(\beta^2 \cdot n^{2\beta}\right)$.[4]

The set of labelled transitions is $LT_k := T_k \times (C_k \cup \{\perp_k\})$ and we have $|LT_k| = |T_k \times (C_k \cup \{\perp_k\})|$ different labelled transitions. We cannot use more channels than we have transitions in the object net, i.e. we could use at most $|T_k|$ different channels from $C_k \cup \{\perp_k\}$. Thus, we have:

$$|LT_k| = |T_k| \cdot (|C_k| + 1) \leq |T_k| \cdot |T_k|$$

From $|T_k| \leq const \cdot \beta^2 \cdot n^{(2\beta)}$ we obtain:

$$|LT_k| \leq \left(const \cdot \beta^2 \cdot n^{2\beta} \right)^2 = const \cdot \beta^4 \cdot n^{(4\beta)}$$

Thus the set of labelled transitions is in $O\left(\beta^4 \cdot n^{(4\beta)}\right) = O\left(n^{(4\beta)}\right)$, i.e. a polynomial in the number of places $n = |P_k|$ where the degree of the polynomial is given by the fan-parameter β.

Since each object net N in $\mathcal{U}_k$ is characterised by its set of labelled transitions and there are $|\mathcal{P}(LT_k)| = 2^{|LT_k|}$ subsets of LT_k, we have at most $2^{O\left(\beta^4 \cdot n^{(4\beta)}\right)}$ different object nets.

Thus the number of different object nets is only single-exponential for fan-bounded EHORNETS – and not double-exponential as in the general case.

Remark 1. Note that the size of the transition set is a polynomial in the number of places m where the degree is given by the fan-parameter $\beta = \beta(m) \leq m$. Of

---

[3] In the following we use *const* to denote some constant. Nevertheless, different occurrences may denote different constants.

[4] Note, that while the bound we have given for the general case in Lemma 2.1 in [10] is strict (i.e. there are Hornets that exactly have this number of object-nets) the calculation given here gives us only an upper bound.

course if we have transitions that use all the places in the pre- or postset, i.e. $\beta = m$ we have an exponential number as before, since:

$$|T_k| = \left(\binom{|P_k|}{0} + \binom{|P_k|}{1} + \cdots + \binom{|P_k|}{m} \right)^2 = \left(2^{|P_k|} \right)^2 = 2^{(2|P_k|)} = 2^{(2m)}$$

This implies the following upper bound for the net universe:

$$|\mathcal{U}_k| = |\mathcal{P}(LT_k)| = 2^{|LT_k|} \le 2^{|T_k|^2} \le 2^{(2^{(2|P_k|)})^2} = 2^{(2^{(2m)})^2} = 2^{(2^{(4m)})}$$

This result is in accordance with Proposition 1. So, the general analysis is just the special case where the fan-parameter β equals the number of places m.

For safe, β-*fan-bounded* EHORNET we can give an upper bound for the number of reachable markings. The number of reachable markings is in $2^{O(n^{(4\beta+1)})}$, i.e. exponential, where the exponent is a polynomial in the number of places n where the degree is given by the fan-parameter β.

Proposition 3. *A safe, β-fan-bounded EHORNET has a finite reachability set: The number of reachable markings is bounded by $2^{O(n^{(4\beta+1)})}$ where n is the maximum of all $|P_k|$ and $|\widehat{P}|$.*

Proof. Analogously to the proof of Lemma 2.1 in [10] we argue that we have at most $(1 + U(m) \cdot 2^m)^{|\widehat{P}|}$ different markings in the safe HORNET, since each reachable marking is of the form $\mu = \sum_{i=1}^{n} \widehat{p}_i[N_i, M_i]$ and each system-net place $\widehat{p}_i$ is either unmarked or marked with a net-token $[N_i, M_i]$. Since each object net $N \in \mathcal{U}_k$ is safe, we know that each net-token has at most $2^{|P_k|} \le 2^m$ different markings M_i, where m is the maximum of all $|P_k|$. Therefore, we have at most $U(m) \cdot 2^m$ different net-tokens. All in all we have at most $(1 + U(m) \cdot 2^m)^{|\widehat{P}|}$ different markings in the safe EHORNET.

For a β-*fan-bounded* EHORNET we have obtained in Proposition 2 a bound for the number of possible object-nets: $|\mathcal{U}_k| \le U(m) = 2^{(const \cdot m^{(4\beta)})}$. Thus the number of different markings in the safe, β-fan-bounded EHORNET is:

$$(1 + U(m) \cdot 2^m)^{|\widehat{P}|} \le \left(1 + 2^{(const \cdot m^{(4\beta)})} \cdot 2^m \right)^{|\widehat{P}|}$$
$$\le \left(2^{(const \cdot m^{(4\beta)} + m)} \right)^{|\widehat{P}|}$$
$$\le \left(2^{(const \cdot m^{\max(4\beta, 1)})} \right)^{|\widehat{P}|}$$
$$= 2^{(const \cdot m^{\max(4\beta, 1)} \cdot |\widehat{P}|)}$$

With $n := \max(m, |\widehat{P}|)$ the bound simplifies to:

$$2^{(const \cdot m^{\max(4\beta, 1)} \cdot |\widehat{P}|)} \le 2^{(const \cdot n^{\max(4\beta, 1)} \cdot n)} = 2^{(const \cdot n^{(\max(4\beta, 1)+1)})}$$

The number of reachable markings is in $2^{O(n^{(\max(4\beta, 1)+1)})}$, i.e. exponential, where the exponent is a polynomial: $const \cdot n^{(\max(4\beta, 1)+1)}$.

The most extreme restriction is to forbid forks and joins at all. In this case we consider elementary HORNETS that have *state-machines* as object-nets only, i.e.

$$\forall k \in K : \forall N \in \mathcal{U}_k : \forall t \in T_N : |{}^\bullet t| \le 1 \wedge |t^\bullet| \le 1$$

An elementary Hornet with this restriction is called ESMHORNET (elementary state-machine HORNET) for short. An ESMHORNET is 1-fan-bounded EHORNET by definition.

Therefore, we obtain the following corollary of Lemma 3 for ESMHORNETS:

Corollary 1. *A safe ESMHORNET has a finite reachability set. The number of reachable markings is bounded by $2^{O(n^5)}$ where n is the maximum of all $|P_k|$ and $|\widehat{P}|$.*

From a complexity theory point of view this is only slightly more complex than reachability of safe p/t nets, where the number of reachable markings is bounded by $2^{O(n)}$ where n is the number of places.

4   Complexity of the Reachability Problem for Fan-Bounded EHORNETS

As safe p/t nets are a special sub-case of fan-bounded EHORNETS (we simply restrict the system net to a single place with the p/t net of interest as the unique net-token) the reachability problem for safe, fan-bounded EHORNETS cannot be simpler than for safe p/t nets, i.e. it is at least PSPACE-hard, since the reachability problem for safe p/t nets is PSPACE-complete. In the following we show that the reachability problem for EHORNETS lies within PSPACE.

Proposition 4. *For safe, β-fan-bounded EHORNETS there exists a non-deterministic algorithm that decides the reachability problem within polynomial space:*

$$\mathsf{Reach}_{\beta-\mathsf{seH}} \in NSpace\left(O\left(n^{(\max(4\beta,1)+1)}\right)\right)$$

where n is the maximum of all $|P_k|$ and $|\widehat{P}|$.

Proof. Whenever μ^* is reachable it is reachable by a firing sequence without loops. The main idea of the algorithm is to guess a firing sequence $\mu_0 \xrightarrow{\theta_1} \mu_1 \xrightarrow{\theta_2} \cdots \xrightarrow{\theta_i} \mu^*$, where μ^* is the marking to be tested for reachability.

By Proposition 3 we know we have at most $maxstep = 2^{const \cdot n^{(\max(4\beta,1)+1)}}$ different markings. Therefore, we can safely cut off the computation after $maxstep$ steps (cf. the Listing in Fig. 5).

For each step $\mu_i \xrightarrow{\theta_i} \mu_{i+1}$ we choose non-deterministically some event θ_i. For a given marking μ_i we guess an event θ_i and a marking μ_{i+1} and test whether $\mu_i \xrightarrow{\theta_i} \mu_{i+1}$ holds.

function *reach*(*EH*: EHORNET, μ^*: Marking): boolean **is**

$c := 2^{const \cdot n^{(max(4\beta,1)+1)}}$

$\mu := \mu_0$

found := ($\mu = \mu^*$)

while ¬found $\wedge$ $c > 0$ **do**

    choose non-deterministically an event $\hat{t}^\alpha[\vartheta](\lambda, \rho)$

    if $\mu \xrightarrow[EH]{\hat{t}^\alpha(\lambda,\rho)}$ **then**

        $\mu := \mu - \lambda + \rho$ // the resulting successor marking

        $c := c - 1$

        found := ($\mu = \mu^*$)

    else

        return false

end while

return found

Fig. 5. Non-deterministic algorithm: reachability for safe EHORNETS

- The markings μ_i and μ_{i+1} can be stored in $O\left(n^{(\max(4\beta,1)+1)}\right)$ bits, i.e. polynomial space.
- The event θ_i can be stored in polynomial bits: The choice for the system net transition $\hat{t}$ fits in polynomial space. The variable binding α selects for each variable in the arc inscriptions some object net from the universe $\mathcal{U}_k$. Since we always have a finite number of variables polynomial space is sufficient. For each kind k we have the multiset of channels $\hat{l}^k_\alpha(\hat{t})$ to synchronise with. In the proof of Proposition 2 we have seen that we have at most $const \cdot n^{\max(4\beta,1)}$ labelled transitions in the object nets, i.e. polynomial space is sufficient. We guess a mode (λ, ρ). (Since we consider safe HORNETS the choice for λ is unique, since there is at most one net-token on each place, which implies that whenever an event $\hat{t}^\alpha[\vartheta]$ is enabled, then λ is uniquely determined.) For the multiset ρ, we use the fact that for each place in the object net N we have at most one token to distribute over all generated net-tokes. For each net $N \in \mathcal{U}_k$ we select one of the net-tokens generated in the postset. All these choices need at most polynomial many bits.
- To check whether the event is enabled we have to whether test $\alpha \sqsubseteq \mu$. This holds iff $\exists \mu'' : \mu = \alpha + \mu''$. Since α and μ are known, this can be tested in-place by 'tagging' all addends from α in μ.

Finally we check whether the successor marking $\mu' = \mu - \lambda + \rho$ is equal to μ_{i+1}. This can be done in-place as $\mu - \lambda$ are those addends, that have not been tagged.

After each step $\mu_i \xrightarrow{\theta_i} \mu_{i+1}$ we decrement a counter (which has been initialised with the maximal sequence length *maxstep*), forget μ_i, and repeat the procedure with μ_{i+1} again until either the marking of interest is reached or the counter reaches zero.

As each step can be tested in polynomial space, the whole algorithm needs at most polynomial many bits to decide reachability.

Now we use the technique of Savitch to construct a deterministic algorithm from the non-deterministic algorithm above.

Proposition 5. *The reachability problem* Reach$_\beta$-seH *for safe* β-fan-bounded EHORNETS *can be solved within polynomial space.*

Proof. We known by Lemma 4 that Reach$_\beta$-seH $\in NSpace(O\left(n^{(\max(4\beta,1)+1)}\right))$. From Savitch's Theorem we obtain:

$$\text{Reach}_\beta\text{-seH} \in DSpace\left(O\left(n^{(\max(4\beta,1)+1)}\right)^2\right)$$
$$= DSpace\left(O\left(n^{2(\max(4\beta,1)+1)}\right)\right)$$

Since we already know by Lipton's result that the problem must be PSPACE-hard, the last proposition is sufficient to prove our central result:

Proposition 6. *The reachability problem for safe, fan-bounded* EHORNETS *is* PSPACE-*complete.*

This result shows that fan-bounded EHORNETS are really simpler since the reachability problem requires exponential space in the general case of safe EHORNETS.

The number of reachable markings is in $2^{O\left(n^{(4\beta+1)}\right)}$ for Fan-Bounded EHOR-NETS, i.e. exponential, where the exponent is a polynomial in the number of places n. We have studied the same situation as before for safe EOS. Therefore we can decide the LTL model-checking problem using the same techniques as in [7] and the CTL model-checking problem analogously to [8]. We obtain:

Proposition 7. *The LTL- and the CTL-model-checking problem for safe, fan-bounded* EHORNETS *are* PSPACE-*complete.*

Since reachability is expressible both with LTL and CTL we obtain that this proposition is in accordance with our previous results from above.

5   Conclusion

In this contribution we described run-time adaption of processes within the nets-within-nets formalism of HORNETS. For run-time verification we are interested in sub-classes of HORNETS with feasible analysis complexity.

In previous contributions we investigated elementary HORNETS as well as their subclass of safe elementary HORNETS. We showed that the reachability problem for safe elementary HORNETS requires at least exponential space. We have also showed that exponential space is sufficient. Of course, an exponential space complexity is not feasible for almost all practical cases – not to mention a verification at run-time.

Therefore, we imposed a structural restriction – here: fan-boundedness – to obtain a better complexity of reachability and related model checking problems. An elementary HORNET is called β-fan-bounded whenever all transitions of all object-nets have at most β places in the pre- and in the postset.

It turns out that reachability is in PSPACE for safe, fan-bounded EHORNETS. This means that we found a structural restriction that establishes a lower complexity. Note, that PSPACE has to be considered as a "good" complexity class for Petri nets, since reachability of 1-safe Petri nets lies within this class.

In future work we like to extend our results to other net-classes, namely workflow nets. We also like to study object-net classes generated by classical process-algebraic operators like sequence, choice, parallelism etc.

References

1. Floerkemeier, C., Langheinrich, M., Fleisch, E., Mattern, F., Sarma, S.E. (eds.): The Internet of Things, First International Conference, IOT 2008, Zurich, Switzerland, March 26–28, 2008. Proceedings. LNCS, vol. 4952. Springer, Heidelberg (2008)
2. Valk, R.: Modelling concurrency by task/flow EN systems. In: 3rd Workshop on Concurrency and Compositionality. Number 191 in GMD-Studien, St. Augustin, Bonn, Gesellschaft für Mathematik und Datenverarbeitung (1991)
3. Valk, R.: Object petri nets: using the nets-within-nets paradigm. In: Desel, J., Reisig, W., Rozenberg, G. (eds.) ACPN 2003. LNCS, vol. 3098, pp. 819–848. Springer, Heidelberg (2004). doi:10.1007/978-3-540-27755-2_23
4. Köhler-Bußmeier, M.: Hornets: nets within nets combined with net algebra. In: Franceschinis, G., Wolf, K. (eds.) PETRI NETS 2009. LNCS, vol. 5606, pp. 243–262. Springer, Heidelberg (2009). doi:10.1007/978-3-642-02424-5_15
5. Köhler-Bußmeier, M., Heitmann, F.: On the expressiveness of communication channels for object nets. Fundamenta Informaticae 93, 205–219 (2009)
6. Köhler, M., Rölke, H.: Properties of object petri nets. In: Cortadella, J., Reisig, W. (eds.) ICATPN 2004. LNCS, vol. 3099, pp. 278–297. Springer, Heidelberg (2004). doi:10.1007/978-3-540-27793-4_16
7. Köhler-Bußmeier, M., Heitmann, F.: Safeness for object nets. Fundamenta Informaticae 101, 29–43 (2010)
8. Köhler-Bußmeier, M., Heitmann, F.: Liveness of safe object nets. Fundamenta Informaticae 112, 73–87 (2011)
9. Köhler-Bußmeier, M.: A survey on decidability results for elementary object systems. Fundamenta Informaticae 130, 99–123 (2014)
10. Köhler-Bußmeier, M.: On the complexity of the reachability problem for safe, elementary Hornets. Fundamenta Informaticae 129, 101–116 (2014). Dedicated to the Memory of Professor Manfred Kudlek
11. Lipton, R.J.: The reachability problem requires exponential space. Research report 62, Department of Computer science (1976)
12. Köhler-Bußmeier, M., Heitmann, F.: An upper bound for the reachability problem of safe, elementary hornets. Fundamenta Informaticae 143, 89–100 (2016)
13. Lomazova, I.A.: Nested Petri nets - a formalism for specification of multi-agent distributed systems. Fundamenta Informaticae 43, 195–214 (2000)
14. Xu, D., Deng, Y.: Modeling mobile agent systems with high level Petri nets. In: IEEE International Conference on Systems, Man, and Cybernetics 2000 (2000)

15. Kummer, O.: Referenznetze. Logos Verlag, Berlin (2002)
16. Hiraishi, K.: PN²: an elementary model for design and analysis of multi-agent systems. In: Arbab, F., Talcott, C. (eds.) COORDINATION 2002. LNCS, vol. 2315, pp. 220–235. Springer, Heidelberg (2002). doi:10.1007/3-540-46000-4_22
17. Bednarczyk, M.A., Bernardinello, L., Pawłowski, W., Pomello, L.: Modelling mobility with petri hypernets. In: Fiadeiro, J.L., Mosses, P.D., Orejas, F. (eds.) WADT 2004. LNCS, vol. 3423, pp. 28–44. Springer, Heidelberg (2005). doi:10.1007/978-3-540-31959-7_2
18. Lakos, C.A.: A petri net view of mobility. In: Wang, F. (ed.) FORTE 2005. LNCS, vol. 3731, pp. 174–188. Springer, Heidelberg (2005). doi:10.1007/11562436_14
19. Hee, K.M., Lomazova, I.A., Oanea, O., Serebrenik, A., Sidorova, N., Voorhoeve, M.: Nested nets for adaptive systems. In: Donatelli, S., Thiagarajan, P.S. (eds.) ICATPN 2006. LNCS, vol. 4024, pp. 241–260. Springer, Heidelberg (2006). doi:10.1007/11767589_14
20. Cardelli, L., Ghelli, G., Gordon, A.D.: Mobility types for mobile ambients. In: Wiedermann, J., Emde Boas, P., Nielsen, M. (eds.) ICALP 1999. LNCS, vol. 1644, pp. 230–239. Springer, Heidelberg (1999). doi:10.1007/3-540-48523-6_20
21. Milner, R., Parrow, J., Walker, D.: A calculus of mobile processes, parts 1–2. Inf. Comput. **100**, 1–77 (1992)
22. Reisig, W.: Petri nets and algebraic specifications. Theor. Comput. Sci. **80**, 1–34 (1991)
23. Hoffmann, K., Ehrig, H., Mossakowski, T.: High-level nets with nets and rules as tokens. In: Ciardo, G., Darondeau, P. (eds.) ICATPN 2005. LNCS, vol. 3536, pp. 268–288. Springer, Heidelberg (2005). doi:10.1007/11494744_16
24. Lomazova, I.A.: Nested petri nets for adaptive process modeling. In: Avron, A., Dershowitz, N., Rabinovich, A. (eds.) Pillars of Computer Science. LNCS, vol. 4800, pp. 460–474. Springer, Heidelberg (2008). doi:10.1007/978-3-540-78127-1_25
25. Taentzer, G.: Distributed graphs and graph transformation. Appl. Categ. Struct. **7**, 431–462 (1999)
26. Ehrig, H., Mahr, B.: Fundamentals of Algebraic Specification. EATCS Monographs on TCS, vol. 6. Springer, Heidelberg (1985)

Petri Nets for Pathways

Synthesis and Analysis of Process Networks by Joint Application of P-graphs and Petri Nets

Rozália Lakner[1]([✉]), Ferenc Friedler[1], and Botond Bertók[2]

[1] Pázmány Péter Catholic University, Szentkirályi 28, Budapest 1088, Hungary
{lakner.rozalia,friedler.ferenc}@ppke.hu
[2] University of Pannonia, Egyetem 10, Veszprém 8200, Hungary
bertok@dcs.uni-pannon.hu

Abstract. Due to the increasing complexity of human developed systems computer aid plays key role in engineering design involving process synthesis and analysis. The P-graph framework provides effective algorithms implemented in software to synthesize optimal process systems constructed from potential building blocks leading from the available resources to the desired targets. P-graph software computes both the optimal structure and the optimal parameter values of a process system, however, does not provide information on the dynamics of the system synthesized. In contrast Petri nets are tools for simulation and analysis of complex systems' dynamic behavior. They can model the operation of a preliminarily well-defined process network, but they are inappropriate for synthesizing the optimal process structure.

The present work suggests joint application of the methods mentioned above combining effective synthesis algorithms from the P-graph framework with the modeling strength of Petri nets, illustrated by identification of feasible reaction pathways.

Keywords: Process network synthesis · P-graph (process graph) · Petri net · Reaction pathway identification

1 Introduction

The Petri net theory and the P-graph framework have been developed for different types of purposes in systems design. While Petri nets are primarily for modeling and analysis of concurrent, asynchronous distributed dynamic systems, P-graph framework has been developed for the synthesis of steady-state processing systems. Even though the purposes of the two approaches are quite different, there are some similarities that makes it possible to use the capabilities of both of them in solving specific problems. The major similarity of the two approaches comes from the structural representation. Both of them use bipartite directed graph for representing structures, the reason of the need of bipartite graph is, however, rather different.

© Springer International Publishing AG 2017
W. van der Aalst and E. Best (Eds.): PETRI NETS 2017, LNCS 10258, pp. 309–329, 2017.
DOI: 10.1007/978-3-319-57861-3_18

Though in process design and analysis, simple directed graphs are capable of properly representing process structures, it is not the case for process synthesis. As far as it has been shown in [1], directed graphs are incapable of unambiguously representing process structures in synthesis.

For example, the directed graph representation of a synthesis problem shown on Fig. 1(a) represents two problems with structurally different solutions. In one of them, all three operating units are required for generating the product (Fig. 1(b)), in the other, there are three structurally different solutions (Fig. 1(c)). Figure 2 shows the P-graph representations of the problems shown on Fig. 1(b) and (c).

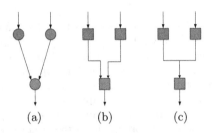

(a)   (b)   (c)

Fig. 1. Structural issue in representing a synthesis problem with directed graph: (a) directed graph, (b) and (c) two related synthesis problems

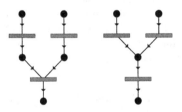

Fig. 2. P-graph representations of the two synthesis problem of Fig. 1(a)

Synthesis by definition is the act of combining components or elements to form a connected whole. P-graph framework is formulated by combinatorial properties of feasible process structures. The so-called combinatorially feasible structures or solution structures are identified by five combinatorial properties given in the form of axioms. The structure of each feasible process must satisfy these axioms, therefore, the search for the optimal structure can be restricted to the set of solution structures. Algorithms of the framework are proved on the axioms. The related softwares are capable of solving different types of industrial problems.

P-graph software provides optimal and alternative process structures for various engineering design problems from chemical process design [2,3] reaction pathway identification (RPI) [4–7], mass exchange network synthesis [8], industrial waste minimization [9,10], supply chain optimization [11–13], business process optimization [14], and crisis management [15–17].

Petri nets (PNs) named after Carl Adam Petri who introduced a mathematical formalism for modeling concurrent, asynchronous, distributed systems [18]. For the last half-century, various extensions for PNs were developed and several successful applications have been done on a wide range of areas. These methods related to both the modeling and the analysis of different fields including process engineering, manufacturing systems and computer sciences [19–21]. Nowadays many Petri net software possess built-in features both for analysis and discrete and continuous simulation, which enables the investigation of different systems [22–24].

The P-graph framework and Petri nets are compared and combined by [25–27]. Both methods have strict formal mathematical definitions and graph-representation. On the basis of the rigorous mathematical fundamentals of the framework, P-graph algorithms provide all of the feasible solution structures of a given synthesis problem, as well as, the optimal or n-best process networks together with their optimal parameter setting. In contrast, Petri nets are applied to determine the behavior of a system with predefined structure.

The present work compares and combines algorithmic process network synthesis by P-graphs and analysis by Petri nets. The proposed method is illustrated by applying it to reaction pathway identification, where a network of elementary reaction steps leading form the starting reactants towards the final products is synthesized by P-graph algorithms; and the startability of the resulted reaction pathways, i.e., the operability of each elementary reaction step included in the pathway, are verified by Petri nets investigating liveness, deadlock and reachability.

After the introduction of process network synthesis in Sect. 2 and Petri nets in Sect. 3, the main similarities and differences between them are discussed in Sect. 4. In Sect. 5 a joint application for reaction pathway identification is presented, that combines both the efficiency of the P-graph algorithms and the simulation and analysis strength of Petri nets. Finally, Sect. 6 concludes our work.

2   Process Network Synthesis - The P-graph Framework

In the early nineties, Friedler and Fan and their collaborators introduced a mathematically rigorous framework called P-graph that yields algorithmically the mathematical programming model of process synthesis problems. The method resorts to the well-established combinatorial mathematics of graph theory and is heavily based on a unique class of graphs in representing unambiguously the structures of process networks. Consequently, a set of axioms can be formulated to express the necessary and sufficient combinatorial properties to which a feasible process structure should conform [1]. In turn, these axioms lead to a set of algorithms implementable effectively on computers [28].

2.1   Definition of PNS Problems

A Process Network Synthesis (PNS) problem is formulated by defining the set
of materials (available raw materials, intermediates, desired products) and candidate operating units, e.g.

$$M = \{M_1, M_3; M_2, M_4, M_5, M_6, M_8, M_9; M_7\},$$
$$O = \{O_1, O_2, O_3, O_4, O_5, O_6\} = \{((\{M_1\}, \{M_4, M_5\}), (\{M_2, M_3\}, \{M_5\}),$$
$$(\{M_3, M_8\}, \{M_5\}), (\{M_4\}, \{M_6, M_7\}), (\{M_5\}, \{M_7, M_8\}), (\{M_5\}, \{M_9\}))\}$$

as it can be seen on the upper left-hand side of Fig. 3.

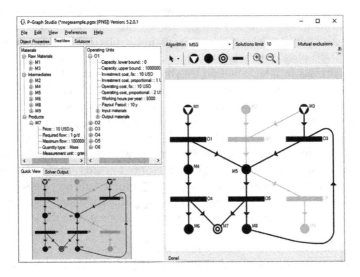

Fig. 3. P-graph representating the maximal structure developed by P-graph
Studio [30]

Various parameters for the operating units and materials are also given. The
candidate operating units are characterized by their input and output materials,
as well as their capacities, i.e., the flow rates of their inlet and outlet streams.
The upper bound on the availability of the raw materials and the lower bound
on the required amount of desired products can be defined as well. For each
intermediate material stream, the gross production must be non-negative, i.e.,
at least the amount consumed must be produced [29].

2.2   P-graph Representation

Besides formal mathematical definition, P-graphs can be visualized as graphs
with two types of node and interconnecting arc. The O-type node representing
the operating units are drawn as horizontal bars, while M-type nodes representing the materials by solid circles. Those circles representing raw materials and

products includes triangles and circles, respectively. The arcs are depicted as lines with triangle shape arrows in the middle, see Fig. 3.

The P-graph representation expresses the structural or combinatorial properties of a PNS problem and resultant structures unambiguously [1]. For instance, if an operating unit has multiple inlet streams, each of the streams needs to be provided for the operation of the unit, which means a logical AND constraint; see, e.g., operating unit O_3 in Fig. 3. If a material can be produced by two or more operating units, then any combination of them can be sufficient for the production of the material, which means a logical OR condition; see, e.g., material M_7 in Fig. 3.

2.3   Axioms of Combinatorially Feasible Process Structures

Each feasible process structure must conform to certain combinatorial properties. The introduction of process graphs or P-graphs rendered it possible to represent the structures of the process networks unambiguously and to extract these universal combinatorial properties that are inherent in all feasible processes. Mathematically, these properties can be stated as a set of axioms. The following set of axioms has been constructed to express the necessary combinatorial properties to which a P-graph must conform to be a combinatorially feasible process structure or solution structure of PNS problem [1].

(S1) Every final product is represented in the graph.

(S2) A vertex of the material type has no input if and only if it represents a raw material.

(S3) Every vertex of the operating unit type represents an operating unit defined in this synthesis problem.

(S4) Every vertex of the operating unit type has at least one path leading to a vertex of the material type representing a final product.

(S5) If a vertex of the material-type belongs to the graph, it must represent an input to or output from at least one operating unit represented in the graph.

A P-graph is defined to be a *combinatorial feasible structure* or *solution structure* for a synthesis problem if and only if it satisfies axioms (S1) through (S5).

As can be seen in Fig. 3, M_2 (and the related O_2) and O_6 (and the related M_9) do not appear in any the solution structure, as they do not satisfy axiom (S2) and (S4), respectively.

2.4   Maximal Structure Generation

The union of the combinatorially feasible solution structures itself is a solution structure and is termed the maximal structure of the problem. Since any optimal structure is among the combinatorial feasible structures, the maximal structure contains the optimal structures. Algorithm MSG (Maximal Structure Generator) directly constructs the maximal structure for a PNS problem in polynomial time, by eliminating exactly those materials and operating units which cannot belong to any combinatorially feasible structure [28] according to the axioms (S1) through (S5). Elimination of one or more materials or operating units from the sets defined in the synthesis problem by algorithm MSG in practice implies, that the input is incomplete or inconsistent. Thus, executing algorithm MSG in P-graph Studio [30] renders it possible to verify whether the input is entered correctly, see Fig. 3. Note that typically no algorithmic support is available in general purpose mathematical modeling tools to ascertain if a part of the model will never be required in the solution.

2.5   Solution Structure Generation

The availability of an algorithm to generate the set of combinatorially feasible solution structures is also of fundamental importance. To generate each solution structure of a synthesis problem exactly once, another highly effective combinatorial algorithm, termed SSG (Solution Structure Generator), has been developed.

By the help of structure generation algorithms from the P-graph framework all the solution structure can be synthesized exhaustively from the predefined sets of the materials and operating units without loss of any potentially feasible structure (Fig. 4). These solution structures can further be analyzed in several aspects by simulation tools, e.g., by Petri nets.

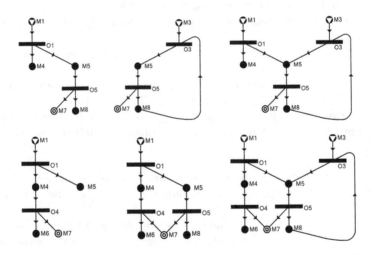

Fig. 4. Solution structures of PNS problem introduced in Fig. 3

2.6   Optimization by P-graphs

In parallel with solution structure algorithms the optimal process structures, as well as the optimal load of the operating units can be computed in software P-graph Studio by Algorithm ABB (Accelerated Bound and Branch). Algorithm

ABB has a major advantage compared to general optimization algorithms. It provides not only the globally optimal, but also the N-best suboptimal structures or flowsheets. The number N is given by the user prior to executing algorithm ABB. A structure is defined to be suboptimal if it is feasible and does not involve a better substructure [29].

3   Petri Nets

Similarly to P-graphs Petri Nets have well defined formal mathematical descriptions and graphical representations as well.

3.1   Formal Definition of Petri Nets

A Petri net can be presented by a four-tuple in the form $PN = < P, T, E, w >$, where P is the set of the places and T is the set of the transitions with $P \cup T \neq \emptyset$ and $P \cap T = \emptyset$. Places act usually as "passive elements" like conditions, states or chemical particles, while transitions represent the "active elements" like actions, events or chemical reactions. The edges of PNs can be from places to transitions and opposite, and they have positive integer weight.

A marking M of a Petri net is a mapping from P to $\mathbb{N}$, where $M(p)$ denotes the state of $p \in P$ defining with the number of tokens in place p. So the state of the Petri net can be represented by a $|P|$-dimensional marking vector M, and M_0 denotes the initial marking representing the initial state of the system, respectively.

The transitions can consume from and also can produce tokens to their input and output places according to w.

Petri nets can be described as bipartite graphs, places are indicated by circles and transitions by rectangles. The places and transitions are connected by weighted directed arcs representing the weight functions.

3.2   Simulation and Analysis of PNs

In state M of the Petri net the transition t is enabled in other word fireable, if all of its input places or preset contain at least the required numbers of tokens defined by the weight function. When a transition t is firing, a defined number of tokens are consumed from its input and produced to its output places, so the state of the net changes producing new marking M'. The enabling and firing of transitions presents the dynamic behavior of a Petri net. Note that the execution of a Petri net is nondeterministic, i.e., when multiple transitions are enabled at the same time, any one of them may fire, and different transition sequences may lead to different states from the same given initial state.

Beyond the simulation of nets, PNs are applicable to system analysis [21,31]. Numerous system properties can be verified by effective solution methods on PNs., e.g., state reachability, boundedness, deadlock or liveness.

The investigated properties can be both structural depending only on the structure of PN and behavioral depending both the structure and the initial marking as well. Most of the structural properties can be easily verified by means of algebraic techniques, and for bounded PNs the behavioral properties can be investigated based on the reachability graph or coverability graph containing the complete state space of Petri net reachable from the initial state M_0.

4   P-graphs and Petri Nets - Similarities and Differences

The similarities between P-graph and Petri nets are mainly comes from their structure representation: both are bipartite directed graphs. Table 1 summarizes the natural correspondences between the specific terms of the two approaches.

Table 1. Corresponding elements of P-graphs and Petri nets

P-graph	Petri net
Operating units	Transitions
Materials	Places
Raw materials	Places without input transitions (source places)
Products	Places without output transitions (sink places)
Intermediates	Places with both input and output transitions

The aim of P-graph framework is to determine the optimal solution of a synthesis problem, where wide range of applications are considered. For example, reaction pathway identification, process design, and supply chain management. The framework considers steady-state models and every operating units in the P-graph can possess their own steady-state models accordingly, where the weights of the related arcs serve as material rates or material flows proportional to the computed loads of the operating units. The solution structures together with the model variables and parameters resulted by the P-graph algorithms can systematically be assigned to Petri nets for further investigation.

The material rates in the P-graph are represented by arc weights in the corresponding Petri net, and the state of the P-graph is represented by tokens in discrete and positive real numbers in continuous models, where the amount of tokens in the Petri net corresponds to the amount of materials in P-graph. Consequently, the initial state of a P-graph where the raw materials are available only, corresponds to a Petri net with tokens available in its source places only.

The P-graph and the corresponding Petri net representation of the example introduced in Sect. 2 is illustrated in Fig. 5. The raw materials and the products of P-graph are highlighted with colored places of Petri net. For construction of Petri net the simulation tool Snoopy [22] was applied.

The combinatorially feasible or solution structures represented by P-graphs satisfy axioms (S1) through (S5) as introduced in Sect. 2. Consequently, both

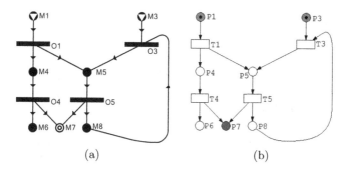

Fig. 5. P-graph (a) and Petri net (b) representation with an initial marking of the maximal structure of the simple example

the P-graph representing a solution structure and the corresponding Petri net transformed from the P-graph possesses a series of structural and behavioral properties [31]. These properties are summarized in Table 2.

Despite of the structural similarities of P-graphs and Petri nets, there are fundamental differences between the target of the application of two methodologies. The P-graph framework provides effective algorithms to synthesize optimal process systems constructed from potential building blocks leading from the available resources to the desired targets and computes both the optimal structure and the optimal parameter values of a process system, however, does not provide information on the dynamics of the system synthesized. In contrast Petri nets are tools for simulation and analysis of complex systems' dynamic behavior. PNs can model the operation of a preliminarily well-defined process network, but they are inappropriate for synthesizing the optimal process structure.

Knowing the similarities and differences of P-graphs and Petri nets it is obvious that the application of the two methods can extend to each other's application areas. The solution structures of P-graph serve as Petri net models that can be investigated with PN's simulation and analysis tools. It is illustrated on Fig. 6 and in the application example as follows in Sect. 5.

5   Application to Reaction Systems

The joint application of the effective synthesis algorithms from the P-graph framework together with the simulation and analysis strength of Petri nets is illustrated by the identification of feasible reaction pathways.

For the investigation of the possible processes in a reaction system, the feasible reaction pathways consists of ordered reaction steps which lead from the raw material to the products have to identified. The analysis and modeling of reaction pathways of a reaction system help us to understand the behavior of complex chemical and biochemical processes, including the catalytic reactions, the fermentation and the enzyme-catalytic biochemical processes as well. For example in the view of reaction pathways quality and quantity of products can

Table 2. Properties of the PNs constructed from P-graphs representing solution structures

Structural properties			
Property	Informal definition	Fulfillment	Remark
Pure	There are no two nodes, directly connected in both directions	Yes	No self-loop
Connected	There is an undirected path between every two nodes	Yes	All materials are directly or indirectly connected with each other through a set of operating units
No input transition	No transitions without pre-places	Yes	No source operating unit
No output transition	No transitions without post-places	Yes	No sink operating unit
No input place	No places without pre-transitions	No	Places without pre-transitions: raw materials
No output place	No places without post-transitions	No	Places without post-transitions: products

Behavioral properties			
Property	Informal definition	Fulfillment	Remark
Structurally bounded	The net is bounded in any initial marking	Yes	No accumulation of materials - mass conservation
Covered by place invariants	Every place belongs to a place invariant	Yes	Mass conservation

be estimated and influenced by the initial materials including the raw materials, catalysts, enzymes.

Moreover, to determine experimentally the reaction pathways of a complex system is extremely difficult, but there are computer-aided methodologies based on mathematical programming fields such as linear programming and graph-theoretic methods. This section introduce methodologies used for design and analysis of feasible structure of the reaction systems.

5.1   The Reaction Pathway Identification Problem

In the investigation of chemical reactions in a reaction system, the chemical properties of the reactants, the conditions under which the reactions take place, and the reaction rates specifying the speed of the reactions are considered to compute the consumption and production of species, i.e., change in their concentrations.

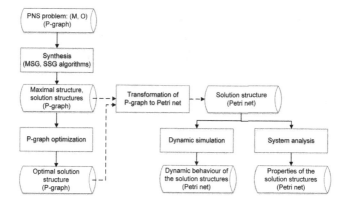

Fig. 6. Joint application of P-graph and Petri net

The relationship between the rate of a reaction and the concentrations of reactants is expressed by the rate law.

The determination of candidate mechanisms for deriving the rate law plays a key role in the study of the kinetics of catalytic reactions. A reaction pathway, comprising the steps of elementary reactions, routes the precursors (starting reactants) of the reaction to the targets (final products) and vice versa; in other words, a reaction pathway signifies the mechanism of the reaction. Any reaction pathway is in the form of a network of the steps of elementary reactions containing a loop or loops. In constituting a pathway, or network, each elementary reaction among plausible elementary reactions contributes the forward, reverse or no step to the network.

According to the classical chemical thermodynamics, the following set of 5 properties of feasible reaction pathways can be formed from the first principles and conditions for any given overall reaction [4].

(R1) Every final product (target) is totally produced by the reaction steps represented in the pathway problem definition, maximal structure, possible structures.

(R2) Every starting reactant (precursor) is totally consumed by the reaction steps represented in the pathway.

(R3) Every active intermediate produced by any reaction step represented in the pathway is totally consumed by one or more reaction steps in the pathway, and every active intermediate consumed by any reaction step represented in the pathway is totally produced by one or more reaction steps in the pathway.

(R4) All reaction steps represented in the pathway are defined a priori.

(R5) The network representing the pathway is acyclic.

Note that focusing on the combinatorial properties of the feasible reaction pathways it straightforward to reduce properties (R1) through (R5) to Axioms (S1) through (S5) established for process-network synthesis [4].

5.2   Synthesis of Reaction Pathways

The Reaction Pathway Identification methods are illustrated with the example of ethylene hydrogenation, where the elementary reactions of the reaction system proposed by Davis and Davis [32] are listed in Table 3.

Table 3. Elementary reactions of ethylene hydrogenation

Elementary reaction
s_{11}: $H_2 + 2l_1 \leftrightarrow 2Hl_1$
s_{12}: $H_2 + 2l_2 \leftrightarrow 2Hl_2$
s_{13}: $C_2H_4 + 2l_1 \leftrightarrow l_1C_2H_4l_1$
s_{14}: $l_1C_2H_4l_1 + Hl_1 \leftrightarrow C_2H_5l_1 + 2l_1$
s_{15}: $l_1C_2H_4l_1 + Hl_2 \leftrightarrow C_2H_5l_1 + l_1 + l_2$
s_{16}: $C_2H_5l_1 + Hl_1 \leftrightarrow C_2H_6 + 2l_1$
s_{17}: $C_2H_5l_1 + Hl_2 \leftrightarrow C_2H_6 + l_1 + l_2$

The maximal structure and the stoichiometrically feasible independent reaction pathways of the reaction system was determined by the help of P-graph Studio [30] based on the P-graph formulation reaction pathways. The maximal structure of the problem is highlighted in Fig. 7 and the eight feasible reaction pathways detailed by Fan at all [33] are summarized in Table 4.

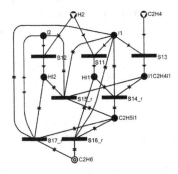

Fig. 7. The maximal structure of reaction pathway identification problem

All of the eight solutions fulfill the axioms of the feasible reaction pathways in P-graph methodology [1, 28] for the overall reaction of the problem

$$C_2H_4 + H_2 \leftrightarrow C_2H_6.$$

Based on the rigorous mathematical conditions defined by the axioms, the stoichiometric exactness of both the elementary reaction steps and the feasible reaction pathways are ensured, and the resulted pathways lead from the starting reactants to the final products of the overall reaction through the sequences of elementary reaction steps.

Table 4. The stoichiometrically feasible independent solutions of reaction pathway identification problem

Feasible reaction pathway
RP_1: $s_{11} + s_{12} + 2s_{13} + 2s_{15} + 2s_{16}$
RP_2: $s_{11} + s_{12} + 2s_{13} + 2s_{14} + 2s_{17}$
RP_3: $s_{11} + s_{13} + s_{14} + s_{16}$
RP_4: $s_{11} + s_{13} + 2s_{14} - s_{15} + s_{17}$
RP_5: $s_{11} + s_{13} + s_{15} + 2s_{16} - s_{17}$
RP_6: $s_{12} + s_{13} - s_{14} + 2s_{15} + s_{16}$
RP_7: $s_{12} + s_{13} + s_{15} + s_{17}$
RP_8: $s_{12} + s_{13} + s_{14} - s_{16} + 2s_{17}$

5.3   Startability of Reaction Pathway

According to the axioms (R1) through (R5), during the operation of a feasible reaction pathway only the species of the overall reaction change in time: the quantities of the starting reactants decrease and the quantities of the final products increase. At the same time the quantities of the intermediates are constants, so the intermediates' sub-system is in steady-state.

Determining of the proper reaction mechanisms of the reaction system it is necessary to investigate whether the steady-state defined by the Reaction Pathway Identification process can be achieved from the initial state where the starting reactants are available, i.e. whether the reaction pathway is startable or not. There are several reason that excludes the startability, for example missing raw materials or unfavorable energetic circumstances. In present work the startability based on structural properties is examined, i.e. structural startability of reaction network is determined, that depends only on the structure of the feasible reaction pathway under investigation including its initial state.

The basic statements for the determination of startability are as follows:

- an elementary reaction step is startable if all of its initial materials (species) are available
- a material is available if it is either a starting reactant or produced by a startable reaction step
- a reaction pathway is startable if all of its elementary reaction steps startable.

The aim of this examination is to explore that all of the reaction steps can be processed or in other words all of the targets including the final products can be reached from the initial state. As the startability depends on the initial state as well, it is necessary to determine the minimal set of the reactants that are necessary for the initiation.

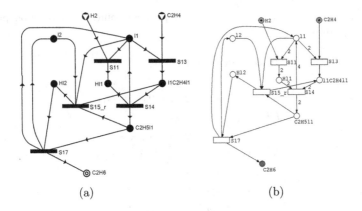

Fig. 8. P-graph (a) and Petri net (b) representation of a feasible independent pathway
$RP_4 : s_{11} + s_{13} + 2s_{14} - s_{15} + s_{17}$

5.4 Analysis of Reaction Pathways

The stoichiometrically feasible reaction pathways can be generated algorithmically by Reaction Pathway Identification based on the P-graph framework for any reaction system. P-graph methodologies serve for synthesizing and optimization purposes of process system in steady-state circumstances, so the dynamic behavior and properties of these solution structures can be investigated with dynamic simulation tools, e.g. by Petri net analysis methods.

For the demonstration of the reaction pathway analysis (i.e. the investigation of startability of reaction pathway) two feasible reaction pathways are selected and highlighted by their P-graph and Petri net representation in Figs. 8 and 9. As can be seen the stoichiometry coefficients and the rates of the elementary reactions defined by weights of the arcs in Petri nets.

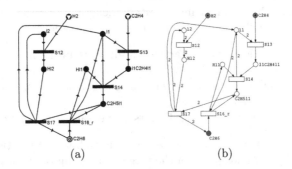

Fig. 9. P-graph (a) and Petri net (b) representation of a feasible independent pathway
$RP_8 : s_{12} + s_{13} + s_{14} - s_{16} + 2s_{17}$

To determine startability it has to be examined whether all of the elementary reactions operate or the products can be produced by the reaction pathway from the given initial materials. These examinations correspond to the determination of liveness or deadlock, and reachability analysis of the corresponding Petri net.

As siphons and traps [21,34–36] play essential role and used extensively for the analysis of the reachability, liveness and deadlock of Petri nets, their main characteristics are summarized as follows.

An important property of the siphon S is, that if it once insufficiently marked, it will never be marked again, i.e., if it loses all tokens, it never get tokens, and all transitions having arcs from the places in S become dead. Consequently, if a Petri net contains a blank siphon, liveness cannot be obtained. So a Petri net without siphons is live, while if the system is in a dead-lock state, it must contain empty siphon.

An essential property of the trap that if it catches tokens, then keeps at least one of them, i.e., if once a trap has any token in one of its places, then the trap remains marked. Firing of the transitions can move tokens, but cannot remove all of the tokens from the trap. Consequently, from the definitions of siphon and trap, if a siphon contains a marked trap, it will never become blank.

In case of a reaction pathway, a siphon can represent both a bounded source of materials and a cyclic structure producing materials by consuming itself; moreover the cyclic structure that is initialized by input materials can be described with trap.

For the siphon and trap analysis of the stoichiometrically feasible reaction pathways the Petri net analysis tool Charlie [23] was applied and the resulted siphons of RP_4 and RP_8 reaction pathways are highlighted in Figs. 10 and 12. The places in the siphons and the postsets of them are denoted by colored circles and rectangles.

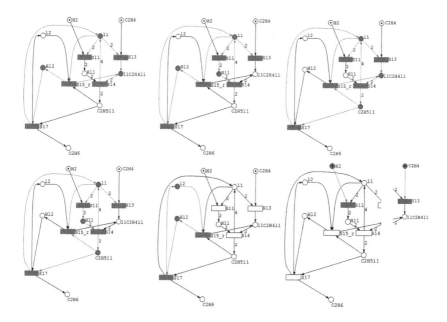

Fig. 10. Siphons of a feasible independent pathway $RP_4 : s_{11} + s_{13} + 2s_{14} - s_{15} + s_{17}$

The feasible independent pathway $RP_4 : s_{11} + s_{13} + 2s_{14} - s_{15} + s_{17}$ contains 7 sets of siphons and one set of trap as summarized in Table 5.

Table 5. The siphons and traps of RP_4 reaction pathway

Siphons	Trap
$S_1: \{l_1, l_1C_2H_4l_1, Hl_2\}$	
$S_2: \{l_1, Hl_1, H_l2\}$	
$S_3: \{l_1, l_1C_2H_4l_1, C_2H_5l_1\}$	
$S_4: \{l_1, Hl_1, C_2H_5l_1\}$	
$S_5: \{l_2, Hl_2\}$	$\tau_1 : \{l_2, Hl_2\}$
$S_6: \{H_2\}$	
$S_7: \{C_2H_4\}$	

In case of siphon S_6 and S_7 their places represent the starting reactants. According to the siphon' properties the transitions in its postsets can be fireable until the starting reactants are available. Siphons S_1–S_5 do not contain any place that represent starting reactant. It means that if the initial state of the Petri net contains only the starting reactants, all of the transitions in their postsets are dead, i.e., all the transitions in S_1–S_5 siphons denoted by colored rectangles cannot be enabled. According to this information the reaction pathway is not startable if only the starting materials are available in the initial state.

A necessary condition to avoid dead-lock state is that every siphon must contain token or active place. Assigning token to l_1, S_1–S_4 siphons fulfill this condition. For siphon S_5 both places (l_2, Hl_2) can be appropriate. As the material set of the reaction system contains two catalysts, namely l_1 and l_2, it is obvious to assign token to them besides the starting reactants in the initial state.

From the initial state where places H_2, C_2H_4, l_1 and l_2 are active, all of the transitions can fire at least once (it means that every elementary reaction steps operate), so the reaction pathway startable when besides the starting reactants the two catalysts are available in the initial state.

The trap analysis of the feasible independent pathway RP_4 shows that the Petri net contains only one trap: $\tau_1 : \{l_2, Hl_2\}$, that is equal to the set of places of siphon S_5. Consequently, although the reaction pathway can be startable with a proper-choosen initial state, but the cyclic behavior of the net is not guaranteed. It means that the net must be controlled for reserving the marking of the other siphons.

Startability can be verified based on such reachability graph or in case of unbounded PN coverability graph as well, that is generated from a predefined initial state. The nodes of a reachability graph represent the states of the system representing the root node as the initial state and the arcs are labeled with the transitions fired.

The observation of startability of reaction pathway based on reachability graph is as follows: if all of the transitions appear on the reachability graph as an arc-label, the system is startable, otherwise not.

Ensuring the tokenization of siphons S_6 and S_7 unbounded amounts of starting reactants are supposed, what is implemented by test arcs or read edges from place H_2 to transition s_{11}, and from place C_2H_4 to transition s_{13}, respectively, where these tokens remain unchanged regardless they initialize their output transitions. The initial tokens of places l_1 and l_2 representing the two catalysts in the system was set to 6 and 1, respectively, according to the minimal requested marking of the siphons S_1–S_4 and S_5.

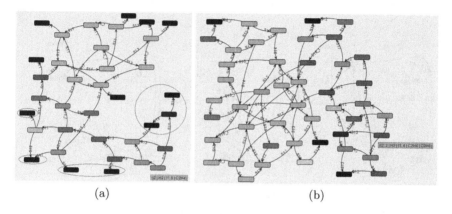

(a)   (b)

Fig. 11. The coverability graph of feasible independent pathway $RP_4 : s_{11} + s_{13} + s_{14} - s_{15} + s_{17}$ (a) and $RP_8 : s_{12} + s_{13} + s_{14} - s_{16} + 2s_{17}$ (b) (the initial states are highlighted in blue boxes) (Color figure online)

The coverability graphs of the feasible reaction pathways generated by Charlie PN analysis tool [23] are highlighted in Fig. 11. As can be seen in the left-hand side picture, all of the elementary reactions represented by transitions and highlighted as arc-labels on the graph appear on the coverability graph, so when the starting reactants and the catalysts are available in the initial state, all the elementary reaction steps can work, i.e., all the transitions can fire. Besides them the ellipses in the left-hand side coverability graph shows the states of the reaction systems, that neither contain product material nor lead to a state that holds products. So the investigation of coverability graph verifies the observa-

Table 6. The siphons and traps of RP_8 reaction pathway

Siphons	Traps
S_1: $\{l_1, C_2H_5l_1, Hl_1\}$	
S_2: $\{l_1, l_1C_2H_4l_1, C_2H_5l_1\}$	τ_1: $\{l_1, l_1C_2H_4l_1, C_2H_5l_1\}$
S_3: $\{Hl_1, C_2H_5l_1, C_2H_6\}$	τ_2: $\{Hl_1, C_2H_5l_1, C_2H_6\}$
S_4: $\{l_2, Hl_2\}$	τ_3: $\{l_2, Hl_2\}$
S_5: $\{H_2\}$	
S_6: $\{C_2H_4\}$	

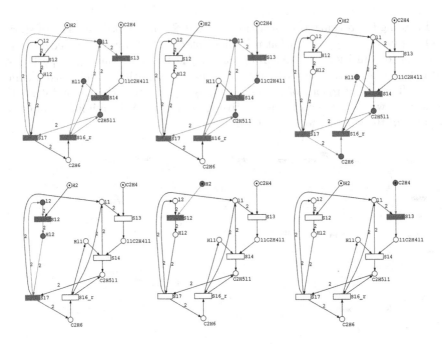

Fig. 12. Siphons of feasible independent pathway $RP_8 : s_{12} + s_{13} + s_{14} - s_{16} + 2s_{17}$

tions based on the siphon and trap analysis, that even thought the system able work cyclic, control is needed for its continuous operation.

The other investigated feasible independent pathway $RP_8 : s_{12} + s_{13} + s_{14} - s_{16} + 2s_{17}$ has six siphons (see in Fig. 12) and three traps as in Table 6:

Defining the starting reactants and the catalysts for the initial state of the reaction pathway, where places H_2, C_2H_4, l_1 and l_2 are active and the amount of the starting reactants H_2, C_2H_4 are infinity, as in the previous example, the siphons are tokenized except siphon S_3. It means that all of the transitions in the postsets of S_3 (i.e. S_{14}, S_{17}, S_{16}_r) are dead, and according to this not all of the elementary reactions is startable, so the reaction pathway is not startable. To resolve the deadlock of S_3 one of the places of it (i.e. Hl_1 or $C_2H_5l_1$ or C_2H_6) have to be marked. According to the structure of PN and siphon S_3, any of these three places can be marked, however as Hl_1 and $C_2H_5l_1$ are catalyst complexes and C_2H_6 represents the product, the tokenization of C_2H_6 is obvious.

Investigating the coverability graph of reaction pathway RP_8 from the defined initial state, where places H_2, C_2H_4, l_1, l_2 and C_2H_6 are active, all elementary reactions can be find as arc label, so the system startable, as it can be seen in the right-hand side of Fig. 11. Moreover, the system serves cyclic behavior, as can be seen in Fig. 11 as well.

6   Concluding Remarks

Process network synthesis by P-graph framework and Petri net based system analysis have been introduced and compared. Besides similar mathematical and graphical representation their complementary capabilities and potentials to joint application have been highlighted and illustrated by reaction pathway identification for the ethylene hydrogenation reaction system.

References

1. Friedler, F., Tarjan, K., Huang, Y.W., Fan, L.T.: Graph-theoretic approach to process synthesis: axioms and theorems. Chem. Eng. Sci. **47**, 1973–1988 (1992)
2. Liu, J., Fan, L.T., Seib, P., Friedler, F., Bertok, B.: Downstream process synthesis for biochemical production of butanol, ethanol, and acetone from grains: generation of optimal and near-optimal flowsheets with conventional operating units. Biotechnol. Prog. **20**, 1518–1527 (2004)
3. Tan, R.R., Cayamanda, C.D., Aviso, K.B.: P-graph approach to optimal operational adjustment in polygeneration plants under conditions of process inoperability. Appl. Energy **135**, 402–406 (2014)
4. Fan, L.T., Bertok, B., Friedler, F.: A graph-theoretic method to identify candidate mechanisms for deriving the rate law of a catalytic reaction. Comput. Chem. **26**, 265–292 (2002)
5. Rosselló, F., Valiente, G.: Graph transformation in molecular biology. In: Kreowski, H.-J., Montanari, U., Orejas, F., Rozenberg, G., Taentzer, G. (eds.) Formal Methods in Software and Systems Modeling. LNCS, vol. 3393, pp. 116–133. Springer, Heidelberg (2005). doi:10.1007/978-3-540-31847-7_7
6. Xu, X., Zhu, C., Ma, Y., Song, H.: A robust combinatorial approach based on P-graph for superstructure generation in downstream bioprocesses. Braz. J. Chem. Eng. **32**(1), 259–267 (2015)
7. Liu, F., Vilaça, P., Rocha, I., Rocha, M.: Development and application of efficient pathway enumeration algorithms for metabolic engineering applications. Comput. Methods Programs Biomed. **118**(2), 134–146 (2015)
8. Lee, S., Park, S.: Synthesis of mass exchange network using process graph theory. Comput. Chem. Eng. **20**, S201–S205 (1996)
9. Kollmann, R., Maier, S., Shahzad, K., Kretschmer, F., Neugebauer, G., Stoeglehner, G., Thomas, E., Narodoslawsky, M.: Waste water treatment plants as regional energy cells-evaluation of economic and ecologic potentials in Austria. Chem. Eng. Trans. **39**, 607–612 (2014)
10. Halim, I., Srinivasan, R.: Systematic waste minimization in chemical processes. 1. Methodology. Ind. Eng. Chem. Res. **41**(2), 196–207 (2002)
11. Kim, Y., Park, S.: Supply network modeling using process graph theory: a framework for analysis. In: 2006 SICE-ICASE International Joint Conference, pp. 1726–1729. IEEE (2006)
12. Lam, H.L., Varbanov, P.S., Klemeš, J.J.: Optimisation of regional energy supply chains utilising renewables: P-graph approach. Comput. Chem. Eng. **34**(5), 782–792 (2010)
13. Prajapat, K., Mahatme, A.: Optimisation into energy supply chain with integration of renewable energy sources. Int. J. Technol. Res. Eng. **4**(1), 154–157 (2016)

14. Tick, J., Imreh, C., Kovács, Z.: Business process modeling and the robust PNS problem. Acta Polytech. Hung. **10**(6), 193–204 (2013)
15. Tan, R.R., Benjamin, M.F.D., Cayamanda, C.D., Aviso, K.B., Razon, L.F.: P-graph approach to optimizing crisis operations in an industrial complex. Ind. Eng. Chem. Res. **55**(12), 3467–3477 (2015)
16. Aviso, K.B., Cayamanda, C.D., Solis, F.D.B., Danga, A.M.R., Promentilla, M.A.B., Yu, K.D.S., Tan, R.R.: P-graph approach for GDP-optimal allocation of resources, commodities and capital in economic systems under climate change-induced crisis conditions. J. Cleaner Prod. **92**, 308–317 (2015)
17. Garcia-Ojeda, J.C., Bertok, B., Friedler, F.: Planning evacuation routes with the P-graph framework. Chem. Eng. Trans. **29**, 1531–1536 (2012)
18. Petri, C.A.: Kommunikation mit Automaten. Rheinisch-Westfälisches Institut für Instrumentelle Mathematik an der Universität Bonn, Dissertation, Schriften des IIM (1963)
19. Peterson, J.L.: Petri Net Theory and the Modeling of Systems. Prentice Hall, New Jersey (1981)
20. Jensen, K., Kristensen, L.M.: Coloured Petri Nets: Modelling and Validation of Concurrent Systems. Springer, Heidelberg (2009)
21. Murata, T.: Petri nets: properties, analysis and applications. Proc. IEEE **77**, 541–580 (1989)
22. Heiner, M., Herajy, M., Liu, F., Rohr, C., Schwarick, M.: Snoopy – a unifying Petri net tool. In: Haddad, S., Pomello, L. (eds.) PETRI NETS 2012. LNCS, vol. 7347, pp. 398–407. Springer, Heidelberg (2012). doi:10.1007/978-3-642-31131-4_22
23. Heiner, M., Schwarick, M., Wegener, J.-T.: Charlie – an extensible Petri net analysis tool. In: Devillers, R., Valmari, A. (eds.) PETRI NETS 2015. LNCS, vol. 9115, pp. 200–211. Springer, Cham (2015). doi:10.1007/978-3-319-19488-2_10
24. Visual Object Net++. http://www.r-drath.de/Home/Visual_Object_Net++.html
25. Gyapay, S., Pataricza, A.: A combination of Petri nets and process network synthesis. Syst. Man Cybern. **2**, 1167–1174 (2003)
26. Gyapay, S., Pataricza, A., Sziray, J., Friedler, F.: Petri-net based optimization of production systems. Intell. Syst. Serv. Mankind **1**, 157–167 (2005)
27. Zapata, M.G., Chacón, R.E., Palacio, B.J.: Intelligent production systems reconfiguration by means of Petri nets and the supervisory control theory. In: Advances in Petri Net Theory and Applications, pp. 75–102 (2010)
28. Friedler, F., Tarjan, K., Huang, Y.W., Fan, L.T.: Combinatorial algorithms for process synthesis. Comput. Chem. Eng. **16**, 313–320 (1992)
29. Bertok, B., Barany, M., Friedler, F.: Generating and analyzing mathematical programming models of conceptual process design by P-graph software. Ind. Eng. Chem. Res. **52**(1), 166–171 (2013)
30. Software P-graph Studio. http://p-graph.org/downloads
31. Blätke, M.A.: Tutorial Petri Nets in Systems Biology. Technical report, Otto-von-Guericke University, Magdeburg (2011)
32. Davis, M.E., Davis, R.J.: Fundamentals of Chemical Reaction Engineering. McGraw-Hill, New York (2003)
33. Fan, L.T., Yu-Chuan, L., Shafie, S., Bertok, B., Friedler, F.: Exhaustive identification of feasible pathways of the reaction catalyzed by a catalyst with multiactive sites via a highly effective graph-theoretic algorithm: application to ethylene hydrogenation. Ind. Eng. Chem. Res. **51**, 2548–2552 (2012)
34. ZhiWu, L., MengChu, Z.: Deadlock Resolution in Automated Manufacturing Systems: A Novel Petri Net Approach. Advances in Industrial Control. Springer, London (2009)

35. Hideki, Y.: On the Structure of Siphons of Petri Nets. Logics, Algebras and Languages in Computer Science. RIMS Kokyuroku, vol. 1915, pp. 132–141. Kyoto University (2014)
36. Karatkevich, A.: Dynamic Analysis of Petri Net-Based Discrete Systems. Springer, Heidelberg (2007)

Parameterized Complexity and Approximability of Coverability Problems in Weighted Petri Nets

Dimitri Watel[1,2(✉)], Marc-Antoine Weisser[3], and Dominique Barth[4]

[1] ENSIIE, Evry, France
dimitri.watel@ensiie.fr
[2] SAMOVAR, Evry, France
[3] LRI, CentraleSupélec, Université Paris-Saclay, Orsay, France
[4] DAVID, Université Versailles Saint-Quentin-en-Yvelines, Versailles, France

Abstract. Many databases have been filled with the chemical reactions found in scientific publications and the associated information (efficiency, chemical products involved...). They can be used to define functions representing costs such as the ecolical impact of the reactions. A major challenge is to use computer driven optimization in order to improve synthesis process and to provide algorithms to help determining a minimum cost pathway (series of reactions) for the synthesis of a molecule.

As, the classical Petri nets do not allows us to consider the optimization component, a weighted model has to be defined and the complexity of the associated problems studied. In this paper we introduce the weighted Petri nets in which each transition is associated with a weight. We define the Minimum Weight Synthesis Problem: find a minimum weight series of transitions to fire to produce a given target component. It mainly differ from classical coverability as it is an optimization problem.

We prove that this problem is EXPSPACE-Complete and that there is no polynomial approximation even when both in and outdegree are fixed to two and the target state is a single component. We also consider a more constraint version of the problem limiting the number of fired transitions. We prove this problem falls into PSPACE and the parametrized versions into XP but it remains not approximable.

Keywords: Petri net coverability problem · Minimum weight synthesis problem · Parameterized complexity · Approximability

1 Introduction

The development of decision support tools for the synthesis of new molecules is a major challenge for organic chemistry and biochemistry [7,17], through the use of databases of reactions that are regularly updated in these scientific fields (such as REAXYS, CHEBI [1,13]). Indeed, the objective is to provide algorithms to help determining a reaction pathway (serie of consecutive reactions) for the synthesis of new molecules by using such reaction databases [7,9]. Usually, a

© Springer International Publishing AG 2017
W. van der Aalst and E. Best (Eds.): PETRI NETS 2017, LNCS 10258, pp. 330–349, 2017.
DOI: 10.1007/978-3-319-57861-3_19

chemist proposes a reaction pathway from a synthesis in the database of a molecule sufficiently similar to the target molecule [16,21]. It is therefore important to determine the optimum reaction pathway of this similar molecule from the reactions recorded in this target database in which each reaction can be associated with a cost depending on the complexity of the reactions or the solvents involved. Thus, the initial molecules in a reaction pathway are usually easy to synthesize or to be bought. Given the cost of these potentially initial molecules and the list of all referenced chemical reactions, the problem is to identify best process to obtain the target molecules.

In this article, we are considering to optimize the cost to obtain or synthesize the target molecules but it can be any additive function such as the ecological footprint if it can be estimated or the time needed if there is no parallelization.

As we say previously, many such chemical databases are used and updated (for example [1,13]), filled with million of reactions found in scientific publications. These databases are maintaining a lot of information such as the efficiency or the chemical products involved in the reaction which may not be reactive but nevertheless necessary (solvent for example). They can be used to define functions representing costs such as environmental impact of the reactions.

This challenge of improving synthesis process by using computer driven optimisation is not specific to chemistry. It can be found in all manufacturing areas as long as one can describe the process as a set of transformations and evaluate the cost of buying resources and the cost of transforming them. We can even find this problem in games. In most of the MMORPG (massively multiplayer online role-playing game), the player have the ability to craft items using resources they find or buy in the game.

Petri nets were introduced by Petri [22] and is a classical model to describe chemical and biological processes [6,12,14,15,19,25]. More generally, it is a way to model transformations of molecular components. Each transformation destroys some components (substrates) and generates some others (products). Considering a quantity (or stock) of such components, represented by a vector containing for each component a non-negative quantity, a transformation may be fired to change this stock into another one.

One of the classical problems with Petri net related to our synthesis problem is the *Coverability* of a stock: starting with an initial stock, is it possible, with a finite list of transformations, to get another stock containing a given target stock? The Coverability problem is decidable [10,11] but requires at least an exponential space complexity in general nets [18,20]. However, in this context, classical Petri nets are not adapted anymore, a weigthed model has to be defined in order to take into account the costs of buying molecules and making the reactions.

To represent this crafting problem with a Petri net, we introduce weighted Petri nets where each transformation is associated with a non-negative weight. This weight allows us to represent both the cost of a transformation and the cost of purchasing a component: a transition transforming an empty set of component into a non empty set. These are two important differences with the coverability problem, thus to avoid confusion, we refer to synthesis problem. The *Minimum Weight Synthesis Problem* (Min–WSP) consists in determining, starting with no component in the stock, which transformation should be fired in order to get, at minimum weight, a stock containing a given target stock.

We have given the practical reasons for our interest in this problem. However, we think that given its simplicity, in terms of definition, it is a problem that deserves to be studied even if given the complexity of coverability problems in classical Petri nets, one can not expect anything that hardness results. Finally, as we have seen with crafting in MMORPG, many optimization problems are linked with the Min–WSP. We focus on the complexity and the approximability of this problem.

Related Works. Priced Petri nets are an extension of standard Petri nets [2–4]. The transitions in such nets have a cost and possibly an aging effect on the current stock. When a token ages, a conservation cost must also be paid. Given an input stock and a target stock, the Priced Coverability problem consists in the search for a minimum cost sequence of transitions transforming the input stock into a stock containing the target stock. This associated decision problem is decidable if and only if the costs are non-negative. This is an extension of our weighted synthesis problem as the conservation cost of the molecules is null and we do not take time into account. Abdulla *et al.* studied the decidability of priced Petri nets problems. Our work considers the approximability and parameterized complexity of our model.

In the works of Abdulla *et al.* or ours, we introduce an optimization component into the problem which try to capture a chemical property. This has also been done in recent work. For example, [5] introduces an NP-Complete problem in which, given an initial stock and some target place, we search for a reachable stock containing a maximum number of tokens in the target place.

Our Contribution. In this paper, we focus on two optimization versions of the Petri Net Coverability problem. The first one is the above-mentionned *Minimum Weight Synthesis Problem* (Min–WSP). We study the complexity, the approximability from a chemist point of view in a sense that we also consider firstly the fact that a chemical reaction has neither a high number ρ of reactants nor a high number π of products and secondly the fact that the number C of target molecules is small. Consequently, in addition to the classical complexity and approximability studies, we also deal with the parameterized complexity and approximability with respect to ρ, π and C.

In Sect. 3, we prove that Min–WSP is EXPSPACE-Complete that determining if an instance of Min–WSP has a feasible solution is polynomial. However, we also prove this problem to be not polynomially approximable to within a poly-logarithmic ratio even if we consider the parameterized versions where $\pi = \rho = 2$ and $C = 1$.

In the second problem, called *Minimum Limited sequence Weighted Synthesis problem* (Min–LWSP), we also search for a minimum transformation cost to cover a target stock. However, contrary to Min–WSP, we consider a human constraint in the sense that we limit the number of transitions we can fire so that the number l of chemical reactions we need and the number of molecules we have to buy in order to synthesis a molecule is reasonable. We study how this new parameter l affects the results of the first problem.

Table 1 summarizes the complexity results for Min–WSP and Min–LWSP given in Sects. 3 and 4.

Table 1. Summary of the results of the paper. The four first lines concern Min–WSP and the others concern Min–LWSP. The four first columns indicate how the parameters of the problems are considerered for the complexity: a unary entry, a binary entry, a fixed constant or a fixed value. Note that l is not defined for Min–WSP thus for the four first lines. The columns Opt. sol. and Feas. sol. respectively specify if the results stands for the search of an optimal solution, the search of the existence of a feasible solution or both.

	l	ρ	π	C	Opt. sol.	Feas. sol.	Result	
Min–WSP	-	2	2	1	×		EXPSPACE-Complete	Theorem 1
	-	2	2	1	×		Polylog-Inapprox	Theorem 4
	-				×	×	P	Theorem 2
Min–LWSP	Binary	2	2	1	×	×	PSPACE-Complete	Theorem 6
	Unary	2	2	1	×	×	NP-Complete	Theorem 7
	cst.				×	×	XP	Theorem 8
	cst.	cst.			×	×	W[2]-Hard	Theorem 9
	cst.			cst.	×	×	W[2]-Hard	Theorem 9
	cst.		cst.			×	W[1]-Complete	Theorem 11
	cst.	cst.	cst.	cst.	×	×	W[1]-Hard	Theorem 10

The hardness results for deciding the existence of a feasible solution of an instance of Min–LWSP immediately proves hardness of approximability for the optimization problem.

The next section is dedicated to the formal definitions of the terminology. In addition, it gives drawing conventions of this paper and details the parameters we focus on in the parameterized complexity study. Sections 3 and 4 are respectively dedicated to the studies of Min–WSP and Min–LWSP.

2 Definitions

This section is dedicated to the formal definitions of the terminology we use and of the problems we study in this paper.

2.1 The Petri Net Coverability Problem

A Petri net is a triplet $(\mathcal{P}, \mathcal{T}, M_0)$ where $\mathcal{P}$ is the finite set of *places* and $\mathcal{T}$ is the finite set of *transitions*. Each place may contain zero, one or more *tokens*. A *state* M maps $\mathcal{P}$ to $\mathbb{N}$, each place x is associated with a non-negative number $M(x)$ of tokens. We write, using classical vector notation [18], $M = \sum_{x \in \mathcal{P}} a_x \cdot x$

where $a_x = M(x)$. We may possibly remove a place x from the sum if a_x is null. Particularly, an empty state is denoted by $\emptyset$. M_0 is called the *initial state* of the Petri net: it defines the initial number of tokens in each place. Each transition $t \in \mathcal{T}$ is a couple of states $t^- = \sum_{x \in \mathcal{P}} t^-(x) \cdot x$ and $t^+ = \sum_{x \in \mathcal{P}} t^-(x) \cdot x$, respectively called the *input state* and the *output state* of t. The set of places for which $t^-(x) > 0$ and the set of places for which $t^+(x) > 0$ are respectively called the *input states* and the *output states*. We denote the transition by $t = t^- \to t^+$.

We say a state M' *covers* another state M if and only if, for all $x \in \mathcal{P}$, $M'(x) \geq M(x)$. Considering a state M of the Petri net, one can *fire* a transition $t \in \mathcal{T}$ if M covers the input state t^-. We say t is *enabled* at M. In that case, the resulting state is $M' = \sum_{x \in \mathcal{P}} (M(x) - t^-(x) + t^+(x)) \cdot x$. We denote this by $M \Rightarrow^t M'$. In other word, firing a transition means transforming some tokens in the input places into tokens in the output places. Similarly, we can define a *sequence* $T = (t_1, t_2, \ldots, t_{|T|})$. This sequence is *enabled at M* if we can successively fire all the transitions of T from t_1 to $t_{|T|}$. In that case, and if firing this sequence produce the state M', we write $M \Rightarrow^T M'$. Note that the sequence T may contain a transition t more than once.

We can now formally define the classical coverability problem in Petri nets.

Problem 1 (Coverability). Given a Petri net $(\mathcal{P}, \mathcal{T}, M_0)$ and a *target state* $\mathcal{C}$, is there an enabled sequence T at M_0 such that $M_0 \Rightarrow^T M$ and M covers $\mathcal{C}$?

We represent an instance of this problem by a bipartite directed graph in which the places are circle nodes and the transitions are squared nodes. For each transition nodes t, we represent the input and output state using incoming and respectively outgoing arcs. An arc (x, t) (resp. (t, x)) is associated with the value $t^-(x)$ (resp. $t^+(x)$). We omit this value when it is 1 and we omit the arc when it is 0. For each target place, i.e. a place x for which $\mathcal{C}(x) \neq 0$, is drawn with a double circle. A dashed outgoing arc, from x, is associated with the number $\mathcal{C}(x)$. Given a state M, $M(x)$ is represented by a value inside the circle node x. An example is given on Fig. 1.

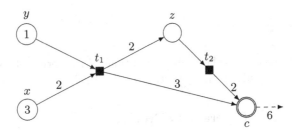

Fig. 1. This figure illustrates an instance of the coverability problem: a Petri Net with four places x, y, z, c and two transitions $t_1 = 2x + y \to 2z + 3c$ and $t_2 = z \to 2c$. The initial state M_0 is $3x + y$. After firing t_1, t_2, t_2 we obtain the state $M = x + 7c$ which is covering the target state $6c$.

2.2   The Weighted Petri Net Synthesis Problem

The Minimum Weighted Synthesis Problem (Min–WSP) insert an optimization part to the previous problem. Each transition $t \in \mathcal{T}$ is associated with a (binary encoded) non-negative weight $w(t) \in \mathbb{N}$. In addition, the initial state M_0 is always $\emptyset$, there is not any token in any place. However, note that the Petri net may contain transitions for which the input state is empty.

We define the weight $w(T)$ of a sequence T of transitions of $\mathcal{T}$ as the sum $w(T) = \sum\limits_{t \in T} w(t)$.

Problem 2 (Minimum Weighted Synthesis, Min-WSP). Given a Petri net $(\mathcal{P}, \mathcal{T}, \emptyset)$, a weight function $w : \mathcal{T} \to \mathbb{N}$ over the transitions and a *target state* $\mathcal{C}$, return a enabled sequence T at $\emptyset$ of $\mathcal{T}$ such that $\emptyset \Rightarrow^T M$, M covers $\mathcal{C}$, and $w(T)$ is minimum.

In addition, we denote by FS–MWSP the problem of determining if there exists a feasible solution for an instance of Min–WSP (not to be confused with the decision version of Min–WSP in which, given an additional integer K, we search for a feasible solution of weight at most K).

We use a representation similar to the classical Petri nets. We add a table indicating the weight of each transition. An example of a Min–WSP instance if is given in Fig. 2.

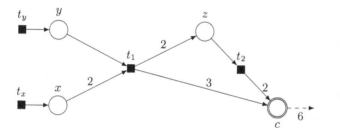

transition	weight
t_x	1
t_y	2
t_1	2
t_2	4

Fig. 2. This figure illustrates a instance of Min–WSP. It is a Petri Net with four places x, y, z, c and four transitions $t_x = \emptyset \to x$, $t_y = \emptyset \to y$, $t_1 = 2x + y \to 2z + 3c$ and $t_2 = z \to 2c$. The initial state M_0 is $\emptyset$. After firing $(t_y, t_y, t_x, t_x, t_x, t_x, t_1, t_1)$ of weight 12 we obtain the state $M = 4z + 6c$ which is covering the target state $6c$.

2.3   Parametrized Version of Min–WSP

In order to analyze the parametrized complexity of the Petri Net Synthesis problem, we introduce four different parameters: ρ and π, respectively the maximum number of input and output tokens among all the transitions of $\mathcal{T}$, C the size of the target state and l the number of transitions fired in a feasible solution. As the three first are constraints on the instances, the last is a constraint on feasible solutions so we will treat it independently.

The two first parameters, ρ and π, limit the maximum number of input and output tokens. More formally,

$$\rho = \max_{t \in \mathcal{T}} \sum_{x \in \mathcal{P}} t^-(x)$$

$$\pi = \max_{t \in \mathcal{T}} \sum_{x \in \mathcal{P}} t^+(x)$$

The third parameter on which we focus is the size $C = \sum_{x \in \mathcal{P}} \mathcal{C}(x)$ of the target state $\mathcal{C}$. From a chemical perspective, these parameters model the limited number of reactants, products of reactions and the number of molecules we want to synthesize, which is likely to be small.

Finally, we define a fourth parameter l to limit the number of molecules we can buy and the number of reactions we can perform to synthesize the target molecules. As introducing this parameter changes the set of feasible solutions for an instance (see Example 1), we define an independent problem: **Minimum Limited sequence Weighted Synthesis problem (Min–LWSP).**

Example 1. We constraint the instance of Fig. 1 by introducing a parameter $l = 6$ to limit the number of fired transitions. As a consequence the sequence $T = (t_y, t_y, t_x, t_x, t_x, t_x, t_1, t_1)$ is not a feasible solution anymore as it contains 8 transitions. This constraint instance contains only one feasible solution: the sequence $T' = (t_y, t_x, t_x, t_1, t_2, t_2)$ of weight 14.

Problem 3 **Limited sequence Weighted Petri Net Synthesis problem (Min–LWSP).** Given a Petri net $(\mathcal{P}, \mathcal{T}, \emptyset)$, a weight function $\omega : \mathcal{T} \to \mathbb{N}$ over the transitions, a *target state* $\mathcal{C}$ and an integer l, return an enabled sequence T at $\emptyset$ of $\mathcal{T}$ such that $\emptyset \Rightarrow^T M$, M covers $\mathcal{C}$, $|T| \leq l$ and $\omega(T)$ is minimum.

Similarly to FS–MWSP, we define FS–MLWSP the problem of determining if there exists a feasible solution for an instance of Min–LWSP.

The reason for which we do not study the parameterized complexity with respect to $|\mathcal{P}|$ and $|\mathcal{T}|$ is that, in the application we consider, the numbers of molecules and reactions in the chemical databases are constantly increasing and exceed one million.

3   Min–WSP

In this section, we study the complexity, the approximability and the parameterized approximability of Min–WSP.

3.1   Complexity and Parameterized Complexity

The next theorem proves that Min–WSP is EXPSPACE-Complete and, in some way, equivalent to the Petri net Coverability problem.

Theorem 1. *The decision version of Min–WSP is EXPSPACE-Complete even if $\pi = \rho = 2$ and $C = 1$.*

Proof. The proof of EXPSPACE-Completeness by two reductions from and to the Petri net Coverability problem. This problem is EXPSPACE-Complete [18,20,24]. Note that this result remains true if the Petri net satisfies $\pi = \rho = 2$ and if the initial state and the target state contain respectively a polynomial number I and a polynomial number C of tokens. We can create an equivalent instance with only one target token and $\pi = \rho = 2$ by firstly adding a new place c and a new transition using all the C target tokens to create one token in c. Finally, transform this transition into $C-1$ transitions and add $C-2$ new places as shown in Fig. 3 so that ρ remains 2. As C is polynomial, this transformation is polynomial too. Similarly, we can reduce the number of initial tokens to 1 in polynomial time.

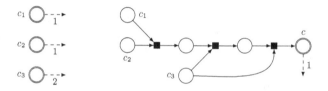

Fig. 3. Example of transformation from an instance (on the left) in which the target state $C = c_1 + c_2 + 2 \cdot c_3$ (and then $C = 4$) to an instance (on the right) satisfying $C = 1$. The weight of every transition is 0.

Let $\mathcal{I} = ((\mathcal{P}, \mathcal{T}, M_0), \mathcal{C})$ be an instance of the Petri net Coverability problems with $\pi = \rho = 2$, $C = 1$ and $M_0 = x$ for some place x. We create an instance $\mathcal{J}$ of Min–WSP in which the Petri net is $(\mathcal{P}, \mathcal{T} \cup \{t\}, \emptyset)$ in which we add a transition $t = \emptyset \rightarrow x$. The weight of t is 1 and the weight of each other transition is 0. The target state is $\mathcal{C}$. Then $\mathcal{C}$ is coverable in $\mathcal{I}$ if and only if there is a feasible solution of weight 1 in $\mathcal{J}$. As a consequence the decision version of Min–WSP is EXPSPACE-hard.

Now given an instance $\mathcal{J} = ((\mathcal{P}, \mathcal{T}), \omega, \mathcal{C})$ of Min–WSP and an integer K, we build an instance $\mathcal{I} = ((\mathcal{P}', \mathcal{T}', M_0'), \mathcal{C}')$ of the Petri net Coverability problem. We firstly add a place w to $\mathcal{P}$. Secondly, for each transition $t \in \mathcal{T}$, we set $t^-(w) = \omega(t)$. Thirdly, $M_0' = K \cdot w$. Finally, $\mathcal{C} = \mathcal{C}'$. Each time a transition t of $\mathcal{T}'$ is fired, it removes $\omega(t)$ tokens from w, thus it is not possible to fire a sequence of cost more than K. Consequently we can cover the target state $\mathcal{C}'$ in $\mathcal{I}$ if and only if there is, in $\mathcal{J}$, a feasible solution of cost at most K, and the decision version of Min–WSP is in EXPSPACE.   □

Remark 1. Theorem 1 shows that Min–WSP is not easier if we fix the three parameters π, ρ and C. As a consequence, there is no parameterized results considering those three parameters.

This second theorem shows that the problem of determining if there exists a feasible solution for an instance of Min–WSP is polynomial.

Theorem 2. *FS–MWSP is polynomial.*

Proof. In order to find a feasible solution, for each transition t for which the input state is empty, we mark all the output places of t. Then, for each transition t for which all the input places are marked, we mark all the output places. We repeat this marking operation until no new place is marked. A place x is marked if and only if there is an enabled sequence $\mathcal{T}$ at $\emptyset$ such that $\emptyset \Rightarrow^{\mathcal{T}} x$ (note that an arbitrary number of tokens can appear in a place while firing $\mathcal{T}$). Consequently there is a feasible solution if and only if all the target places are marked. Note that this algorithm is not correct if the initial marking is not empty.   □

Note that Theorem 2 does not explain how to build a feasible solution. In fact, even if we can easily adapt the algorithm given in the proof to return such a solution, for some instances, no feasible solution contains a polynomial number of transitions. See, for example, the instance on Fig. 4 or the instance given in [20] to prove the EXPSPACE-Hardness of the Coverability problem, in which any feasible solution contains respectively $O(2^{|\mathcal{P}|})$ and $O(2^{2^{|\mathcal{P}|}})$ transitions if such a solution exists. On the other hand, [24] proves that if an instance $\mathcal{I}$ of Min–WSP contains a feasible solution, it contains a solution of double exponential size $f(|\mathcal{I}|)$. It means that the optimum cost is less than $U = f(|\mathcal{I}|) \cdot \max_{t \in \mathcal{T}} \omega(t)$ and that we can iterate the decision version of Min–WSP with at most an exponential space in order to find the optimum cost even if we cannot store the associated optimal solution in exponential space.

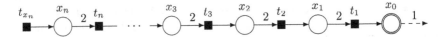

Fig. 4. Example of instance for which the number of transitions is exponential. Indeed, in order to put a token in the place x_0, we need to buy 2^n tokens for x_n using the transition t_{x_n}, then fire 2^{n-1} times the transition t_n, then fire 2^{n-2} times the transition t_{n-1}, and so on until we fire once the transition t_1. This sequence contains then 2^n transitions.

3.2 Approximability

We show in this subsection that Min–WSP cannot be approximated within a polylogarithmic ratio in polynomial time. Basically, the best ratio an approximation algorithm may achieve is at least polynomial in the size of the instance. Considering that there exist instances in which no feasible solution has a polynomial number of transitions (see the end of the previous subsection), the search for an approximation algorithm seems pointless. However, we show that the inapproximability result holds even if there is no circuit in the net and if there exists a polynomial size feasible solution that can be built, for example, with the algorithm described by Theorem 2. In order to prove this inapproximability result for Min–WSP, we build, in this subsection, a reduction from the MMSA$_h$ problem.

Problem 4 Minimum Monotone Satisfying Assignment (MMSA$_h$). Given a set Y of boolean variables and a monotone boolean formula φ of depth h (this formula has h levels of alternating AND and OR gates, where the top level is an AND gate), minimize the number of true variables such that φ is satisfied.

We respectively call $D(\varphi)$ and $C(\varphi)$ the set of OR and AND gates in the formula.

Theorem 3 [27]. *Unless $P = NP$, there is no polynomial approximation for MMSA$_3$ with a ratio $Q(\log(|Y|), \log(|D(\varphi)|), \log(|C(\varphi)|))$ where Q is any polynomial.*

We now detail and prove a reduction from MMSA$_h$ to Min–WSP. An example is given on Fig. 5. Let $\mathcal{I} = (Y, \varphi)$ be an instance of MMSA$_h$, we build the following instance $\mathcal{J}$:

- add one place x_0 and a transition $t_0 = \emptyset \to x_0$;
- for each variable y, add one place x_y and a transition $t_y = x_0 \to l_y \cdot x_y$ where l_y is the number of literals y in φ;
- add one place x_g for each gate g;
- for each OR gate $g = \bigvee_i \varphi_i$, where φ_i are either gates or variables, add, for each i, a transition $t_g^i = x_{\varphi_i} \to x_g$;
- for each AND gate $g = \bigwedge_i \varphi_i$, where φ_i are either gates or variables, add a transition $t_g = \sum_i x_{\varphi_i} \to x_g$;
- set the target state to $\mathcal{C} = x_g$ where g is the top level AND gate;
- set the weight of t_0 to 1 and the weight of every other transition to 0.

Lemma 1. *If there is a feasible solution for $\mathcal{I}$ with $\omega \geq 1$ true variables, there is a feasible solution for $\mathcal{J}$ of weight ω.*

Proof. The solution consists in firing ω times t_0 (this way, we put ω tokens in the place x_0) and then using all the transitions of the true gates and variables in the formula, starting with the variables and the lower gates and terminating with the top level AND gate. The proof that, when a transition is fired, all the input places contain a token (and then that the solution is feasible) can be done by induction on the height of each gate. □

Lemma 2. *If there is a feasible solution for $\mathcal{J}$ of weight $\omega \geq 1$, there is a feasible solution for $\mathcal{I}$ with at most ω true variables.*

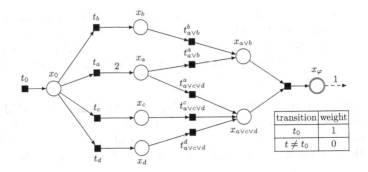

Fig. 5. Example of reduction from MMSA$_2$ to Min–WSP with the boolean formula $\varphi = (a \vee b) \wedge (a \vee c \vee d)$.

Proof. Let $T = (t_1, t_2, \ldots, t_{|T|})$ be a feasible solution for $\mathcal{J}$ of cost $\omega \geq 1$. We now prove that assigning true to all the variables $y \in Y$ such that $t_y \in T$ is a feasible solution for $\mathcal{I}$ of cost at most ω. Let f be the boolean function associating to each variable and each gate the value *true* or *false*. We have to check that $f(g)$ is true where g is the top level AND gate.

Firstly, there are at most ω distinct variables for which the transition is fired in T. Indeed, in order to fire the transition t_y associated with the variable $y \in Y$, we have to fire the transition t_0 of weight 1 first in order to put a token in x_0. As the weight of T is ω, there are at most ω variables set to true.

Secondly, for each $1 \leq i \leq |T|$ such that $t_i \neq t_0$, the transition t_i is associated either with a variable y or a gate g. Considering how we set the true and false variables in $\mathcal{I}$, if the transition is associated with a variable y, then $f(y)$ is true. We now prove by induction on i that, on the other case, $f(g)$ is true. Let $\varphi(t)$ be the variable or the gate associated with the transition t, for $t \neq t_0$. Similarly, $\varphi(x)$ is the variable or the gate associated to the place x, if $x \neq x_0$. Note that the first transition t_i for which $t_i \neq t_0$ is necessarily associated with a variable. We now assume that, for every $j \leq i$, either $t_j = t_0$ or $f(\varphi(t_j))$ is true. We also assume, without loss of generality that $t_{i+1} \neq t_0$ and that $g = \varphi(t_{i+1})$ is an OR gate: $g = \varphi_1 \vee \varphi_2 \vee \cdots \vee \varphi_k$. Thus, t_{i+1} has one input place $x \neq x_0$ such that $\varphi(x) = \varphi_\kappa$ for some $\kappa \in [\![1; k]\!]$ (and $t_{i+1} = t_g^{\varphi_\kappa}$). Before this transition is fired, x contains a token otherwise T would not be a feasible solution for $\mathcal{J}$. As $x \neq x_0$, the token in x was added by a reaction $t_j \neq t_0$ for some $j \leq i$ and $\varphi(x) = \varphi(t_j) = \varphi_\kappa$. By the inductive hypothesis, $f(\varphi(t_j))$ is true, then $f(g)$ is true. A similar argument occurs if g is an AND gate. Consequently, there is a feasible solution for $\mathcal{I}$ of cost at most ω. $\qquad\square$

Theorem 4. *Unless $P = NP$, there is no polynomial approximation for Min–WSP with a ratio $Q(\log(|\mathcal{P}|), \log(|\mathcal{T}|))$ where Q is any polynomial even if $\pi = \rho = 2$, $C = 1$, the net has no circuit and there exists a feasible solution with a polynomial size.*

Proof. Let Q be a polynomial. We assume that the cost of an optimal solution for $\mathcal{I}$ is ω^*. We can use the previous reduction to build an instance $\mathcal{J}$. By Lemmas 1 and 2, the cost of an optimal solution for $\mathcal{J}$ is ω^*. We can then transform, in polynomial time, that instance to ensure that $\rho = 2$ as it was done in the proof of Theorem 1. Note that $\pi = C = 1$ and that the net is acyclic. In addition, there exists a polynomial size feasible solution consisting in firing t_0 and t_x for each variable x and then firing t_g for each gate of the formula.

If there is a $Q(\log(n), \log(m))$-approximation for Min–WSP, we can use it to build a solution for $\mathcal{J}$ of cost at most $Q(\log(n), \log(m)) \cdot \omega^*$, and then use Lemma 2 to build a feasible solution for $\mathcal{I}$ of cost at most $Q(\log(n), \log(m)) \cdot \omega^*$.

Finally note that, in the reduction $m = |C(\phi)| + |D(\phi)|(|D(\phi)| + |C(\phi)| + |Y|) + |Y|$ and $n = 1 + |C(\phi)| + |D(\phi)| + |Y|$, thus there is a polynomial Q' such that $Q(\log(n), \log(m)) \leq Q'(\log(|Y|), \log(|D(\varphi)|), \log(|C(\varphi)|))$. As a consequence, we have built a $Q'(\log(|Y|), \log(|D(\varphi)|), \log(|C(\varphi)|))$-approximation for MMSA$_h$. By Theorem 3, this is a contradiction. □

4   Min–LWSP

In this section, we study the complexity, the approximability and the parameterized approximability of Min–LWSP.

4.1   Complexity

Theorem 5. *Min–LWSP and FS–MLWSP are in PSPACE.*

Proof. Let K be any integer. We search for the existence of a feasible solution of weight less than K. To achieve this, we provide a non-deterministic algorithm that runs in polynomial space.

We start with a state where all the places are empty. At each iteration, we non-deterministically choose a transition t. If t is not enabled at the current state or if the maximum weight K is lower than the current weight, then return NO, otherwise, fire the t. If $l + 1$ transitions were fired, return NO. If the target state is covered, return YES. If none of those cases occur, we start a new iteration.

At each iteration, the algorithm must store, for each place, the number of tokens in that place. Those numbers are no more than $l \cdot \pi$ as a transition can produce at most π tokens. It must also store the current total weight and the number of the current transition, which are respectively no more than K and l. Consequently, this algorithm runs in polynomial space and Min–LWSP is in NPSPACE. As PSPACE = NPSPACE [26], Min–LWSP is in PSPACE. The proof for FS–MLWSP is the same except that we do not consider the weights. □

Theorem 6. *Min–LWSP and FS–MLWSP are PSPACE-complete, even if $\rho = \pi = 2$ and $C = 1$.*

Proof. The proof of Theorem 1 of [18], page 287, gives a reduction from the Turing halting problem in polynomial space to the Reachability problem (and the Coverability problem) for 1-Conservative Petri nets with $\rho = \pi = 2$ and $C = 1$. The same reduction can be used to prove our theorem. Some states encode the tape and others encode the states of the automata. Each transition function is encoded by a transition of the Petri net of weight 0. As the machine cannot use more that $P(|x|)$ cells of the tape, where P is a polynomial and x is the input word, it cannot use more than $2^{P(|x|)}|Q|$ transitions where $|Q|$ is the size of the automata otherwise the machine loops indefinitely. Thus the Petri net must cover the target state by firing at most that number of transitions. The initial state of the Petri net of the proof of [18] encodes the word x written on the tape and the initial state of the automata. In this version, we add a transition t_0 of weight 1 that creates that initial state from nothing. We can then transform t_0 into multiple transitions as we did in Theorem 1 so that π remains 2. The machine halts without using more than $P(|x|)$ cells if and only if the Petri net covers the target state with at most $1 + 2^{P(|x|)}|Q|$ transitions of total weight at most 1. Thus the decision version of Min–LWSP is PSPACE-hard. By Theorem 5, the decision version of Min–LWSP is PSPACE-Complete, even if $\rho = \pi = 2$ and $C = 1$.

In order to prove that FS–MLWSP is also PSPACE-hard, we must prevent the transition t_0 from being fired twice in a feasible solution. To do so, we add a place x_0 as input of t_0 and a construction as the one given in Fig. 4 so that we need to fire at least $2^{P(|x|)+1}|Q|$ transitions in order to put a token in the place x_0. We then set $l = 2^{P(|x|)+1}|Q| + 2^{P(|x|)}|Q| + 1$ so that any feasible solution cannot place more than one token in x_0 and then cannot fire t_0 twice.   □

The same ideas show the following theorem.

Theorem 7. *If the encoding of l is unary, the decision versions of Min–LWSP and FS–MLWSP are NP-Complete, even if $\rho = \pi = 2$ and $C = 1$.*

4.2   Parameterized Complexity and Approximability

We present in this section four theorems describing the parameterized complexity of Min–LWSP and FS–MLWSP. There are proved using reduction from and to the set cover problem and the partitioned clique problem.

Problem 5 **Set Cover.** Given an integer K, a set E and a set $S \subset 2^E$, find a subset S' of S covering E such that $|S'| \leq K$.

Problem 6 **Partitioned clique.** Given an undirected graph $G = (V, E)$ and a partition $V_1, V_2, \ldots, V_k$ of V, find a clique of size k with exactly one node in each set V_i.

Set Cover problem is W[2]-Complete with respect to the parameter K [8]. Partitioned clique problem is W[1]-complete with respect to the parameter k [23].

Theorem 8. *Min–LWSP is XP with respect to the parameter l.*

Proof. One can search for an optimal solution by exhaustively enumerating all the m^l sequences of transitions.   □

Theorem 9. *FS–MLWSP is W[2]-hard with respect to the parameters l and ρ and is W[2]-hard with respect to the parameters l and C.*

Proof. This proof is an FPT reduction from the set cover problem parameterized with K. Let $\mathcal{I} = (K, E, S)$ be an instance of Set Cover. We now build an instance $\mathcal{J}$ of FS–MLWSP parameterized with l and ρ.

We create for each element e in E a place x_e. For each set s in S, we create a transition $t_s = \emptyset \rightarrow \sum\limits_{e \in s} x_e$. The target state is $C = \sum\limits_{e \in E} x_e$. We finally set $l = K$. This reduction satisfies $\rho = 0$. A feasible solution S' for $\mathcal{I}$ can be transformed into a feasible solution for $\mathcal{J}$ by firing every transition t_s for $s \in S'$ and, conversely, from a feasible solution for $\mathcal{J}$, we can build a feasible solution for $\mathcal{I}$ by selecting the sets for which the transition is fired. As this reduction is FPT with respect to K, FS–MLWSP is W[2] with respect to l and ρ.

If we now add to this instance a new place c and a new transition $\sum\limits_{e \in E} x_e \rightarrow c$, if the target state is $C = c$ and if we set $l = K + 1$, we get a new instance of FS–MLWSP in which $C = 1$. Note that ρ does not polynomially depend on the parameter K. As this reduction is also FPT with respect to K, FS–MLWSP is W[2] with respect to l and C. $\qquad\square$

Theorem 10. *FS–MLWSP is W[1]-hard with respect to l, ρ, π and C.*

Proof. Given an instance $\mathcal{I} = (G, V_1, V_2, \ldots, V_k)$ of Partitioned Clique, we now build the following instance $\mathcal{J}$ of FS–MLWSP parameterized with l, ρ, π and C:

- add one place x_0 and a transition $t_0 = \emptyset \rightarrow x_0$;
- add one place x_v and a transition $t_v = x_0 \rightarrow (k-1) \cdot x_v$ for each node $v \in V$;
- add one place $c_{i,j}$ for each $i < j \in [\![1; k]\!]$;
- add, for each edge $e = (u, v)$ such that $u \in V_i, v \in V_j$ and $i < j$, a transition $t_e = x_u + x_v \rightarrow c_{i,j}$;
- set the target state to $C = \sum\limits_{i=1}^{k-1} \sum\limits_{j=i+1}^{k} c_{i,j}$;
- set l to $2k + \frac{k \cdot (k-1)}{2}$.

An example is given Fig. 6.

This reduction is polynomial and l, C, ρ and π depends only on k. Thus it is FPT with respect to k.

If there is a clique $(v_1, v_2, \ldots, v_k)$ of size k in G satisfying $v_i \in V_i$ for $i \in [\![1; k]\!]$, there is a feasible solution for $\mathcal{J}$ consisting in buying k tokens for the place x_0 with the transition t_0, firing the k transitions t_{v_i} for $i \in [\![1; k]\!]$ and then firing the $\frac{k \cdot (k-1)}{2}$ transitions $t_{(v_i, v_j)}$ for $i < j \in [\![1; k]\!]$. Those transitions exist and are enabled as $(v_1, v_2, \ldots, v_k)$ is a clique.

We now assume there is a feasible solution $T = (t_1, t_2, \ldots, t_{|T|})$ for $\mathcal{J}$. It satisfies $|T| \leq l$. Let $\mathcal{T}_V$ and $\mathcal{T}_E$ be respectively the set of transitions $\{t_v, v \in V\}$ and $\{t_e, e \in E\}$. Let $(M_0 = \emptyset, M_1, M_2, \ldots, M_{|T|})$ be the successive states of $\mathcal{J}$ after firing the transitions of T. Note that $\emptyset \Rightarrow^T M_{|T|}$, and, as a consequence, this

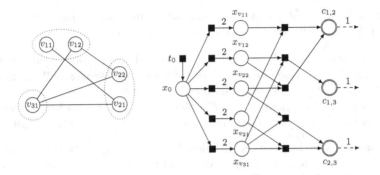

Fig. 6. Example of reduction from Partitioned Clique to FS–MLWSP. On the left, the three dashed ellipses describe the partition of the nodes.

state $M_{|T|}$ contains at least $\mathcal{C}(c_{i,j}) = 1$ token in each place $c_{i,j}$ for $i < j \in [\![1;k]\!]$. Only the transitions of $\mathcal{T}_E$ can create such tokens. As none of those transitions create more than one such token, there are, in T, at least $\frac{k \cdot (k-1)}{2}$ transitions of $\mathcal{T}_E$. As $l = 2 \cdot k + \frac{k \cdot (k-1)}{2}$, there are at most $2k$ transitions of $\{t_0\} \cup \mathcal{T}_V$ in T. As there must be a token in x_0 before a transition of $\mathcal{T}_V$ can be fired, there are at most k transitions of $\mathcal{T}_V$ in T.

In addition, there is, for each $i \in [\![1;k]\!]$, at least one node v_i in V_i and an integer l such that $M_l(x_{v_i}) \geq 1$. Indeed, otherwise, no transition of $\mathcal{T}_E$ placing a token in c_{ji} or c_{ij} for all $j \neq i$ could have been fired. Thus, there are in T exactly k transitions of $\mathcal{T}_V$. Each one is associated with one node $v_i \in V_i$ for $i \in [\![1;k]\!]$.

Finally, $(v_1, v_2, \ldots, v_k)$ is a clique, otherwise, some transition $t_{(v_i,v_j)}$ would not exist and consequently no token could have been placed in $c_{i,j}$.

This conclude the reduction. FS–MLWSP is W[1]-Hard with respect to the parameters l, C, π and ρ. $\square$

We finally prove that FS–MLWSP belongs to the W[1] class if parameterized with l and π. We first give an intermediate lemma proving that, if l and π are fixed, we can consider that ρ and C are fixed too.

Lemma 3. *There exists an FPT-reduction from FS–MLWSP parameterized with l and π to FS–MLWSP parameterized with l, π, ρ and C.*

Proof. As there are at most l transitions in a feasible solution and as every transition may produce at most π tokens, a feasible solution may produce at most $l \cdot \pi$ tokens. Consequently, if $C > l \cdot \pi$ there is no feasible solution and the problem is solved. In addition, if a transition needs more than $l \cdot \pi$ input tokens, this transition may be removed from the instance as it is not possible to fire it. We then necessarily get an instance where $C \leq l \cdot \pi$ and $\rho \leq l \cdot \pi$. $\square$

Theorem 11. *FS-MLWSP is W[1]-complete with respect to l and π.*

Due to its length, the complete proof is given in Appendix A. It is based on a reduction to the partitioned clique problem.

Remark 2. Note that Theorem 11 does not prove any parameterized result on Min–LWSP. Determining if Min–LWSP is W[1]-Complete with respect to l and π and with respect to l, ρ, π and C are open questions.

Finally, the complexity of the determing if there exists feasible solutions for Min–LWSP allows us conclude this section with the following corollary.

Corollary 1. *Let Q be a polynomial.*

- *Unless $P = PSPACE$, there is no polynomial approximation for Min–LWSP with a ratio $2^{Q(|\mathcal{P}|,|\mathcal{T}|)}$ even if $\rho = \pi = 2$ and $C = 1$.*
- *Unless $P = NP$, there is no polynomial approximation for Min–LWSP with a ratio $2^{Q(|\mathcal{P}|,|\mathcal{T}|)}$ even if $\rho = \pi = 2$ and $C = 1$ and if the encoding of l is unary.*
- *Unless $FPT = W[1]$, there is no FPT approximation for Min–LWSP with ratio $2^{Q(|\mathcal{P}|,|\mathcal{T}|)}$, with respect to l, ρ, π and C.*

Proof. Those results are respectively deduced from Theorems 6, 7 and 10.   □

5   Conclusion

In this paper we present the Minimum Weight Synthesis problem, a variant of the classical Coverability problem introducing weights on transitions. We provide a deep analysis of the complexity and parametrized complexity. Our results are summarized in Table 1. They illustrate how hard this problem is even when most parameters are constrained. In the last section, we prove that using approximation algorithm for solving this problem is not adequate as there is no constant ratio or small variable ratio approximation algorithm.

From a theoretical perspective, there are a few cases of parameterized complexity which are still open questions. In particular, Theorems 9 and 10 provide W[1]-hard and W[2]-hard results. It would be interesting to find other reductions to achieve completeness results.

From a more practical perspective, as the problem is hard to solve and to approximate, we should now study different heuristic algorithms.

Acknowledgment. *We thank the three anonymous reviewers for their constructive comments that helped to improve the quality of this paper and of future work.*

A   Proof of Theorem 12

Theorem 11. FS–MLWSP is W[1]-complete with respect to l and π.

Proof. By Lemma 3 and Theorem 10, we have to prove that FS–MLWSP is W[1] with respect to l, ρ, π and C. To do so, we describe a reduction to the partitioned clique problem. Let $\mathcal{I} = ((\mathcal{P}, \mathcal{T}, \emptyset), \omega, \mathcal{C}, l)$ be an instance of FS–MLWSP. We assume that $\mathcal{I}$ contains a fake transition t_0 such that $t_0^- = t_0^+ = \emptyset$ so that $\mathcal{I}$ contains a feasible solution of size lower than l if and only if it contains a feasible solution of size exactly l. We now create an instance $\mathcal{J} = (G, V_1, V_2, \ldots, V_l, V_{l+1})$ of the partitioned clique problem such that $\mathcal{J}$ contains a feasible solution if and only if $\mathcal{I}$ does. An example is given in Fig. 7.

In the remaining of this proof, given a state M, the ordered set of states $\{\alpha_1, \alpha_2, \ldots, \alpha_k\}$ is called a *decomposition* of M if and only if $\sum_{j=1}^{k} \alpha_j = M$. The state α_j may be empty.

Let t be a transition of $\mathcal{I}$. For each $i \in [\![2; l]\!]$, we create at most $(i-1)^\rho \cdot (l-(i+1))^\pi$ nodes in V_i, one per decomposition of t^- in $i-1$ states and per decomposition of t^+ in $l-i+1$ states. If $t^- = \emptyset$, we also create at most l^π nodes in V_1, one per decomposition of t^+ into l states. Finally, we add at most l^C nodes to V_{l+1}, one for each decomposition of $\mathcal{C}$ into l sets. For example, in Fig. 7, $t_1^- = \emptyset$ and $t_1^+ = x + 2y$. We add six nodes to V_1 as there are six possible decompositions of t_i^+ into 2 states : $\{\emptyset, x+2y\}, \{x, 2y\}, \{x+y, y\}$ and the symmetrical decompositions. Note that the number of nodes in G is FPT with respect to the parameters l, ρ, π and C.

Let $i < j \in [\![1; l]\!]$, and $v_i \in V_i$ and $v_j \in V_j$ be two nodes of G. The node v_i is associated with a transition t_i, a decomposition of t_i^- and a decomposition $\{\alpha_{i+1}, \alpha_{i+2}, \ldots, \alpha_{l+1}\}$ of t_i^+. Similarly, the node v_j is associated with a transition t_j, a decomposition $\{\beta_1, \beta_2, \ldots, \beta_{j-1}\}$ of t_j^- and a decomposition of t_j^+. We add to G the edge (v_i, v_j) if and only if α_j covers β_i.

Similarly, let $i \in [\![1; l]\!]$, and $v_i \in V_i$ and $v_{l+1} \in V_{l+1}$ be two nodes of G. The node v_i (respectively v_{l+1}) is associated with a transition t_i, a decomposition of t_i^- and a decomposition $\{\alpha_{i+1}, \alpha_{i+2}, \ldots, \alpha_{l+1}\}$ of t_i^+ (resp. a decomposition $\{\beta_1, \beta_2, \ldots, \beta_l\}$ of $\mathcal{C}$). We add to G the edge (v_i, v_{l+1}) if and only if α_{l+1} covers β_i.

For example, in Fig. 7, the last node of V_1 and the second node of V_2 are respectively associated with the decomposition $\{x+2y, \emptyset\}$ of t_1^+ and the decomposition $\{x+y\}$ of t_2^-. The two nodes are linked as $x + 2y$ covers $x + y$.

We now prove that $\mathcal{J}$ contains a feasible solution if and only if $\mathcal{I}$ has an enabled sequence at $\emptyset$ with l transitions such that the resulting state covers $\mathcal{C}$.

We first assume there is a clique of G containing a node v_i of V_i for every $i \in [\![1; l+1]\!]$. Let $T = (t_1, t_2, \ldots, t_l)$ be the sequence such that t_i is the transition associated with v_i for $i \leq l$. Let $\{\beta_{i,1}, \beta_{i,2}, \ldots, \beta_{i,i-1}\}$ and $\{\alpha_{i,i+1}, \alpha_{i,i+2}, \ldots, \alpha_{i,l+1}\}$ be respectively the decompositions of t_i^- and t_i^+ associated with v_i and let $\{\mathcal{C}_1, \mathcal{C}_2, \ldots, \mathcal{C}_l\}$ be the decomposition of $\mathcal{C}$ associated with v_{l+1}.

We now show that T is enabled at $\emptyset$. As $v_1 \in V_1$, then $t_1^- = \emptyset$ and t_1 is enabled at $\emptyset$. Let $i \in [\![1; l-1]\!]$. As $(v_1, v_2 \ldots v_i, v_{i+1})$ is a clique of G, then, by construction, $\alpha_{j,i+1}$ covers $\beta_{j,i+1}$ for every $j \in [\![1; i]\!]$. For each place x of $\mathcal{P}$:

$$\sum_{j=1}^{i}(t_j^+(x) - t_j^-(x)) \geq \sum_{j=1}^{i}\left(\alpha_{j,i+1}(x) + \sum_{k=j+1}^{i}\alpha_{j,k}(x) + \sum_{k=1}^{j-1}\beta_{k,j}(x)\right)$$

$$\geq \sum_{j=1}^{i}\alpha_{j,i+1}(x) + \sum_{j<k\leq i}(\alpha_{j,k}(x) - \beta_{j,k})(x)$$

$$\geq \sum_{j=1}^{i} \alpha_{j,i+1}(x) = t_{i+1}^{-}(x)$$

Consequently, for every $i \in [\![1;l]\!]$, $(t_1, t_2, \ldots, t_i)$ is enabled at $\emptyset$. Finally, we can similarly show that $\sum_{j=1}^{l}(t_j^{+}(x) - t_j^{-}(x)) \geq \sum_{j=1}^{l} \alpha_{j,l+1}(x)$ and, as (v_i, v_{l+1}) is an edge of G for $i \leq l + 1$, then, by construction, $\sum_{j=1}^{l} \alpha_{j,l+1}(x) \geq \sum_{j=1}^{l} C_j(x) = C(x)$ for every place x. Thus, when firing T, the resulting state covers C and T is a feasible solution of $\mathcal{I}$.

We now assume there exists such a feasible solution $T = (t_1, t_2, \ldots, t_l)$ of $\mathcal{I}$ and prove $\mathcal{J}$ contains a clique of size $l + 1$. Let $\gamma_{i,j}$, for $i < j \in [\![1;l]\!]$ be the states describing the tokens produced by t_i and consumed by t_j ; let $\gamma_{i,l+1}$ be the tokens produced by t_i, not consumed by any next transition and used

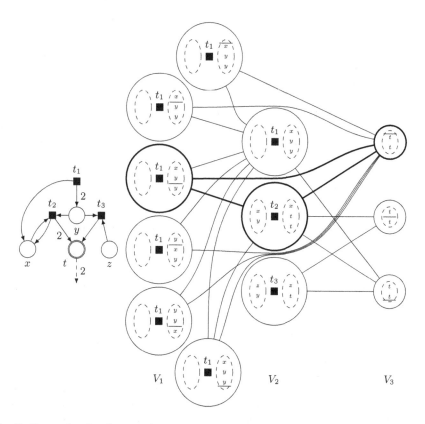

Fig. 7. Example of reduction from an instance $\mathcal{I}$ of FS–MLWSP with $l = 2$ on the left to an instance $\mathcal{J}$ of Partitioned Clique on the right. Due to lack of space, the fake transition is not part of $\mathcal{I}$. Each node of the clique instance is either a transition t with decompositions of t^- (on the left) and t^+ (on the right) or an decomposition of C into 2 states. The sequence (t_1, t_2) is a feasible solution of $\mathcal{I}$. The bold clique on the right is a feasible solution of $\mathcal{J}$ associated with that sequence.

to cover $\mathcal{C}$; and finally let $\gamma'_{i,l+1}$ be the not consumed tokens of t_i^+ that are not used to cover $\mathcal{C}$. Thus, we have firstly $t_i^+ = \gamma'_{i,l+1} + \sum_{j=i+1}^{l+1} \gamma_{i,j}$, secondly $t_j^- = \sum_{i=1}^{j-1} \gamma_{i,j}$ and thirdly $\sum_{i=1}^{l} \gamma_{i,l+1} = \mathcal{C}$. For each set V_i with $i \leq l$, we select the node v_i associated with t_i, the decomposition $\{\gamma_{j,i}, j \leq i-1\}$ of t_i^- and the decomposition $\{\gamma_{i,i+1}, \ldots, \gamma_{i,l}, \gamma_{i,l+1} + \gamma'_{i,l+1}\}$ of t_i^+. We finally choose the node v_{l+1} of V_{l+1} associated with the decomposition $\{\gamma_{j,l+1}, j \leq l\}$ of $\mathcal{C}$. If $i < j \leq l$, then $\gamma_{i,j}$ is the j-th state of the decomposition of t_i^+ and the i-th state of the decomposition of t_j^-. By construction the edge (v_i, v_j) belongs to G. Moreover, if $i \leq l$, the last state $\gamma_{i,l+1} + \gamma'_{i,l+1}$ of the decomposition of t_i^+ covers the i-th state $\gamma_{i,l+1}$ of the decomposition of $\mathcal{C}$. By construction the edge (v_i, v_{l+1}) belongs to G. Consequently, $\{v_1, v_2, \ldots, v_{l+1}\}$ is a clique of size of $l+1$ in $\mathcal{J}$.

As a result and by Theorem 10, FS–MLWSP is W[1]-Complete in l and π. $\square$

References

1. Reaxys. Elsevier (2016). https://www.elsevier.com/solutions/reaxys
2. Abdulla, P.A., Mayr, R.: Minimal cost reachability/coverability in priced timed petri nets. In: Alfaro, L. (ed.) FoSSaCS 2009. LNCS, vol. 5504, pp. 348–363. Springer, Heidelberg (2009). doi:10.1007/978-3-642-00596-1_25
3. Abdulla, P.A., Mayr, R.: Computing optimal coverability costs in priced timed Petri nets. In: Proceedings of the Symposium on Logic in Computer Science, pp. 399–408 (2011)
4. Abdulla, P.A., Mayr, R.: Priced timed Petri nets. Logical Methods Comput. Sci. 9(4), 1–51 (2013)
5. Andersen, J.L., Flamm, C., Merkle, D., Stadler, P.F.: Maximizing output and recognizing autocatalysis in chemical reaction networks is NP-complete. J. Syst. Chem. 3(1), 1–9 (2012). http://www.jsystchem.com/content/3/1/1
6. Angeli, D., De Leenheer, P., Sontag, E.: A Petri Net approach to the study of persistence in chemical reaction networks. Math. Biosci. 210(2), 598–618 (2007). http://arxiv.org/abs/q-bio/0608019
7. Bøgevig, A., Federsel, H.J., Huerta, F., Hutchings, M.G., Kraut, H., Langer, T., Löw, P., Oppawsky, C., Rein, T., Saller, H.: Route design in the 21st century: the IC SYNTH software tool as an idea generator for synthesis prediction. Org. Process Res. Dev. 19(2), 357–368 (2015)
8. Downey, R., Fellows, M.: Parameterized Complexity, vol. 3. Springer, New York (1999). https://www.dagstuhl.de/Reports/01/01311.pdf
9. Eigner-Pitto, V., Huerta, F.F., Hutchings, M.G., Saller, H., Loew, P.: Reaction prediction tools for both idea generation in new synthesis route planning and for de novo molecule design. In: 12th German Conference on Chemoinformatics (2016)
10. Finkel, A.: The minimal coverability graph for Petri nets. In: Rozenberg, G. (ed.) ICATPN 1991. LNCS, vol. 674, pp. 210–243. Springer, Heidelberg (1993). doi:10. 1007/3-540-56689-9_45
11. Finkel, A., Leroux, J.: Recent and simple algorithms for Petri nets. Softw. Syst. Model. 14(2), 719–725 (2015)
12. Genrich, H., Küffner, R., Voss, K.: Executable Petri net models for the analysis of metabolic pathways. Int. J. Softw. Tools Technol. Transf. 3(4), 394–404 (2001)

13. Hastings, J., de Matos, P., Dekker, A., Ennis, M., Harsha, B., Kale, N., Muthukrishnan, V., Owen, G., Turner, S., Williams, M., Steinbeck, C.: The chebi reference database and ontology for biologically relevant chemistry: enhancements for 2013. Nucleic Acids Res. **41**(D1), D456 (2012). http://dx.doi.org/10.1093/nar/gks1146

14. Heiner, M.: Preface: Petri nets for systems and synthetic biology. Natural Comput. **10**(3), 987–992 (2011)

15. Hofestädt, R.: A Petri net application to model metabolic processes. Syst. Anal. Model. Simul. **16**(2), 113–122 (1994)

16. Horvath, D., Jeandenans, C.: Molecular similarity and virtual screening. In silico methods to retrieve active analogs in the context of discovering therapeutic compounds. Actual. Chim. **9**, 64–67 (2000)

17. Johnson, A.P., Marshall, C.: Starting material oriented retrosynthetic analysis in the LHASA program. 2. Mapping the SM and target structures. J. Chem. Inf. Comput. Sci. **32**(5), 418–425 (1992)

18. Jones, N.D., Landweber, L.H., Edmund Lien, Y.: Complexity of some problems in Petri nets. Theoret. Comput. Sci. **4**(3), 277–299 (1977)

19. Koch, I.: Petri nets-a mathematical formalism to analyze chemical reaction networks. Mol. Inform. **29**(12), 838–843 (2010)

20. Lipton, R.J.: The Reachability Problem Requires Exponential Space. Technical report, Yale Research Report #63 (1976)

21. Nouleho, S., Barth, D., David, O., Watel, D., Weisser, M.: A new definition of molecule similarity to determine molecular construction. Poster in 12th German Conference on Chemoinformatics (2016)

22. Petri, C.A.: Kommunikation mit Automaten. Ph.D. Thesis, Universität Hamburg (1962). http://epub.sub.uni-hamburg.de/informatik/volltexte/2011/160/

23. Pietrzak, K.: On the parameterized complexity of the fixed alphabet shortest common supersequence and longest common subsequence problems. J. Comput. Syst. Sci. **67**(4), 757–771 (2003)

24. Rackoff, C.: The covering and boundedness problems for vector addition systems. Theoret. Comput. Sci. **6**(2), 223–231 (1978). http://linkinghub.elsevier.com/retrieve/pii/0304397578900361

25. Reddy, V.N., Mavrovouniotis, M.L., Liebman, M.N.: Petri net representations in metabolic pathways. In: Proceedings of the International Conference on Intelligent Systems for Molecular Biology, vol. 1, pp. 328–336 (1993)

26. Savitch, W.J.: Relationships between nondeterministic and deterministic tape complexities. J. Comput. Syst. Sci. **4**, 177–192 (1970)

27. Watel, D., Weisser, M.A.: A note on the inapproximability of the Minimum Monotone Satisfying Assignment problem. Technical report, HAL (2016). https://hal.archives-ouvertes.fr/hal-01377704

Author Index

Printed in the United States
By Bookmasters